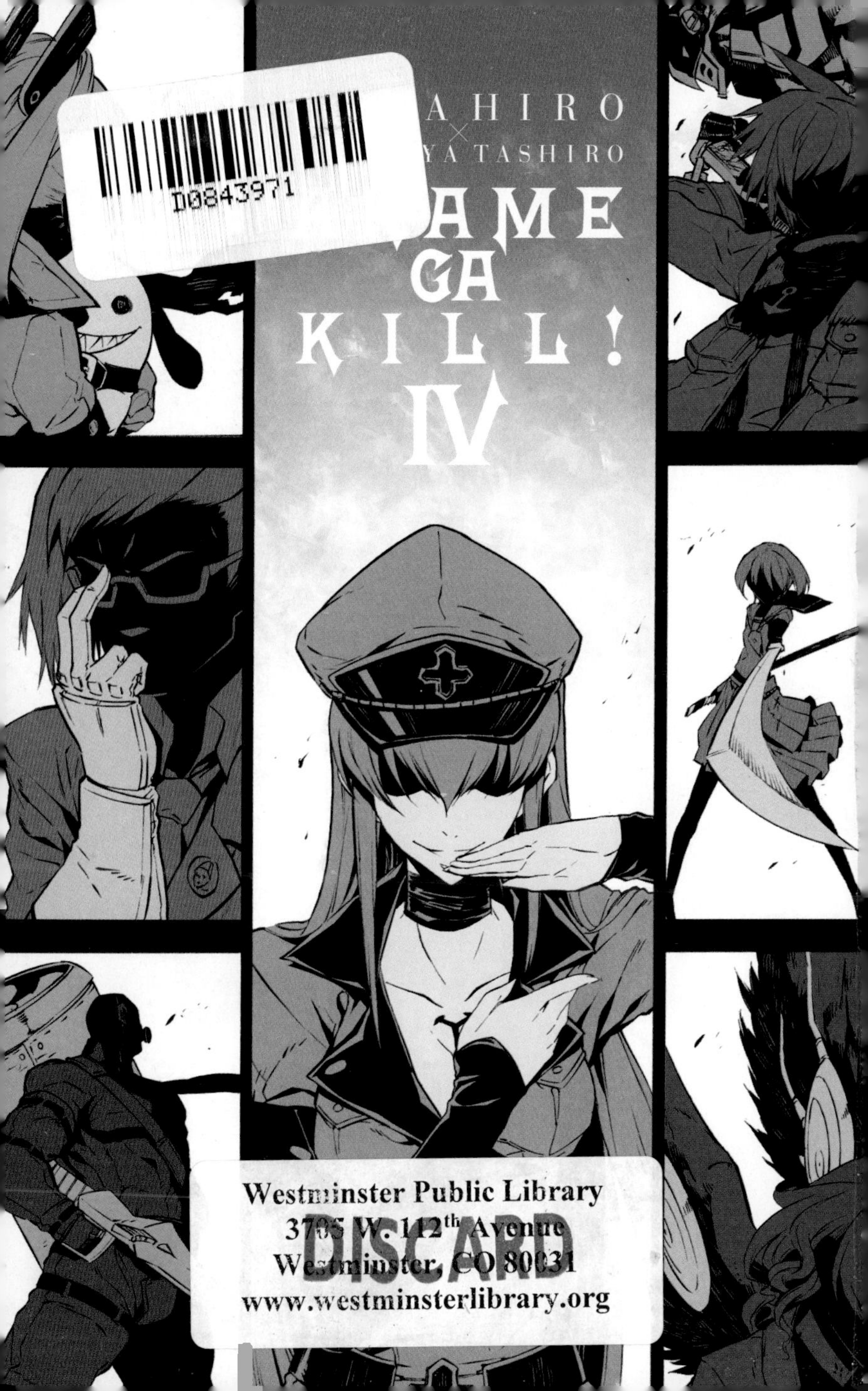
AHIRO
×
YA TASHIRO
AME
GA
KILL!
IV

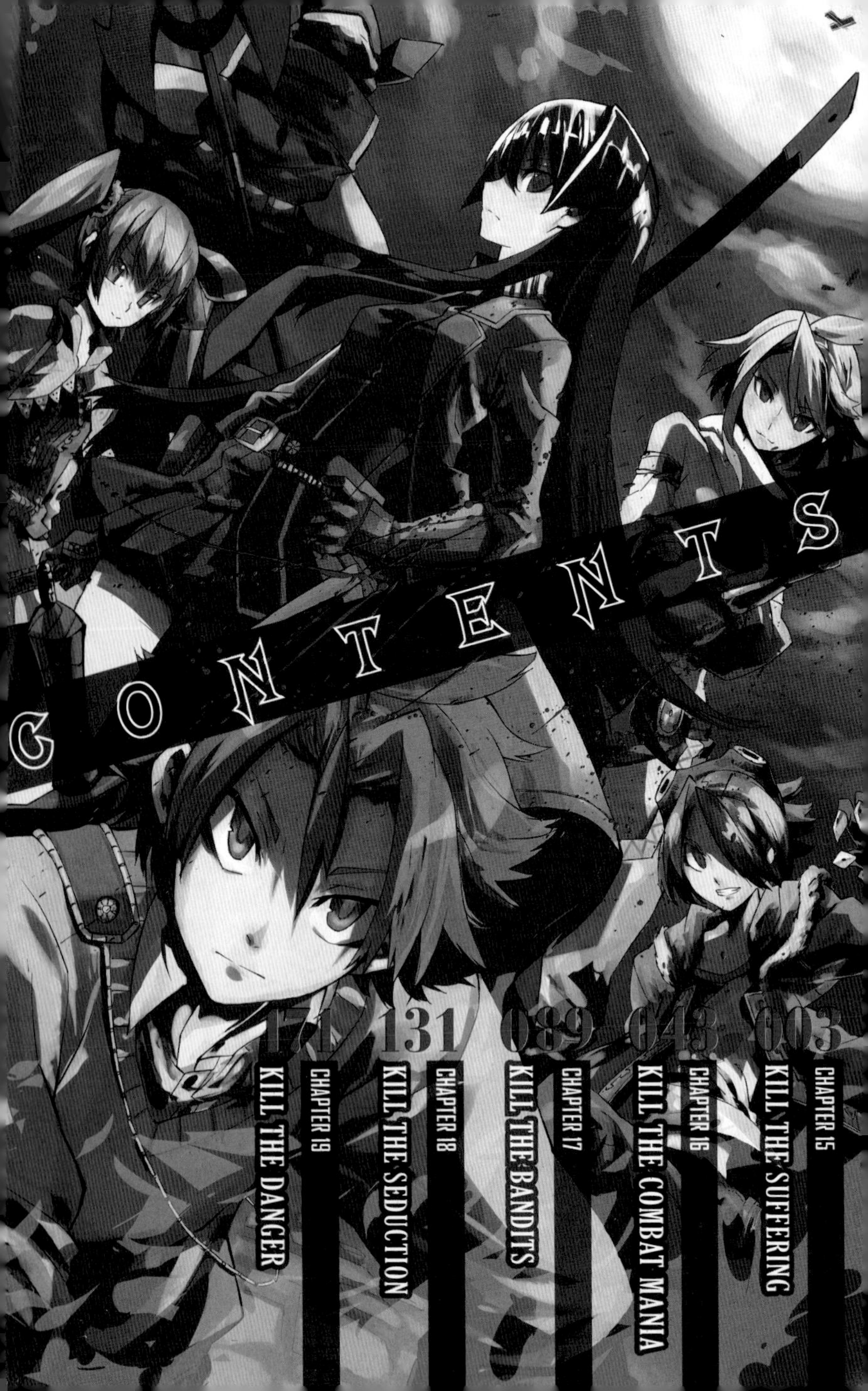

CONTENTS

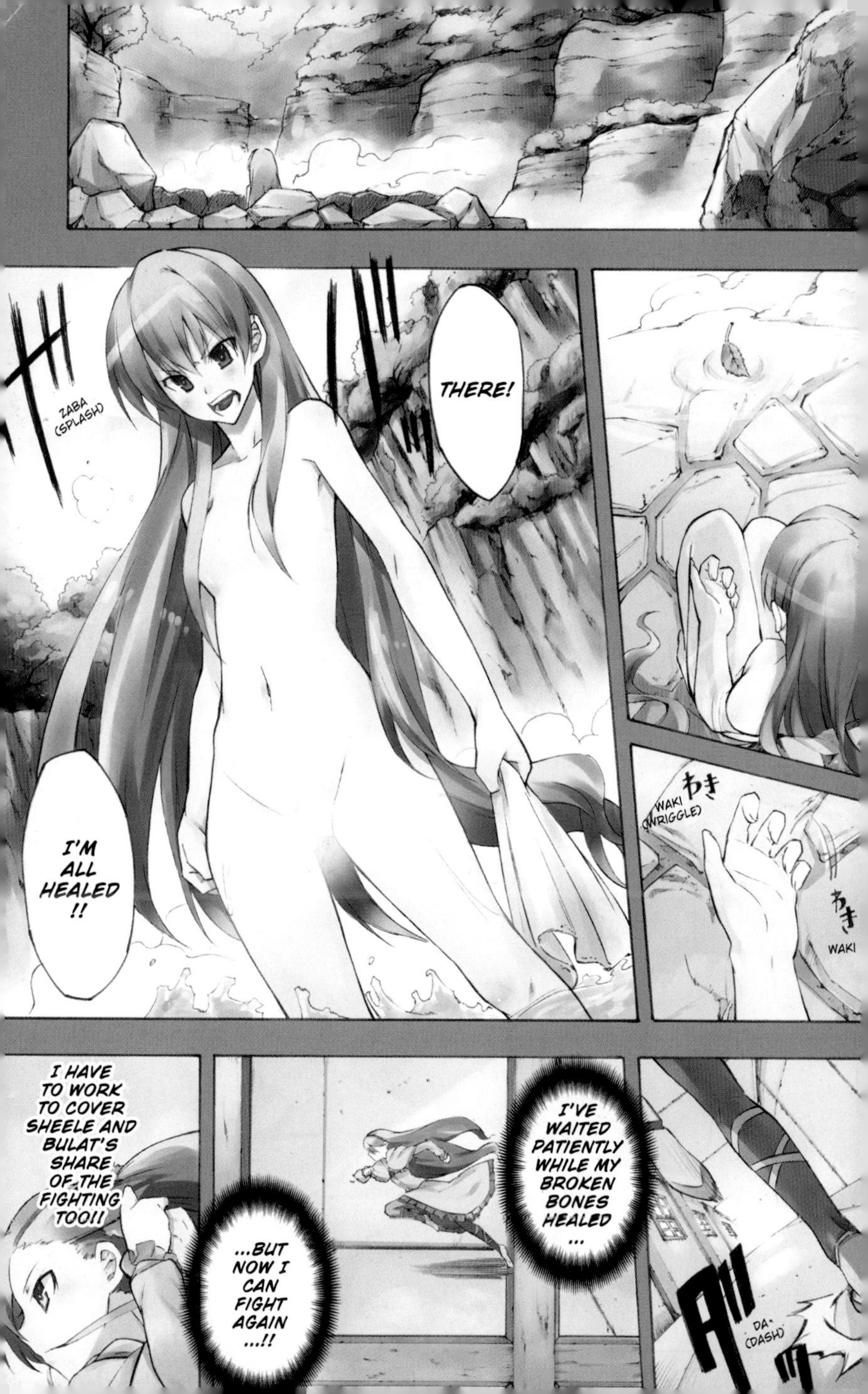

わき
WAKI (WRIGGLE)
わき
WAKI
ZABA (SPLASH)
THERE!
I'M ALL HEALED !!
DA (DASH)
I'VE WAITED PATIENTLY WHILE MY BROKEN BONES HEALED ...
...BUT NOW I CAN FIGHT AGAIN ...!!
I HAVE TO WORK TO COVER SHEELE AND BULAT'S SHARE OF THE FIGHTING TOO!!

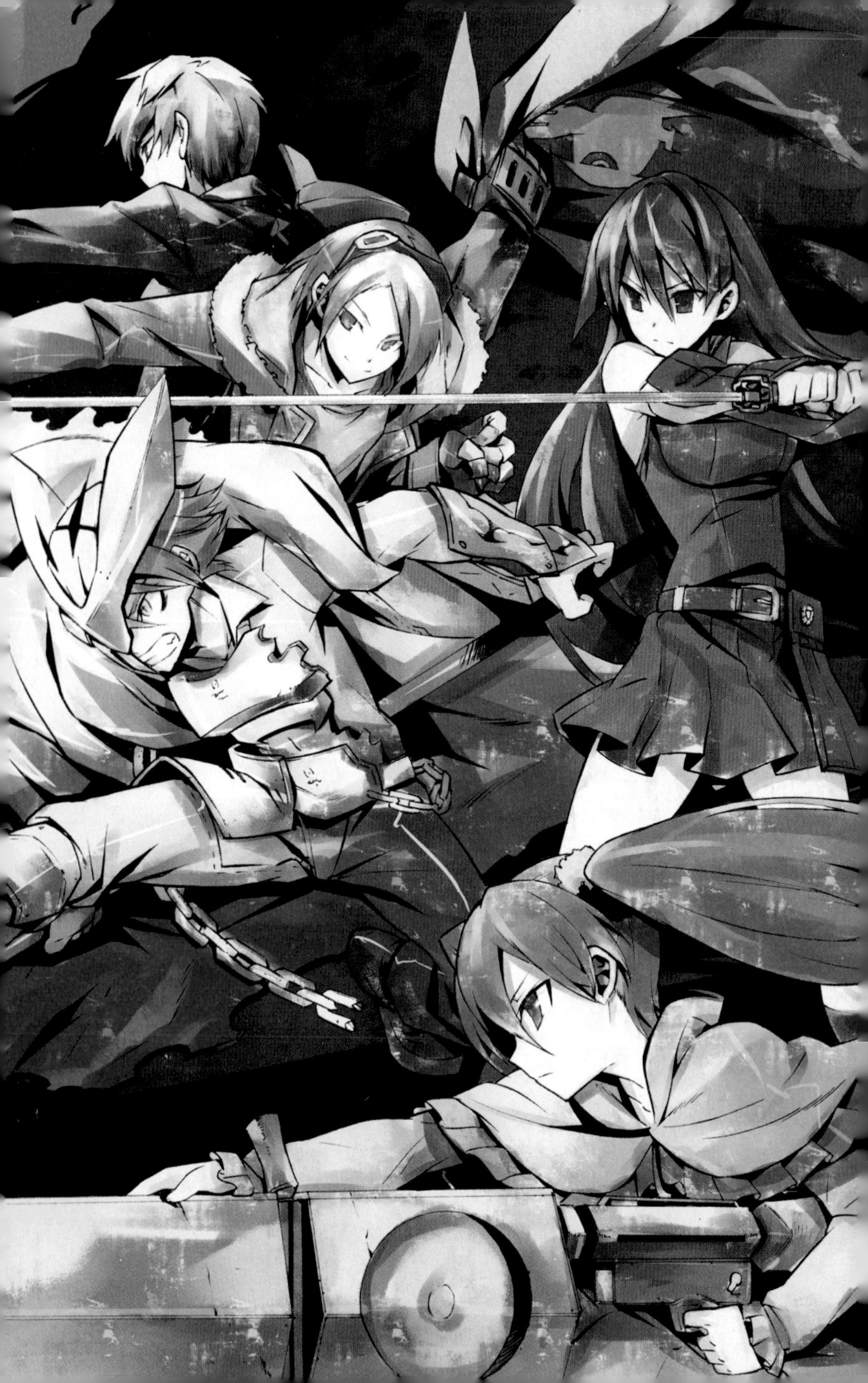

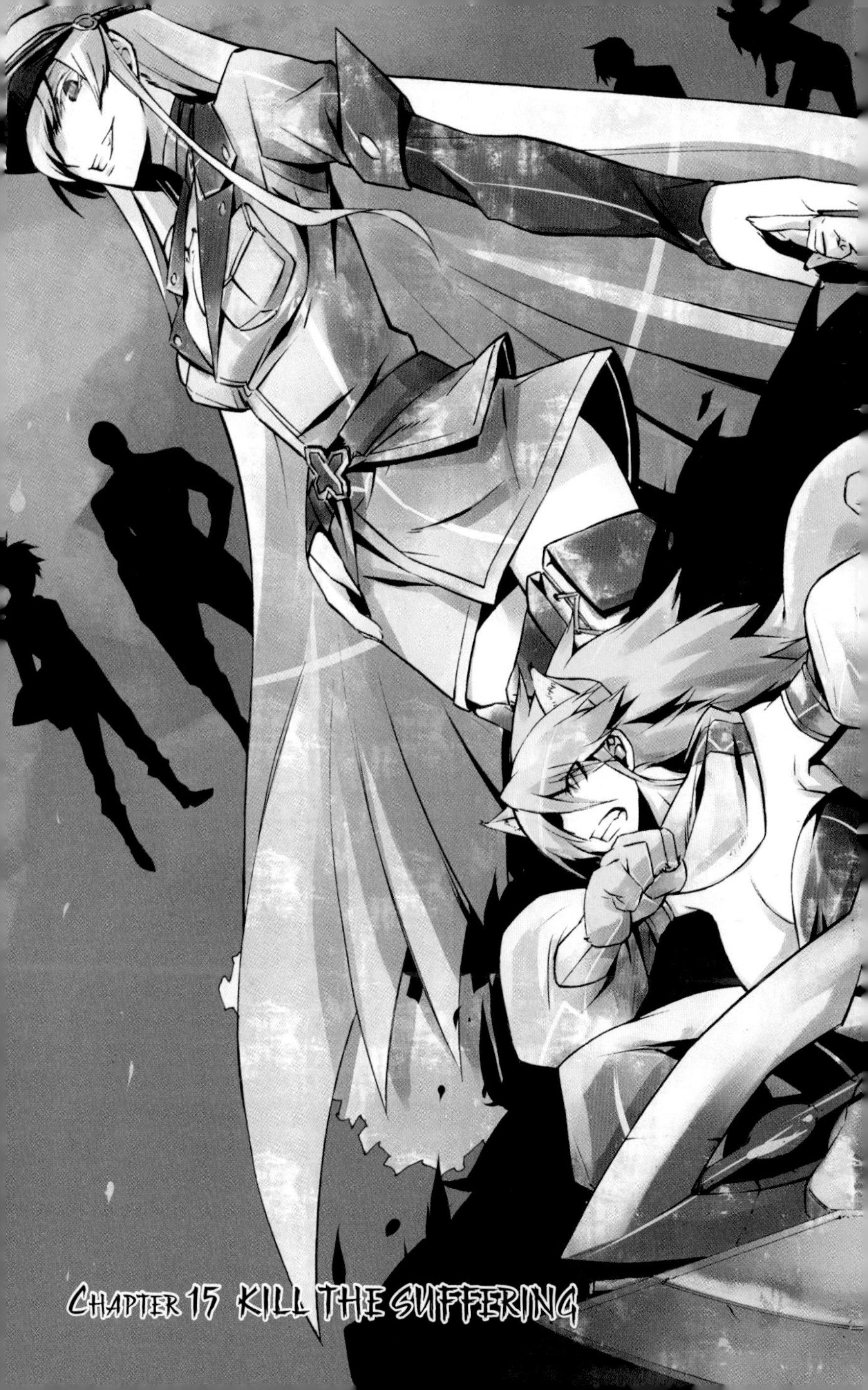

Chapter 15 Kill the Suffering

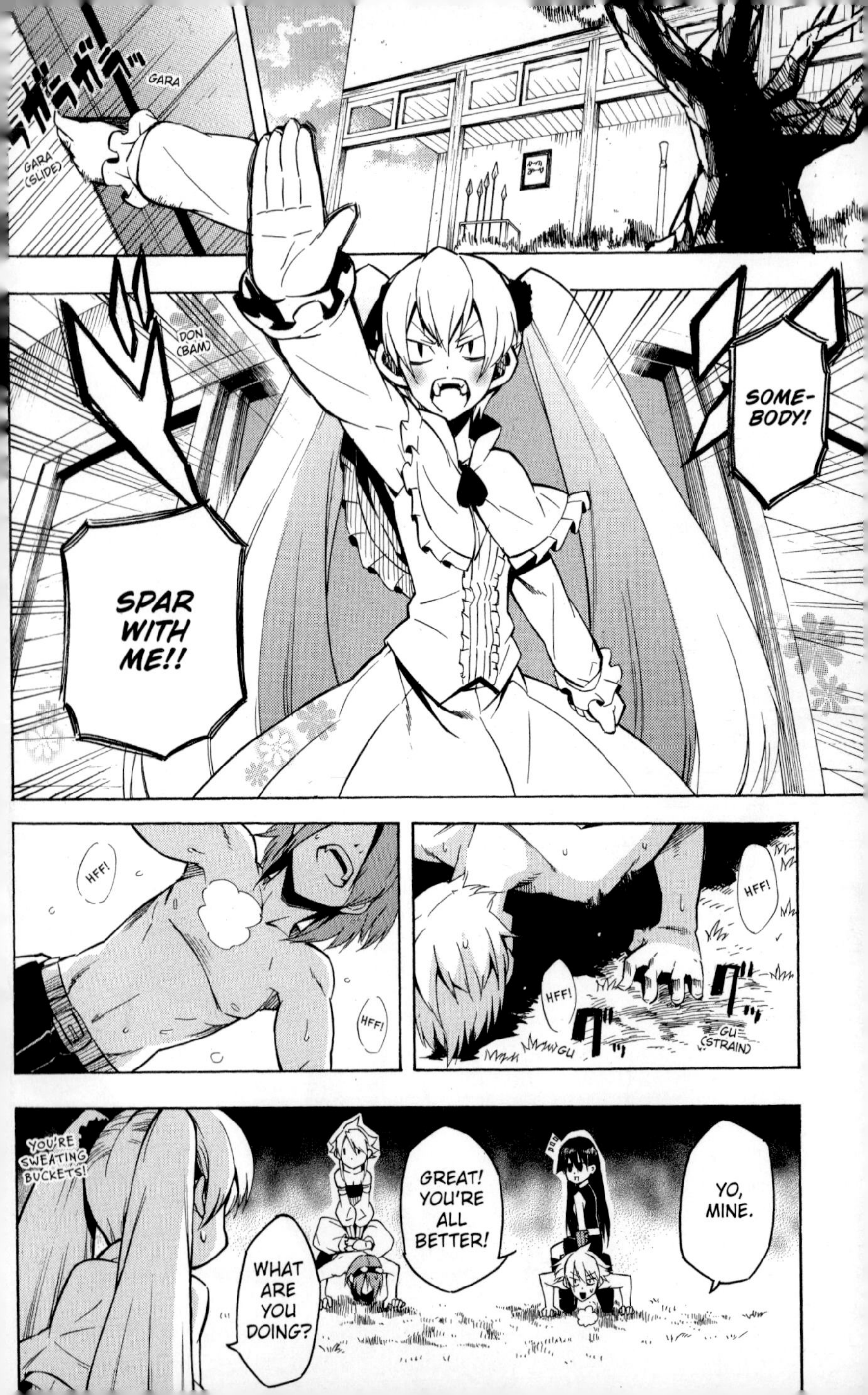
GARA
GARA (SLIDE)
DON (BAM)
SOME-BODY!
SPAR WITH ME!!
HFF!
HFF!
GU
GU (STRAIN)
HFF!
HFF!
YO, MINE.
GREAT! YOU'RE ALL BETTER!
WHAT ARE YOU DOING?
YOU'RE SWEATING BUCKETS!

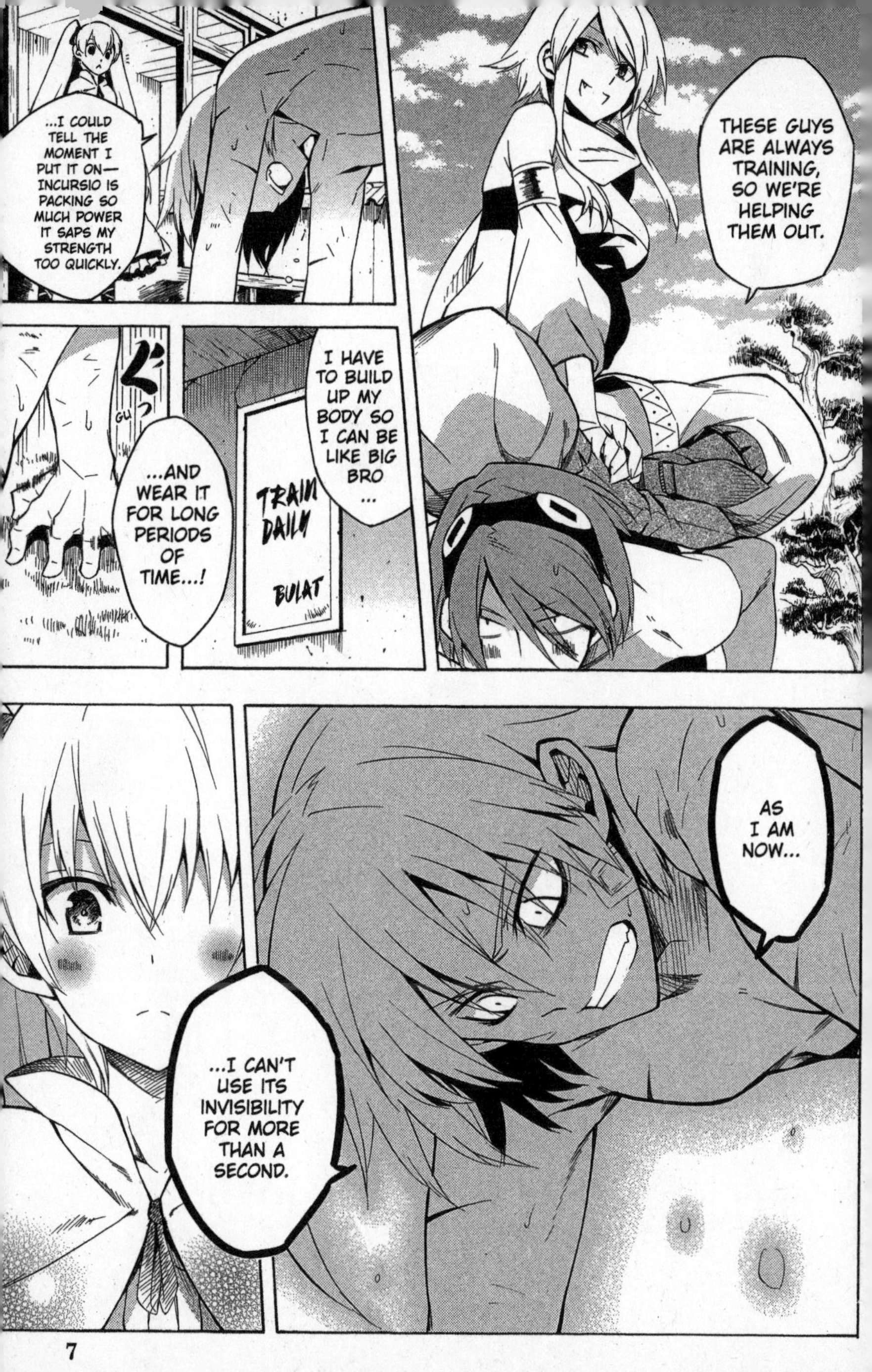
THESE GUYS ARE ALWAYS TRAINING, SO WE'RE HELPING THEM OUT.
...I COULD TELL THE MOMENT I PUT IT ON—INCURSIO IS PACKING SO MUCH POWER IT SAPS MY STRENGTH TOO QUICKLY.
I HAVE TO BUILD UP MY BODY SO I CAN BE LIKE BIG BRO ...
ぐ
GU
...AND WEAR IT FOR LONG PERIODS OF TIME...!
TRAIN DAILY
BULAT
AS I AM NOW...
...I CAN'T USE ITS INVISIBILITY FOR MORE THAN A SECOND.

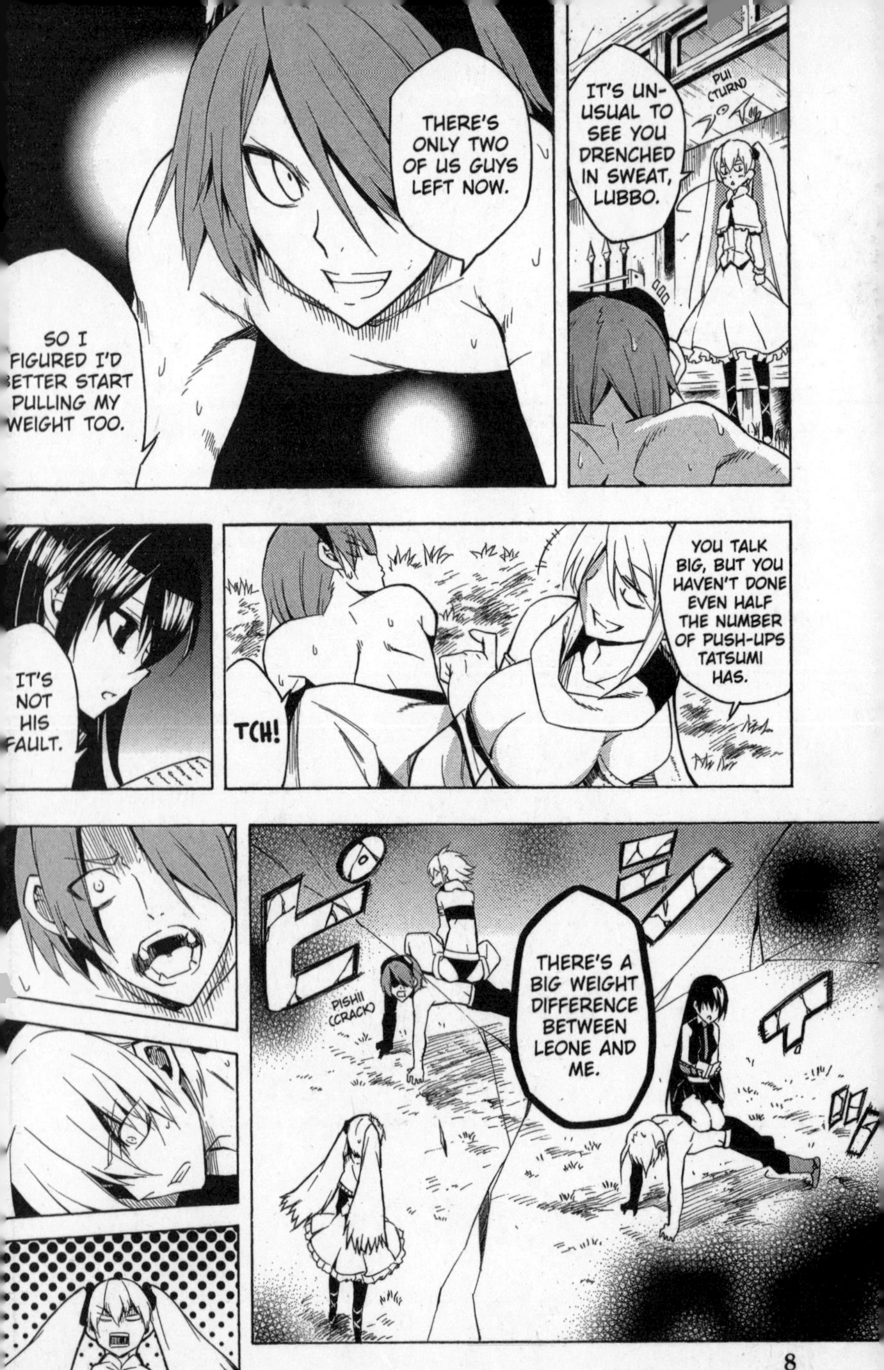
PUI (TURN)
IT'S UN-USUAL TO SEE YOU DRENCHED IN SWEAT, LUBBO.
THERE'S ONLY TWO OF US GUYS LEFT NOW.
SO I FIGURED I'D BETTER START PULLING MY WEIGHT TOO.
YOU TALK BIG, BUT YOU HAVEN'T DONE EVEN HALF THE NUMBER OF PUSH-UPS TATSUMI HAS.
TCH!
IT'S NOT HIS FAULT.
THERE'S A BIG WEIGHT DIFFERENCE BETWEEN LEONE AND ME.
PISHII (CRACK)

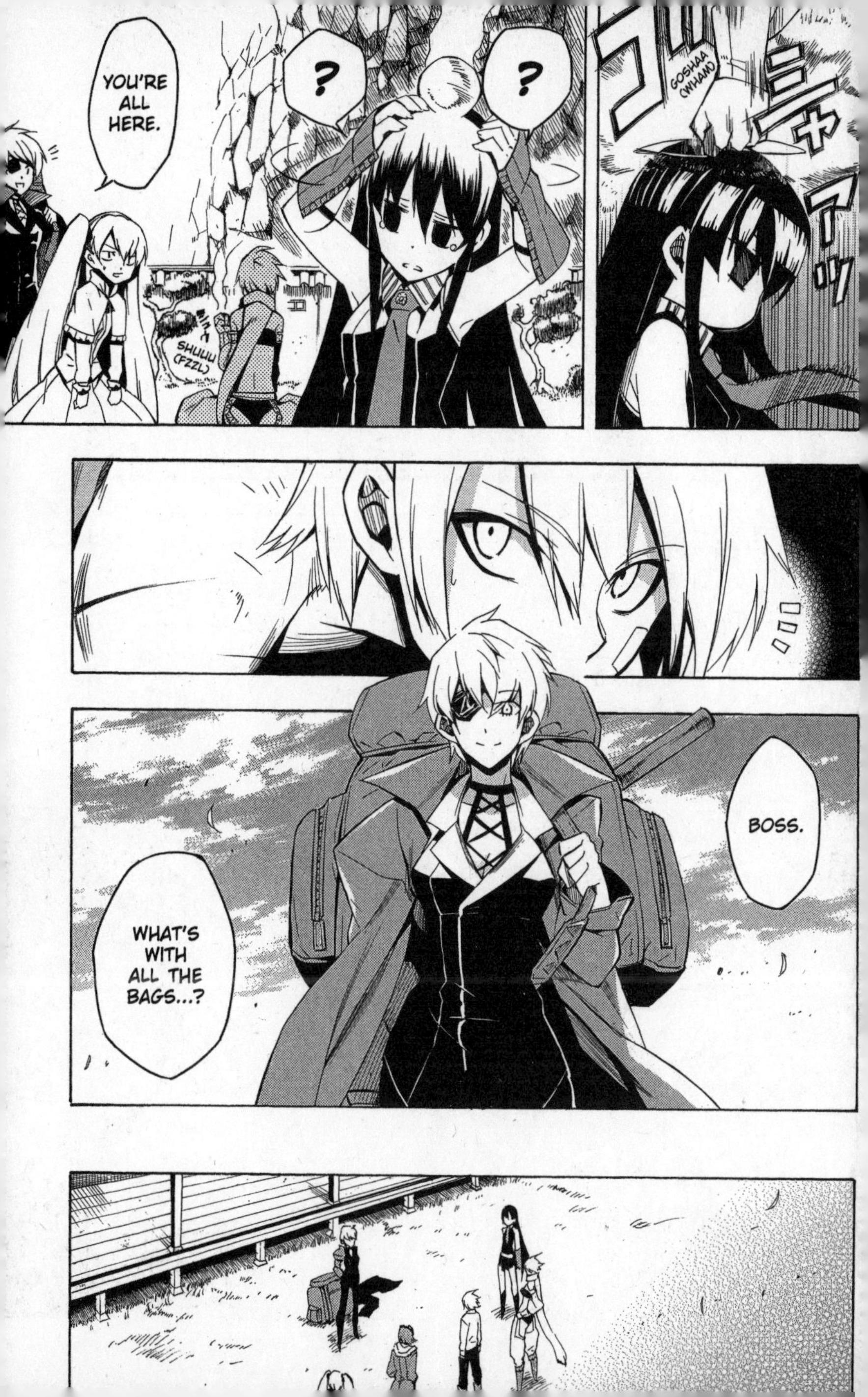

GOSHAA (WHAM)
?
?
YOU'RE ALL HERE.
SHUUU (FZZL)
BOSS.
WHAT'S WITH ALL THE BAGS...?

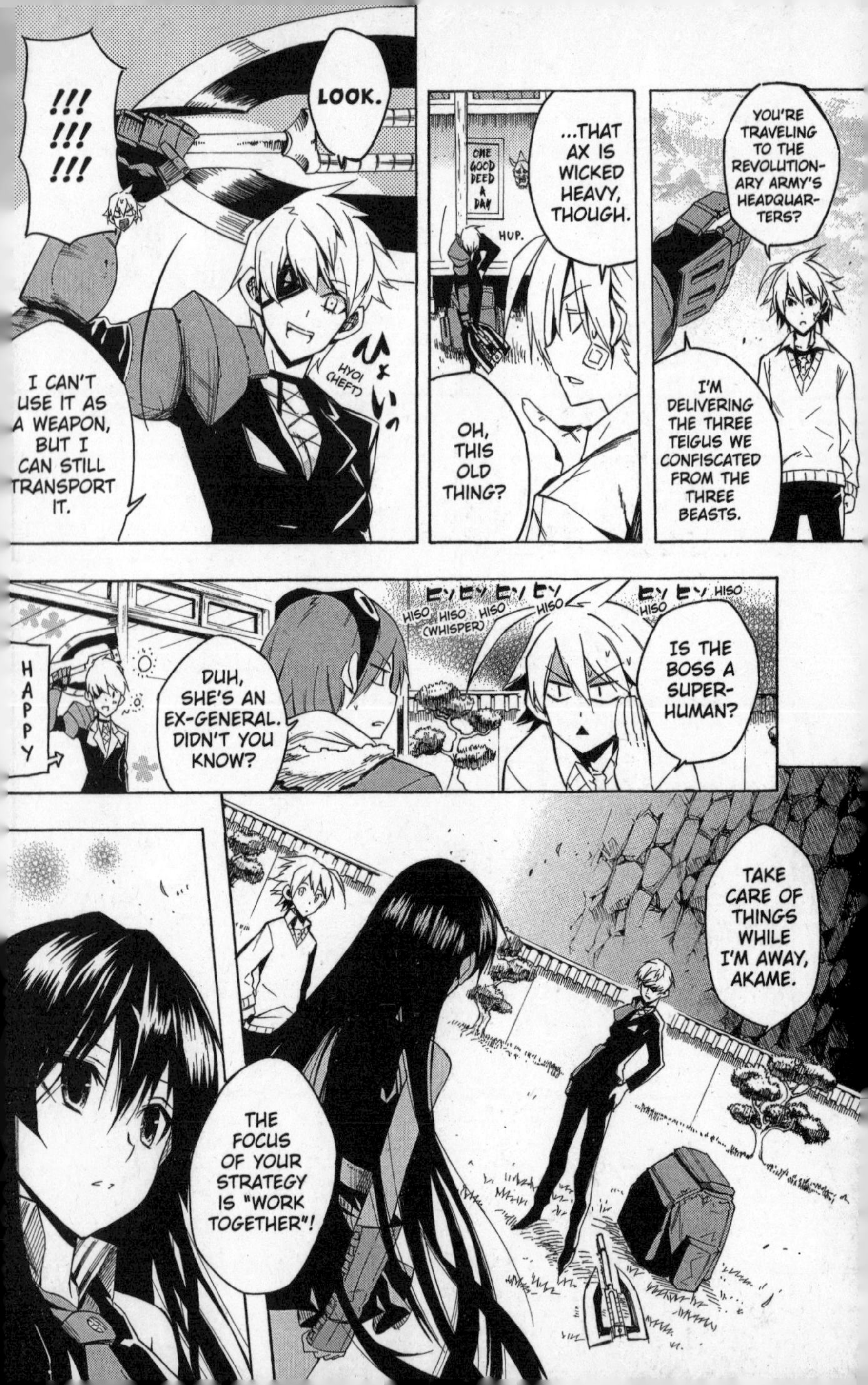
YOU'RE TRAVELING TO THE REVOLUTIONARY ARMY'S HEADQUARTERS?
I'M DELIVERING THE THREE TEIGUS WE CONFISCATED FROM THE THREE BEASTS.
...THAT AX IS WICKED HEAVY, THOUGH.
ONE GOOD DEED A DAY
HUP.
OH, THIS OLD THING?
LOOK.
!!! !!! !!!
HYOI (HEFT)
I CAN'T USE IT AS A WEAPON, BUT I CAN STILL TRANSPORT IT.
HISO HISO
IS THE BOSS A SUPERHUMAN?
HISO HISO HISO (WHISPER) HISO
DUH, SHE'S AN EX-GENERAL. DIDN'T YOU KNOW?
HAPPY
TAKE CARE OF THINGS WHILE I'M AWAY, AKAME.
...
THE FOCUS OF YOUR STRATEGY IS "WORK TOGETHER"!

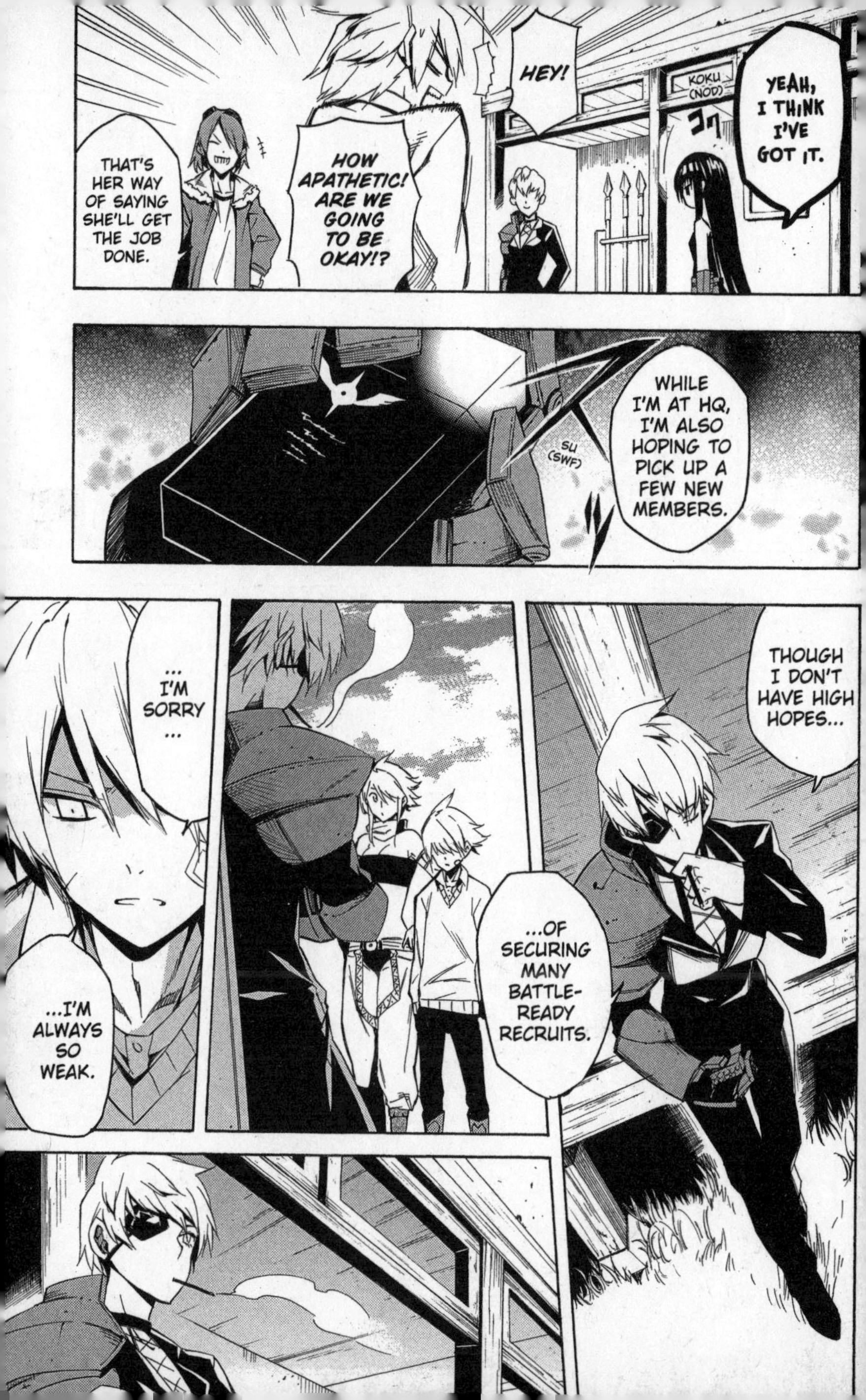
YEAH, I THINK I'VE GOT IT.
KOKU (NOD)
HEY!
HOW APATHETIC! ARE WE GOING TO BE OKAY!?
THAT'S HER WAY OF SAYING SHE'LL GET THE JOB DONE.
WHILE I'M AT HQ, I'M ALSO HOPING TO PICK UP A FEW NEW MEMBERS.
SU (SWF)
THOUGH I DON'T HAVE HIGH HOPES...
...OF SECURING MANY BATTLE-READY RECRUITS.
...I'M SORRY...
...I'M ALWAYS SO WEAK.

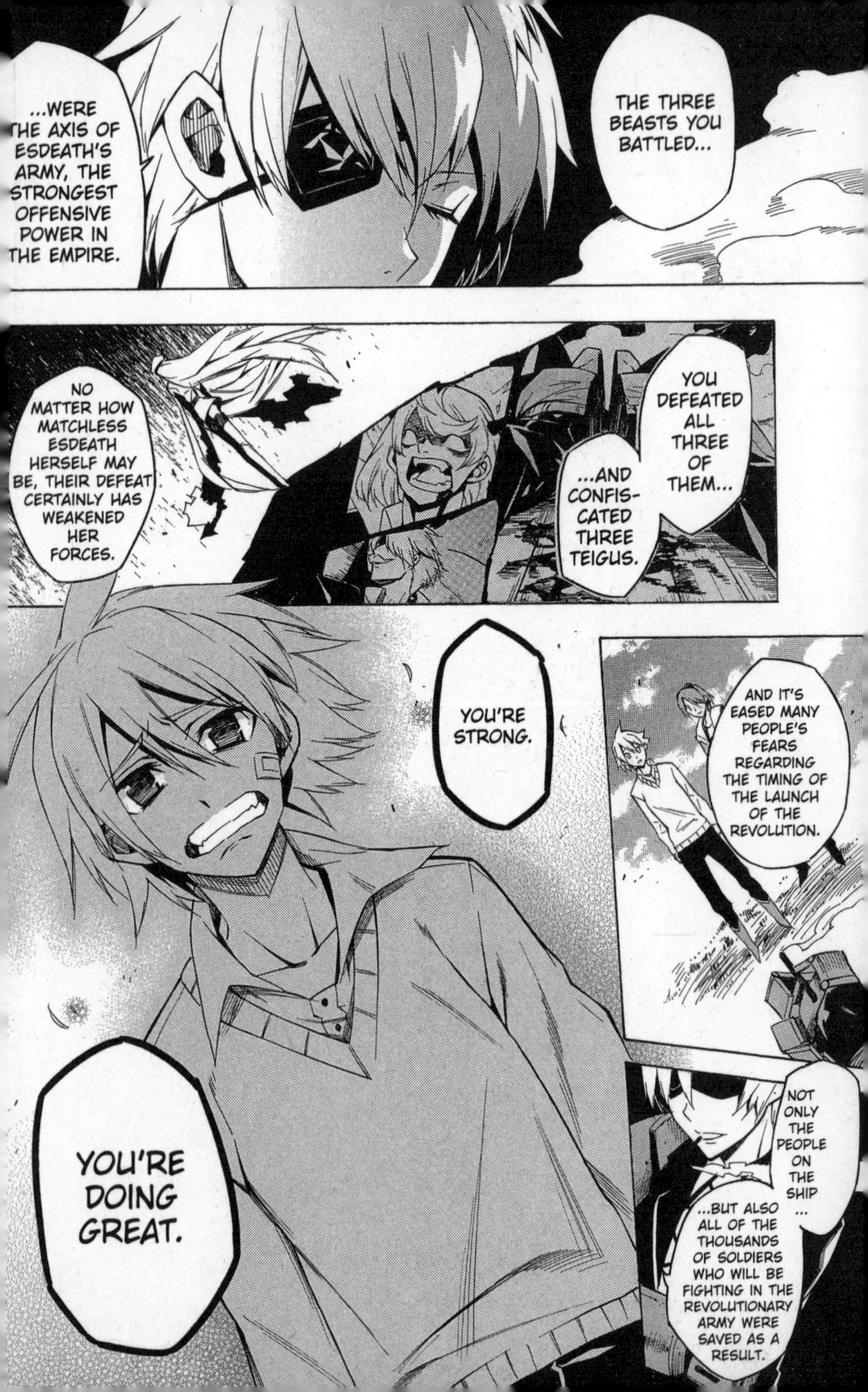
THE THREE BEASTS YOU BATTLED...
...WERE THE AXIS OF ESDEATH'S ARMY, THE STRONGEST OFFENSIVE POWER IN THE EMPIRE.
YOU DEFEATED ALL THREE OF THEM...
...AND CONFISCATED THREE TEIGUS.
NO MATTER HOW MATCHLESS ESDEATH HERSELF MAY BE, THEIR DEFEAT CERTAINLY HAS WEAKENED HER FORCES.
AND IT'S EASED MANY PEOPLE'S FEARS REGARDING THE TIMING OF THE LAUNCH OF THE REVOLUTION.
YOU'RE STRONG.
NOT ONLY THE PEOPLE ON THE SHIP...
...BUT ALSO ALL OF THE THOUSANDS OF SOLDIERS WHO WILL BE FIGHTING IN THE REVOLUTIONARY ARMY WERE SAVED AS A RESULT.
YOU'RE DOING GREAT.

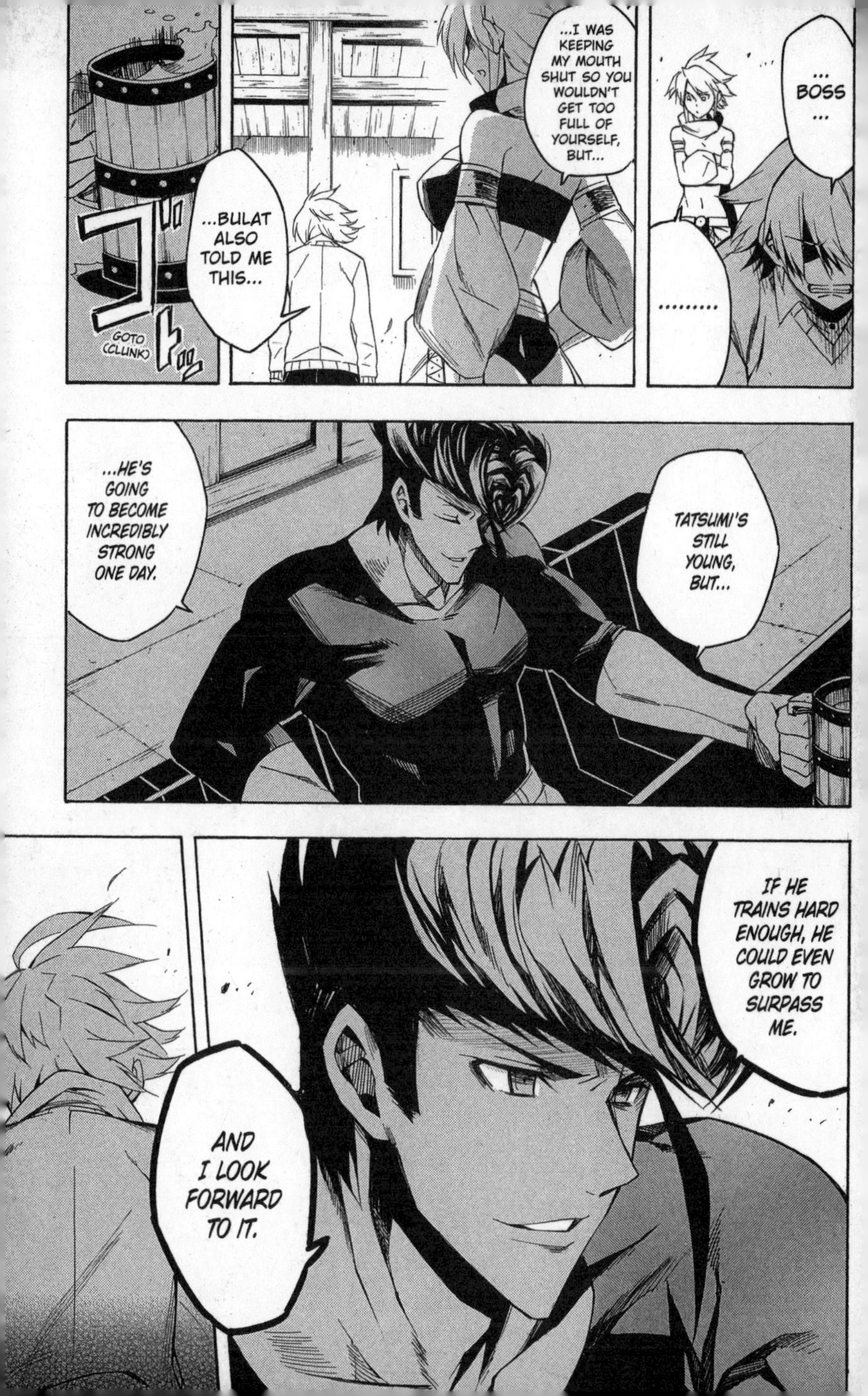
...BOSS...
....
...I WAS KEEPING MY MOUTH SHUT SO YOU WOULDN'T GET TOO FULL OF YOURSELF, BUT...
...BULAT ALSO TOLD ME THIS...
GOTO (CLUNK)
TATSUMI'S STILL YOUNG, BUT...
...HE'S GOING TO BECOME INCREDIBLY STRONG ONE DAY.
IF HE TRAINS HARD ENOUGH, HE COULD EVEN GROW TO SURPASS ME.
AND I LOOK FORWARD TO IT.

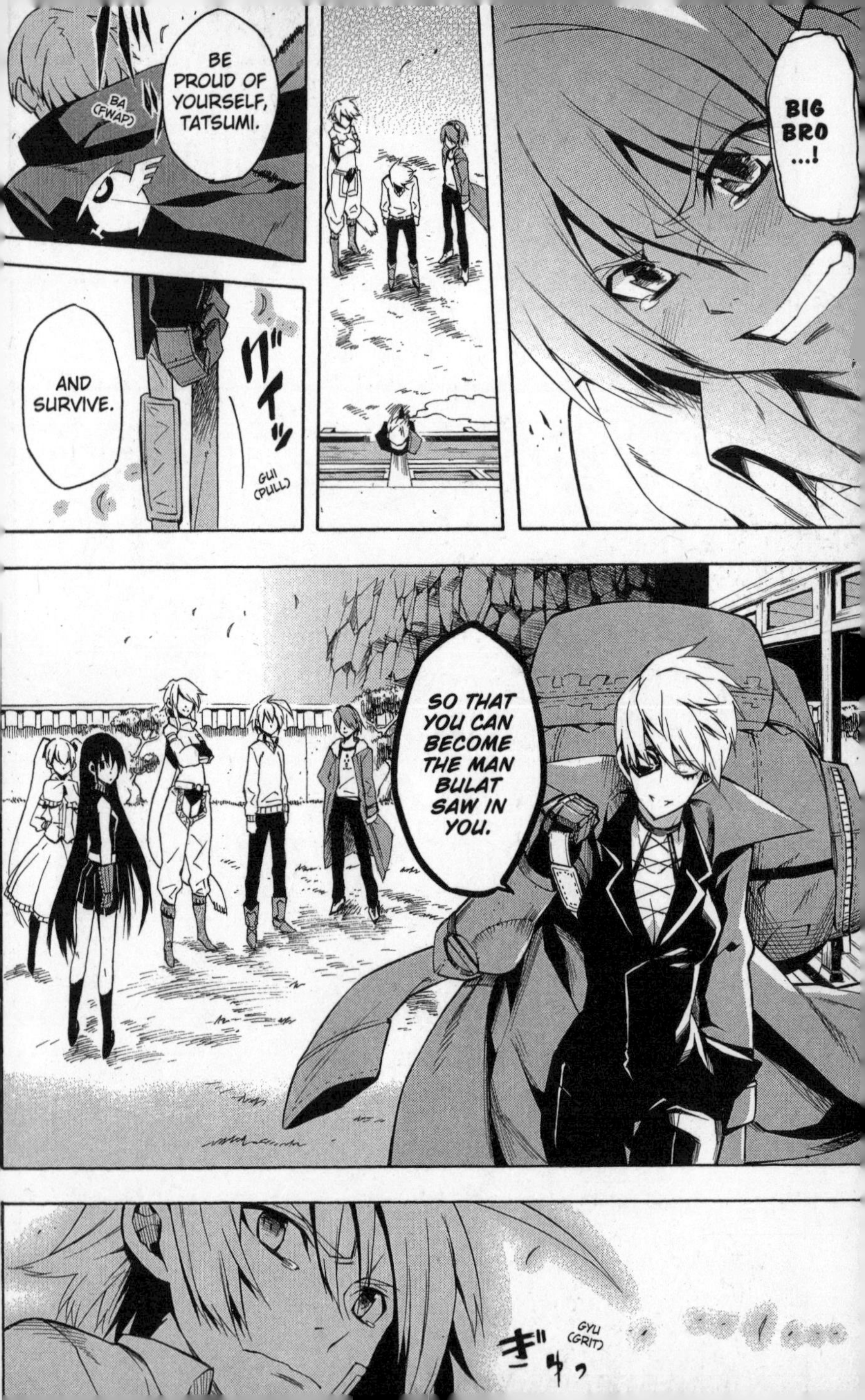
BIG BRO ...!
BE PROUD OF YOURSELF, TATSUMI.
BA (FWAP)
AND SURVIVE.
GUI (PULL)
SO THAT YOU CAN BECOME THE MAN BULAT SAW IN YOU.
GYU (GRIT)

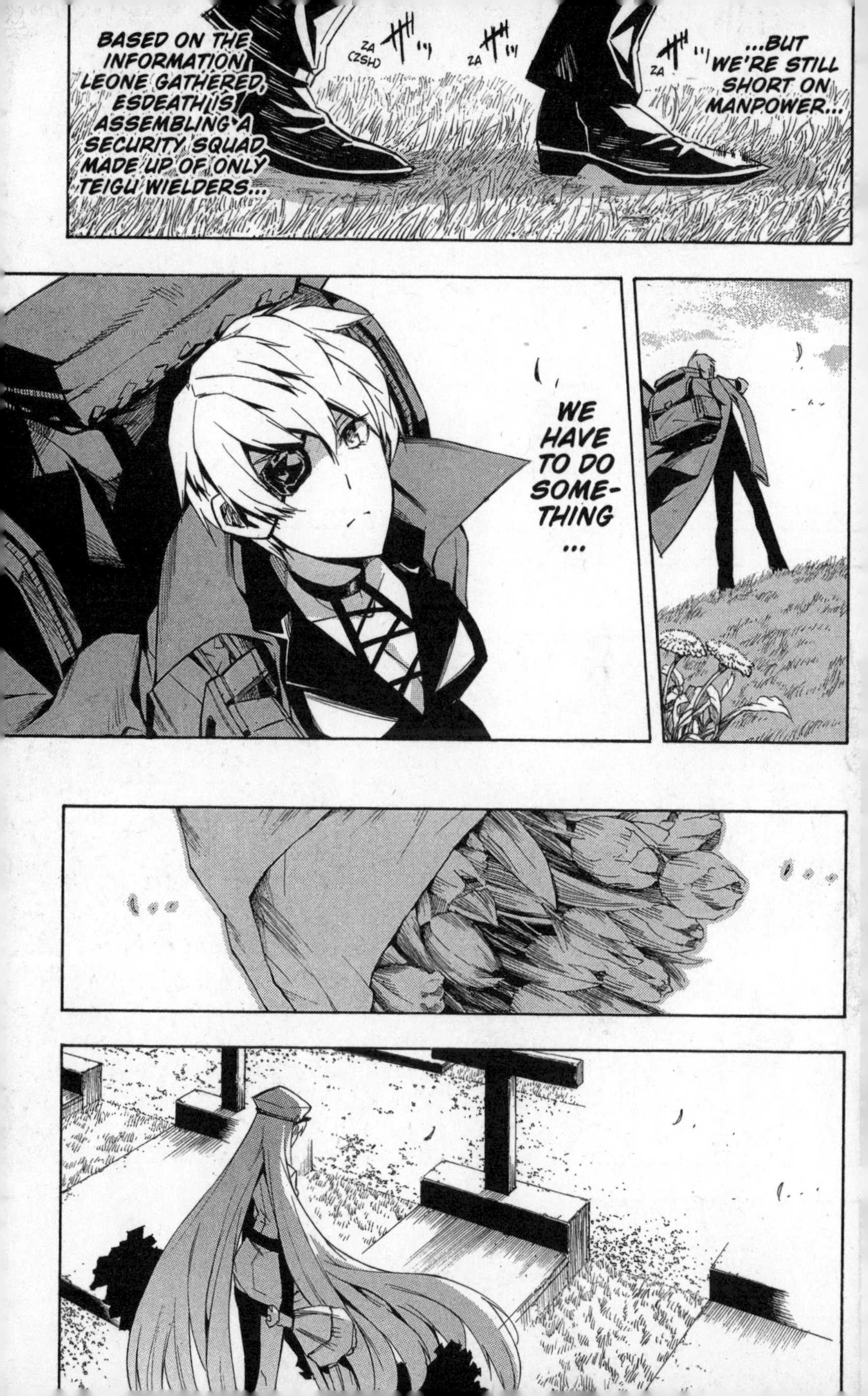
BASED ON THE INFORMATION LEONE GATHERED, ESDEATH IS ASSEMBLING A SECURITY SQUAD MADE UP OF ONLY TEIGU WIELDERS...
ZA (ZSH)
ZA
ZA
...BUT WE'RE STILL SHORT ON MANPOWER...
WE HAVE TO DO SOME-THING ...
...

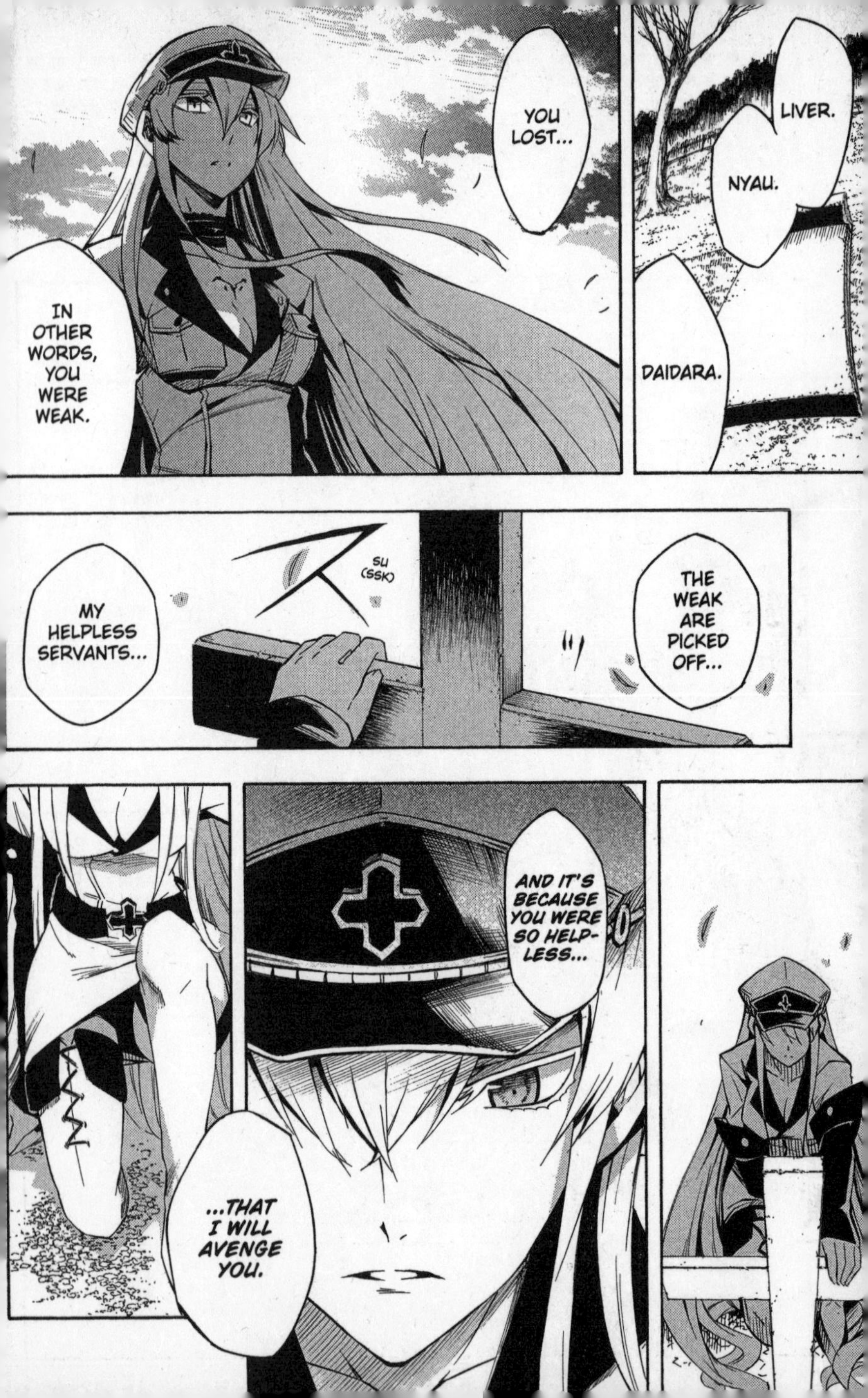
LIVER.
NYAU.
DAIDARA.
YOU LOST...
IN OTHER WORDS, YOU WERE WEAK.
THE WEAK ARE PICKED OFF...
SU (SSK)
MY HELPLESS SERVANTS...
AND IT'S BECAUSE YOU WERE SO HELP-LESS...
...THAT I WILL AVENGE YOU.

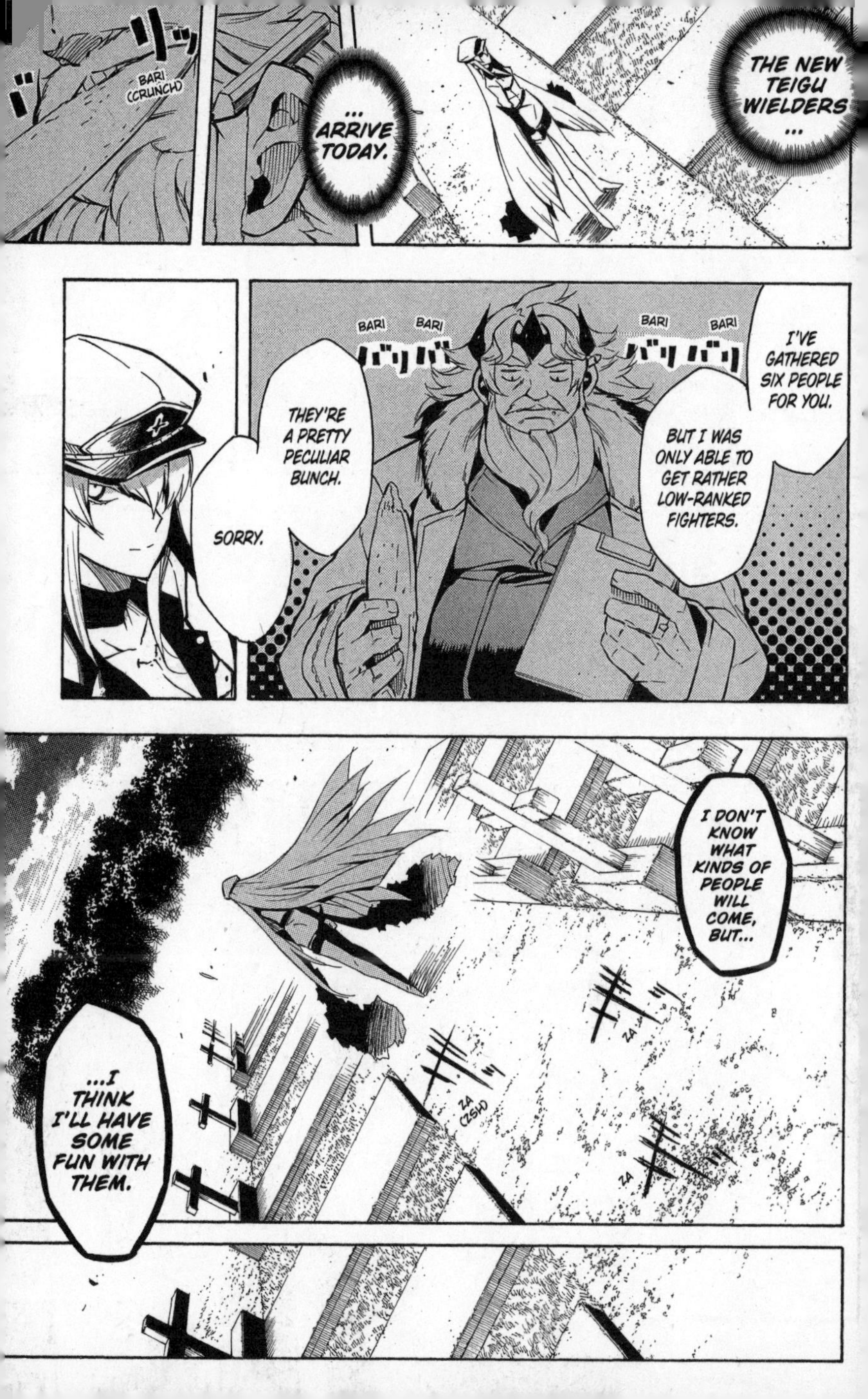
THE NEW TEIGU WIELDERS...
...ARRIVE TODAY.
BARI (CRUNCH)
BARI BARI BARI BARI
I'VE GATHERED SIX PEOPLE FOR YOU.
BUT I WAS ONLY ABLE TO GET RATHER LOW-RANKED FIGHTERS.
THEY'RE A PRETTY PECULIAR BUNCH.
SORRY.
I DON'T KNOW WHAT KINDS OF PEOPLE WILL COME, BUT...
...I THINK I'LL HAVE SOME FUN WITH THEM.
ZA
ZA (ZSH)
ZA

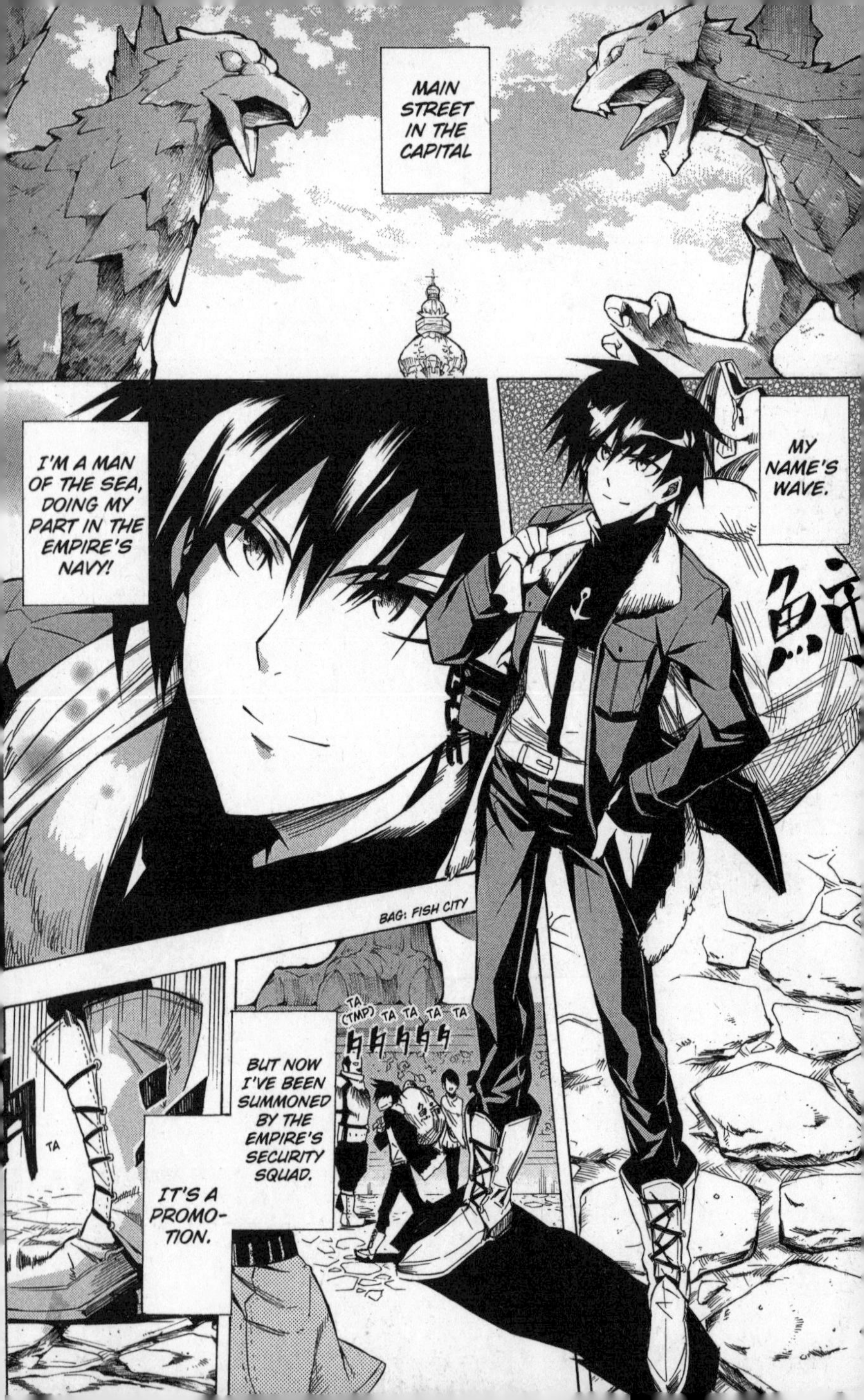
MAIN STREET IN THE CAPITAL
MY NAME'S WAVE.
I'M A MAN OF THE SEA, DOING MY PART IN THE EMPIRE'S NAVY!
BAG: FISH CITY
TA (TMP) TA TA TA TA
BUT NOW I'VE BEEN SUMMONED BY THE EMPIRE'S SECURITY SQUAD.
IT'S A PROMOTION.
TA

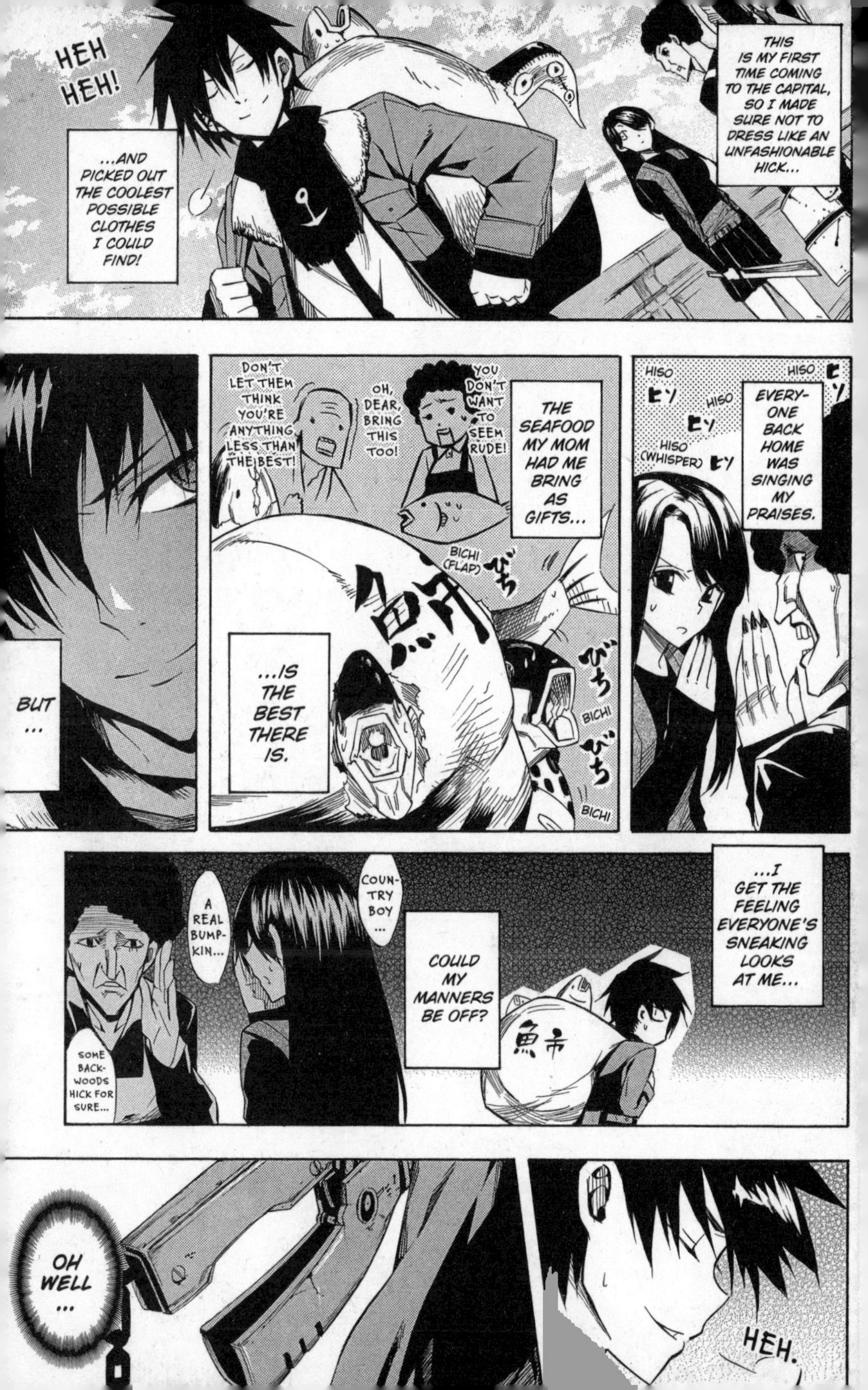
THIS IS MY FIRST TIME COMING TO THE CAPITAL, SO I MADE SURE NOT TO DRESS LIKE AN UNFASHIONABLE HICK...
...AND PICKED OUT THE COOLEST POSSIBLE CLOTHES I COULD FIND!
HEH HEH!
HISO HISO HISO HISO (WHISPER)
EVERY-ONE BACK HOME WAS SINGING MY PRAISES.
THE SEAFOOD MY MOM HAD ME BRING AS GIFTS...
YOU DON'T WANT TO SEEM RUDE!
OH, DEAR, BRING THIS TOO!
DON'T LET THEM THINK YOU'RE ANYTHING LESS THAN THE BEST!
BICHI (FLAP)
BICHI
BICHI
...IS THE BEST THERE IS.
BUT...
...I GET THE FEELING EVERYONE'S SNEAKING LOOKS AT ME...
COULD MY MANNERS BE OFF?
COUN-TRY BOY...
A REAL BUMP-KIN...
SOME BACK-WOODS HICK FOR SURE...
HEH.
OH WELL...

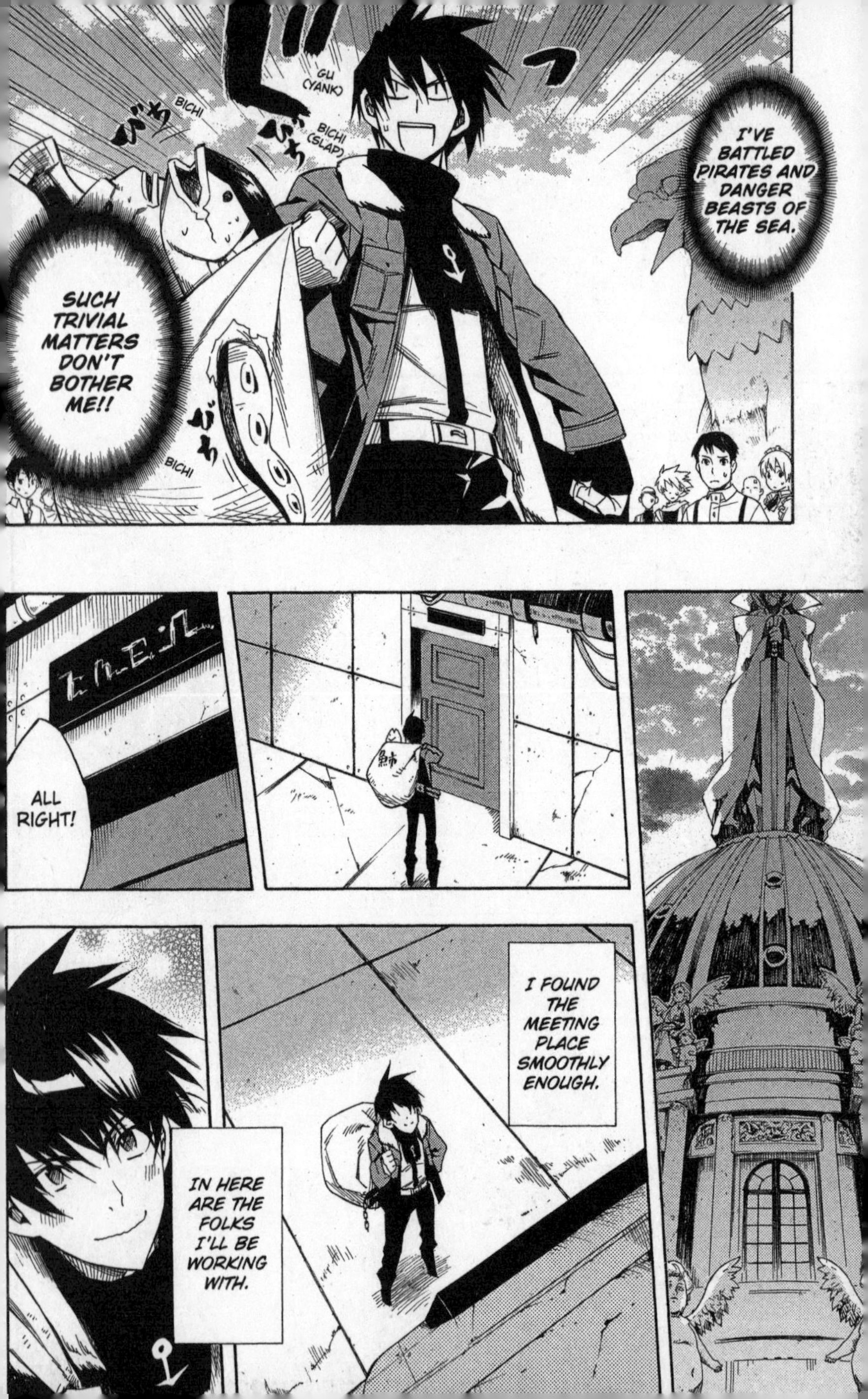
I'VE BATTLED PIRATES AND DANGER BEASTS OF THE SEA.
GU (YANK)
BICHI (SLAP)
BICHI
SUCH TRIVIAL MATTERS DON'T BOTHER ME!!
BICHI
ALL RIGHT!
I FOUND THE MEETING PLACE SMOOTHLY ENOUGH.
IN HERE ARE THE FOLKS I'LL BE WORKING WITH.

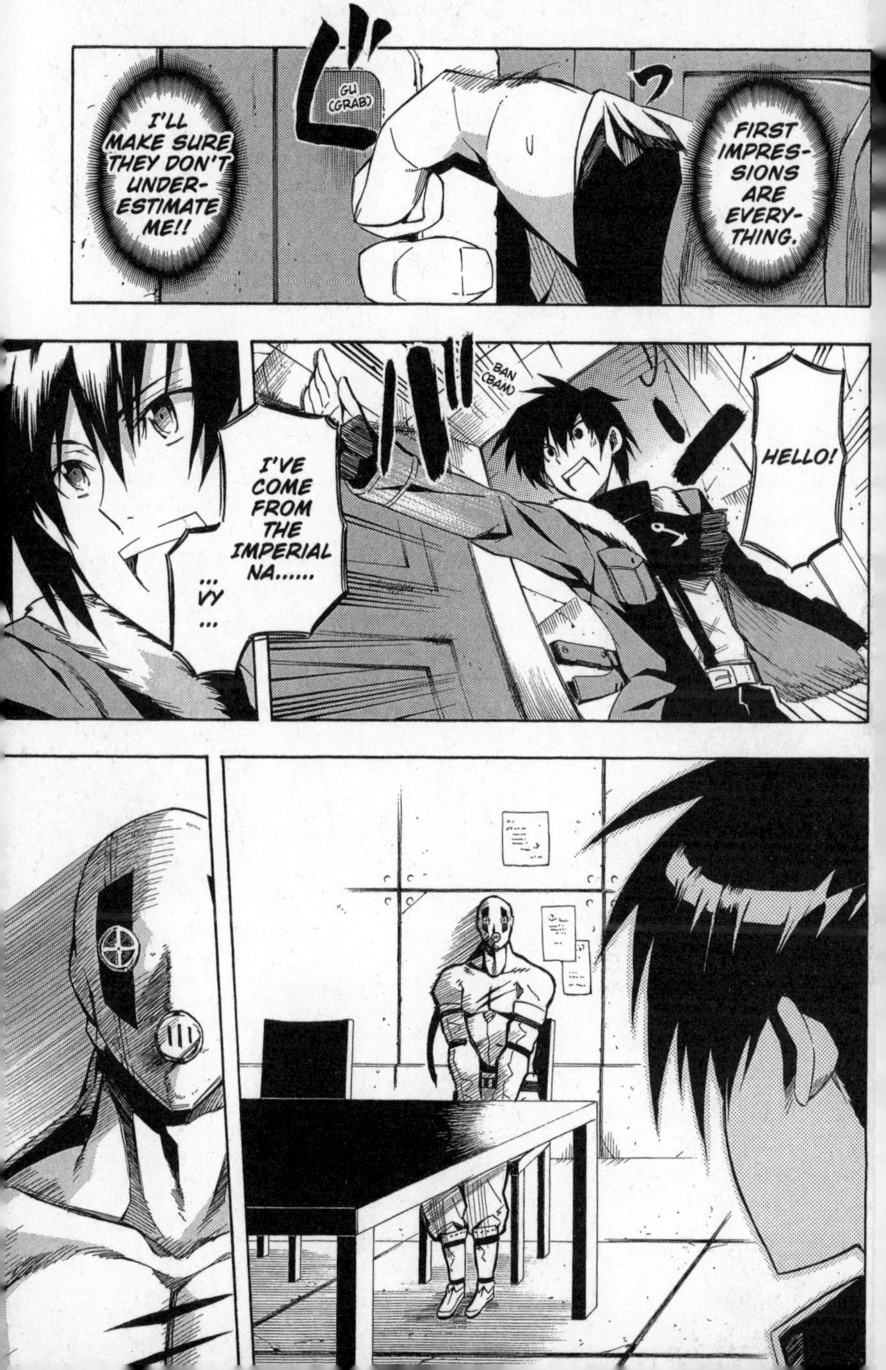
FIRST IMPRES-SIONS ARE EVERY-THING.
GU (GRAB)
I'LL MAKE SURE THEY DON'T UNDER-ESTIMATE ME!!
HELLO!
BAN (BAM)
I'VE COME FROM THE IMPERIAL NA......
...VY...

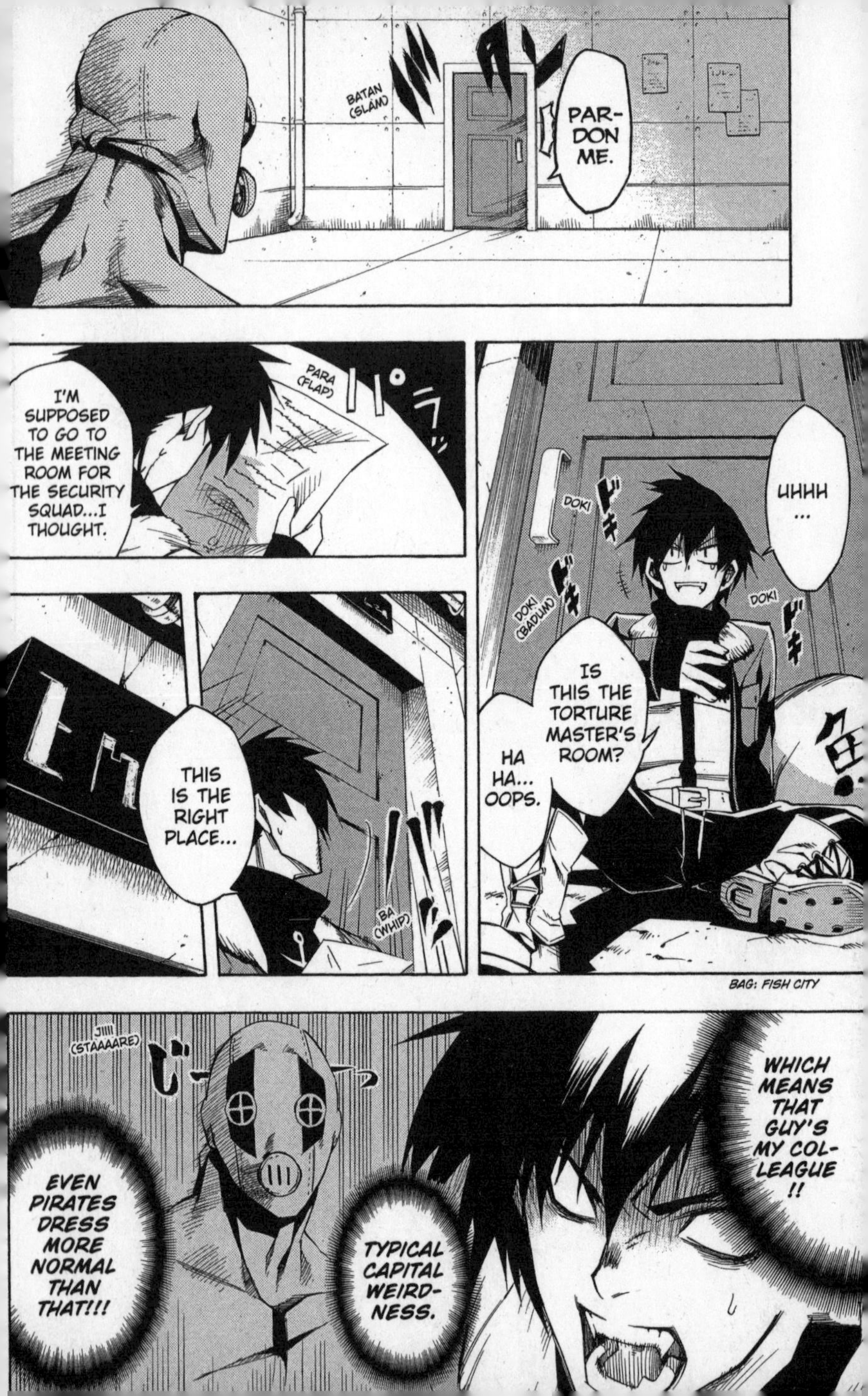
PAR-DON ME.
BATAN (SLAM)
UHHH ...
DOKI
DOKI (BADUM)
DOKI
IS THIS THE TORTURE MASTER'S ROOM?
HA HA... OOPS.
PARA (FLAP)
I'M SUPPOSED TO GO TO THE MEETING ROOM FOR THE SECURITY SQUAD...I THOUGHT.
THIS IS THE RIGHT PLACE...
BA (WHIP)
BAG: FISH CITY
WHICH MEANS THAT GUY'S MY COL-LEAGUE !!
JIIII (STAAAARE)
TYPICAL CAPITAL WEIRD-NESS.
EVEN PIRATES DRESS MORE NORMAL THAN THAT!!!

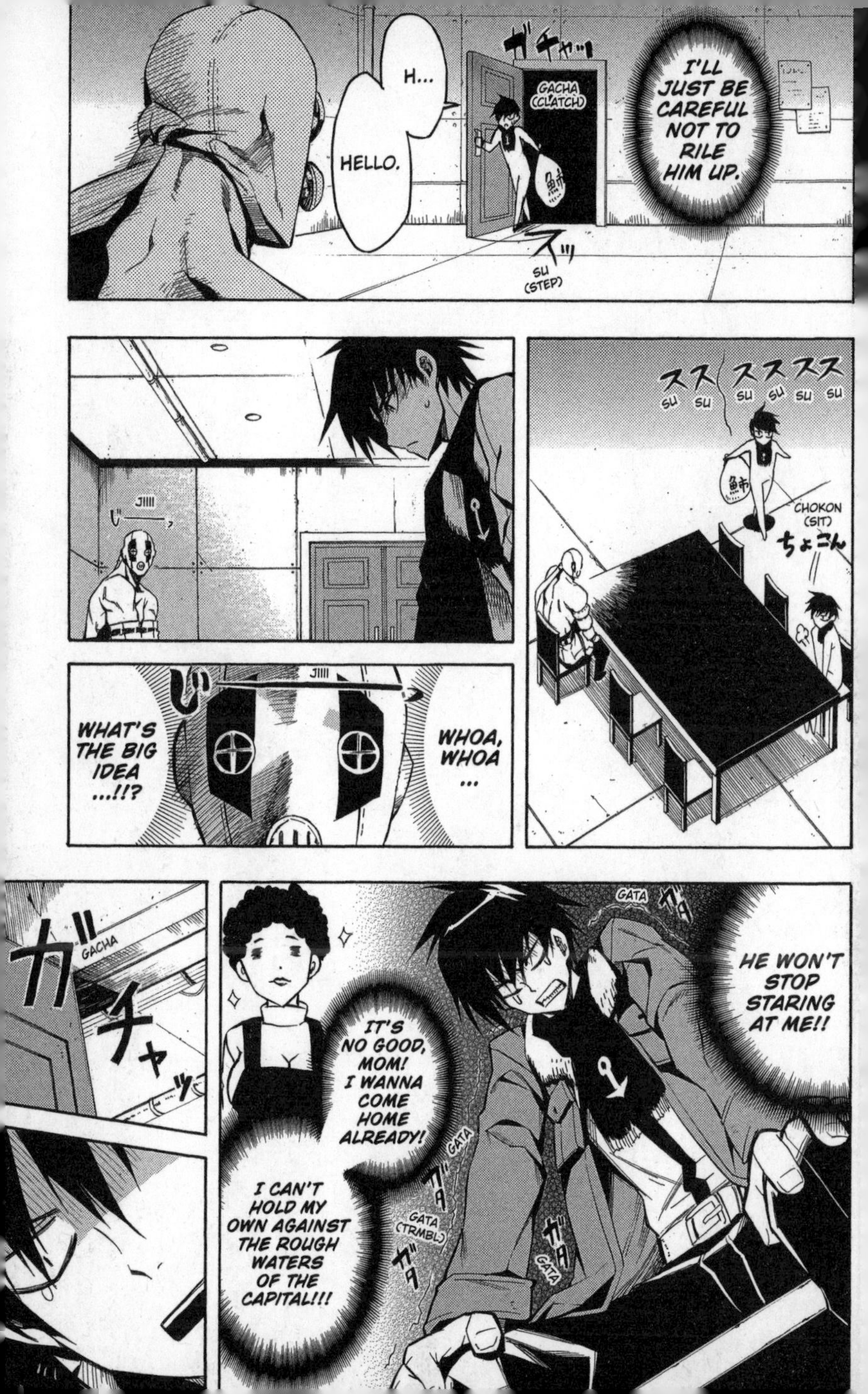
I'LL JUST BE CAREFUL NOT TO RILE HIM UP.
GACHA (CLATCH)
H...
HELLO.
SU (STEP)
SU SU SU SU SU SU
CHOKON (SIT)
JIIII
JIIII
WHOA, WHOA ...
WHAT'S THE BIG IDEA ...!!?
GATA
HE WON'T STOP STARING AT ME!!
IT'S NO GOOD, MOM! I WANNA COME HOME ALREADY!
GATA
GATA (TRMBL)
GATA
I CAN'T HOLD MY OWN AGAINST THE ROUGH WATERS OF THE CAPITAL!!!
GACHA

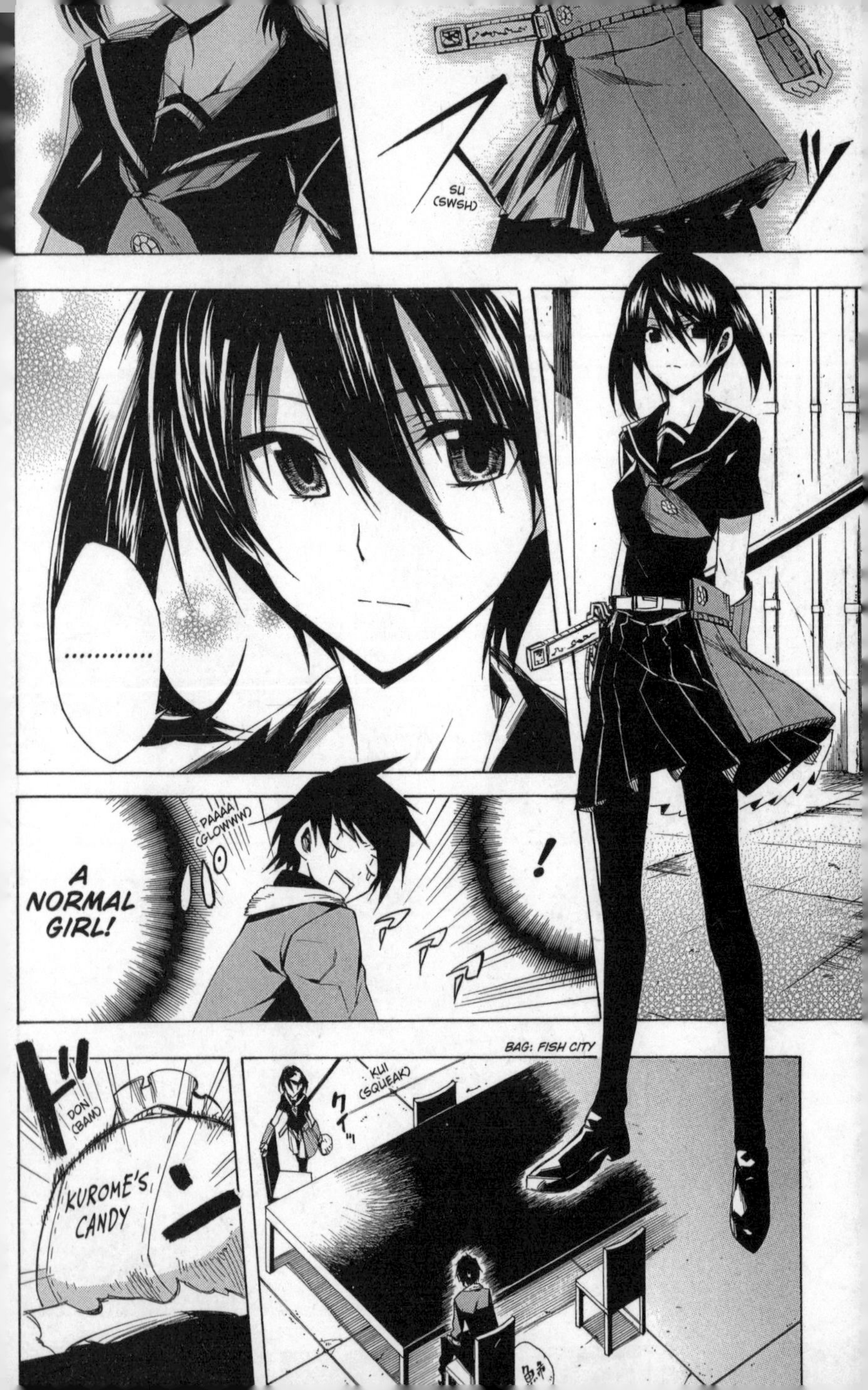
SU (SWSH)
....
PAAAA (GLOWWW)
!
A NORMAL GIRL!
BAG: FISH CITY
KUI (SQUEAK)
DON (BAM)
KUROME'S CANDY

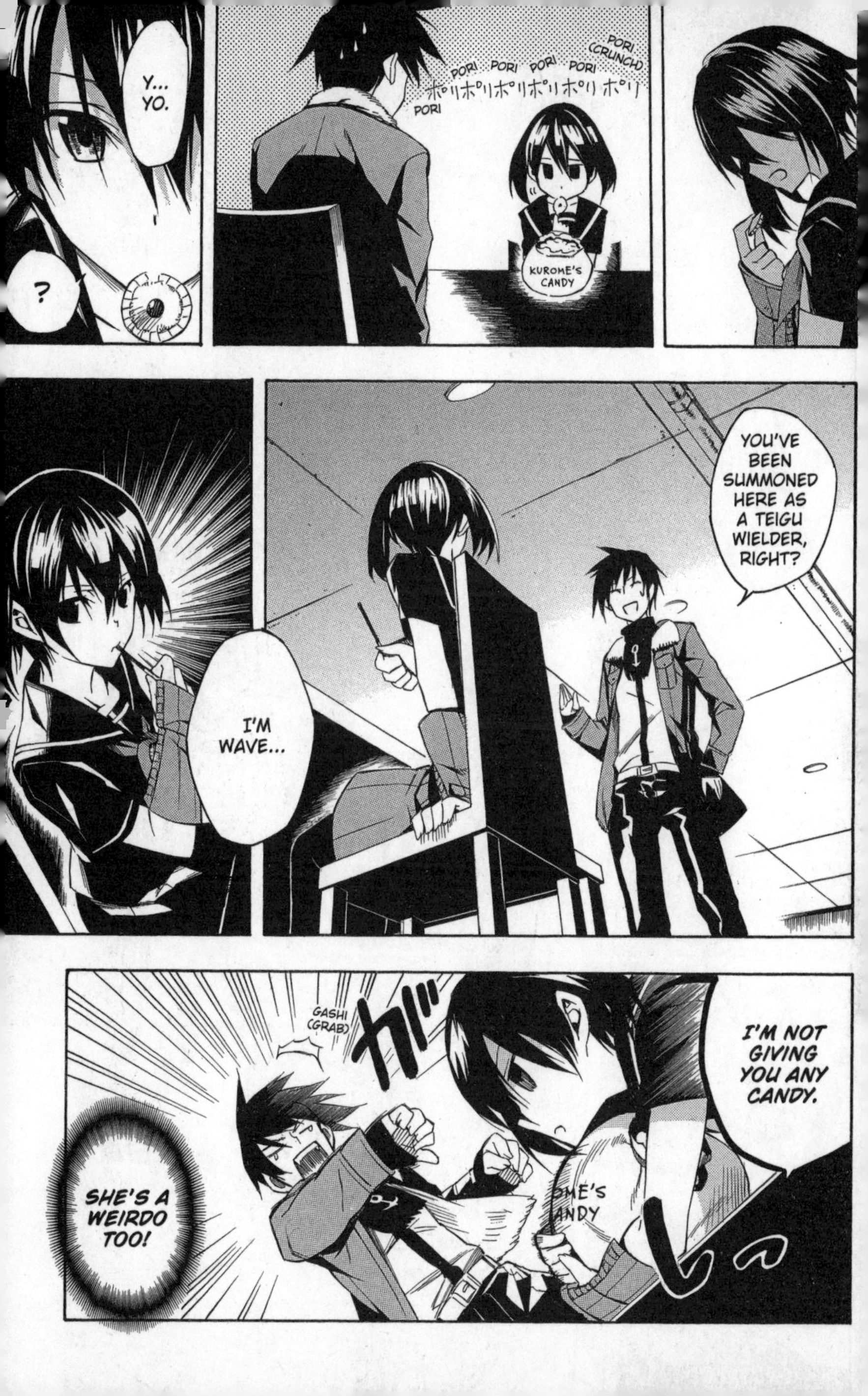
PORI PORI PORI PORI PORI
PORI (CRUNCH)
ポリポリポリポリポリ ポリ
KUROME'S CANDY
Y... YO.
?
YOU'VE BEEN SUMMONED HERE AS A TEIGU WIELDER, RIGHT?
I'M WAVE...
I'M NOT GIVING YOU ANY CANDY.
GASHI (GRAB)
OME'S
ANDY
SHE'S A WEIRDO TOO!

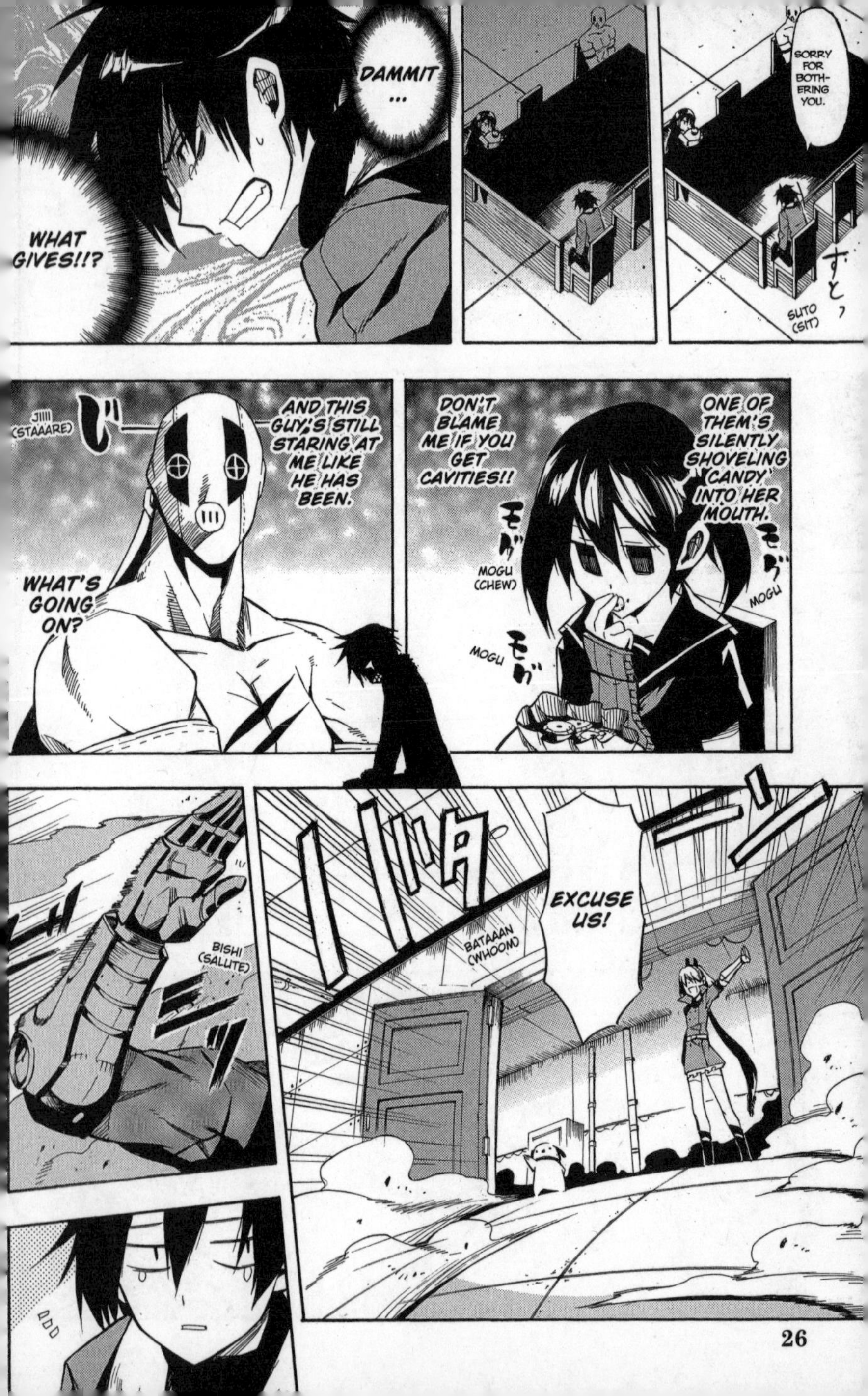

SORRY FOR BOTHERING YOU.
すとっ
SUTO (SIT)
DAMMIT ...
WHAT GIVES!!?
ONE OF THEM'S SILENTLY SHOVELING 'CANDY' INTO HER MOUTH.
DON'T BLAME ME IF YOU GET CAVITIES!!
もぐ
MOGU
もぐ
MOGU (CHEW)
もぐ
MOGU
AND THIS GUY'S STILL STARING AT ME LIKE HE HAS BEEN.
じ
JIIII (STAAARE)
WHAT'S GOING ON?
EXCUSE US!
BATAAAN (WHOOM)
BISHI (SALUTE)

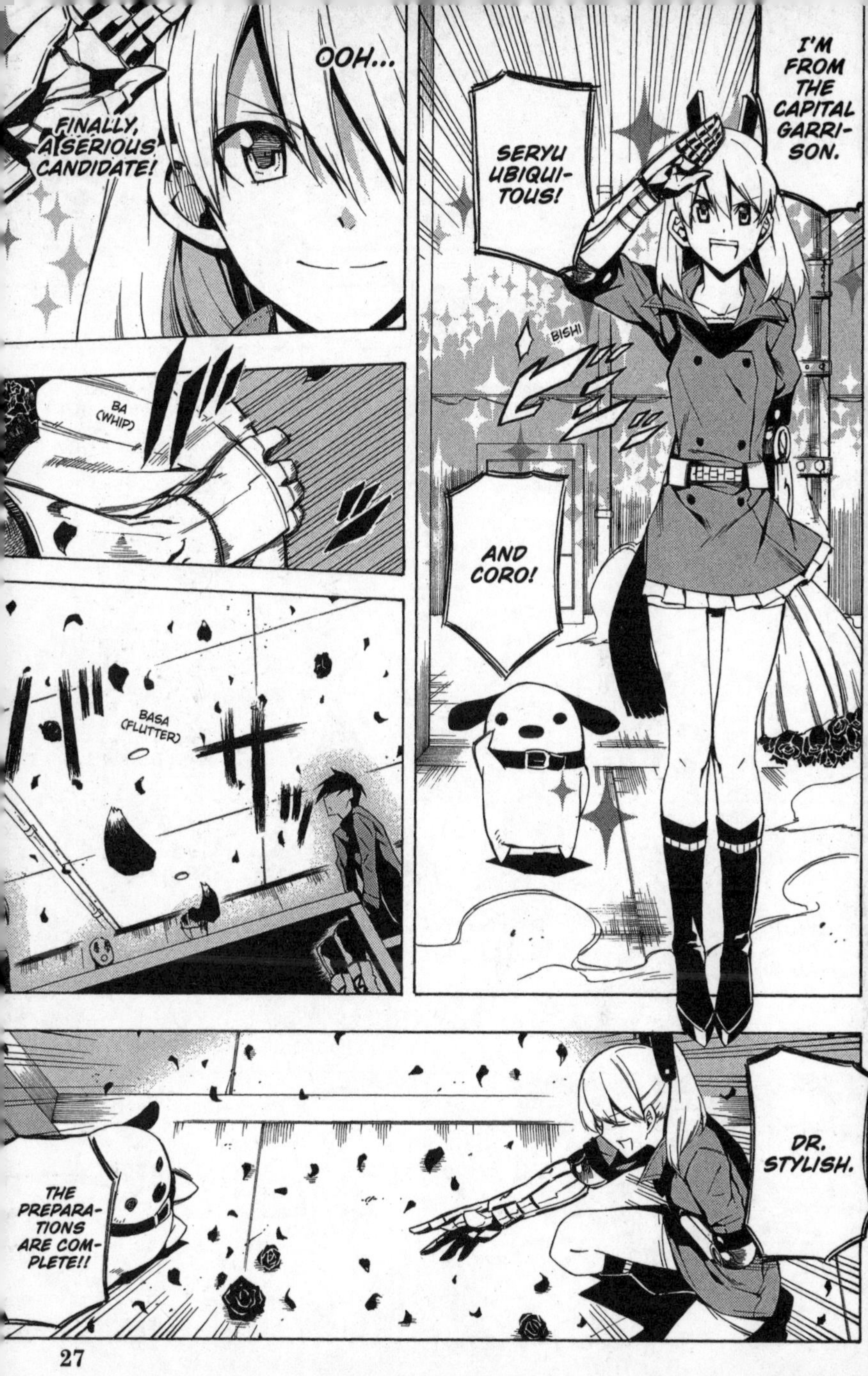
I'M FROM THE CAPITAL GARRI-SON.
SERYU UBIQUI-TOUS!
BISHI
AND CORO!
OOH...
FINALLY, A SERIOUS CANDIDATE!
BA (WHIP)
BASA (FLUTTER)
DR. STYLISH.
THE PREPARA-TIONS ARE COM-PLETE!!

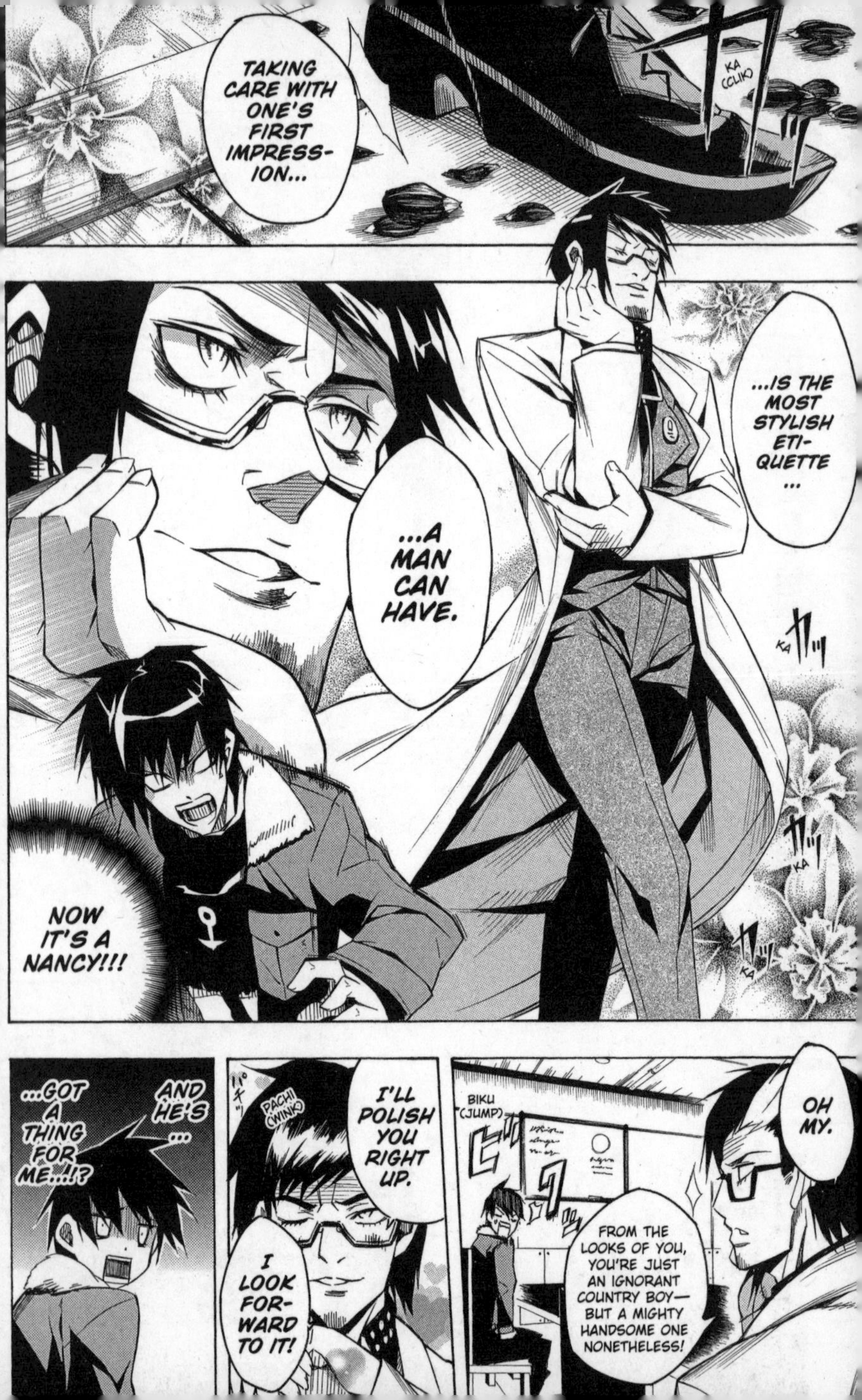
TAKING CARE WITH ONE'S FIRST IMPRESS-ION...
KA (CLIK)
...IS THE MOST STYLISH ETI-QUETTE ...
...A MAN CAN HAVE.
KA
KA
KA
NOW IT'S A NANCY!!!
OH MY.
BIKU (JUMP)
FROM THE LOOKS OF YOU, YOU'RE JUST AN IGNORANT COUNTRY BOY—BUT A MIGHTY HANDSOME ONE NONETHELESS!
I'LL POLISH YOU RIGHT UP.
PACHI (WINK)
I LOOK FOR-WARD TO IT!
AND HE'S ...
...GOT A THING FOR ME...!?

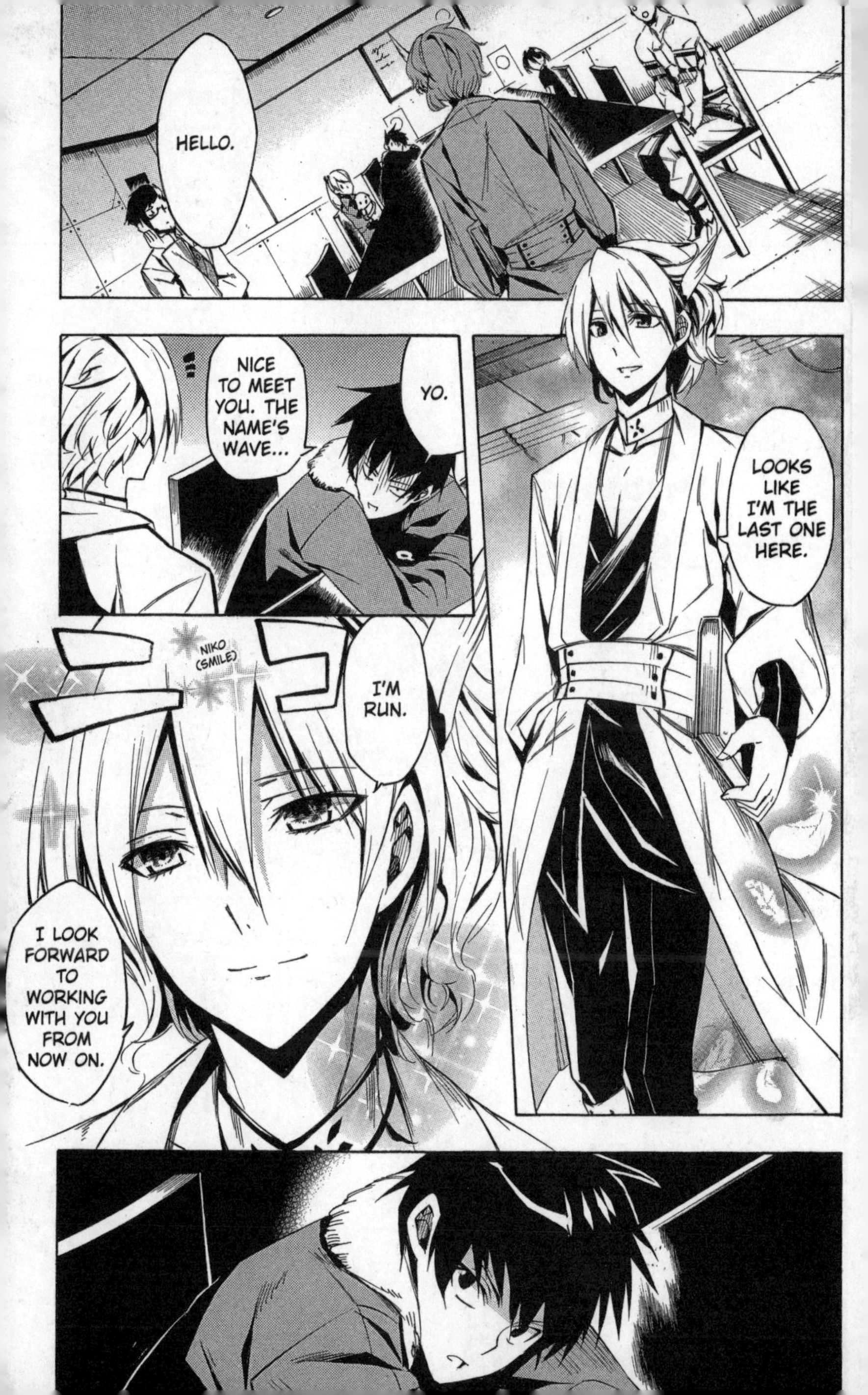
HELLO.
LOOKS LIKE I'M THE LAST ONE HERE.
YO.
NICE TO MEET YOU. THE NAME'S WAVE...
I'M RUN.
NIKO (SMILE)
I LOOK FORWARD TO WORKING WITH YOU FROM NOW ON.

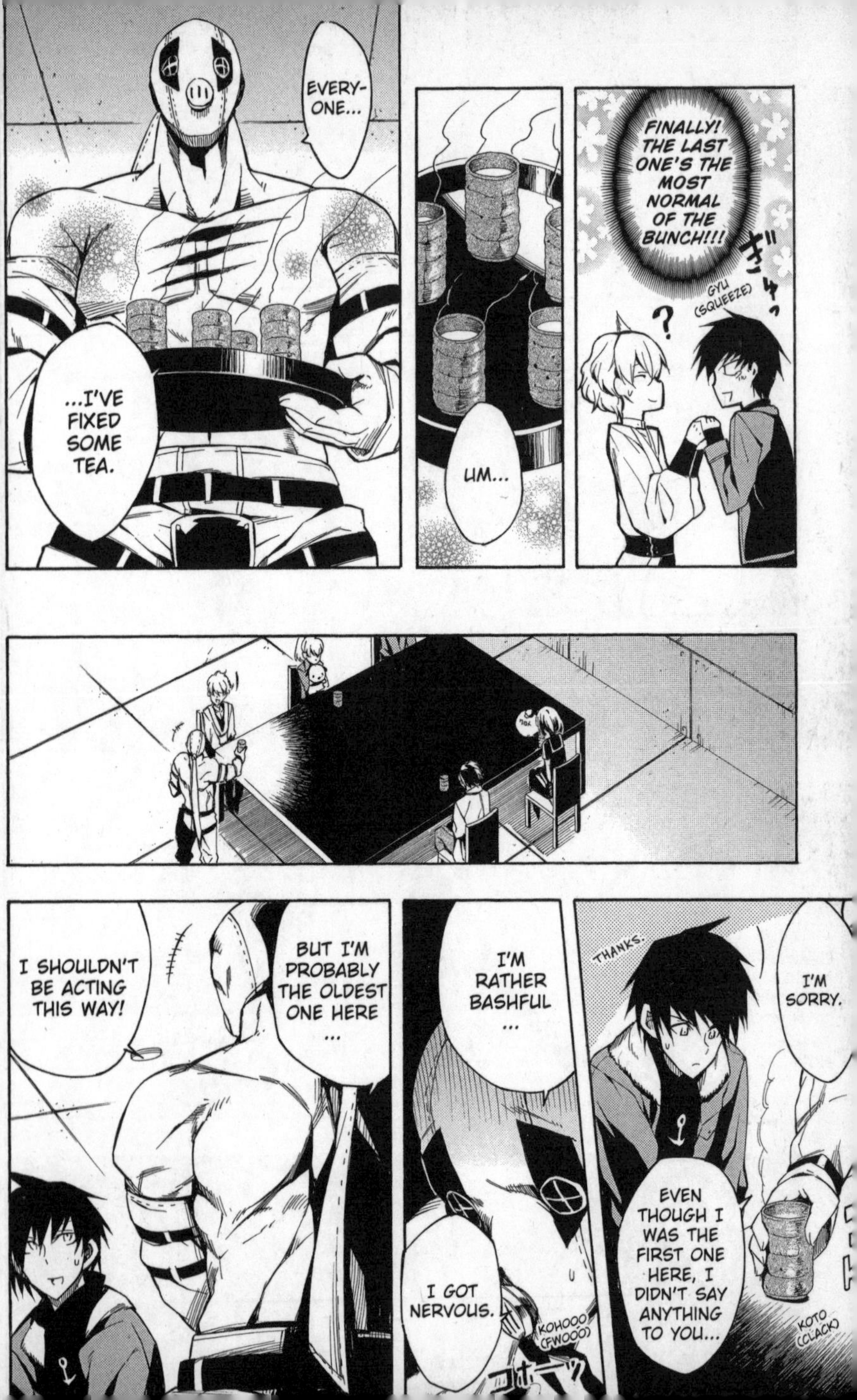
FINALLY! THE LAST ONE'S THE MOST NORMAL OF THE BUNCH!!!
GYU (SQUEEZE)
?
UM...
EVERY-ONE...
...I'VE FIXED SOME TEA.
I'M SORRY.
THANKS.
EVEN THOUGH I WAS THE FIRST ONE HERE, I DIDN'T SAY ANYTHING TO YOU...
KOTO (CLACK)
I'M RATHER BASHFUL ...
I GOT NERVOUS.
KOHOOO (FWOOO)
BUT I'M PROBABLY THE OLDEST ONE HERE ...
I SHOULDN'T BE ACTING THIS WAY!

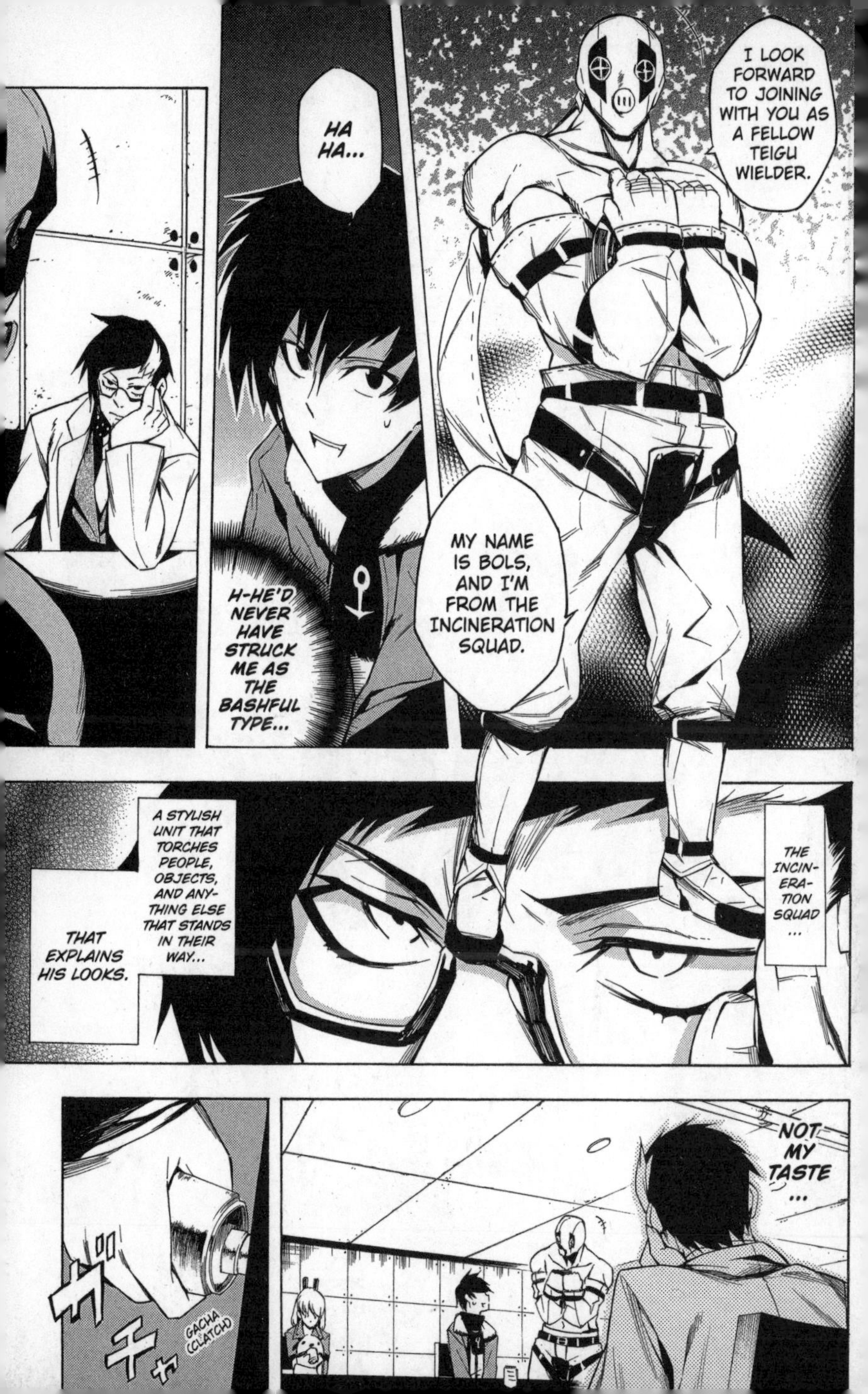
I LOOK FORWARD TO JOINING WITH YOU AS A FELLOW TEIGU WIELDER.
MY NAME IS BOLS, AND I'M FROM THE INCINERATION SQUAD.
HA HA...
H-HE'D NEVER HAVE STRUCK ME AS THE BASHFUL TYPE...
THE INCIN-ERA-TION SQUAD ...
A STYLISH UNIT THAT TORCHES PEOPLE, OBJECTS, AND ANY-THING ELSE THAT STANDS IN THEIR WAY...
THAT EXPLAINS HIS LOOKS.
NOT MY TASTE ...
ガチャ
GACHA (CLATCH)

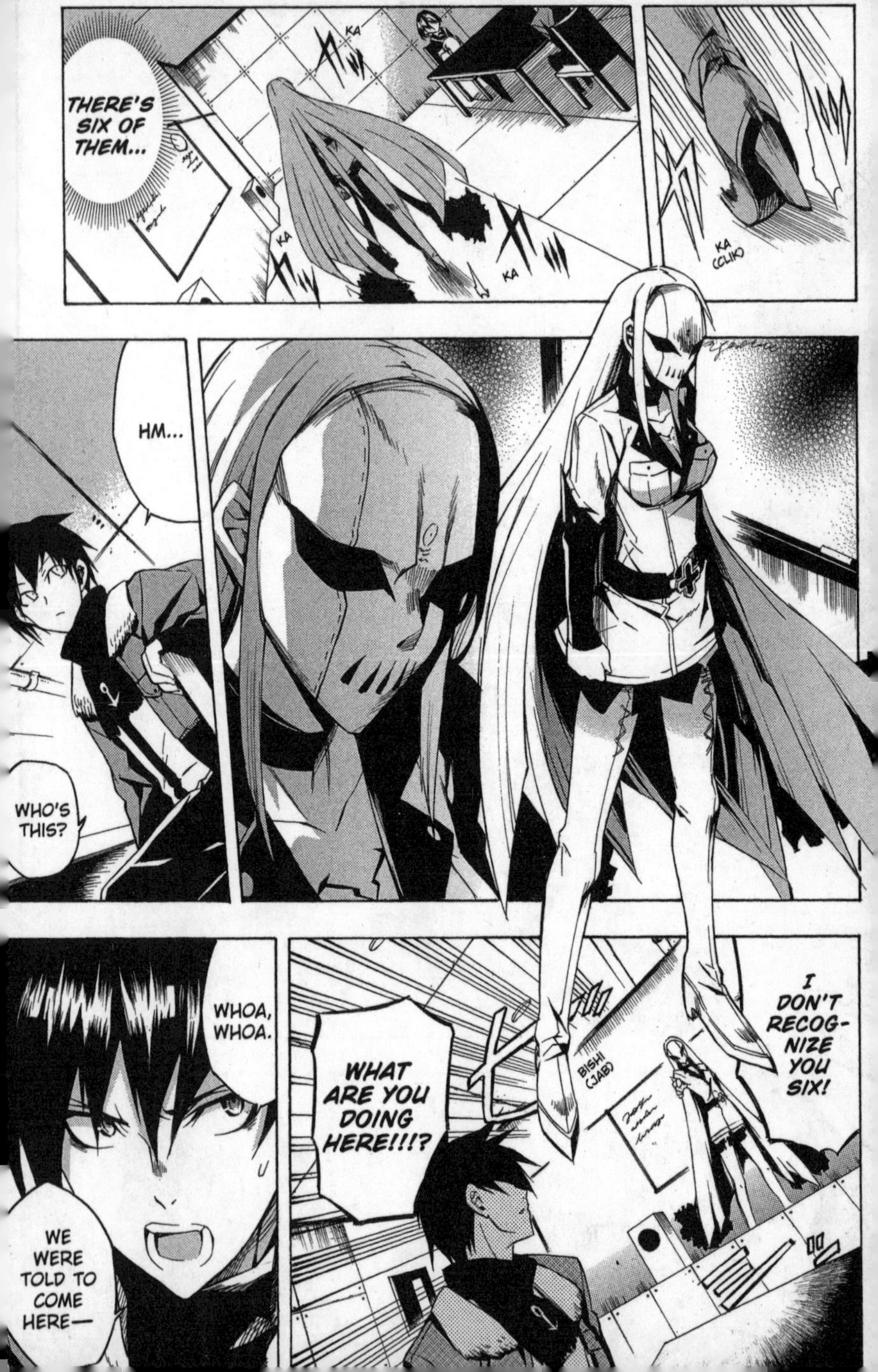
KA (CLIK)
KA
THERE'S SIX OF THEM...
KA
KA
HM...
WHO'S THIS?
I DON'T RECOG-NIZE YOU SIX!
BISHI (JAB)
WHAT ARE YOU DOING HERE!!!?
WHOA, WHOA.
WE WERE TOLD TO COME HERE—

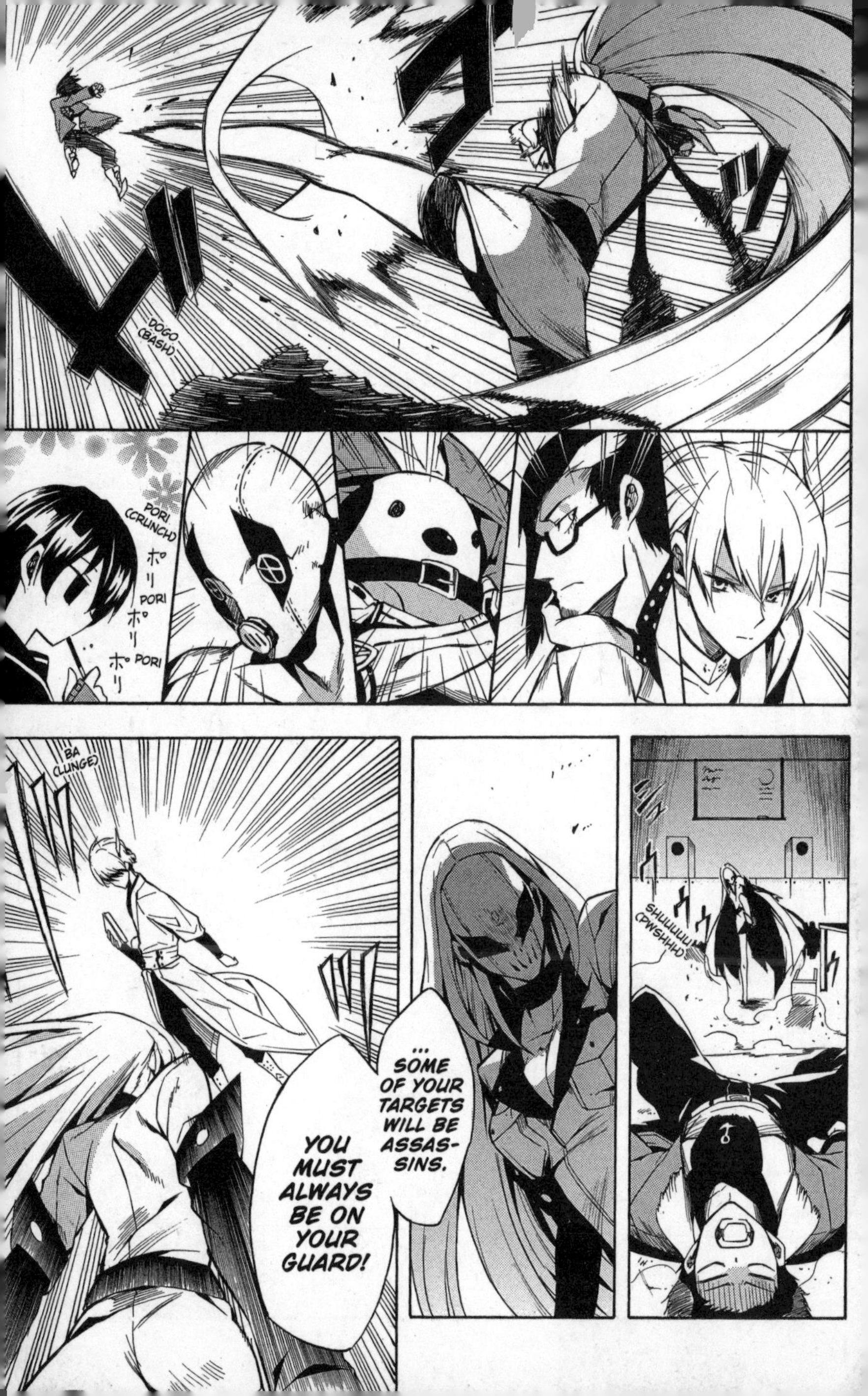
DOGO (BASH)
PORI (CRUNCH)
ポリ
PORI
ポリ
ポリ
PORI
SHUUUUUU (PWSHHH)
...
...
... SOME OF YOUR TARGETS WILL BE ASSAS-SINS.
YOU MUST ALWAYS BE ON YOUR GUARD!
BA (LUNGE)

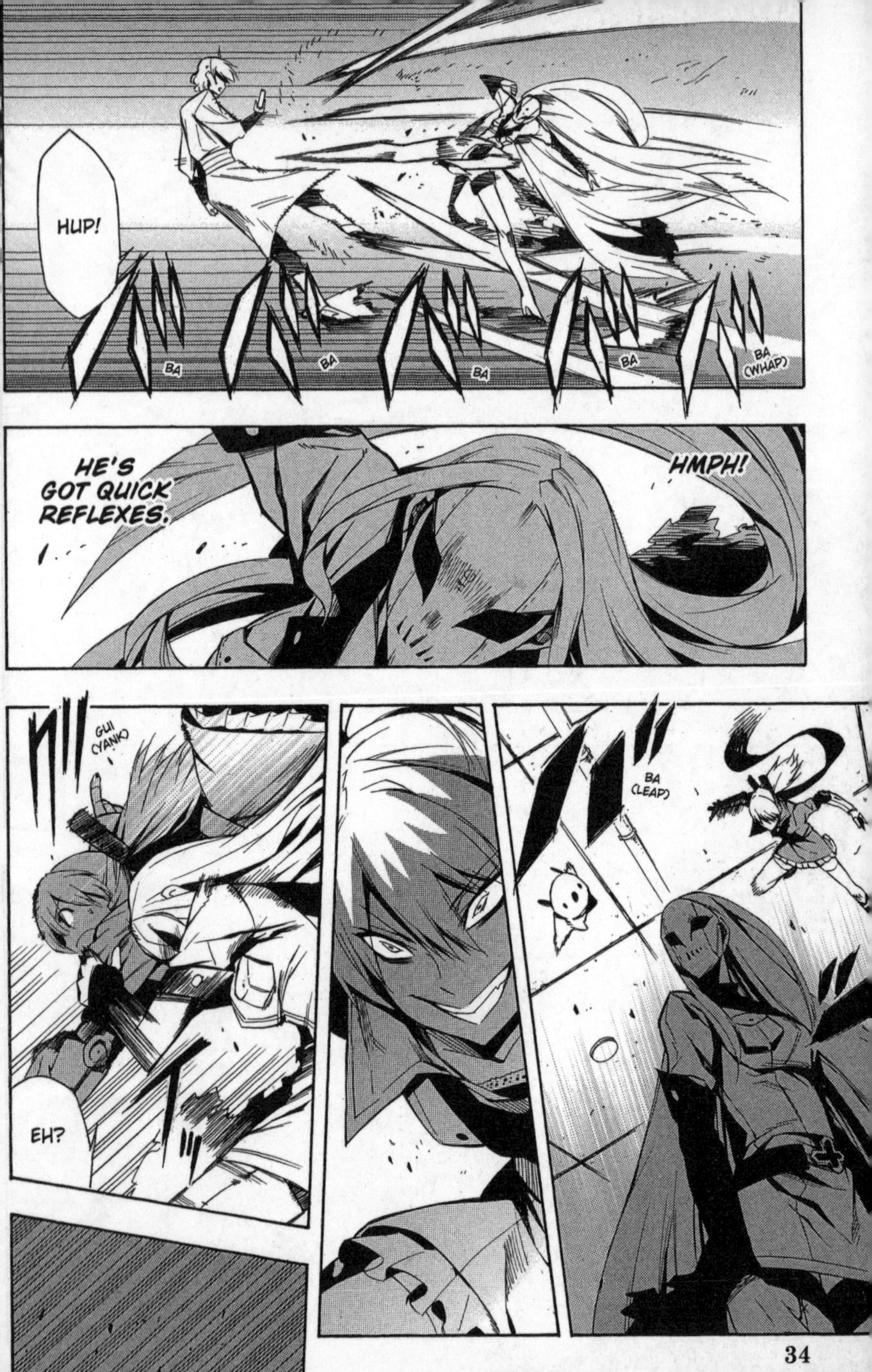
HUP!
BA (WHAP)
BA
BA
BA
BA
HMPH!
HE'S GOT QUICK REFLEXES.
BA (LEAP)
GUI (YANK)
EH?

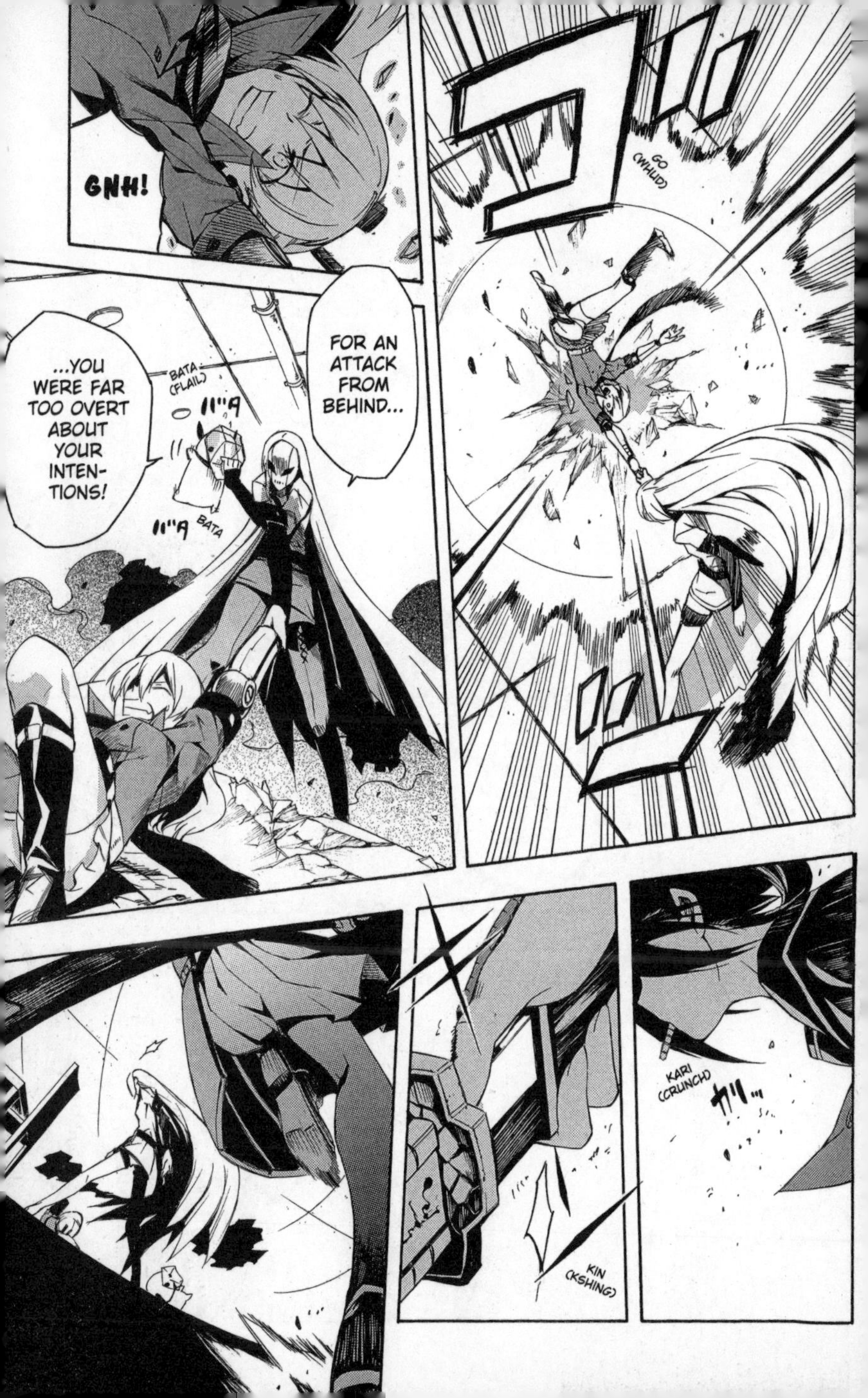
GO
(WHUD)
GNH!
FOR AN ATTACK FROM BEHIND...
BATA
(FLAIL)
BATA
...YOU WERE FAR TOO OVERT ABOUT YOUR INTEN-TIONS!
KARI
(CRUNCH)
KIN
(KSHING)

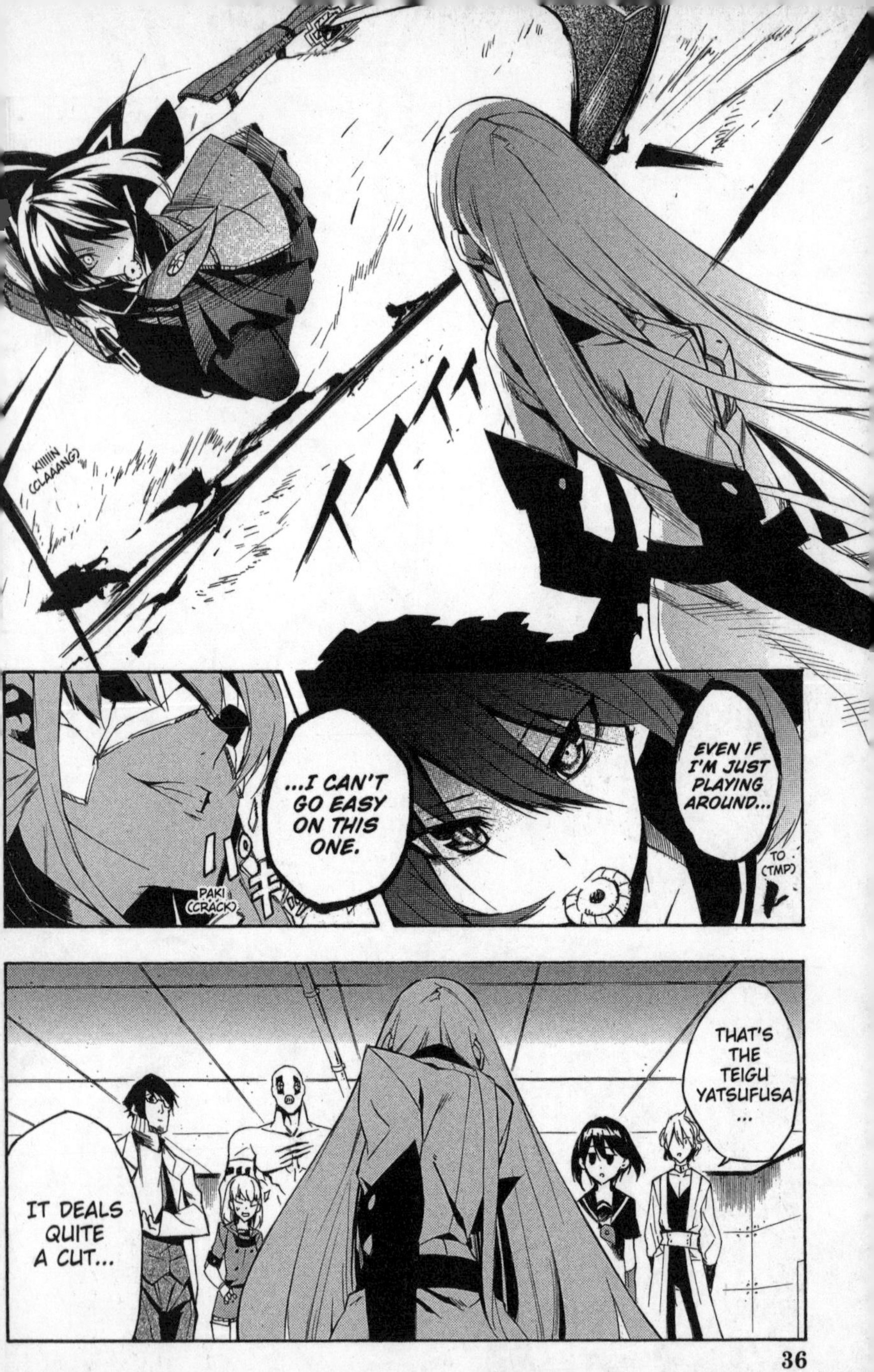
KIIIIIN (CLAAANG)
EVEN IF I'M JUST PLAYING AROUND...
TO (TMP)
...I CAN'T GO EASY ON THIS ONE.
PAKI (CRACK)
THAT'S THE TEIGU YATSUFUSA ...
IT DEALS QUITE A CUT...

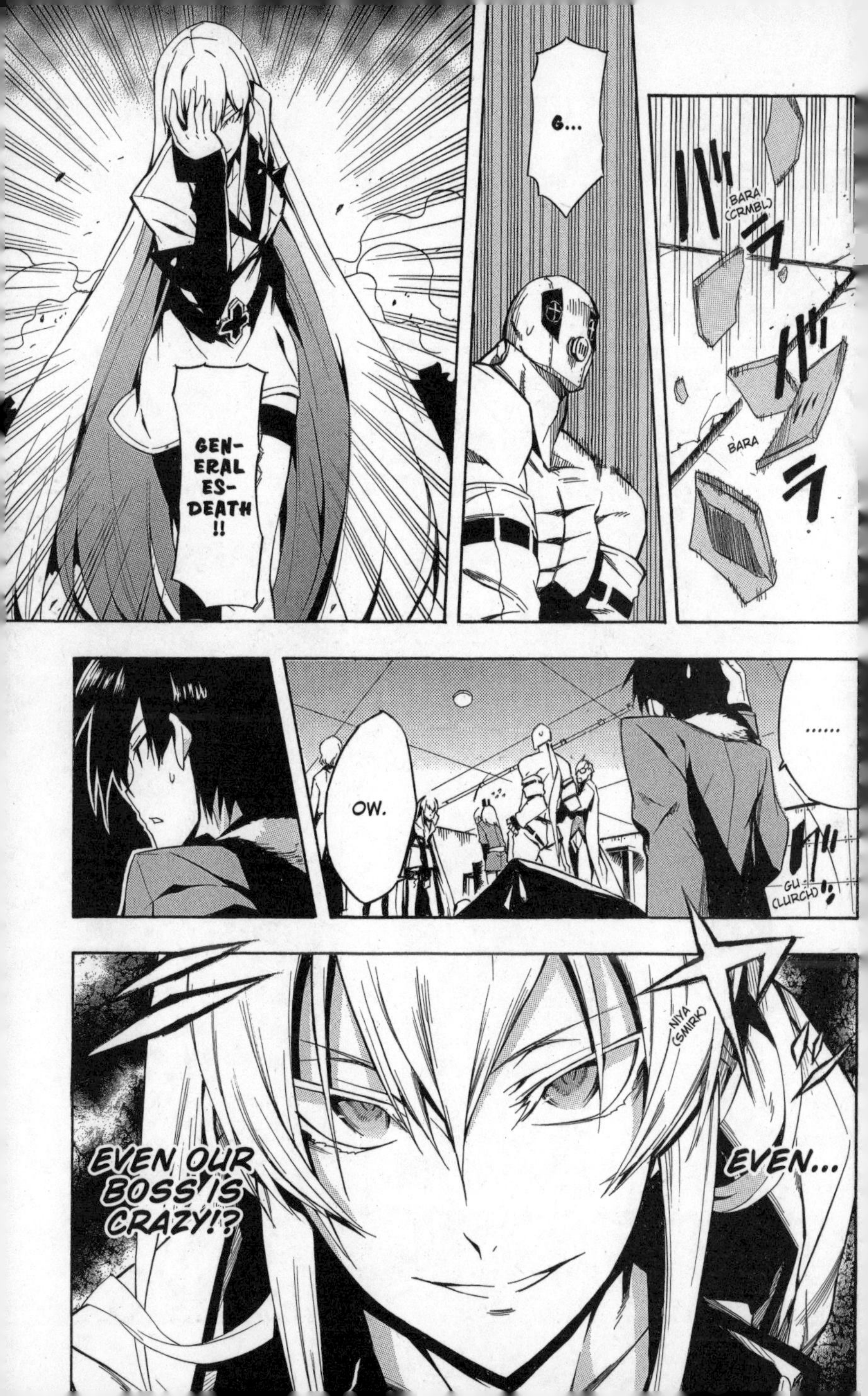
BARA (CRMBL)
BARA
G...
GEN-ERAL ES-DEATH!!
......
GU (LURCH)
OW.
NIYA (SMIRK)
EVEN...
EVEN OUR BOSS IS CRAZY!?

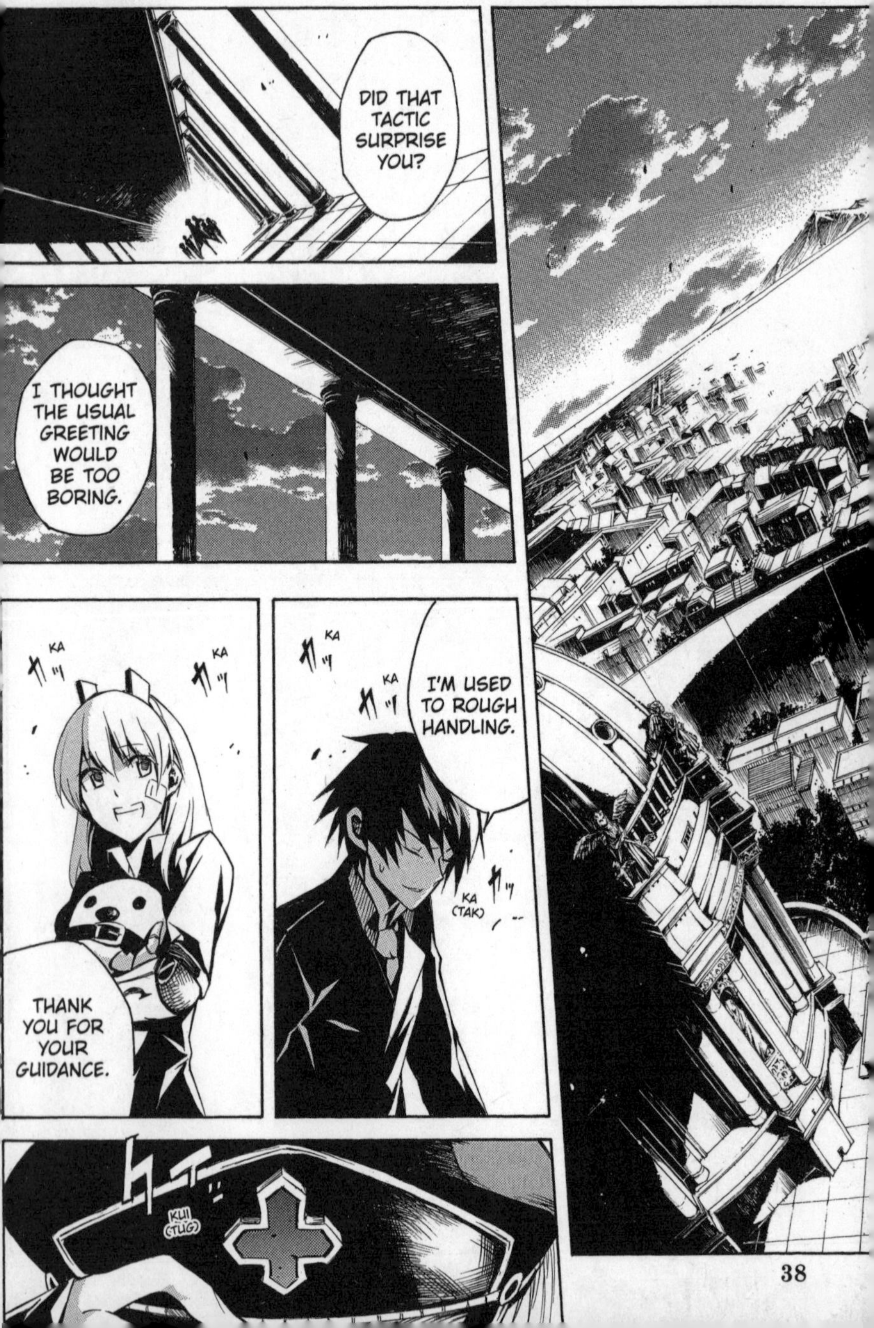
DID THAT TACTIC SURPRISE YOU?
I THOUGHT THE USUAL GREETING WOULD BE TOO BORING.
KA
KA
I'M USED TO ROUGH HANDLING.
KA (TAK)
KA
KA
THANK YOU FOR YOUR GUIDANCE.
KUI (TUG)

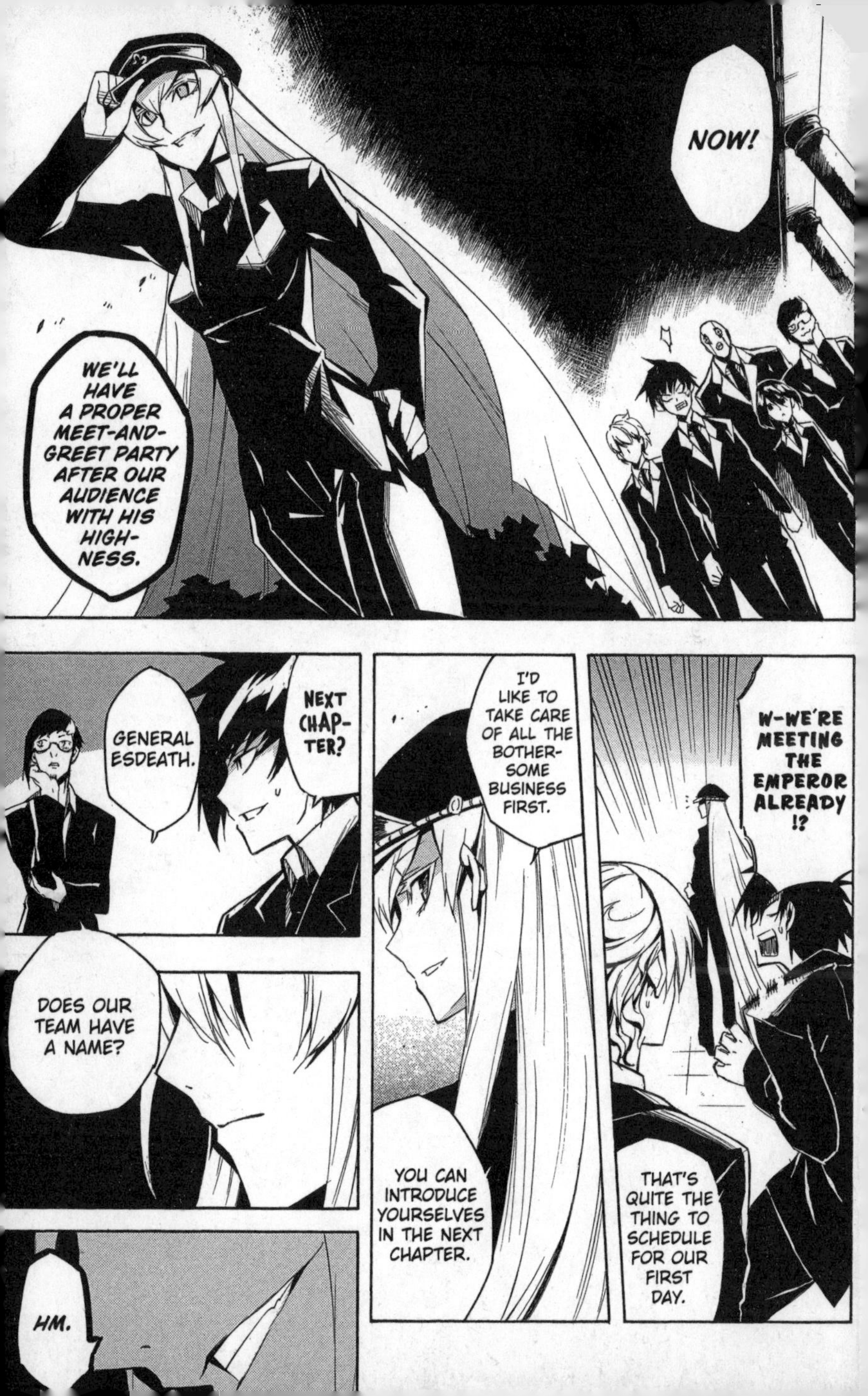
NOW!
WE'LL HAVE A PROPER MEET-AND-GREET PARTY AFTER OUR AUDIENCE WITH HIS HIGHNESS.
W-WE'RE MEETING THE EMPEROR ALREADY!?
THAT'S QUITE THE THING TO SCHEDULE FOR OUR FIRST DAY.
I'D LIKE TO TAKE CARE OF ALL THE BOTHERSOME BUSINESS FIRST.
YOU CAN INTRODUCE YOURSELVES IN THE NEXT CHAPTER.
NEXT CHAPTER?
GENERAL ESDEATH.
DOES OUR TEAM HAVE A NAME?
HM.

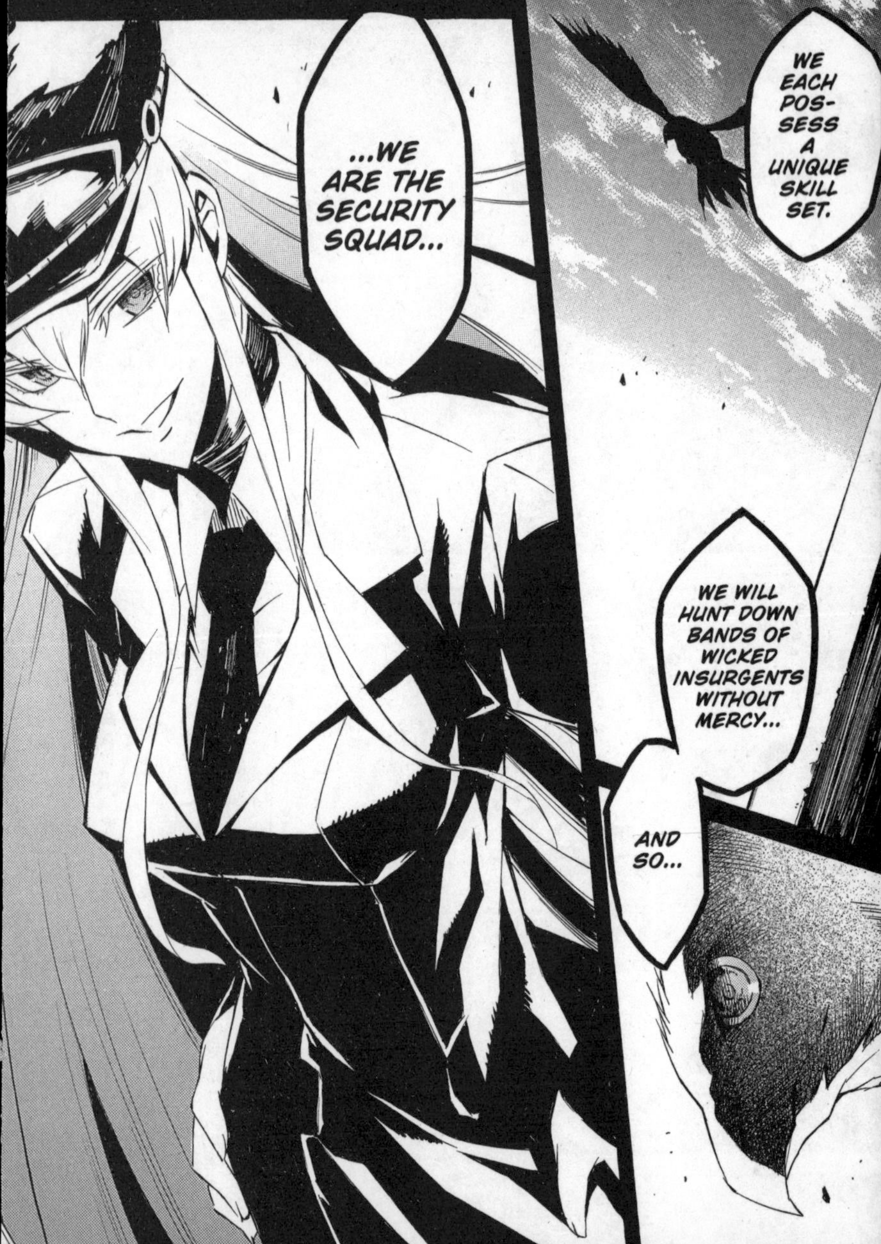
...WE ARE THE SECURITY SQUAD...
WE EACH POS-SESS A UNIQUE SKILL SET.
WE WILL HUNT DOWN BANDS OF WICKED INSURGENTS WITHOUT MERCY...
AND SO...

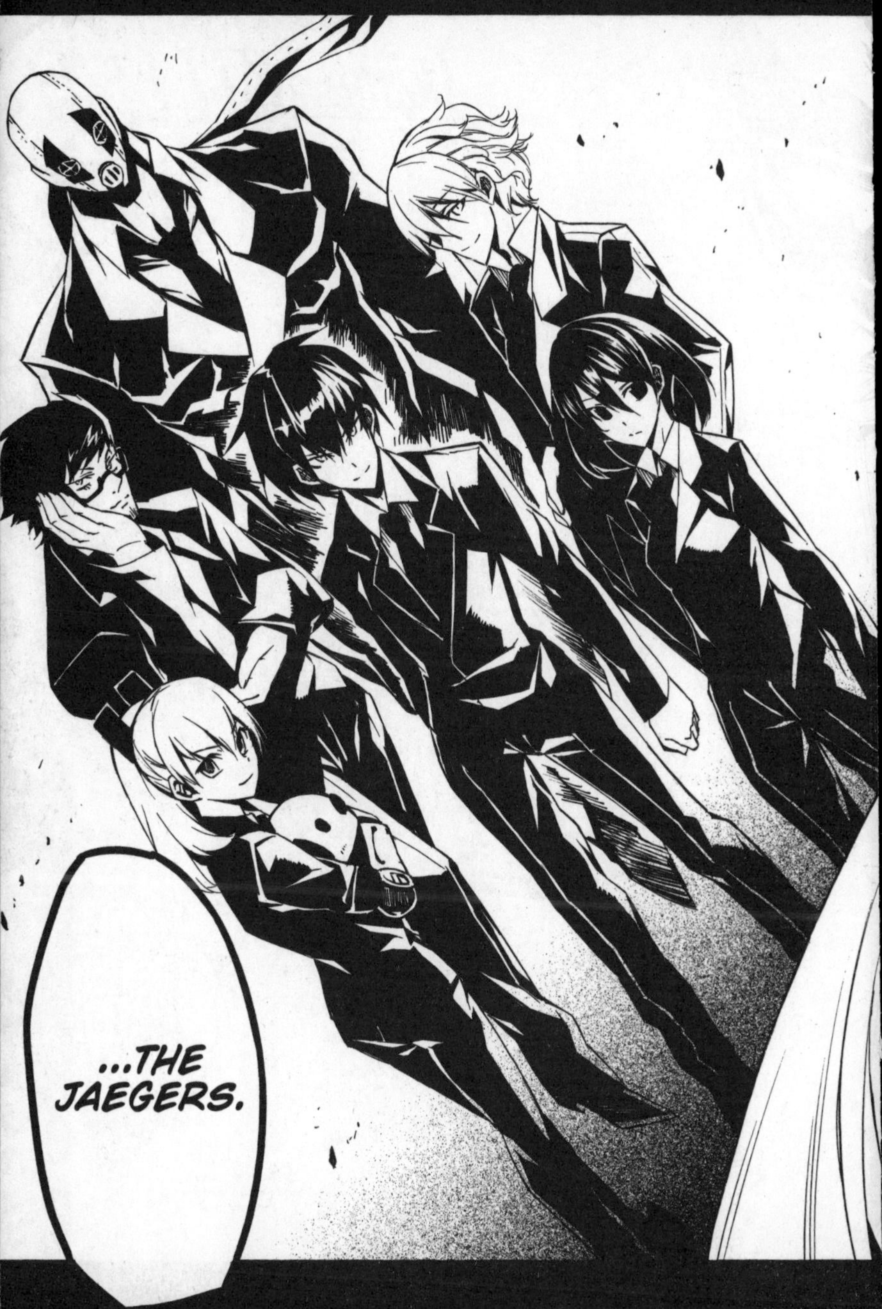
...THE JAEGERS.

Akame ga KILL!
Rough Sketches 1

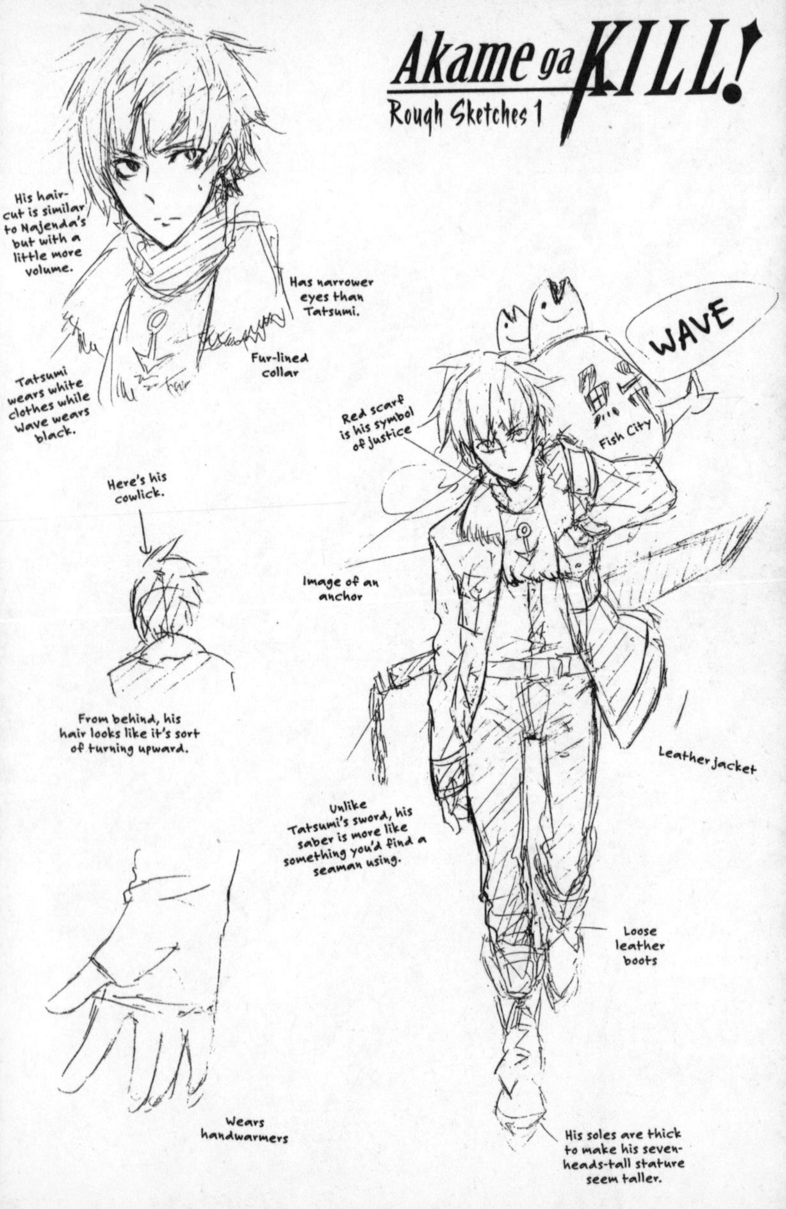

His hair-cut is similar to Najenda's but with a little more volume.
Has narrower eyes than Tatsumi.
Fur-lined collar
Tatsumi wears white clothes while Wave wears black.
WAVE
Red scarf is his symbol of justice
Fish City
Here's his cowlick.
Image of an anchor
From behind, his hair looks like it's sort of turning upward.
Leather jacket
Unlike Tatsumi's sword, his saber is more like something you'd find a seaman using.
Loose leather boots
Wears handwarmers
His soles are thick to make his seven-heads-tall stature seem taller.

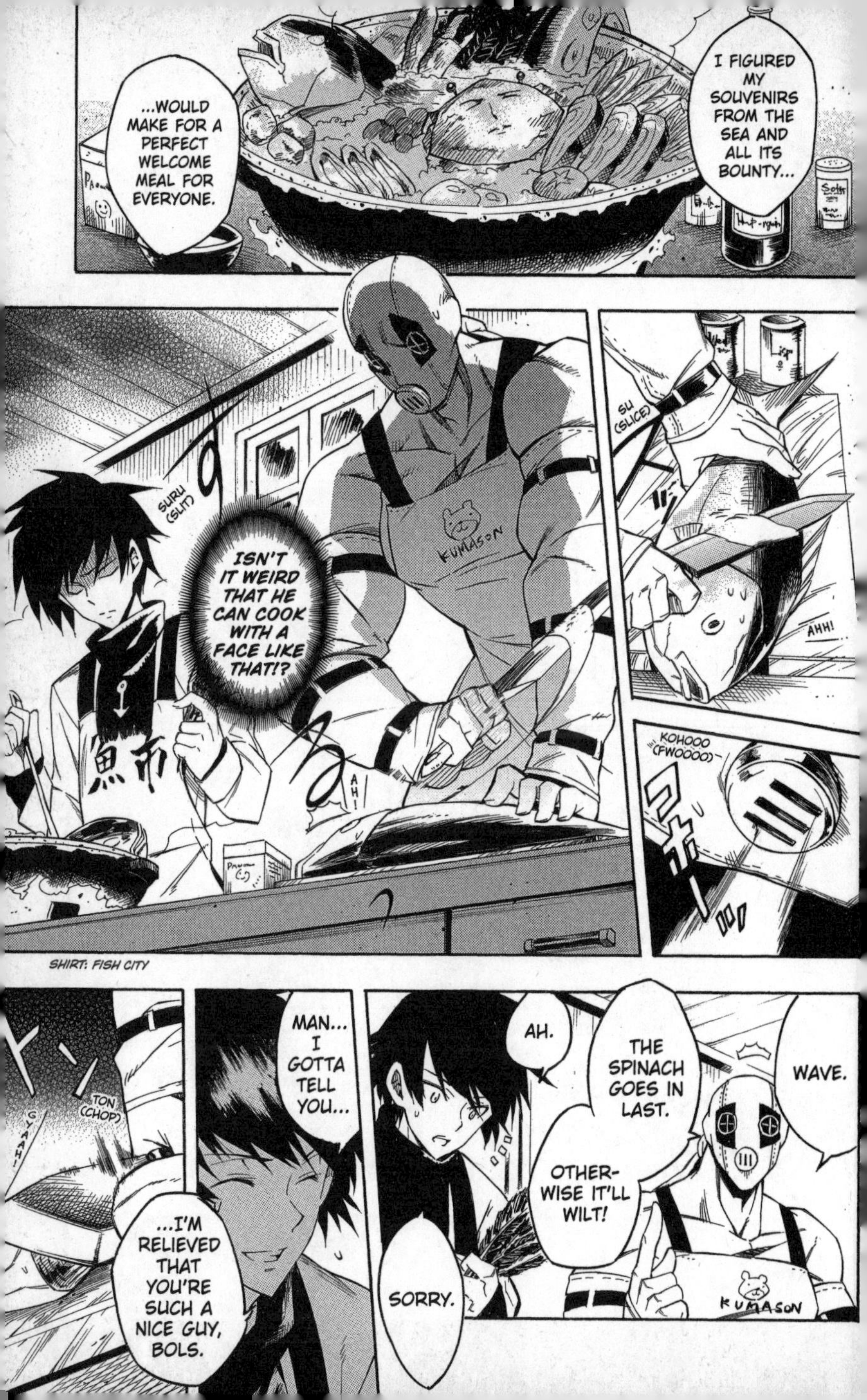
I FIGURED MY SOUVENIRS FROM THE SEA AND ALL ITS BOUNTY...
...WOULD MAKE FOR A PERFECT WELCOME MEAL FOR EVERYONE.
SU (SLICE)
AHH!
KOHOOO (FWOOOO)
SURU (SLIT)
ISN'T IT WEIRD THAT HE CAN COOK WITH A FACE LIKE THAT!?
AH!
KUMASON
魚市
SHIRT: FISH CITY
WAVE.
THE SPINACH GOES IN LAST.
OTHER-WISE IT'LL WILT!
AH.
SORRY.
MAN... I GOTTA TELL YOU...
...I'M RELIEVED THAT YOU'RE SUCH A NICE GUY, BOLS.
TON (CHOP)
GYAAH!

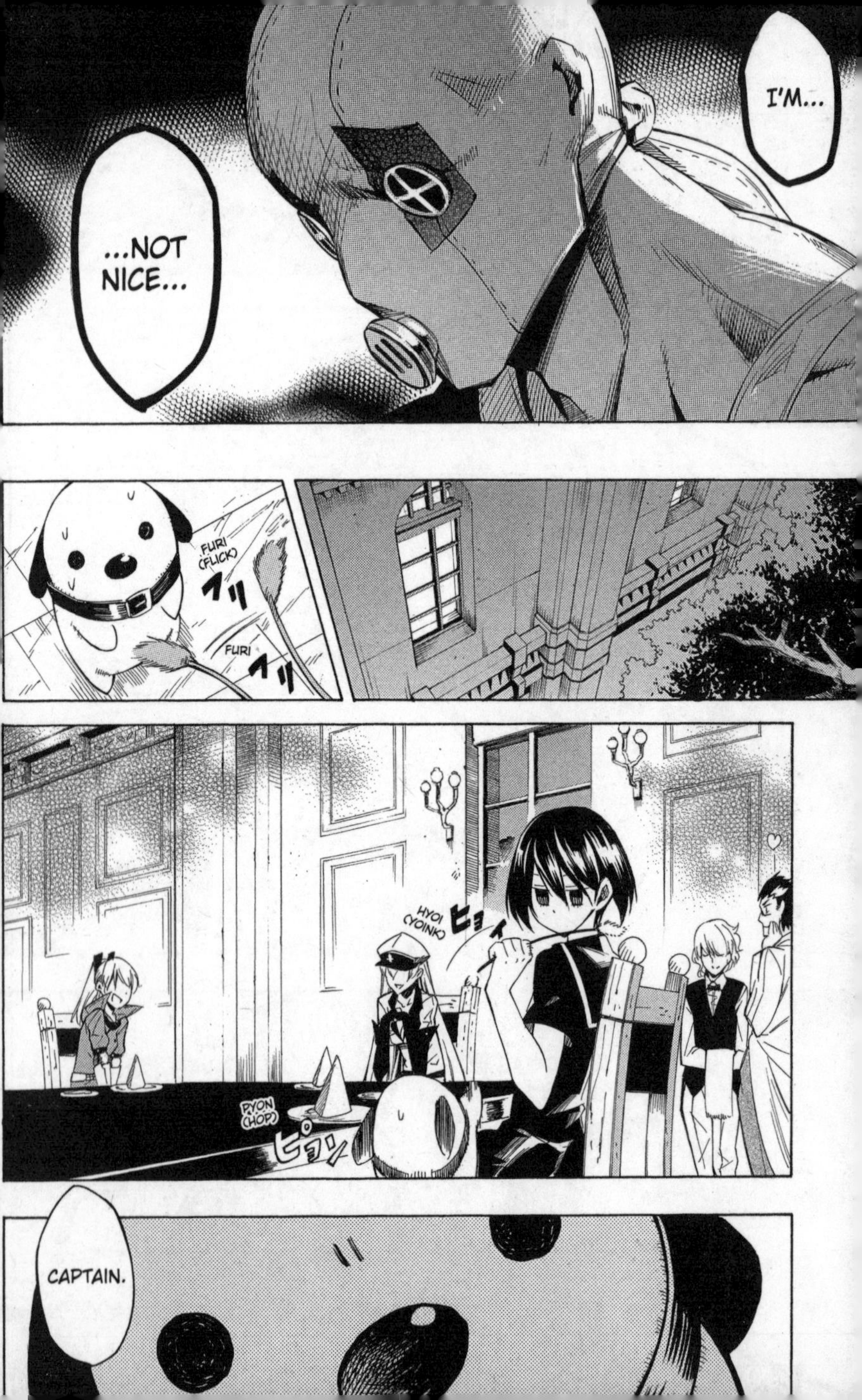
I'M...
...NOT NICE...
FURI (FLICK)
FURI
HYOI (YOINK)
PYON (HOP)
CAPTAIN.

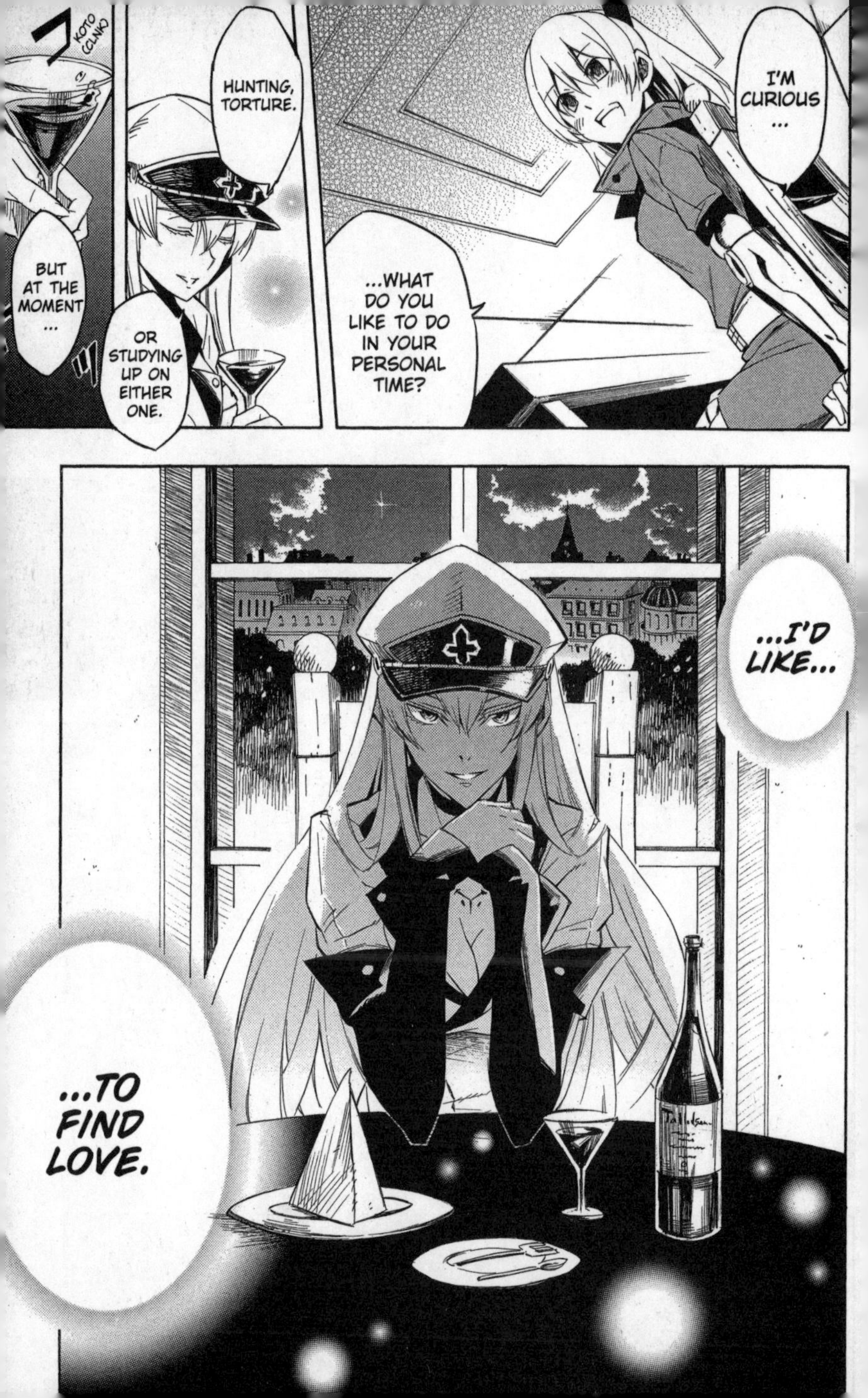
I'M CURIOUS...
...WHAT DO YOU LIKE TO DO IN YOUR PERSONAL TIME?
HUNTING, TORTURE.
OR STUDYING UP ON EITHER ONE.
KOTO (CLNK)
BUT AT THE MOMENT...
...I'D LIKE...
...TO FIND LOVE.

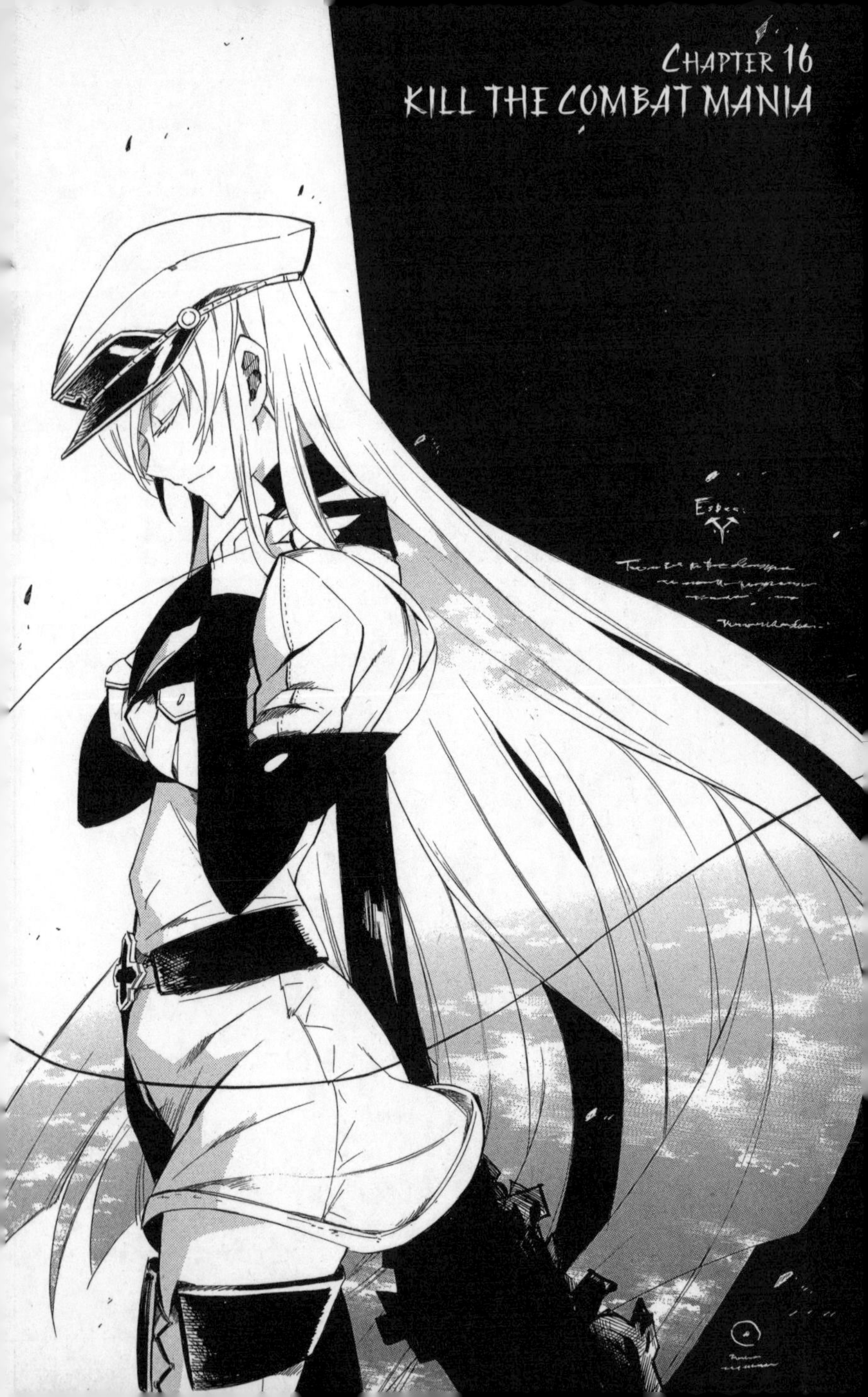
CHAPTER 16
KILL THE COMBAT MANIA

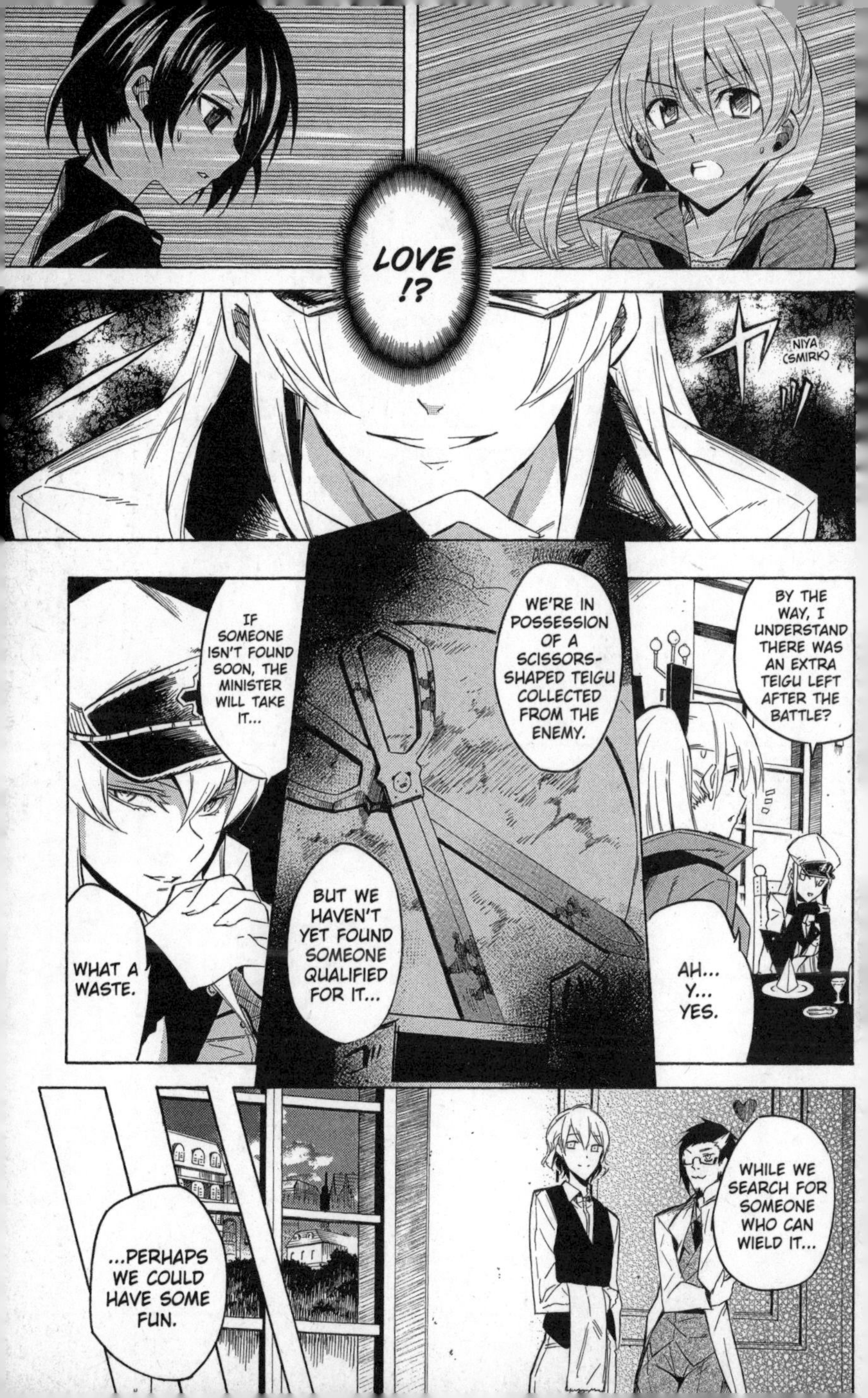
LOVE !?
NIYA (SMIRK)
BY THE WAY, I UNDERSTAND THERE WAS AN EXTRA TEIGU LEFT AFTER THE BATTLE?
AH... Y... YES.
WE'RE IN POSSESSION OF A SCISSORS-SHAPED TEIGU COLLECTED FROM THE ENEMY.
BUT WE HAVEN'T YET FOUND SOMEONE QUALIFIED FOR IT...
IF SOMEONE ISN'T FOUND SOON, THE MINISTER WILL TAKE IT...
WHAT A WASTE.
WHILE WE SEARCH FOR SOMEONE WHO CAN WIELD IT...
...PERHAPS WE COULD HAVE SOME FUN.

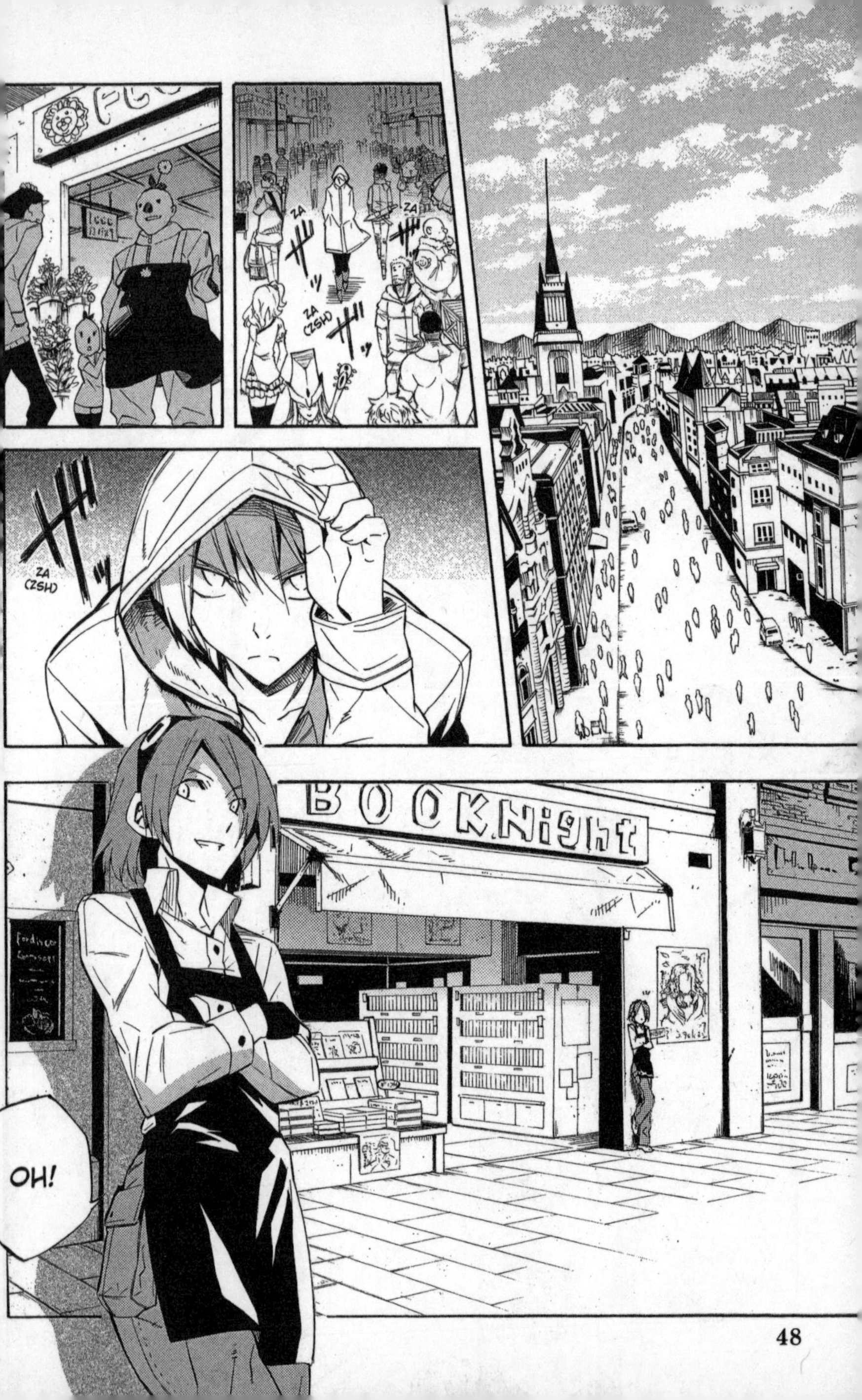
ZA
ZA
ZA (ZSH)
ZA (ZSH)
BOOKNight
OH!

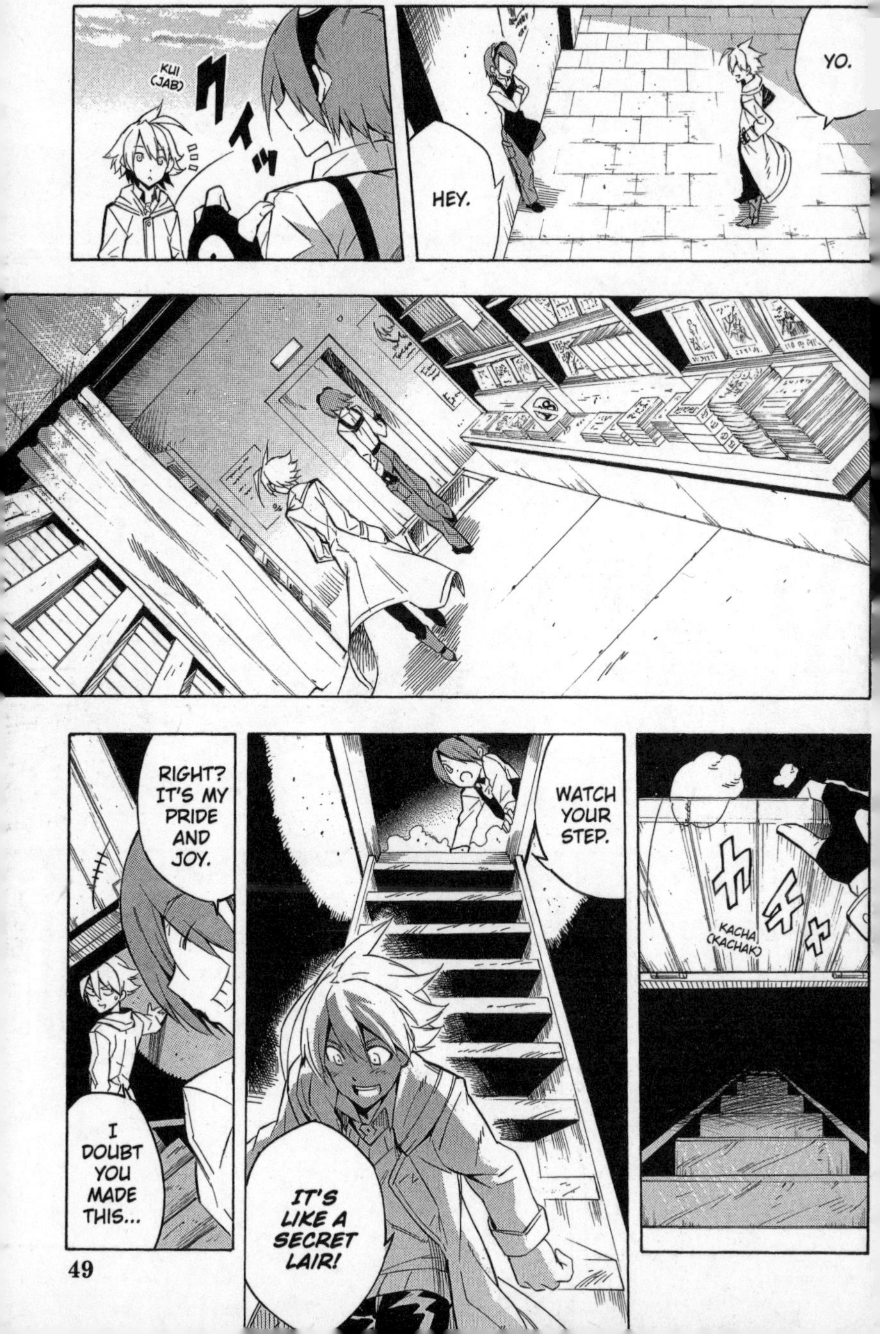

YO.
HEY.
KUI (JAB)
WATCH YOUR STEP.
KACHA (KACHAK)
IT'S LIKE A SECRET LAIR!
RIGHT? IT'S MY PRIDE AND JOY.
I DOUBT YOU MADE THIS...

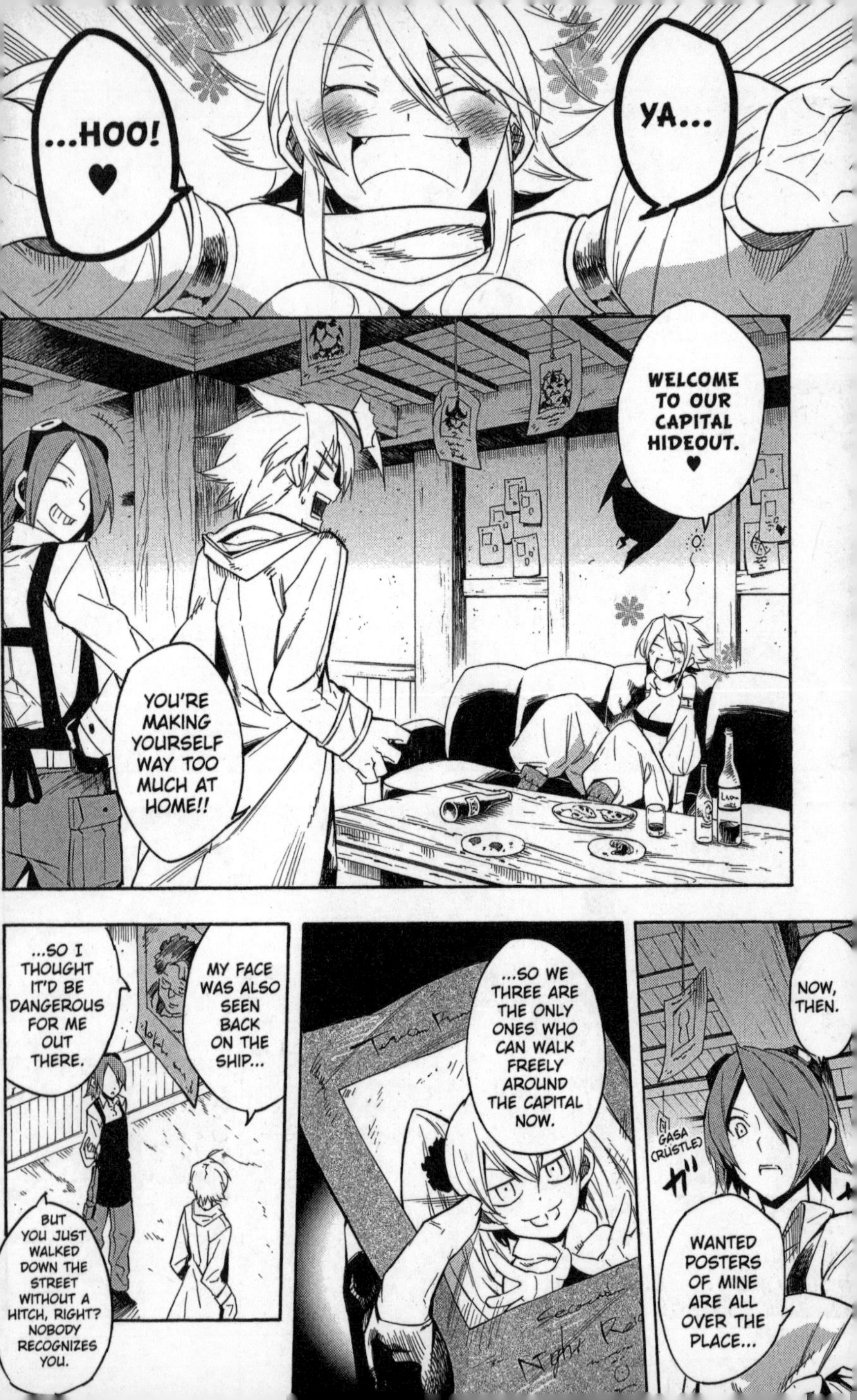

YA...
...HOO! ♥
WELCOME TO OUR CAPITAL HIDEOUT. ♥
YOU'RE MAKING YOURSELF WAY TOO MUCH AT HOME!!
NOW, THEN.
GASA (RÜSTLE)
WANTED POSTERS OF MINE ARE ALL OVER THE PLACE...
...SO WE THREE ARE THE ONLY ONES WHO CAN WALK FREELY AROUND THE CAPITAL NOW.
MY FACE WAS ALSO SEEN BACK ON THE SHIP...
...SO I THOUGHT IT'D BE DANGEROUS FOR ME OUT THERE.
BUT YOU JUST WALKED DOWN THE STREET WITHOUT A HITCH, RIGHT? NOBODY RECOGNIZES YOU.

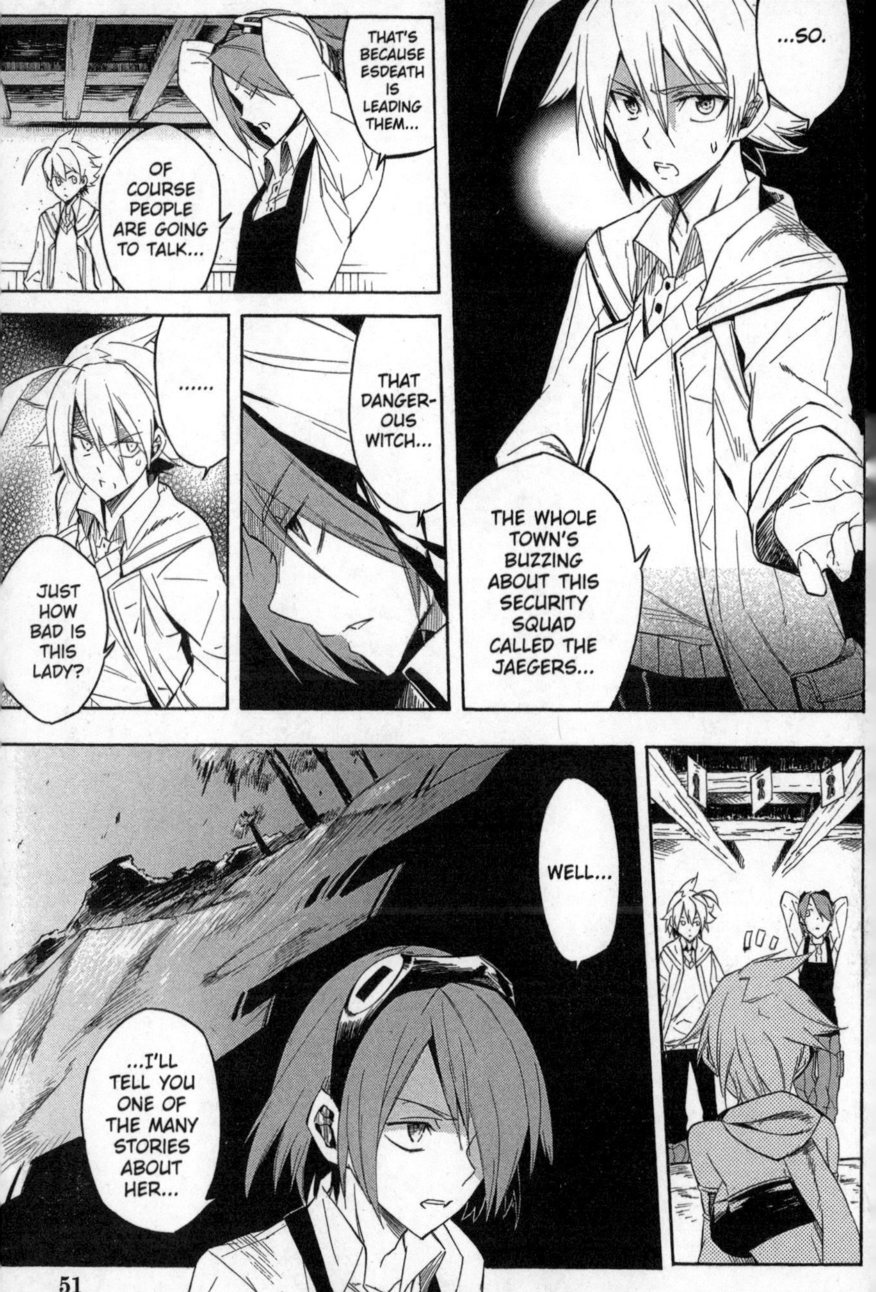
...SO.
THE WHOLE TOWN'S BUZZING ABOUT THIS SECURITY SQUAD CALLED THE JAEGERS...
THAT'S BECAUSE ESDEATH IS LEADING THEM...
OF COURSE PEOPLE ARE GOING TO TALK...
THAT DANGEROUS WITCH...
......
JUST HOW BAD IS THIS LADY?
WELL...
...I'LL TELL YOU ONE OF THE MANY STORIES ABOUT HER...

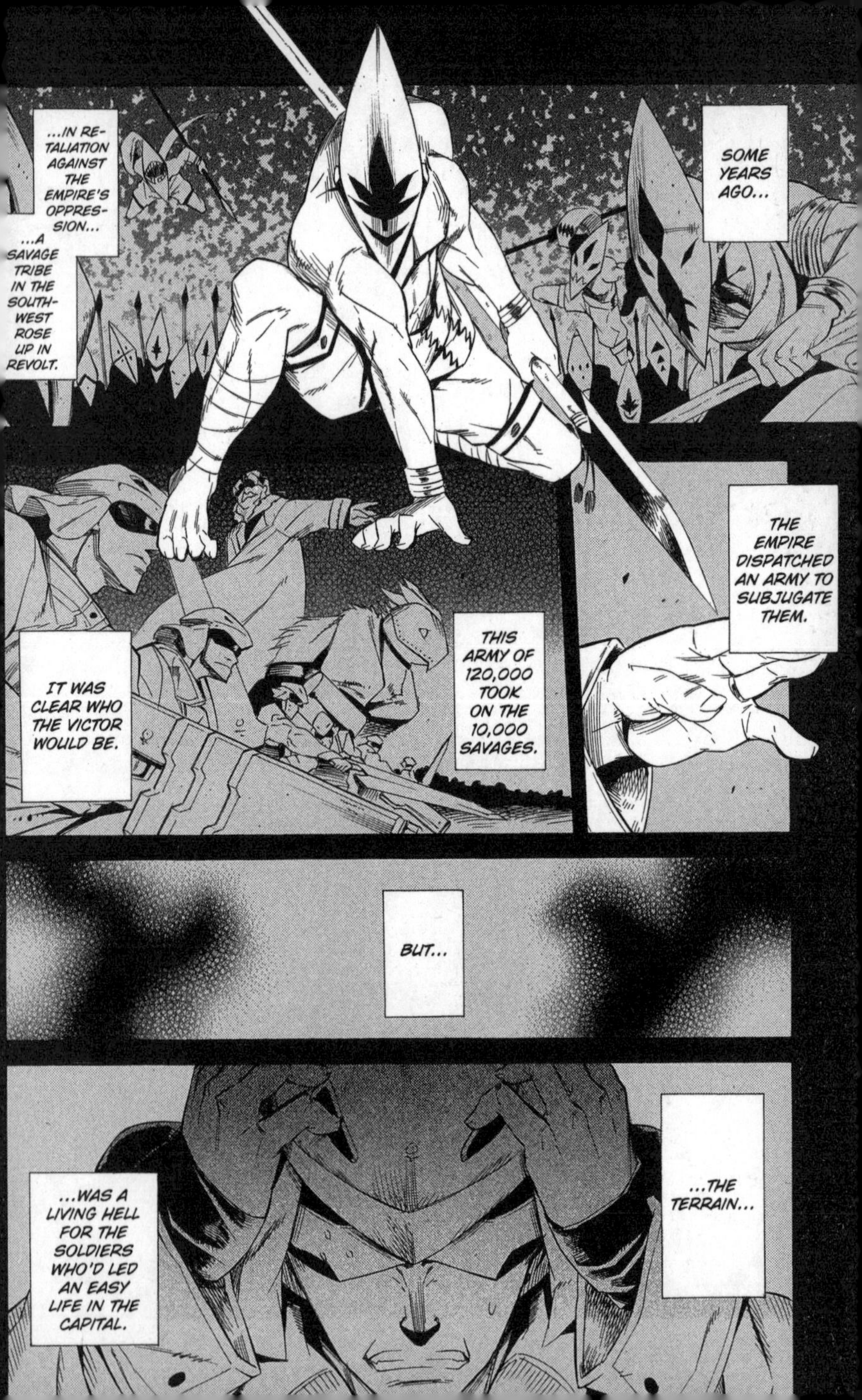
SOME YEARS AGO...
...IN RETALIATION AGAINST THE EMPIRE'S OPPRESSION...
...A SAVAGE TRIBE IN THE SOUTHWEST ROSE UP IN REVOLT.
THE EMPIRE DISPATCHED AN ARMY TO SUBJUGATE THEM.
THIS ARMY OF 120,000 TOOK ON THE 10,000 SAVAGES.
IT WAS CLEAR WHO THE VICTOR WOULD BE.
BUT...
...THE TERRAIN...
...WAS A LIVING HELL FOR THE SOLDIERS WHO'D LED AN EASY LIFE IN THE CAPITAL.

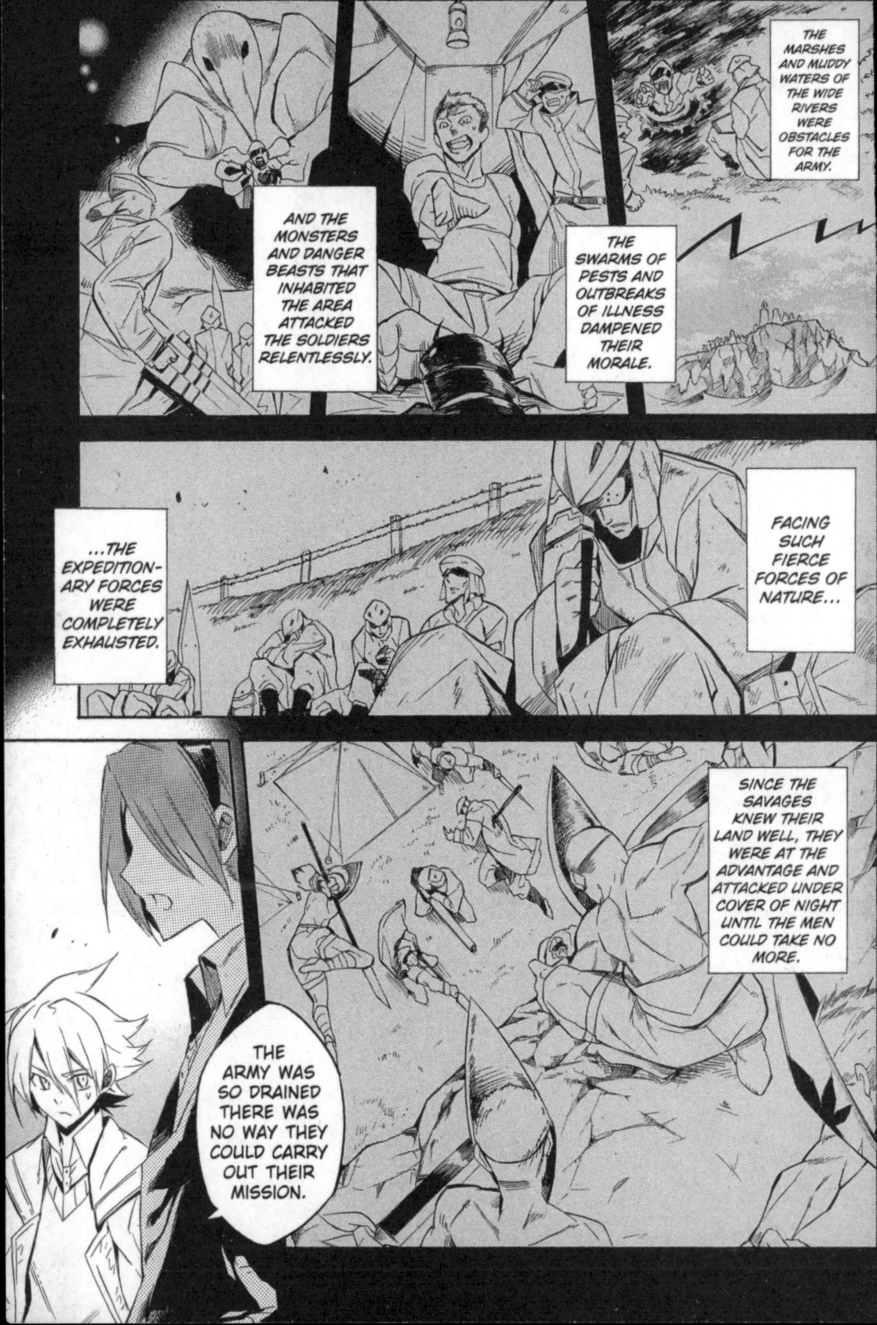
THE MARSHES AND MUDDY WATERS OF THE WIDE RIVERS WERE OBSTACLES FOR THE ARMY.
THE SWARMS OF PESTS AND OUTBREAKS OF ILLNESS DAMPENED THEIR MORALE.
AND THE MONSTERS AND DANGER BEASTS THAT INHABITED THE AREA ATTACKED THE SOLDIERS RELENTLESSLY.
FACING SUCH FIERCE FORCES OF NATURE...
...THE EXPEDITION-ARY FORCES WERE COMPLETELY EXHAUSTED.
SINCE THE SAVAGES KNEW THEIR LAND WELL, THEY WERE AT THE ADVANTAGE AND ATTACKED UNDER COVER OF NIGHT UNTIL THE MEN COULD TAKE NO MORE.
THE ARMY WAS SO DRAINED THERE WAS NO WAY THEY COULD CARRY OUT THEIR MISSION.

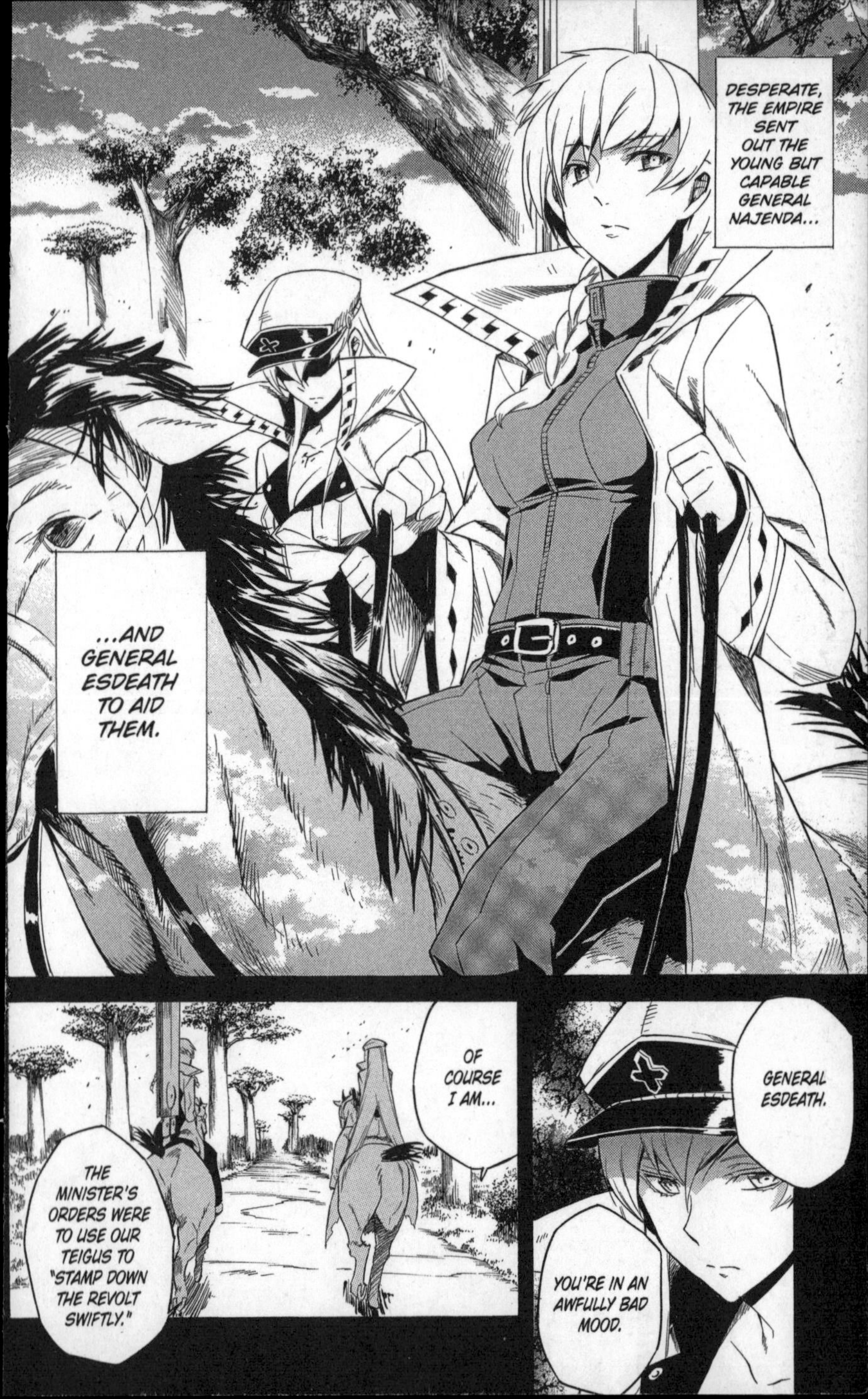
DESPERATE, THE EMPIRE SENT OUT THE YOUNG BUT CAPABLE GENERAL NAJENDA...
...AND GENERAL ESDEATH TO AID THEM.
GENERAL ESDEATH.
YOU'RE IN AN AWFULLY BAD MOOD.
OF COURSE I AM...
THE MINISTER'S ORDERS WERE TO USE OUR TEIGUS TO "STAMP DOWN THE REVOLT SWIFTLY."

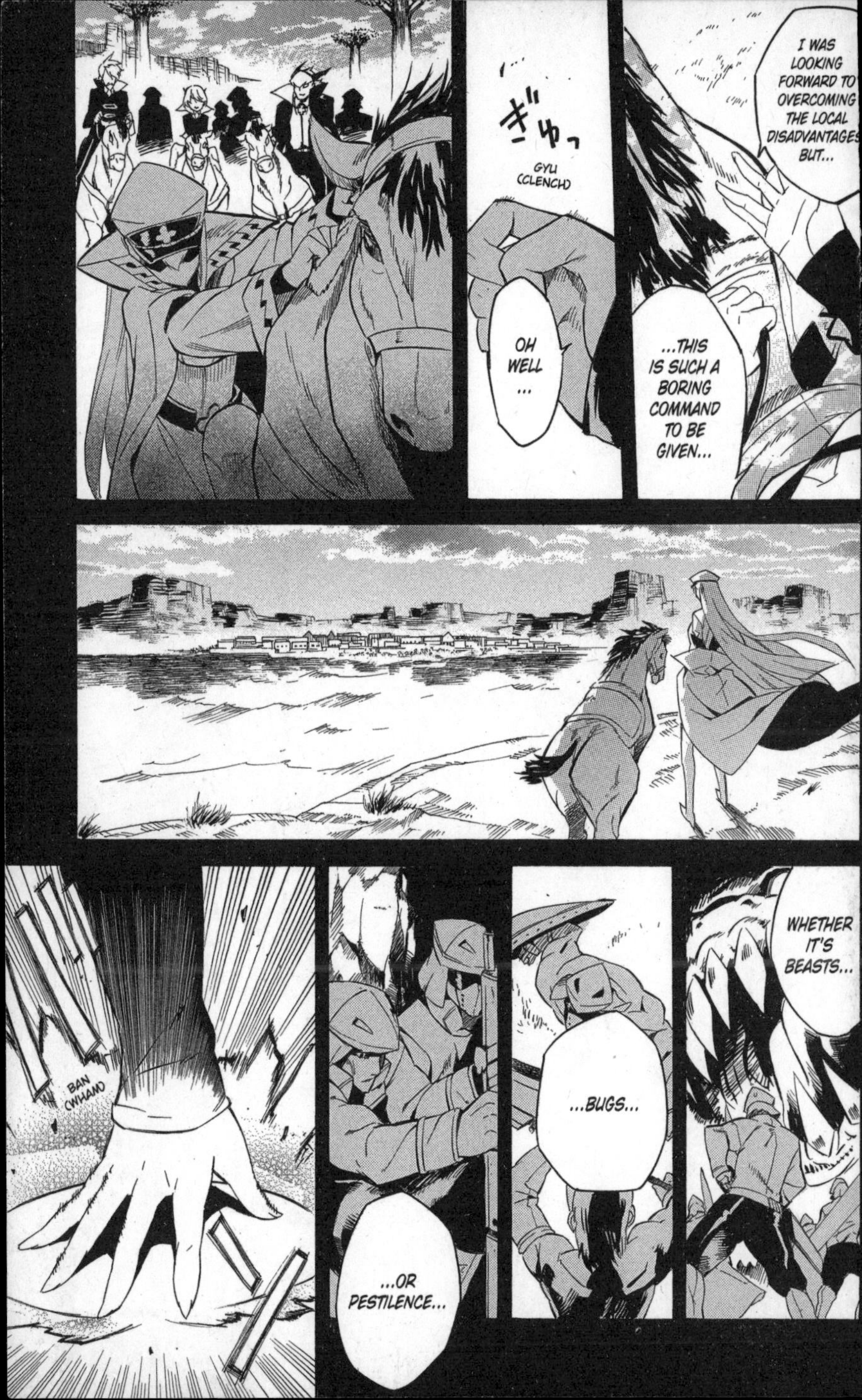
I WAS LOOKING FORWARD TO OVERCOMING THE LOCAL DISADVANTAGES BUT...
...THIS IS SUCH A BORING COMMAND TO BE GIVEN...
ぎゅっ
GYU (CLENCH)
OH WELL...
WHETHER IT'S BEASTS...
...BUGS...
...OR PESTILENCE...
BAN (WHAM)

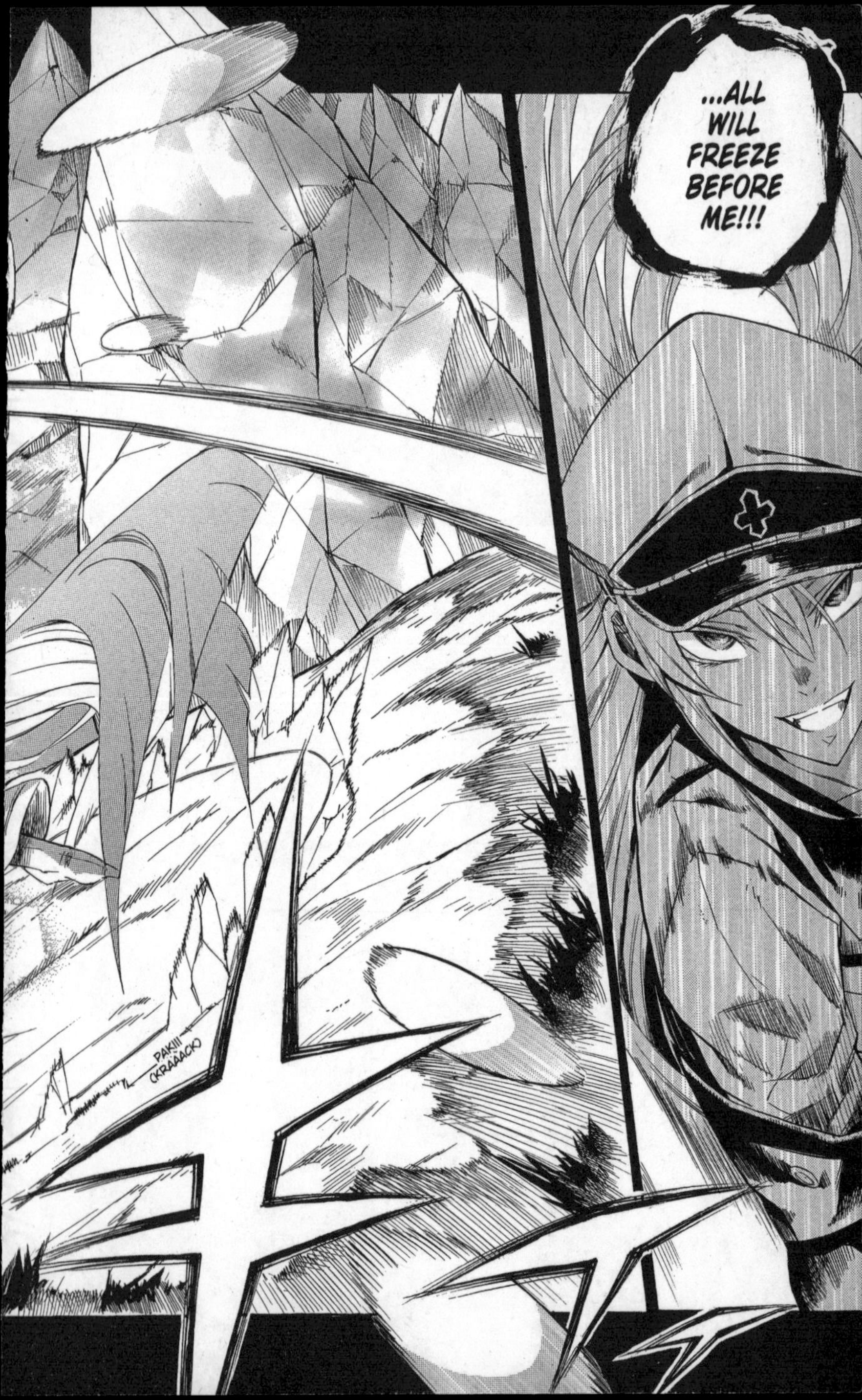
...ALL WILL FREEZE BEFORE ME!!!
PAKIII
(KRÄÄACK)

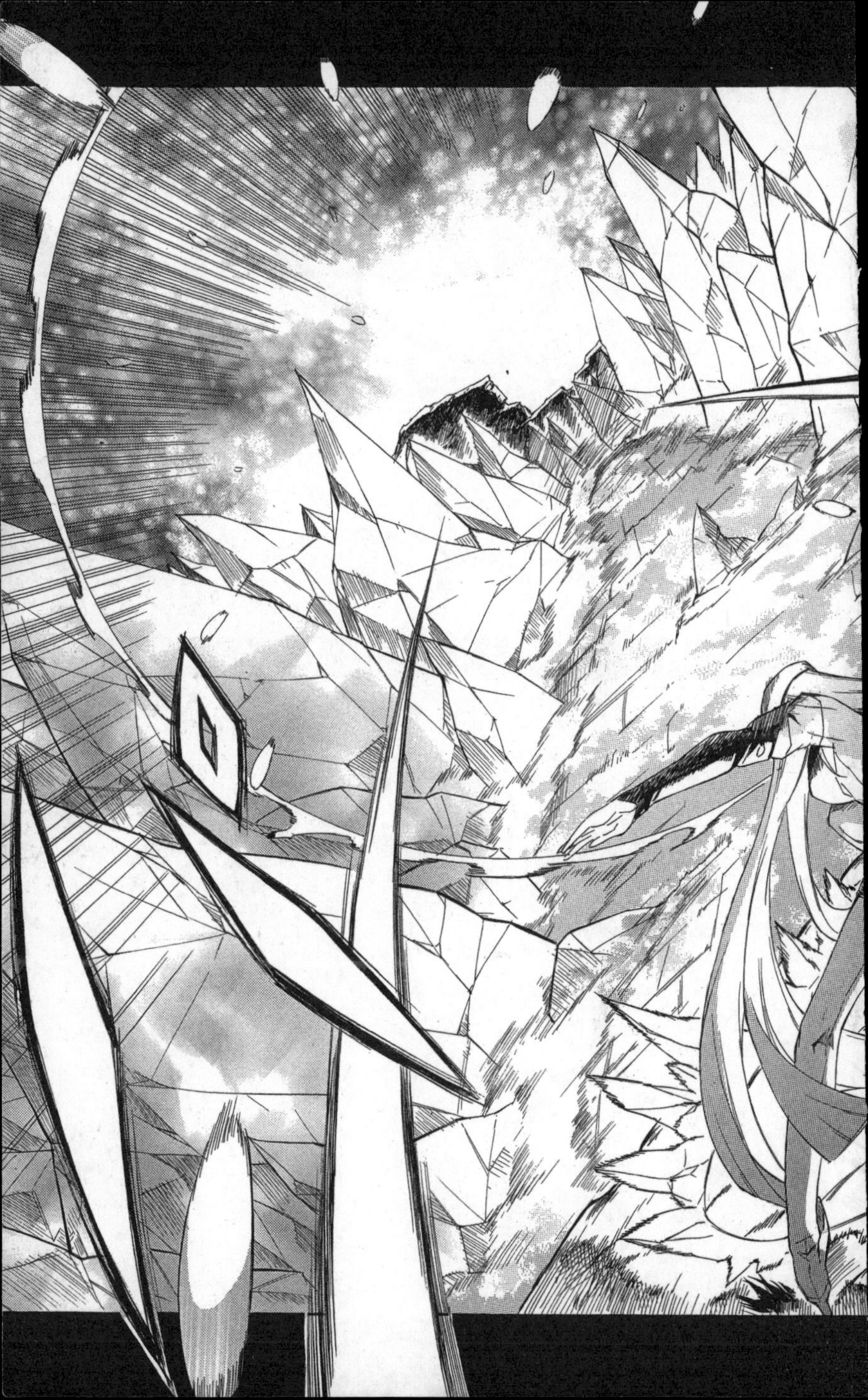

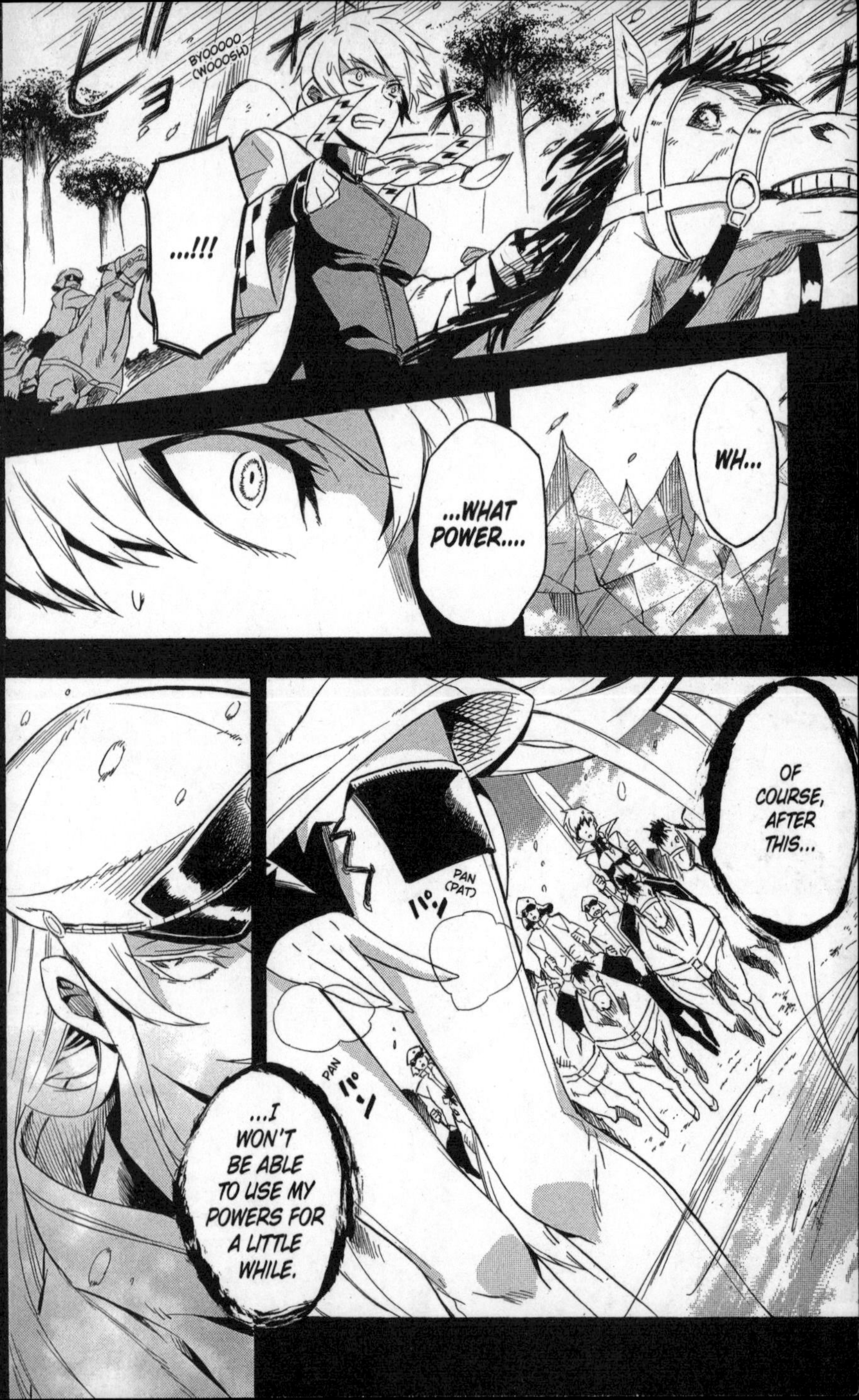
BYOOOOO (WOOOSH)
...!!!
WH...
...WHAT POWER....
OF COURSE, AFTER THIS...
PAN (PAT)
PAN
...I WON'T BE ABLE TO USE MY POWERS FOR A LITTLE WHILE.

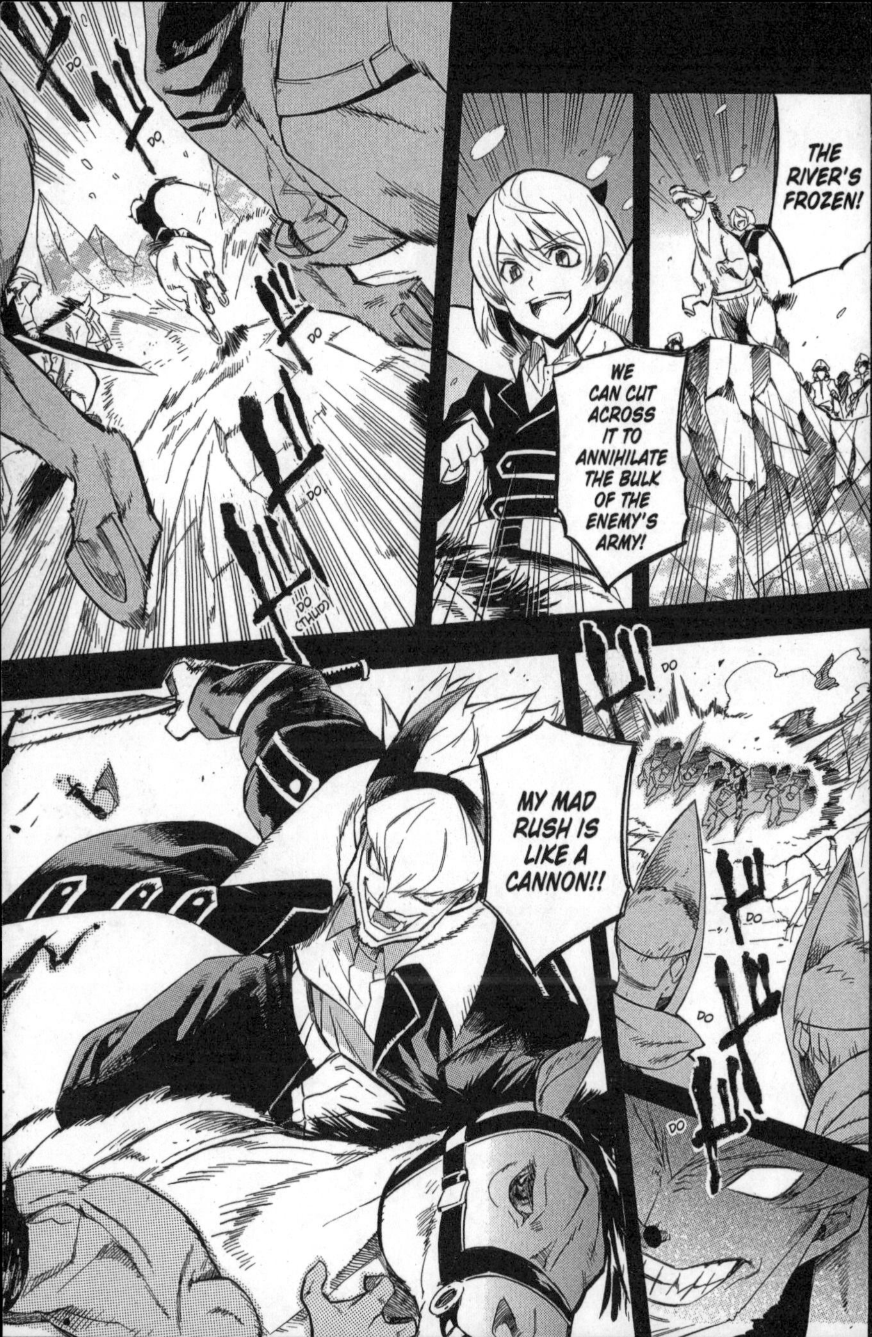
THE RIVER'S FROZEN!
WE CAN CUT ACROSS IT TO ANNIHILATE THE BULK OF THE ENEMY'S ARMY!
DO
DO
DO
DO
DO (THUD)
DO
MY MAD RUSH IS LIKE A CANNON!!
DO
DO
DO

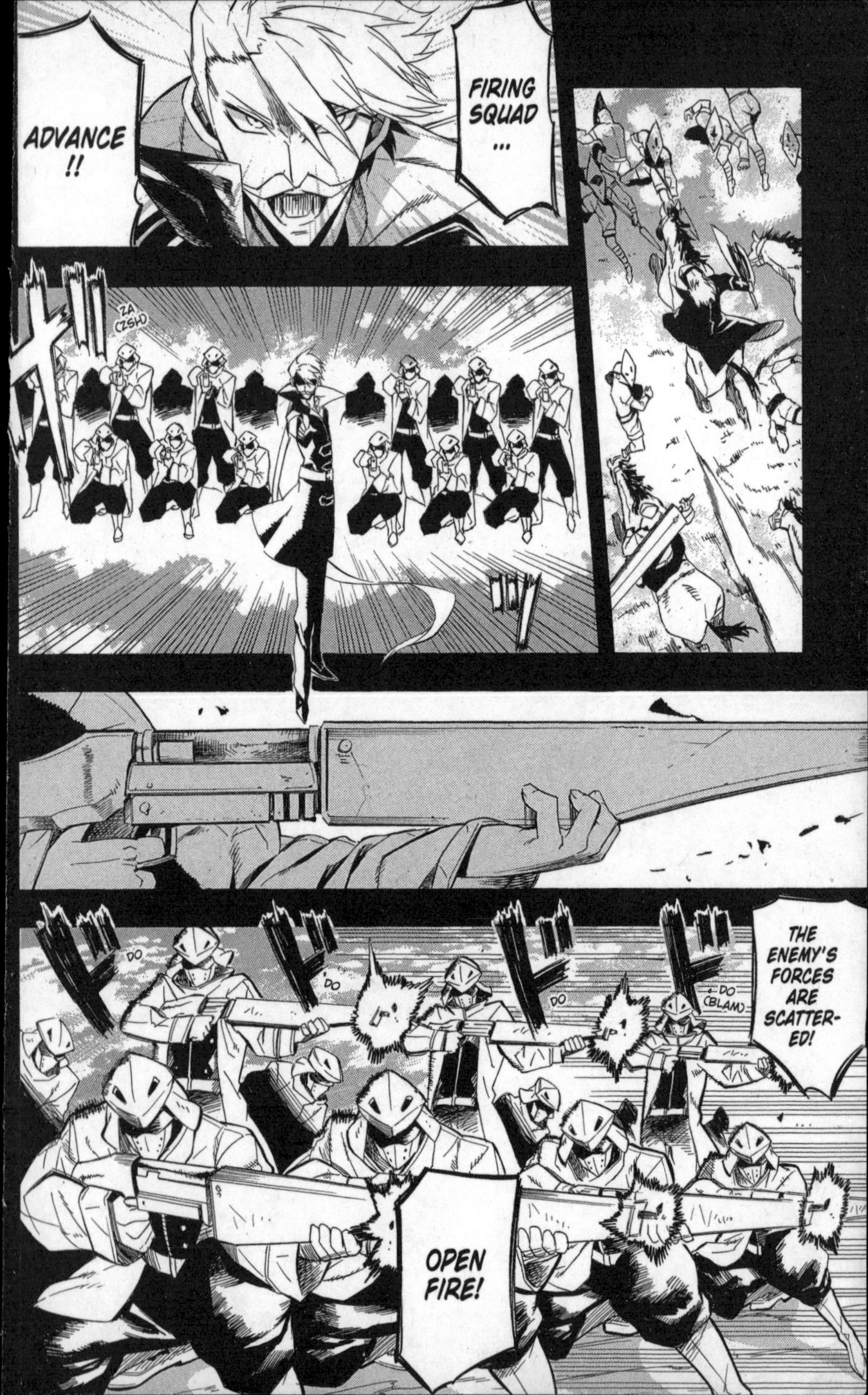
FIRING SQUAD ...
ADVANCE !!
ZA CZSH
THE ENEMY'S FORCES ARE SCATTER-ED!
DO (BLAM)
DO
DO
DO
OPEN FIRE!

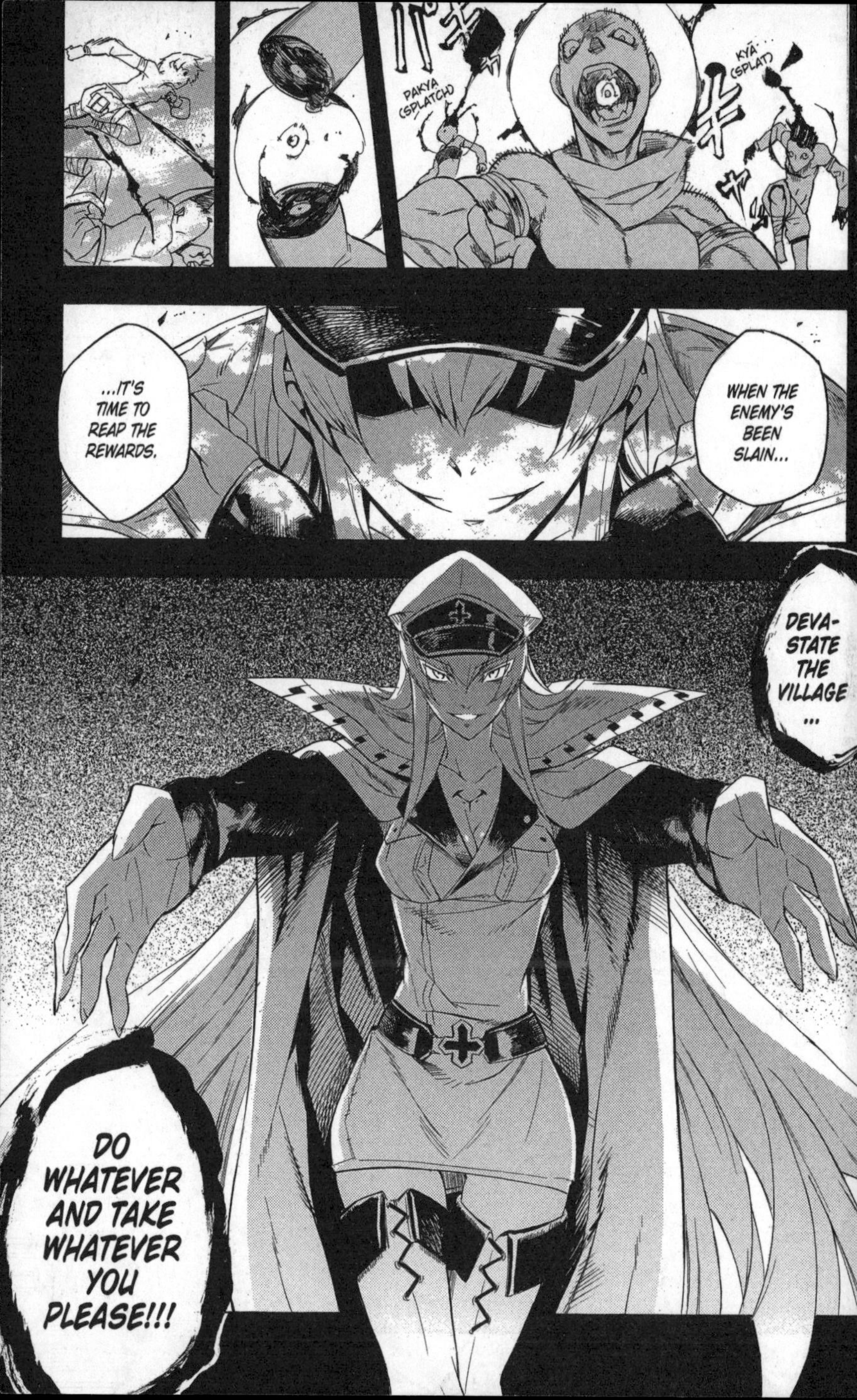
KYĀ (SPLAT)
PAKYA (SPLATCH)
WHEN THE ENEMY'S BEEN SLAIN...
...IT'S TIME TO REAP THE REWARDS.
DEVA-STATE THE VILLAGE...
DO WHATEVER AND TAKE WHATEVER YOU PLEASE!!!

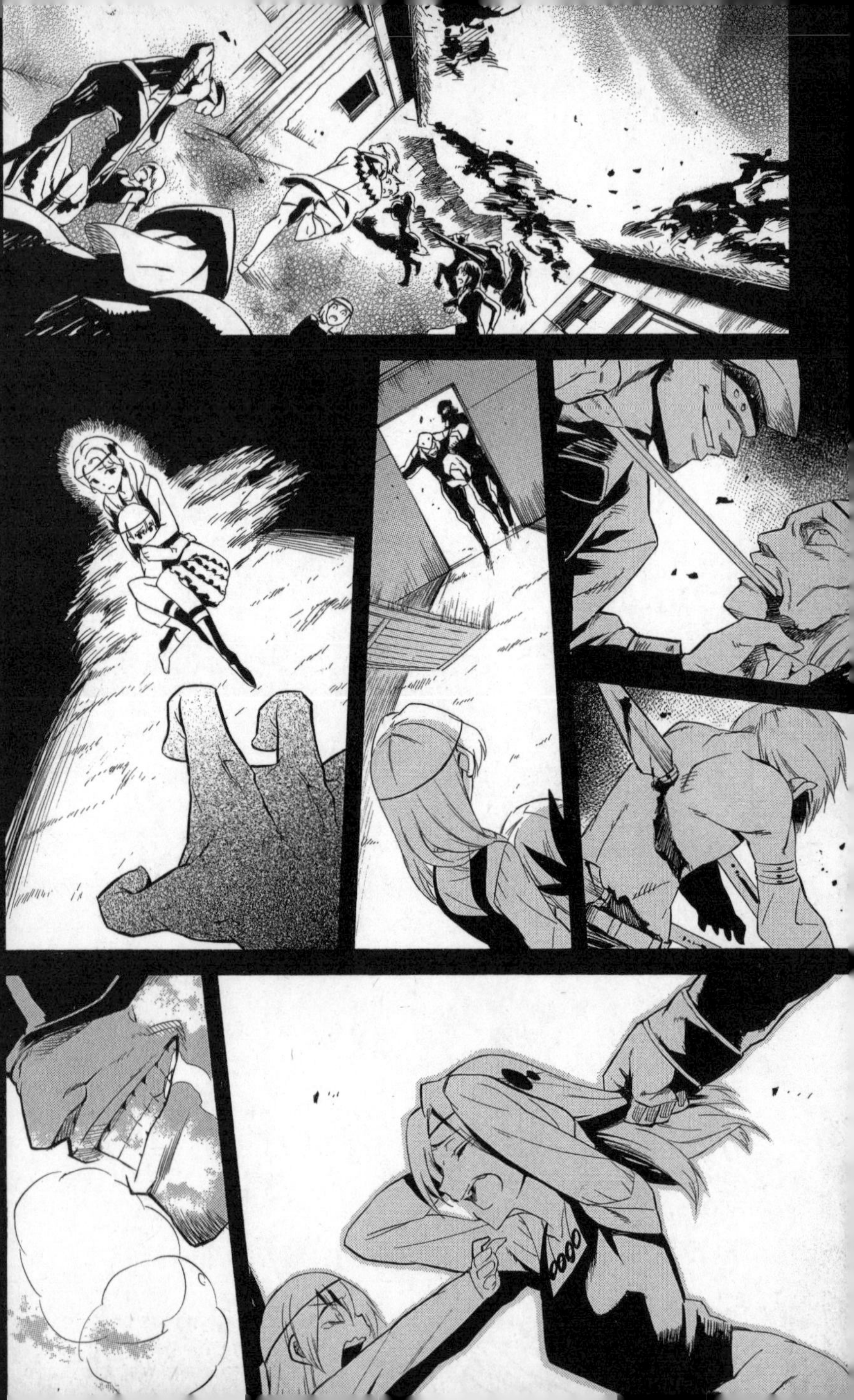

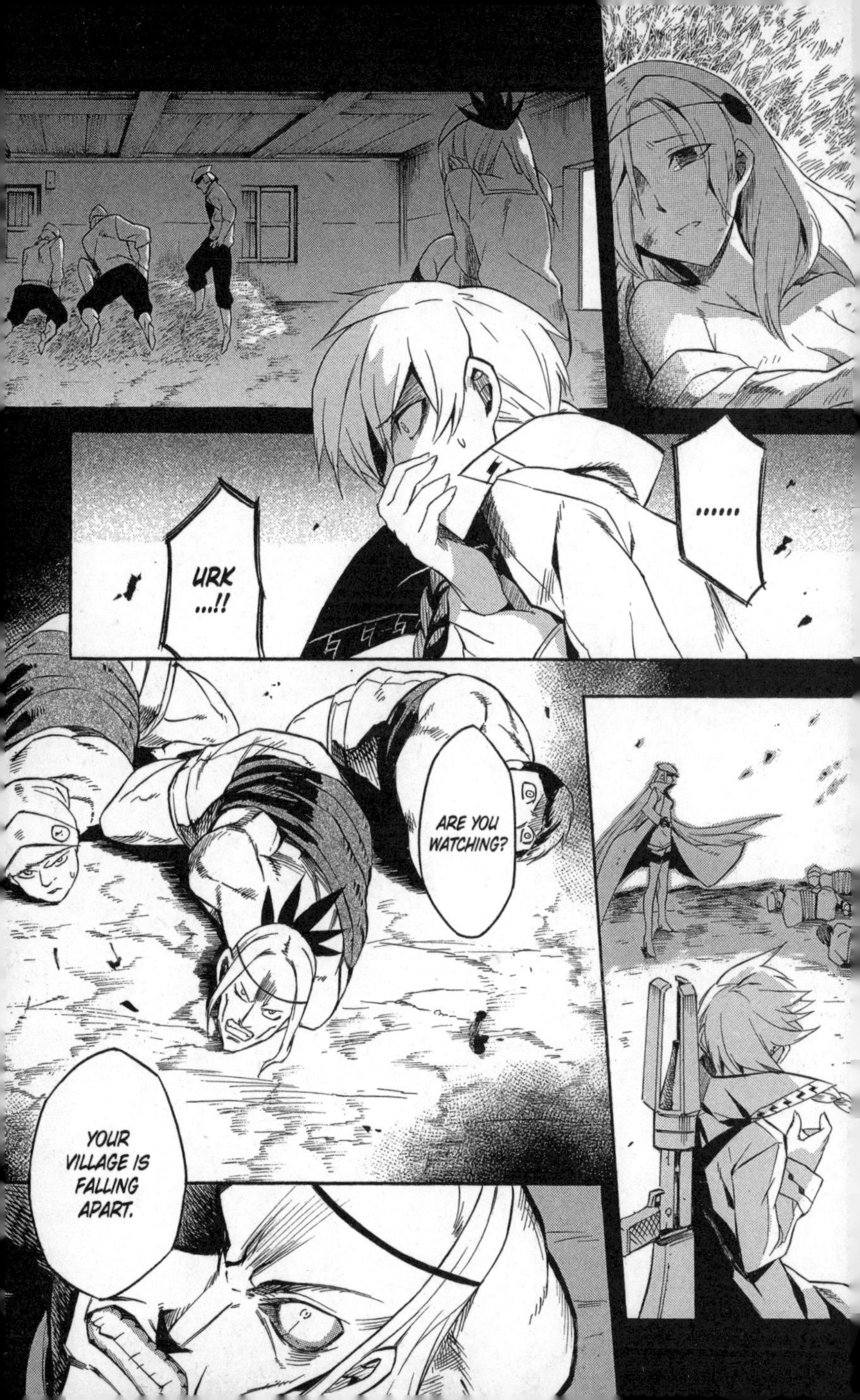
......
URK ...!!
ARE YOU WATCHING?
YOUR VILLAGE IS FALLING APART.

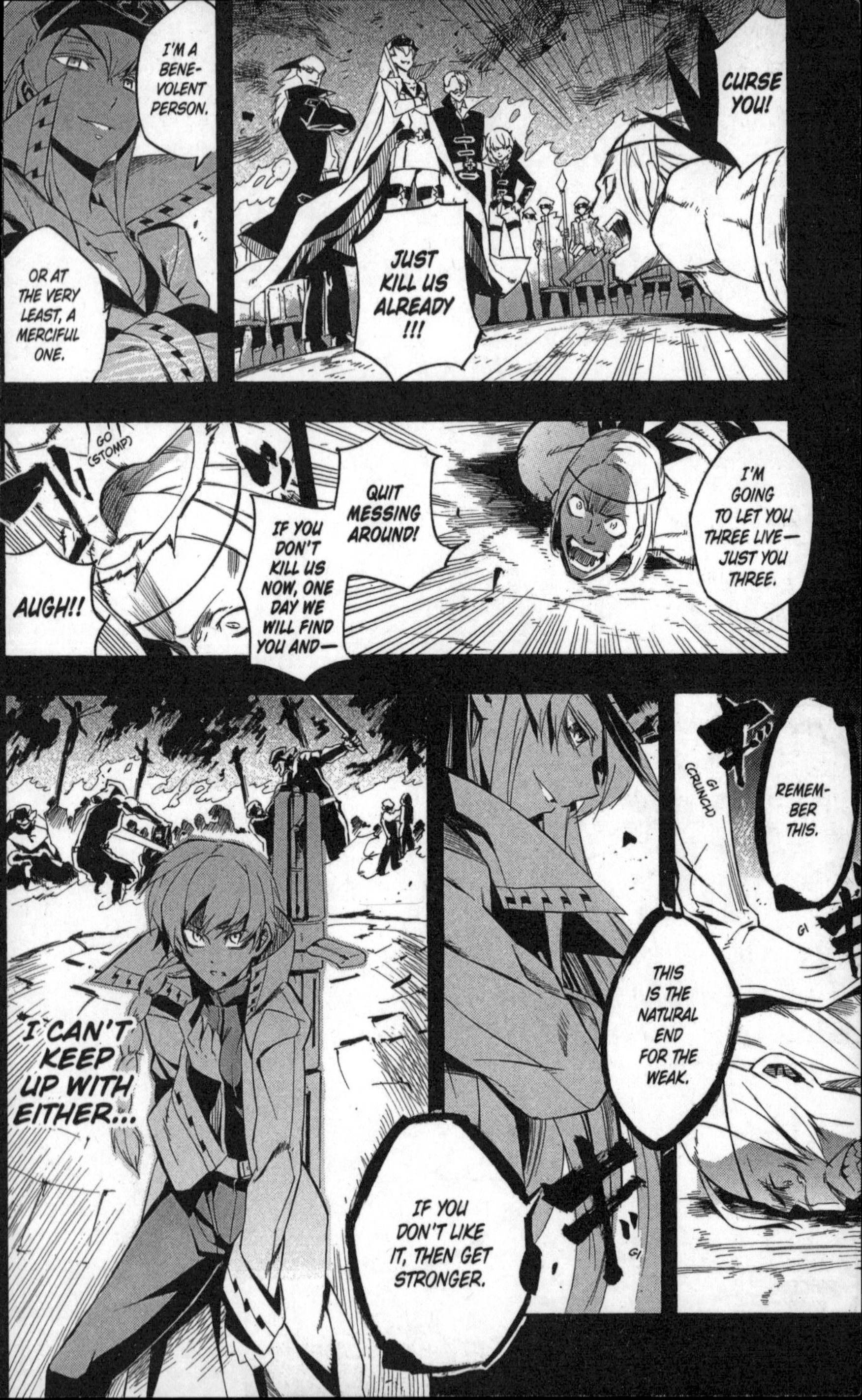
CURSE YOU!
JUST KILL US ALREADY !!!
I'M A BENEVOLENT PERSON.
OR AT THE VERY LEAST, A MERCIFUL ONE.
I'M GOING TO LET YOU THREE LIVE—JUST YOU THREE.
QUIT MESSING AROUND!
IF YOU DON'T KILL US NOW, ONE DAY WE WILL FIND YOU AND—
GO (STOMP)
AUGH!!
GI (CRUNCH)
REMEMBER THIS.
GI
THIS IS THE NATURAL END FOR THE WEAK.
IF YOU DON'T LIKE IT, THEN GET STRONGER.
GI
I CAN'T KEEP UP WITH EITHER...

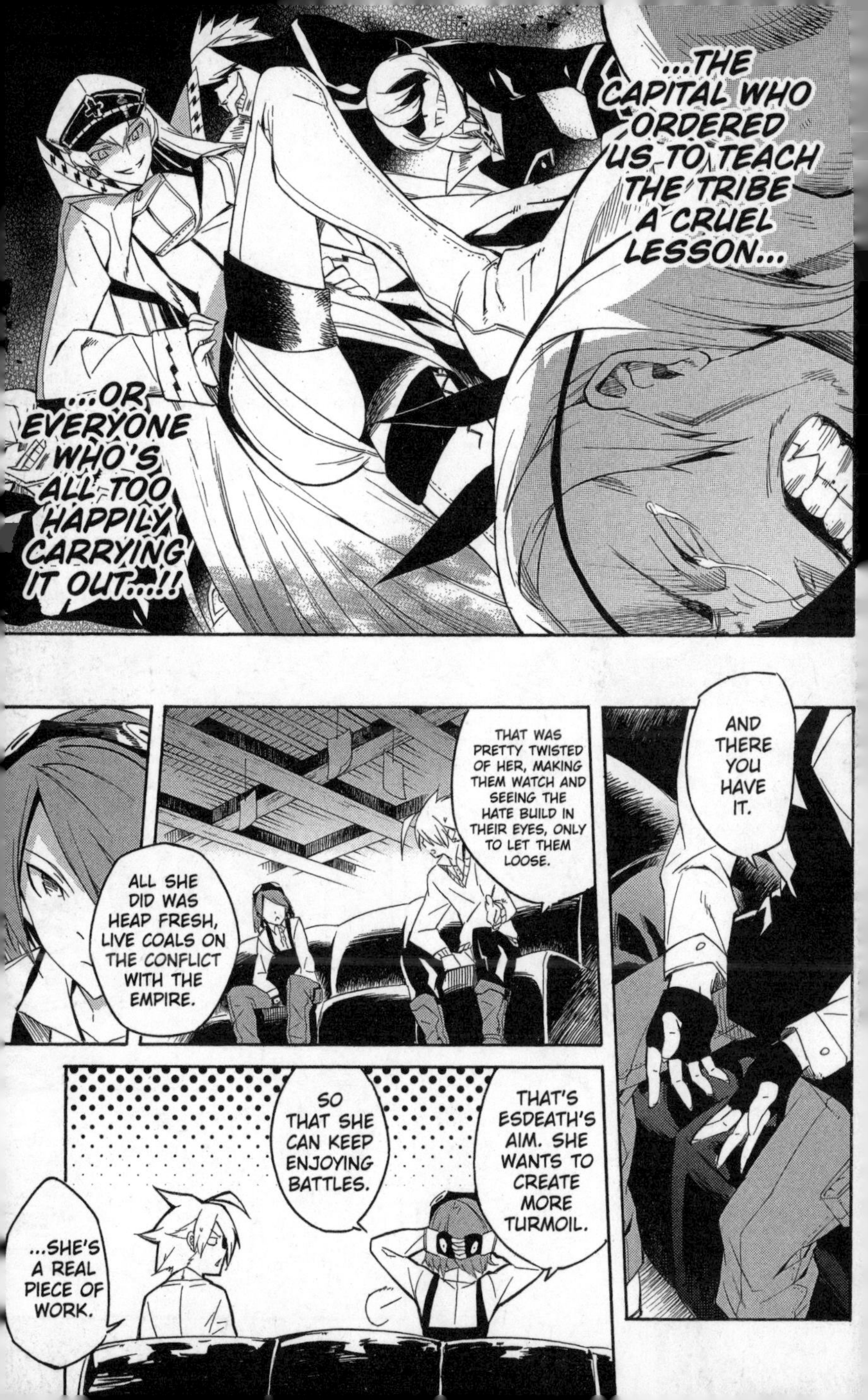
...THE CAPITAL WHO ORDERED US TO TEACH THE TRIBE A CRUEL LESSON...
...OR EVERYONE WHO'S ALL TOO HAPPILY CARRYING IT OUT...!!
AND THERE YOU HAVE IT.
THAT WAS PRETTY TWISTED OF HER, MAKING THEM WATCH AND SEEING THE HATE BUILD IN THEIR EYES, ONLY TO LET THEM LOOSE.
ALL SHE DID WAS HEAP FRESH, LIVE COALS ON THE CONFLICT WITH THE EMPIRE.
THAT'S ESDEATH'S AIM. SHE WANTS TO CREATE MORE TURMOIL.
SO THAT SHE CAN KEEP ENJOYING BATTLES.
...SHE'S A REAL PIECE OF WORK.

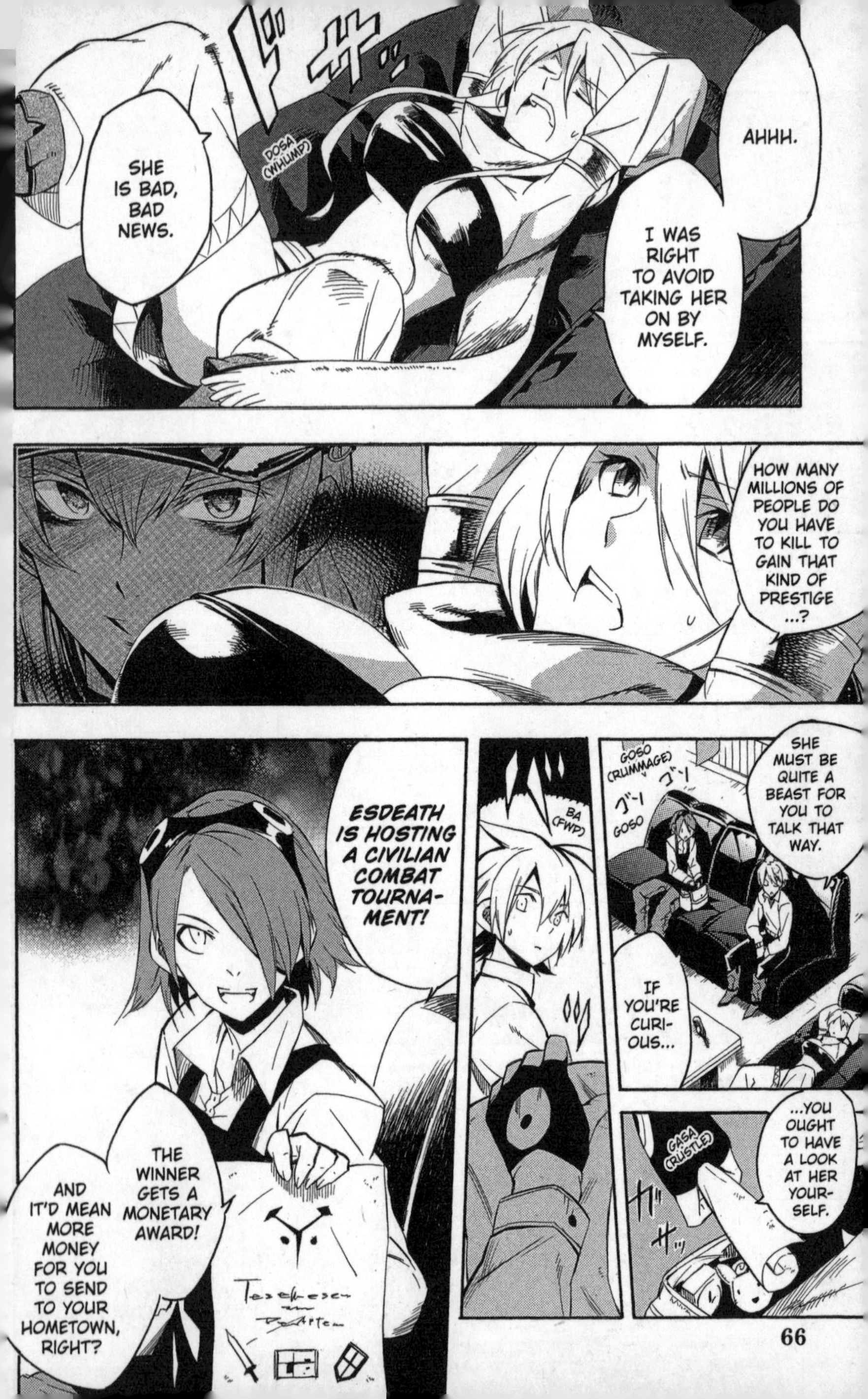
AHHH.
I WAS RIGHT TO AVOID TAKING HER ON BY MYSELF.
DOSA (WHUMP)
SHE IS BAD, BAD NEWS.
HOW MANY MILLIONS OF PEOPLE DO YOU HAVE TO KILL TO GAIN THAT KIND OF PRESTIGE ...?
SHE MUST BE QUITE A BEAST FOR YOU TO TALK THAT WAY.
GOSO (RUMMAGE)
GOSO
IF YOU'RE CURIOUS...
GASA (RUSTLE)
...YOU OUGHT TO HAVE A LOOK AT HER YOURSELF.
BA (FWP)
ESDEATH IS HOSTING A CIVILIAN COMBAT TOURNAMENT!
THE WINNER GETS A MONETARY AWARD!
AND IT'D MEAN MORE MONEY FOR YOU TO SEND TO YOUR HOMETOWN, RIGHT?

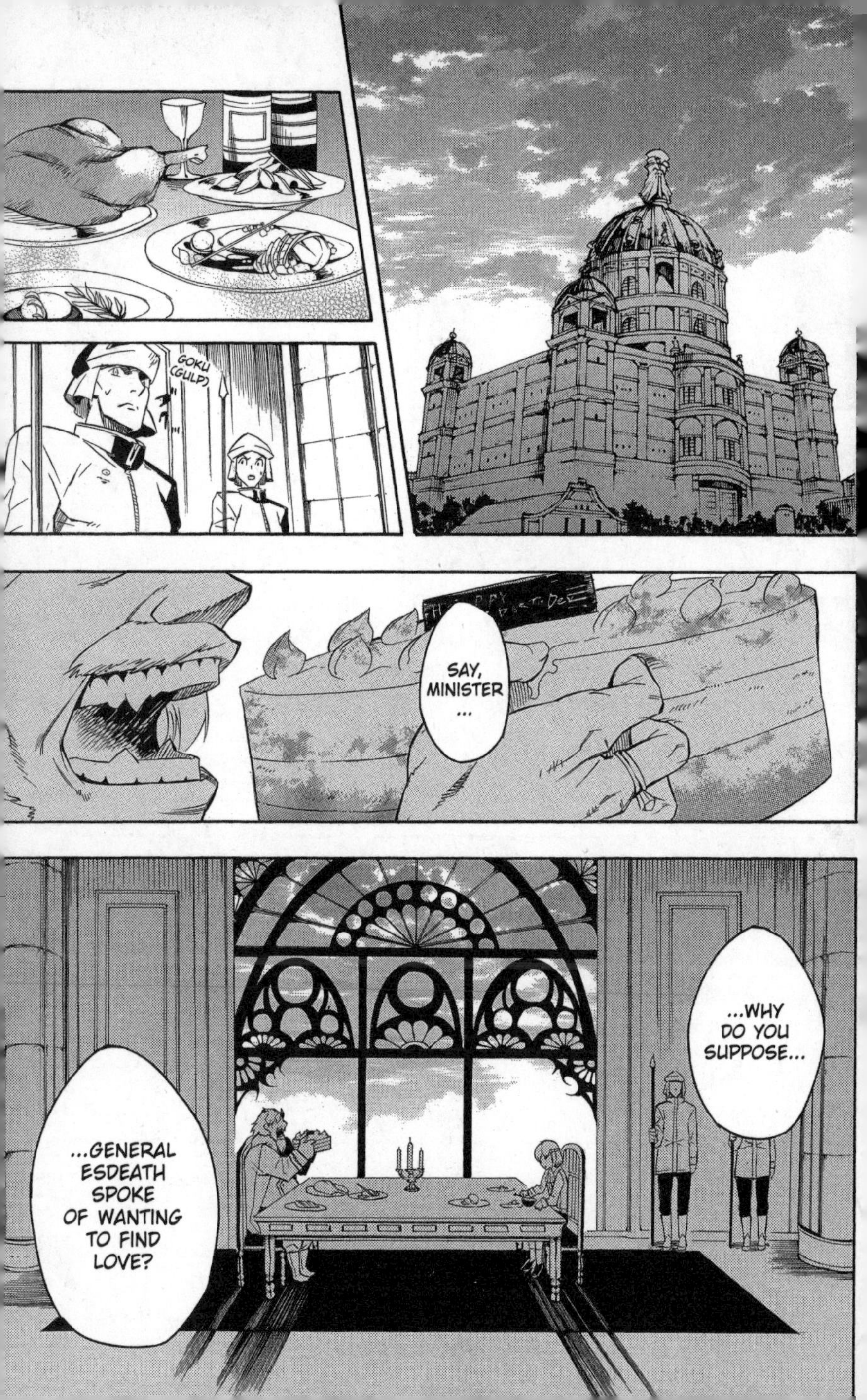
GOKU (GULP)
SAY, MINISTER ...
...WHY DO YOU SUPPOSE...
...GENERAL ESDEATH SPOKE OF WANTING TO FIND LOVE?

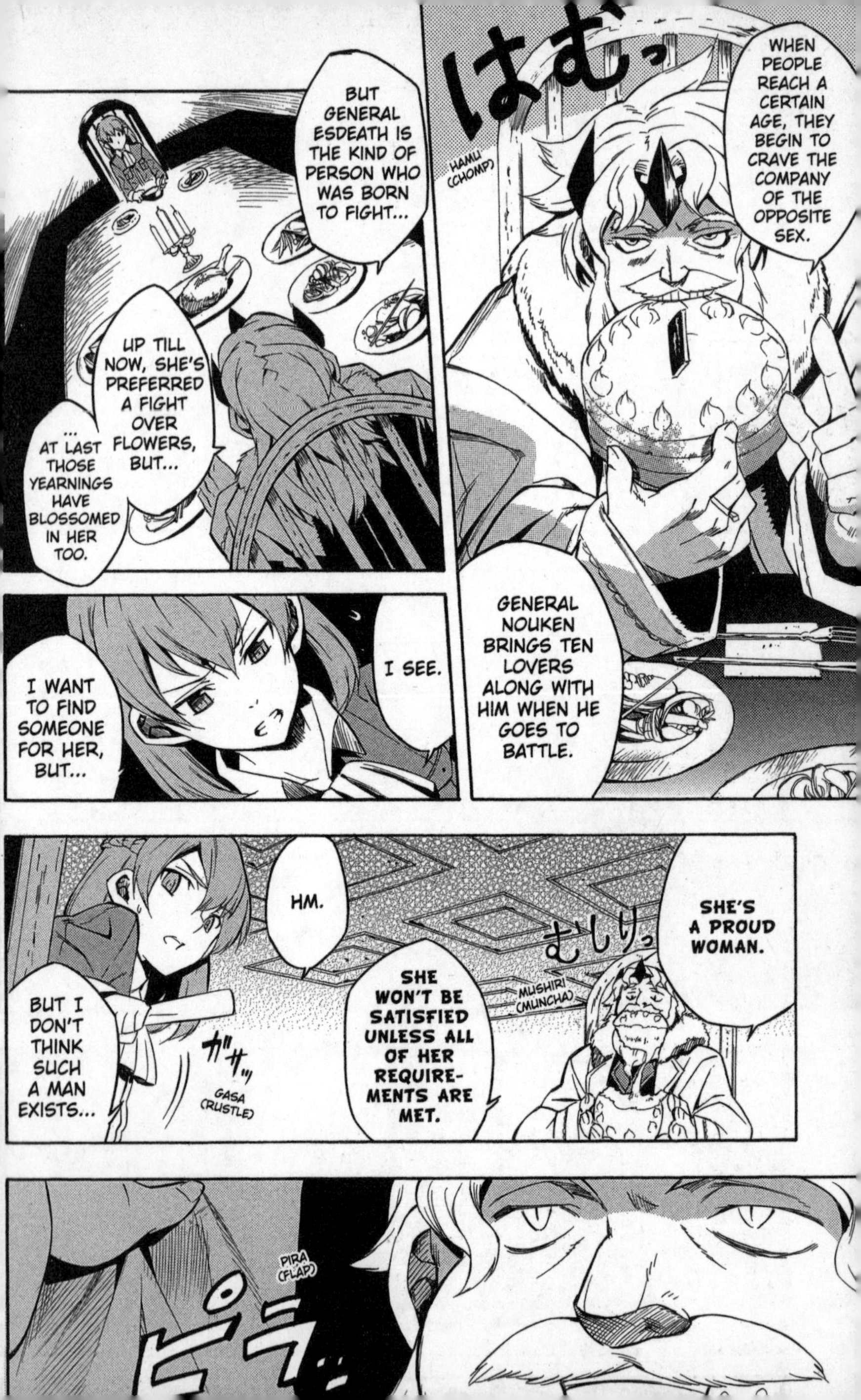
はむっ
HAMU (CHOMP)
WHEN PEOPLE REACH A CERTAIN AGE, THEY BEGIN TO CRAVE THE COMPANY OF THE OPPOSITE SEX.
BUT GENERAL ESDEATH IS THE KIND OF PERSON WHO WAS BORN TO FIGHT...
UP TILL NOW, SHE'S PREFERRED A FIGHT OVER FLOWERS, BUT...
... AT LAST THOSE YEARNINGS HAVE BLOSSOMED IN HER TOO.
GENERAL NOUKEN BRINGS TEN LOVERS ALONG WITH HIM WHEN HE GOES TO BATTLE.
I SEE.
I WANT TO FIND SOMEONE FOR HER, BUT...
SHE'S A PROUD WOMAN.
むしりっ
MUSHIRI (MUNCHA)
SHE WON'T BE SATISFIED UNLESS ALL OF HER REQUIRE-MENTS ARE MET.
HM.
BUT I DON'T THINK SUCH A MAN EXISTS...
ガサッ
GASA (RUSTLE)
PIRA (FLAP)
ピラッ

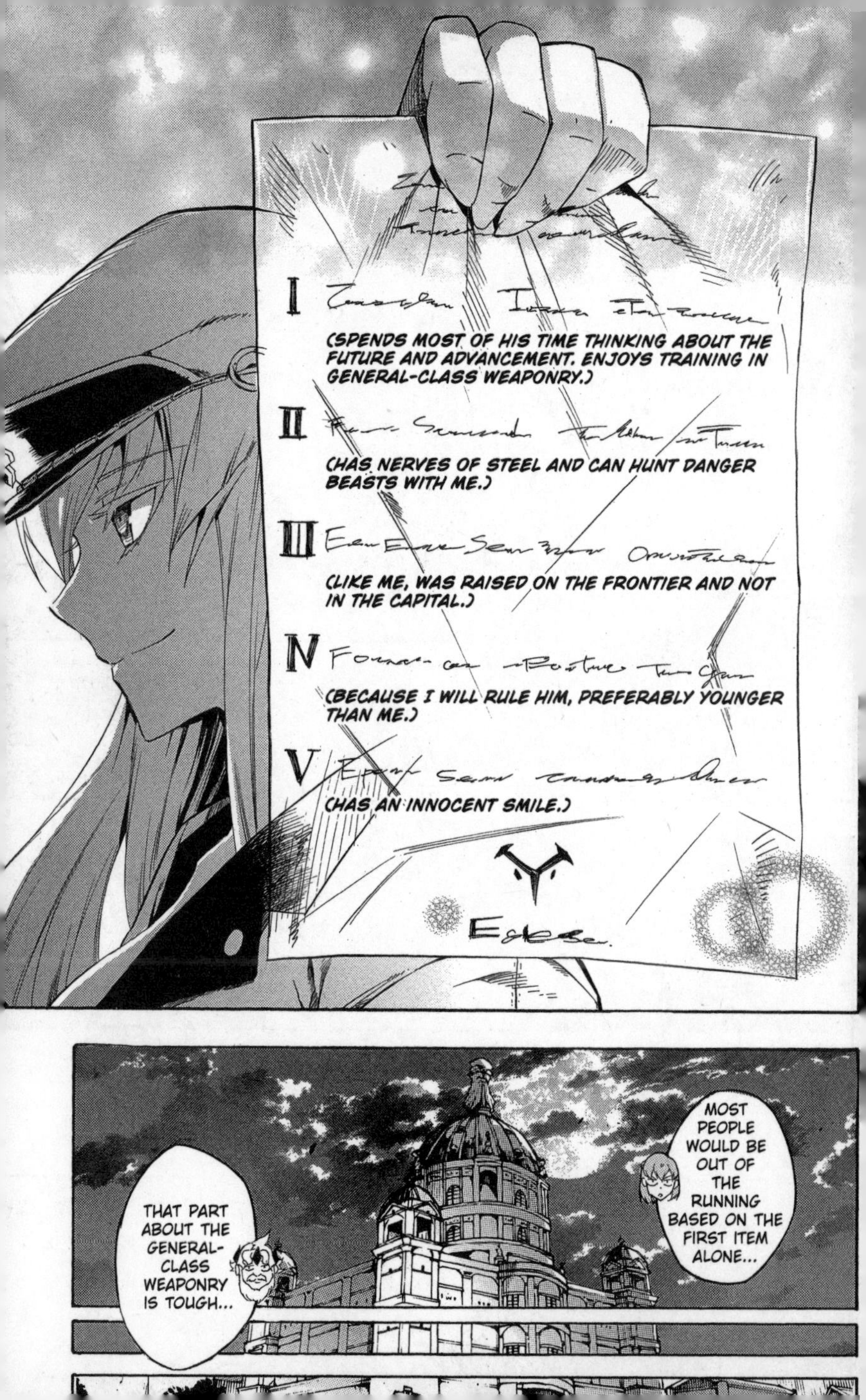
I
(SPENDS MOST OF HIS TIME THINKING ABOUT THE FUTURE AND ADVANCEMENT. ENJOYS TRAINING IN GENERAL-CLASS WEAPONRY.)
II
(HAS NERVES OF STEEL AND CAN HUNT DANGER BEASTS WITH ME.)
III
(LIKE ME, WAS RAISED ON THE FRONTIER AND NOT IN THE CAPITAL.)
IV
(BECAUSE I WILL RULE HIM, PREFERABLY YOUNGER THAN ME.)
V
(HAS AN INNOCENT SMILE.)
MOST PEOPLE WOULD BE OUT OF THE RUNNING BASED ON THE FIRST ITEM ALONE...
THAT PART ABOUT THE GENERAL-CLASS WEAPONRY IS TOUGH...

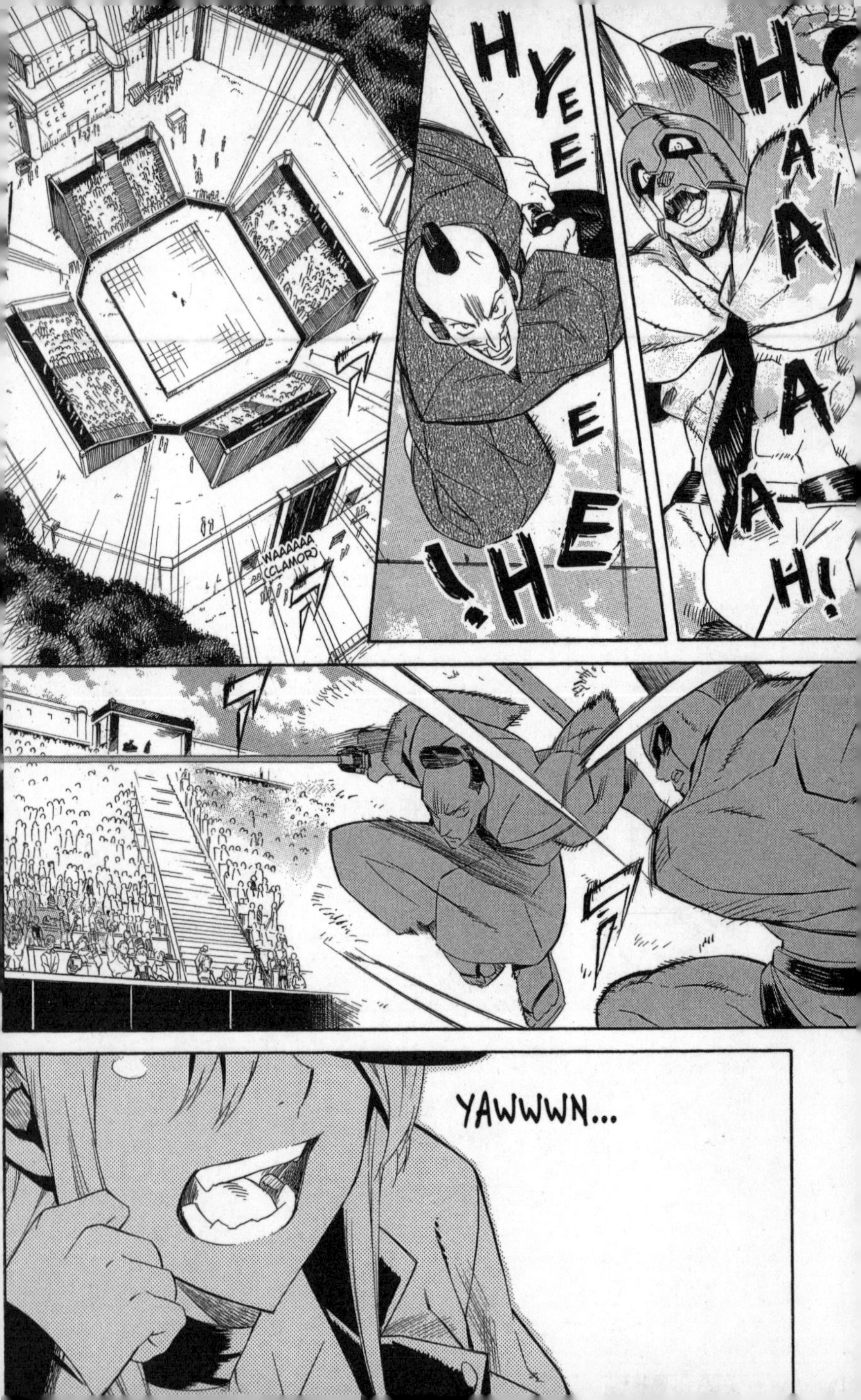
HAAAAH!
HYEE EHEH!
WAAAAAA (CLAMOR)
YAWWWN...

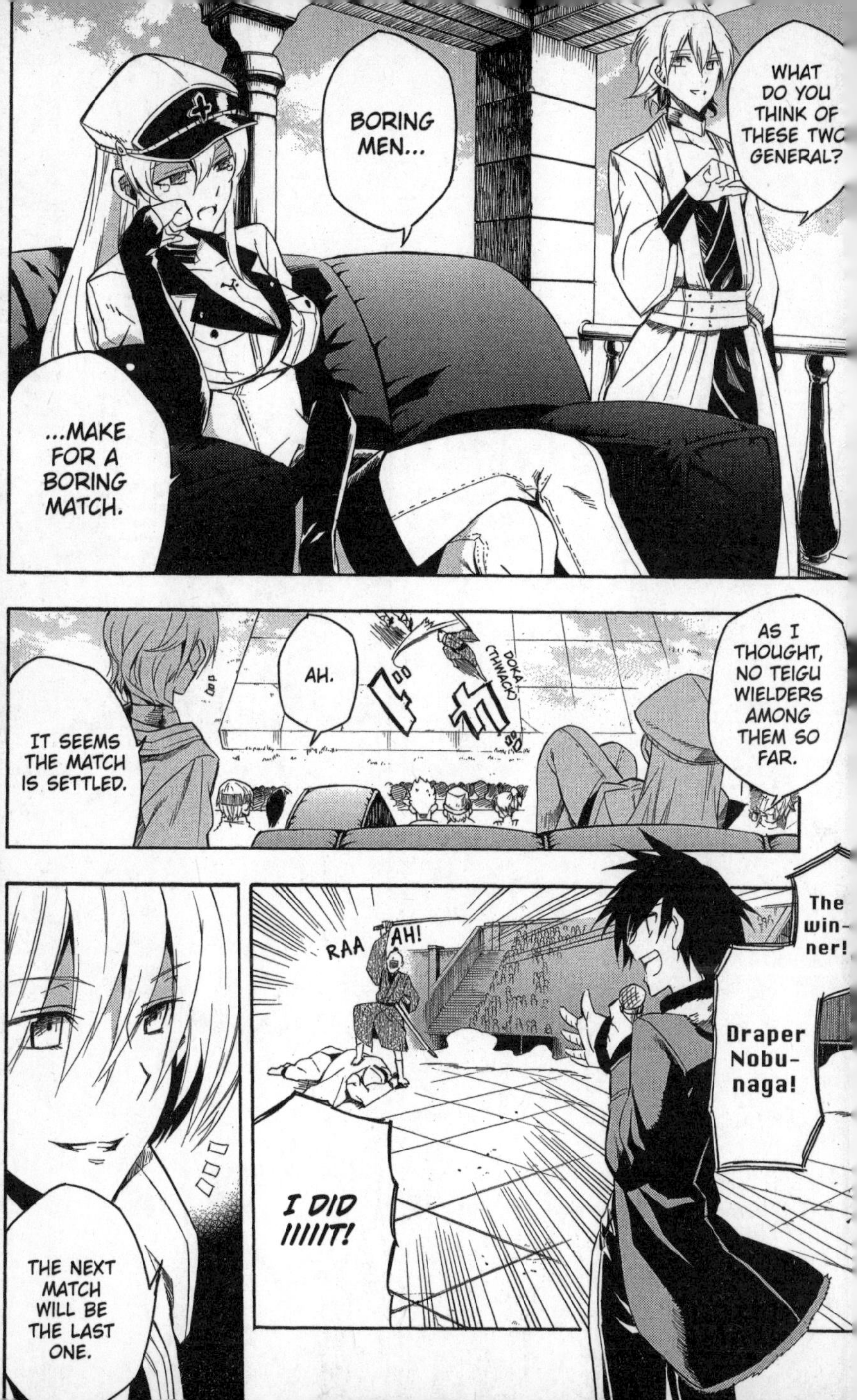
WHAT DO YOU THINK OF THESE TWO GENERAL?
BORING MEN...
...MAKE FOR A BORING MATCH.
AS I THOUGHT, NO TEIGU WIELDERS AMONG THEM SO FAR.
DOKA CTHWACK
AH.
IT SEEMS THE MATCH IS SETTLED.
The winner!
Draper Nobunaga!
RAAAH!
I DID IIIIIIT!
THE NEXT MATCH WILL BE THE LAST ONE.

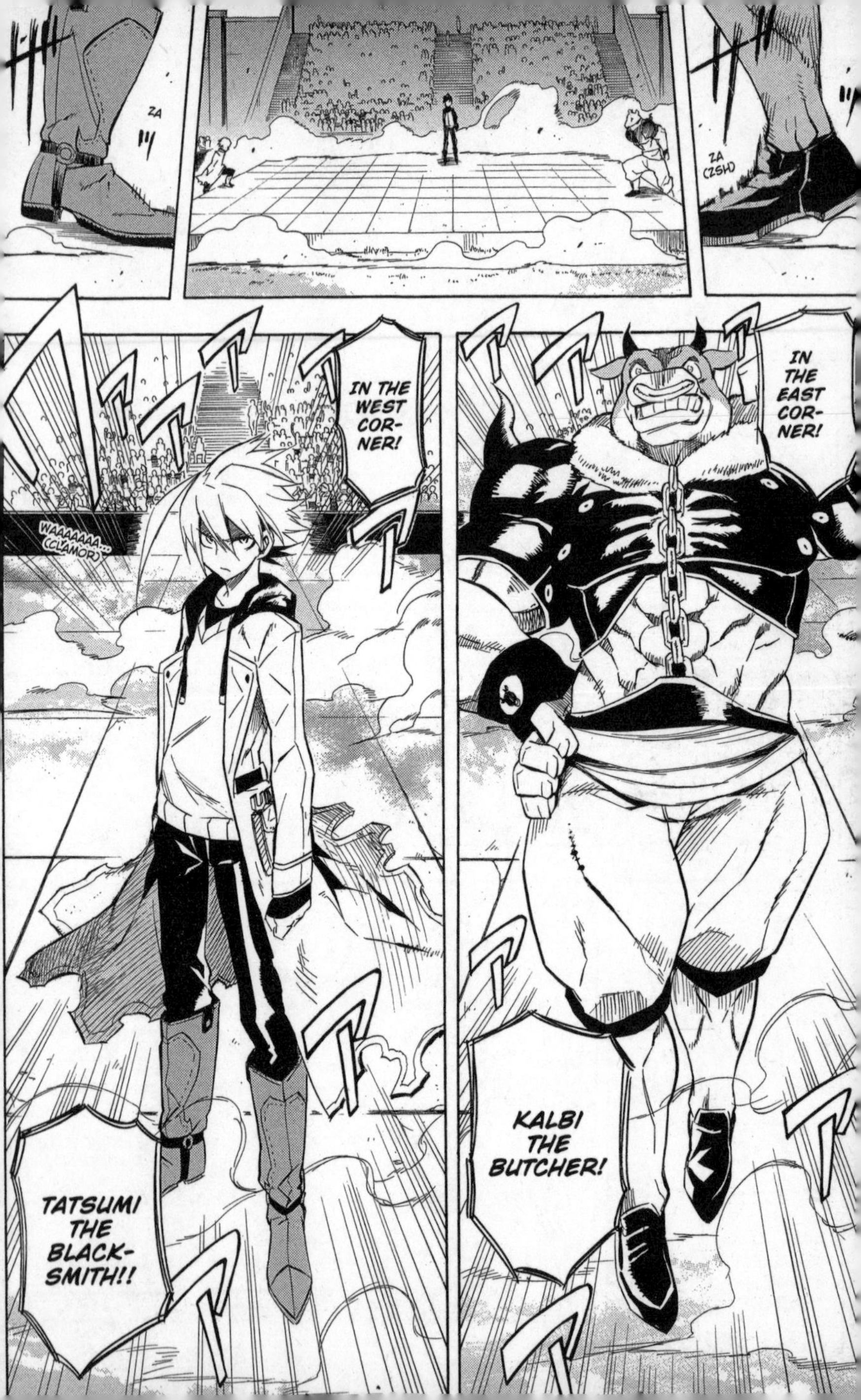
ZA (ZSH)
ZA
IN THE EAST CORNER!
KALBI THE BUTCHER!
IN THE WEST CORNER!
WAAAAAAA... (CLAMOR)
TATSUMI THE BLACK-SMITH!!

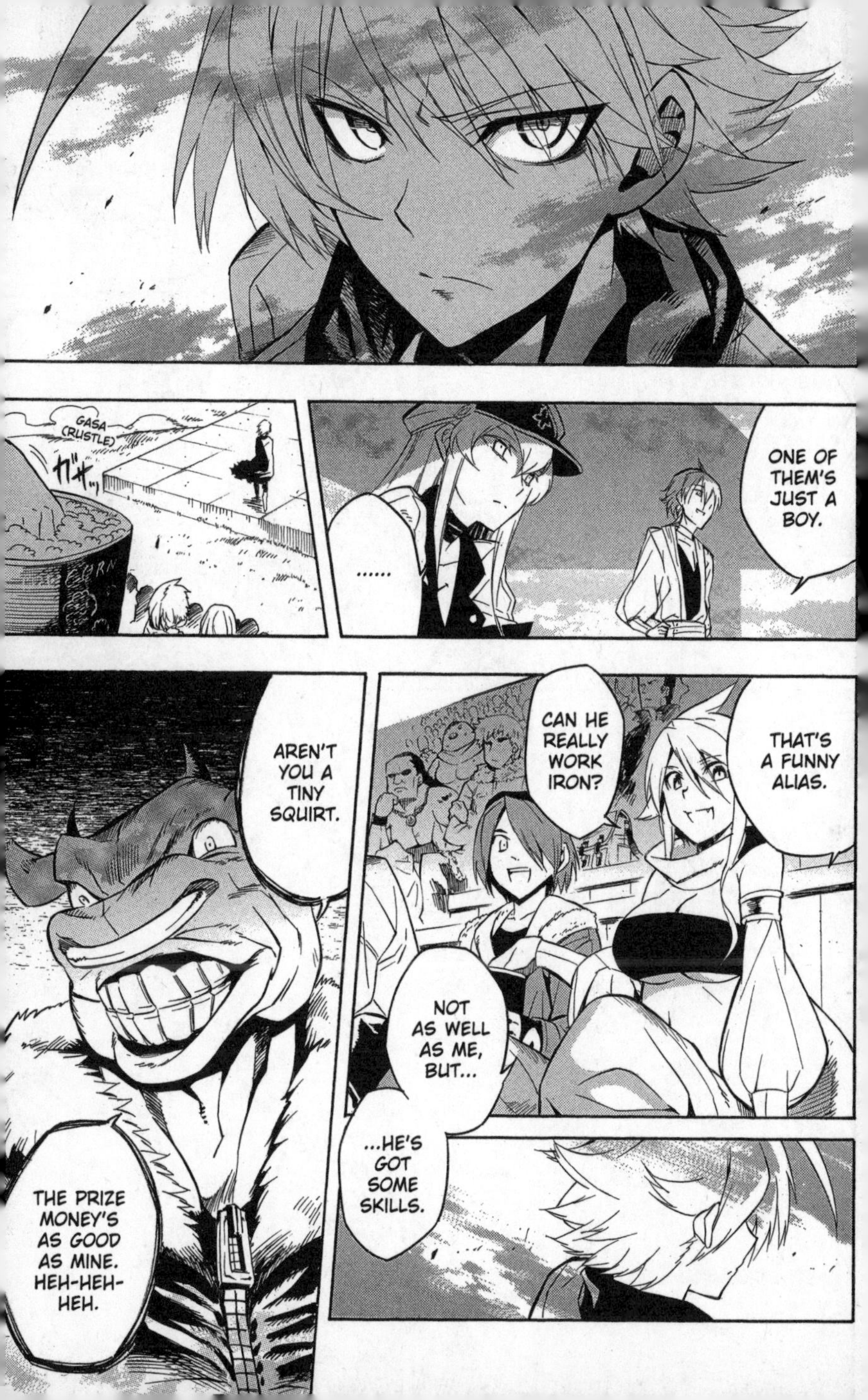
ONE OF THEM'S JUST A BOY.
......
GASA (RUSTLE)
THAT'S A FUNNY ALIAS.
CAN HE REALLY WORK IRON?
NOT AS WELL AS ME, BUT...
...HE'S GOT SOME SKILLS.
AREN'T YOU A TINY SQUIRT.
THE PRIZE MONEY'S AS GOOD AS MINE. HEH-HEH-HEH.

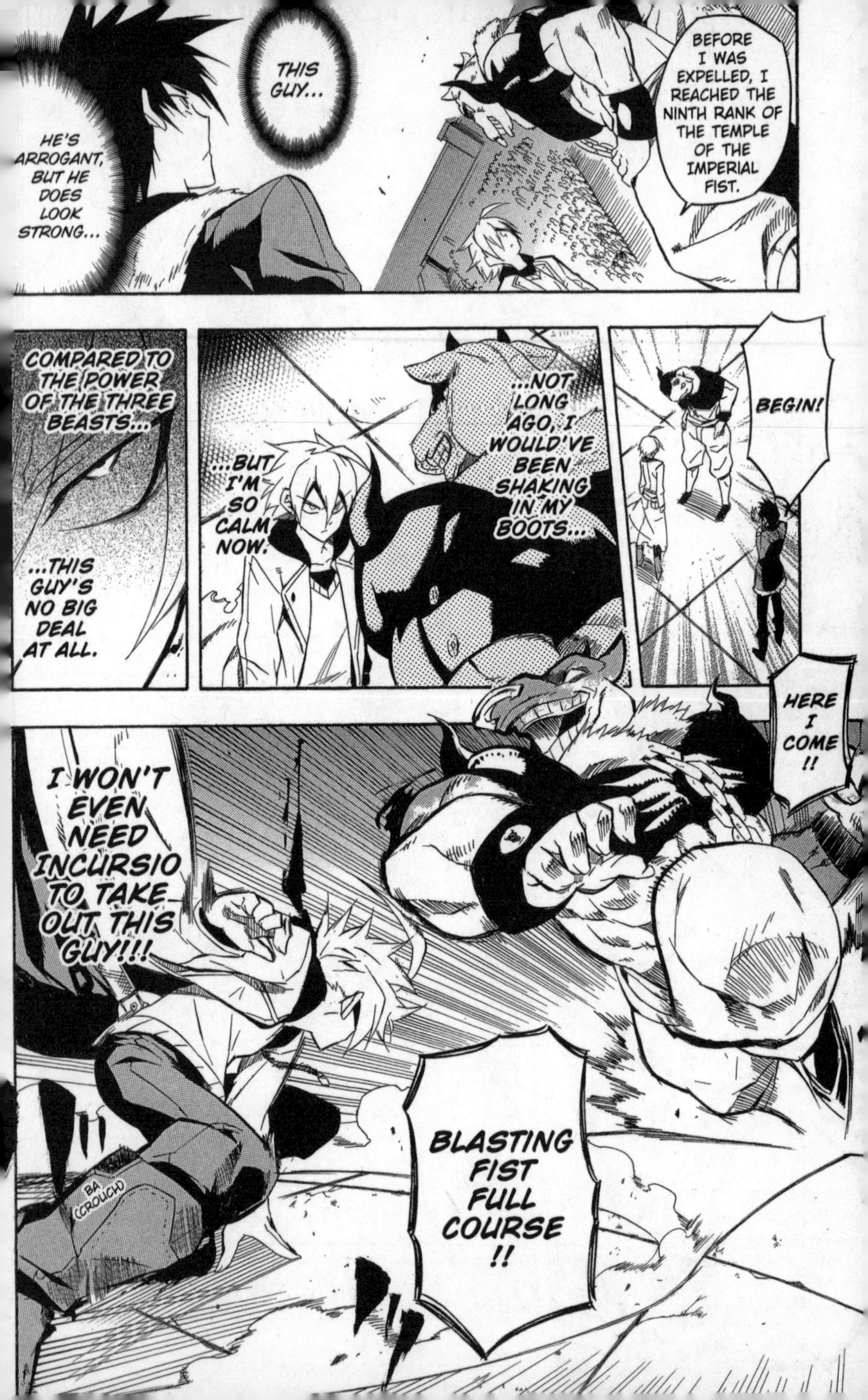
BEFORE I WAS EXPELLED, I REACHED THE NINTH RANK OF THE TEMPLE OF THE IMPERIAL FIST.
THIS GUY...
HE'S ARROGANT, BUT HE DOES LOOK STRONG...
BEGIN!
...NOT LONG AGO, I WOULD'VE BEEN SHAKING IN MY BOOTS...
...BUT I'M SO CALM NOW.
COMPARED TO THE POWER OF THE THREE BEASTS...
...THIS GUY'S NO BIG DEAL AT ALL.
HERE I COME!!
BLASTING FIST FULL COURSE!!
I WON'T EVEN NEED INCURSIO TO TAKE OUT THIS GUY!!!
BA (CROUCH)

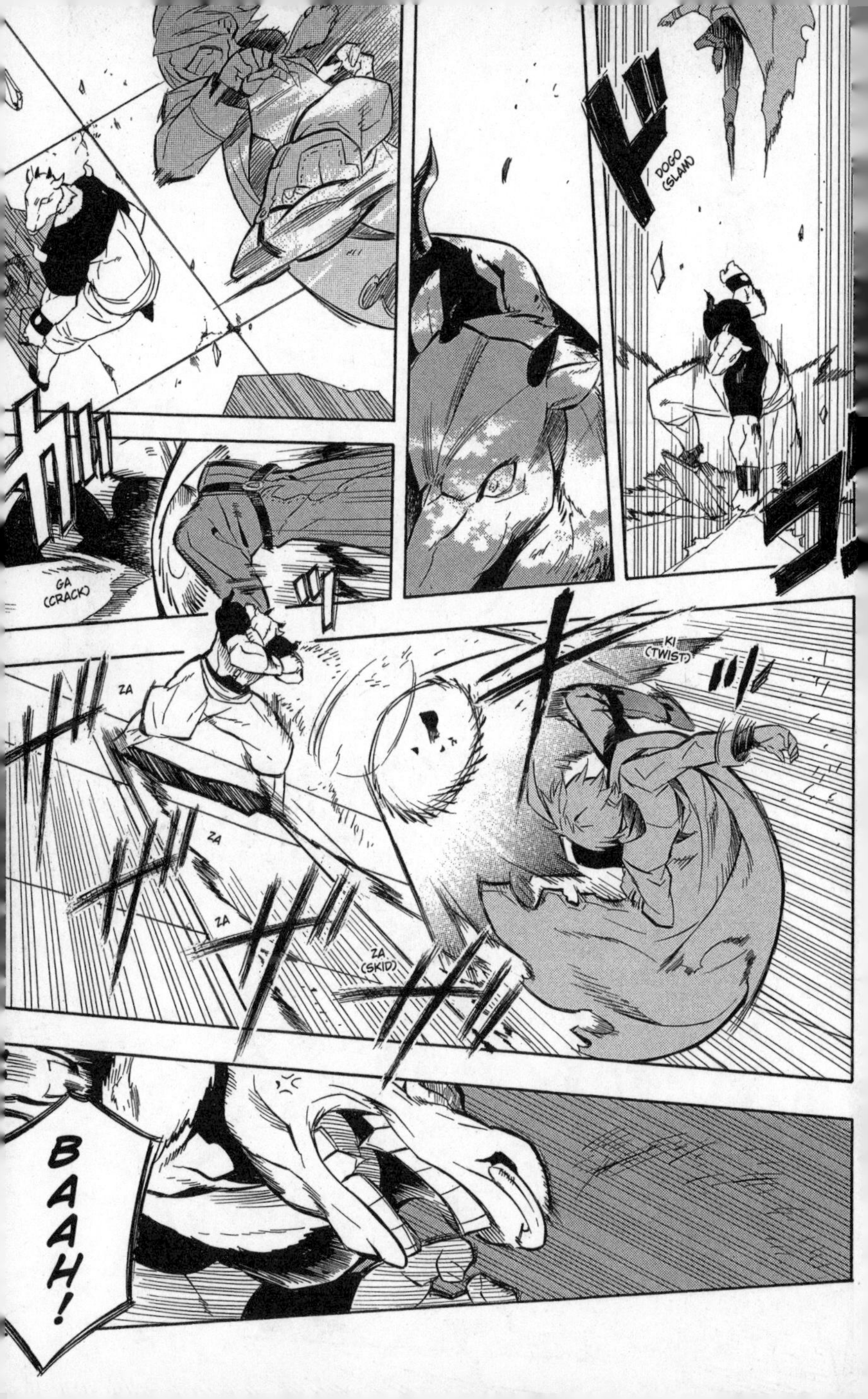
DOGO (SLAM)
GA (CRACK)
KI (TWIST)
ZA
ZA
ZA
ZA (SKID)
BAAAH!

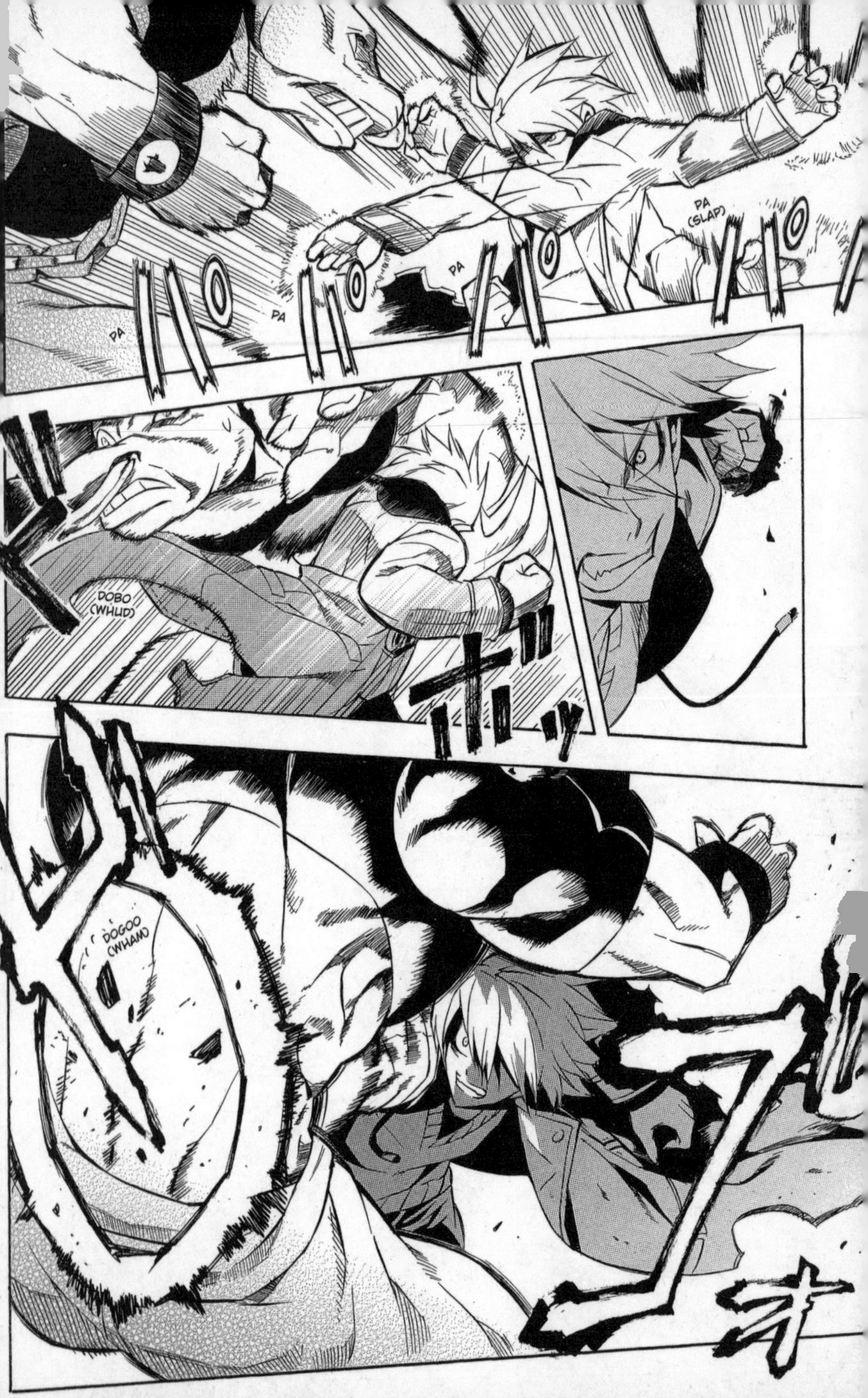
PA
(SLAP)
PA
PA
PA
DOBO
(WHUD)
DOGOO
(WHAM)

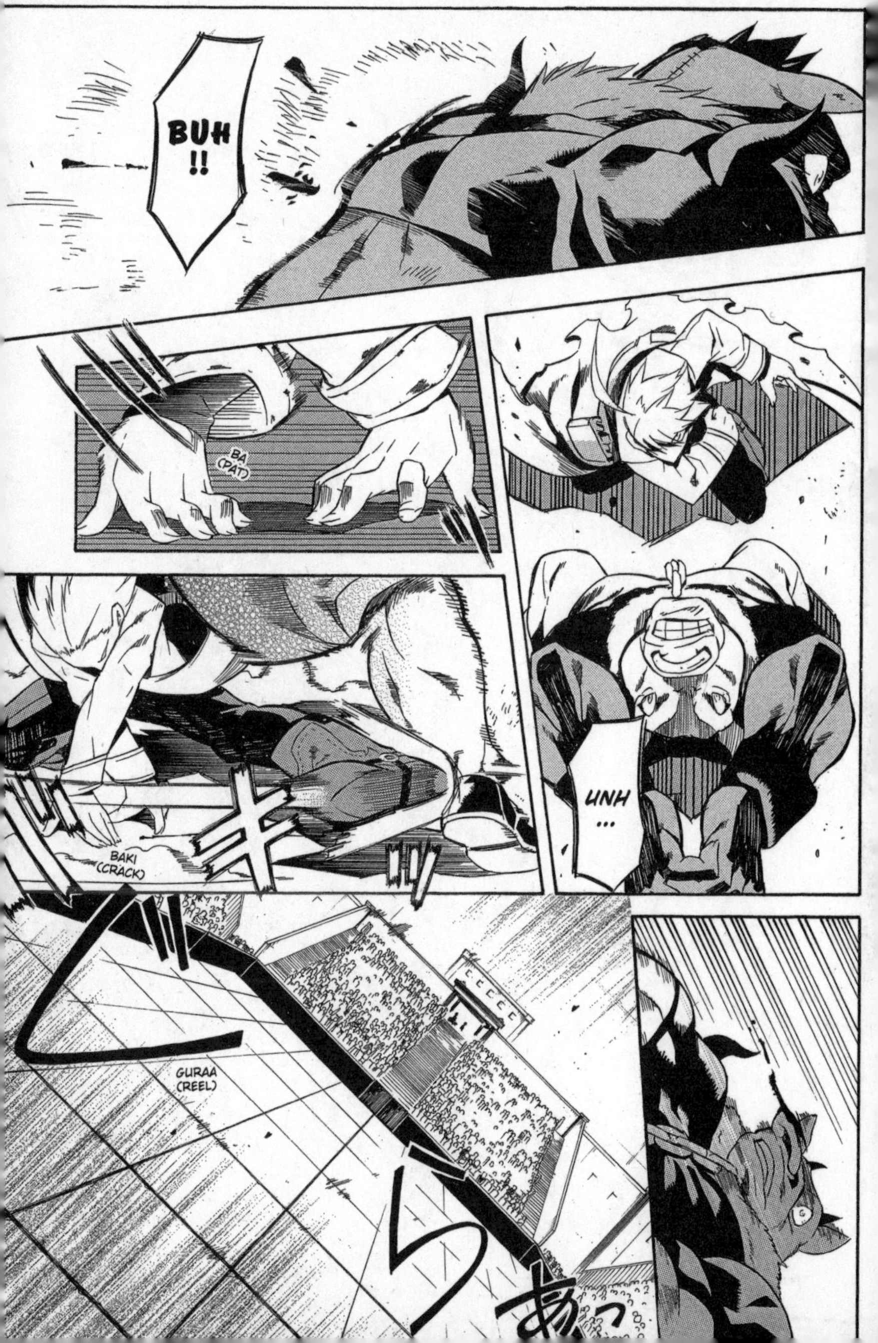
BUH!!
BA (PAT)
UNH...
BAKI (CRACK)
あっ
GURAA (REEL)

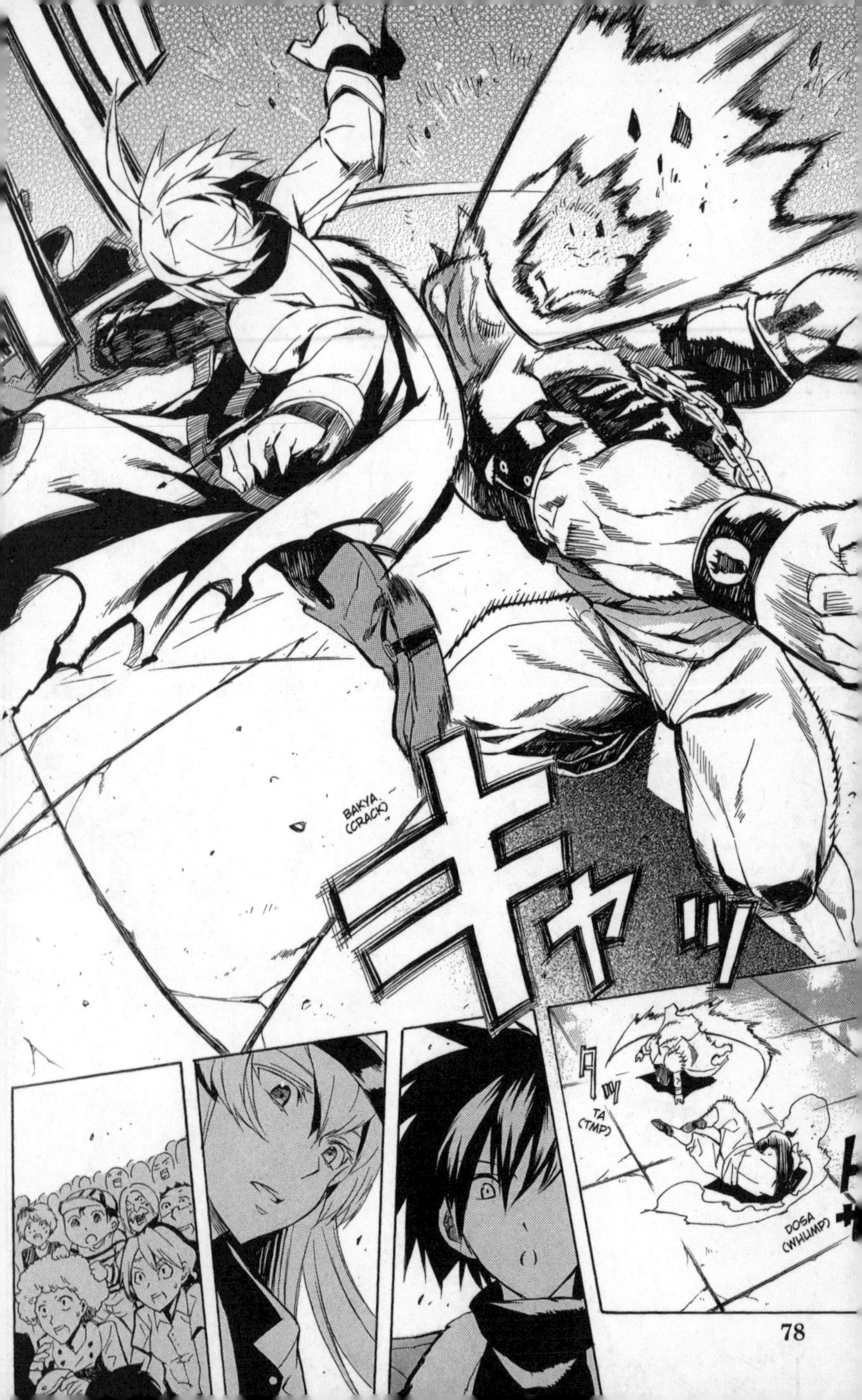

BAKYA (CRACK)
ギャッ
タッ
TA (TMP)
DOSA (WHUMP)

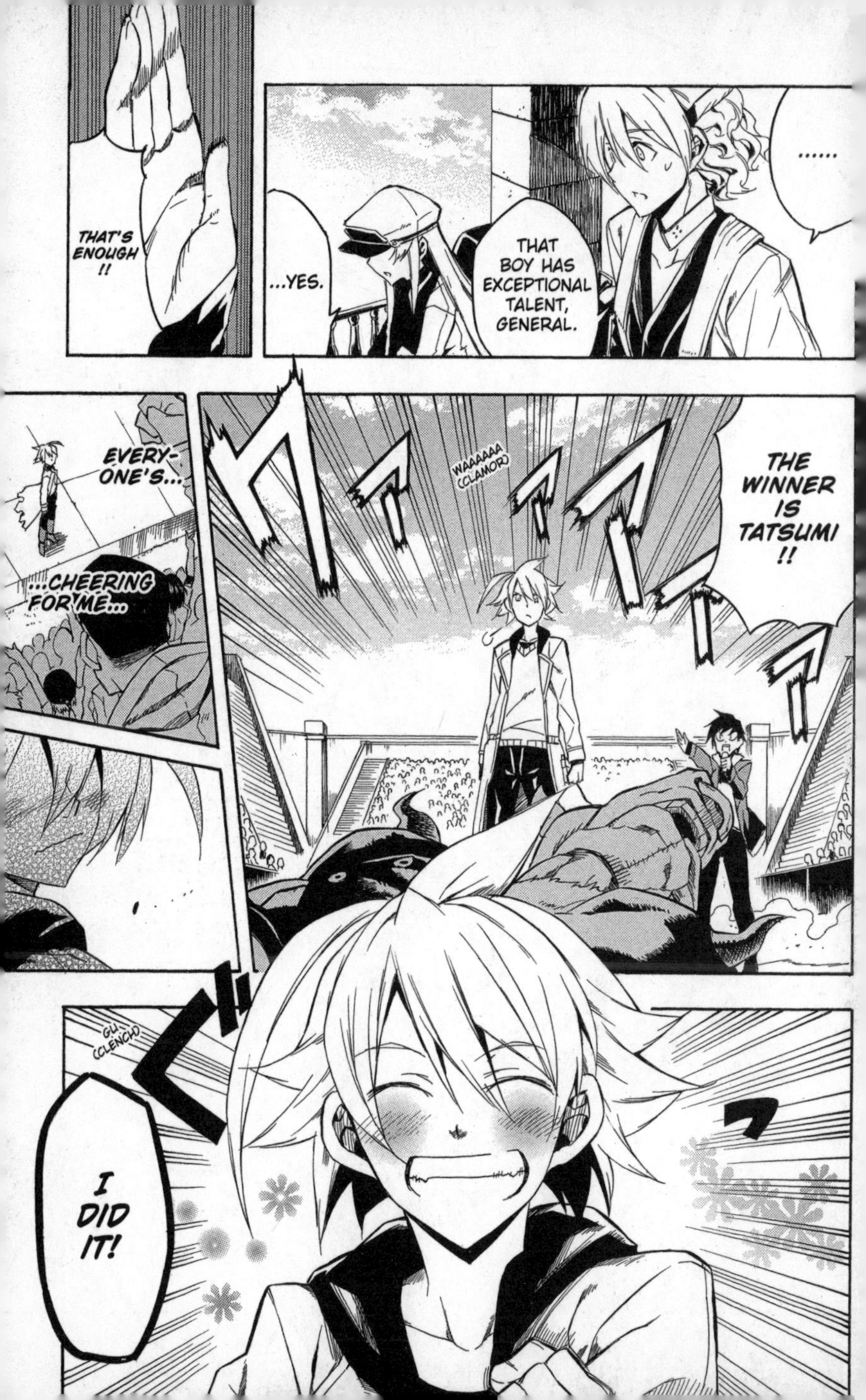
......
THAT BOY HAS EXCEPTIONAL TALENT, GENERAL.
...YES.
THAT'S ENOUGH !!
THE WINNER IS TATSUMI !!
WAAAAAA (CLAMOR)
EVERY-ONE'S...
...CHEERING FOR ME...
GU (CLENCH)
I DID IT!

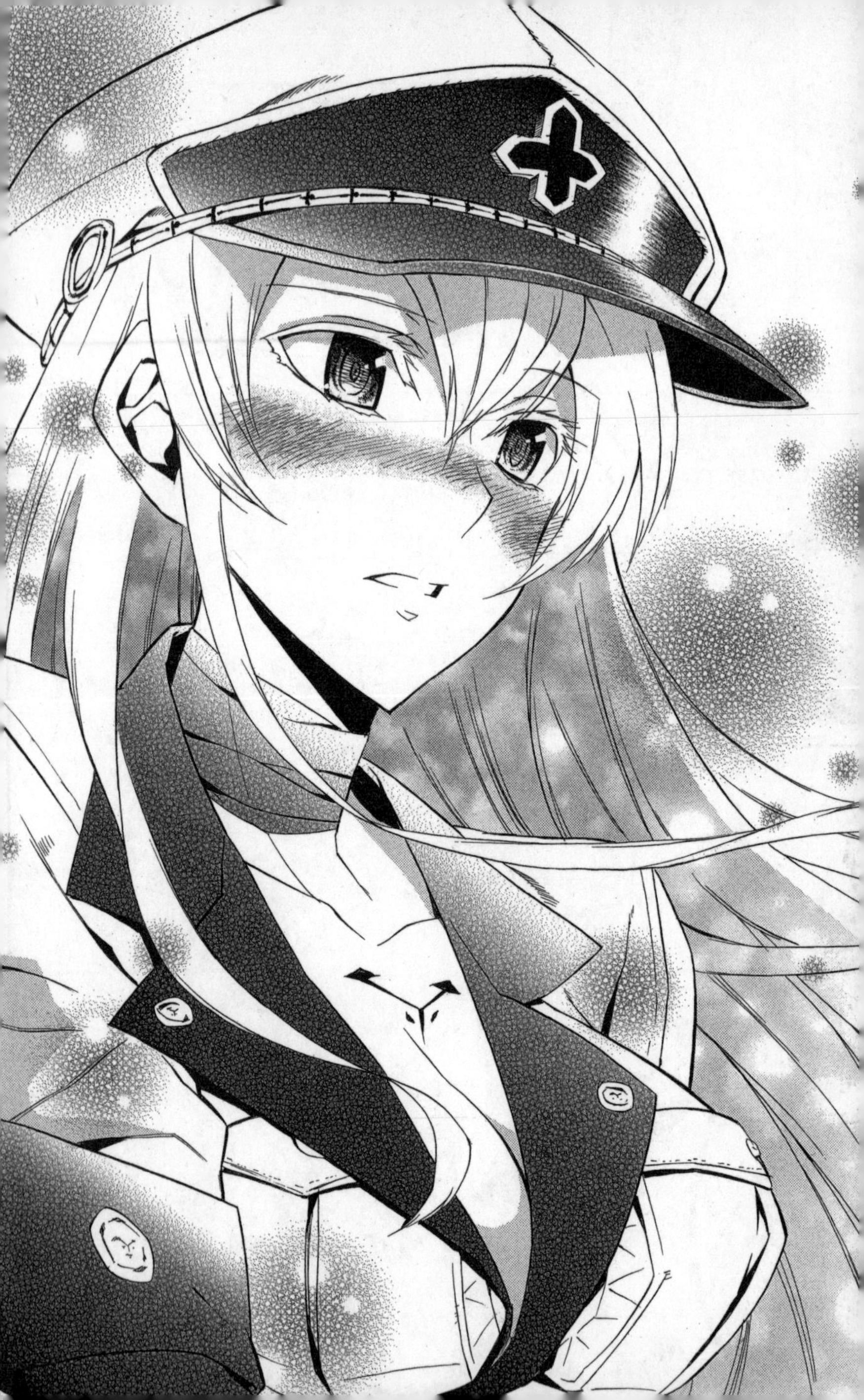

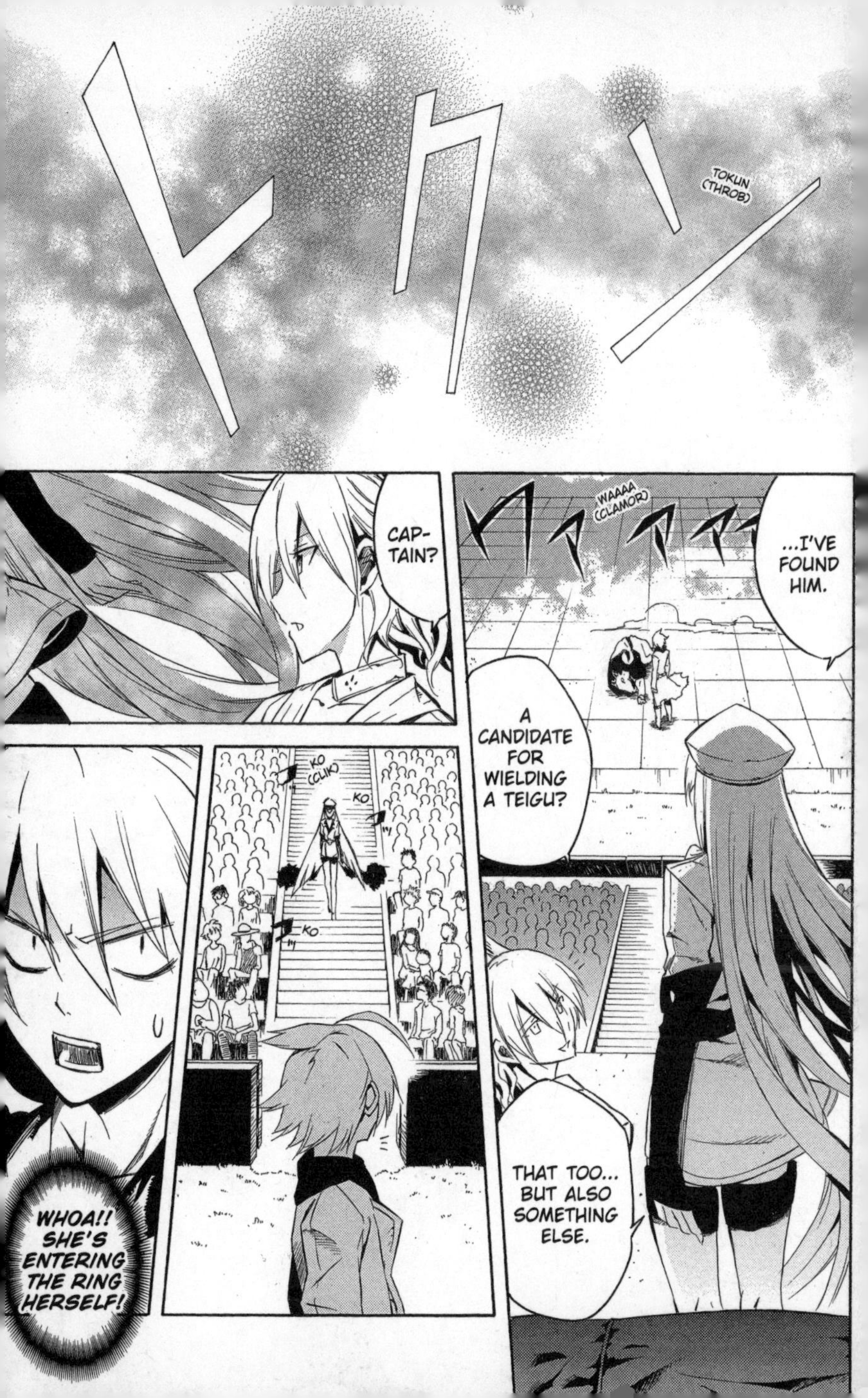
TOKUN (THROB)
WAAAA (CLAMOR)
...I'VE FOUND HIM.
A CANDIDATE FOR WIELDING A TEIGU?
CAP-TAIN?
THAT TOO... BUT ALSO SOMETHING ELSE.
KO (CLIK)
KO
KO
WHOA!! SHE'S ENTERING THE RING HERSELF!

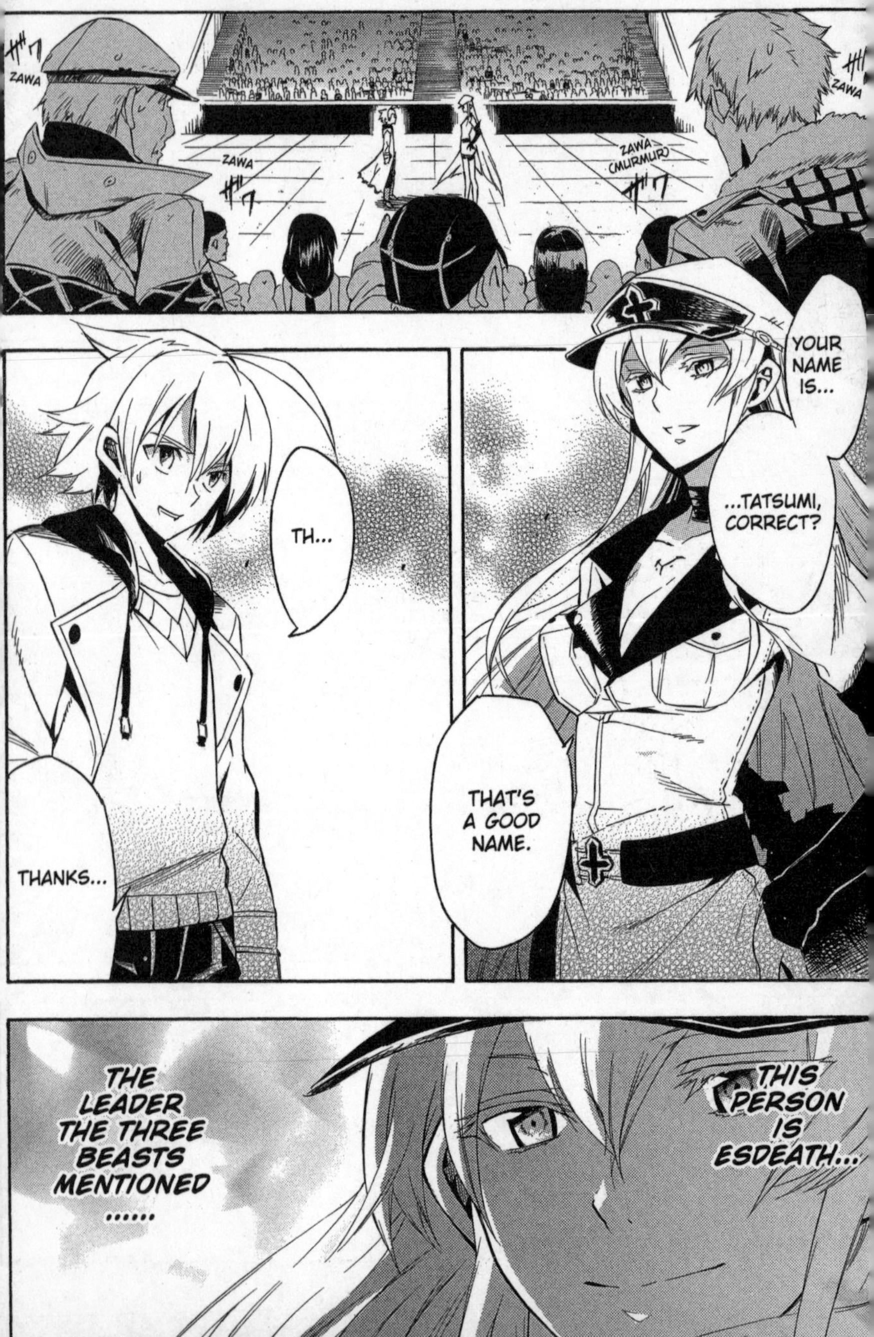
ZAWA
ZAWA (MURMUR)
ZAWA
ZAWA
YOUR NAME IS...
...TATSUMI, CORRECT?
TH...
THAT'S A GOOD NAME.
THANKS...
THIS PERSON IS ESDEATH...
THE LEADER THE THREE BEASTS MENTIONED ......

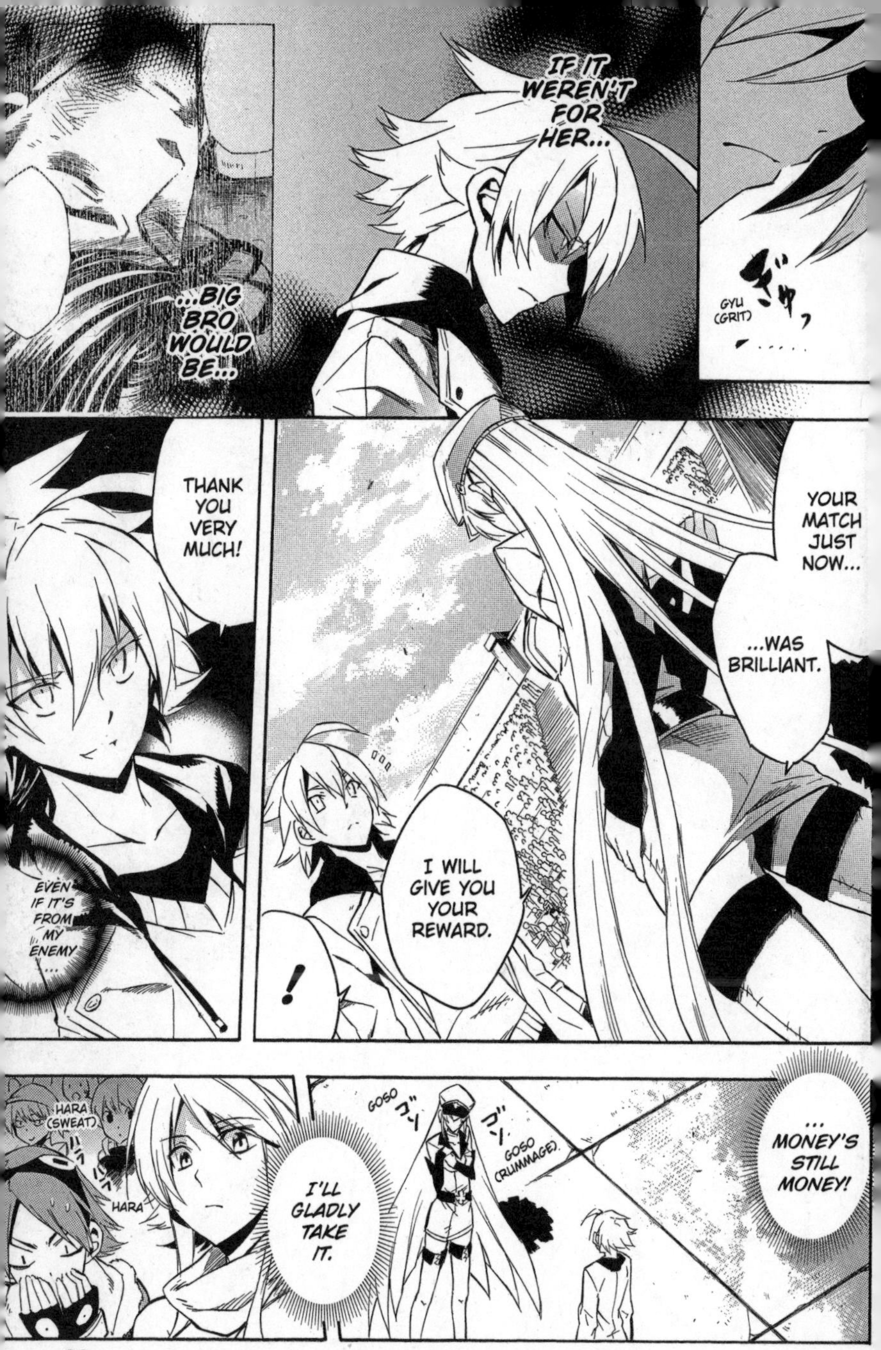
GYU (GRIT)
IF IT WEREN'T FOR HER...
...BIG BRO WOULD BE...
YOUR MATCH JUST NOW...
...WAS BRILLIANT.
I WILL GIVE YOU YOUR REWARD.
!
THANK YOU VERY MUCH!
EVEN IF IT'S FROM MY ENEMY...
...MONEY'S STILL MONEY!
GOSO (RUMMAGE)
GOSO
I'LL GLADLY TAKE IT.
HARA (SWEAT)
HARA

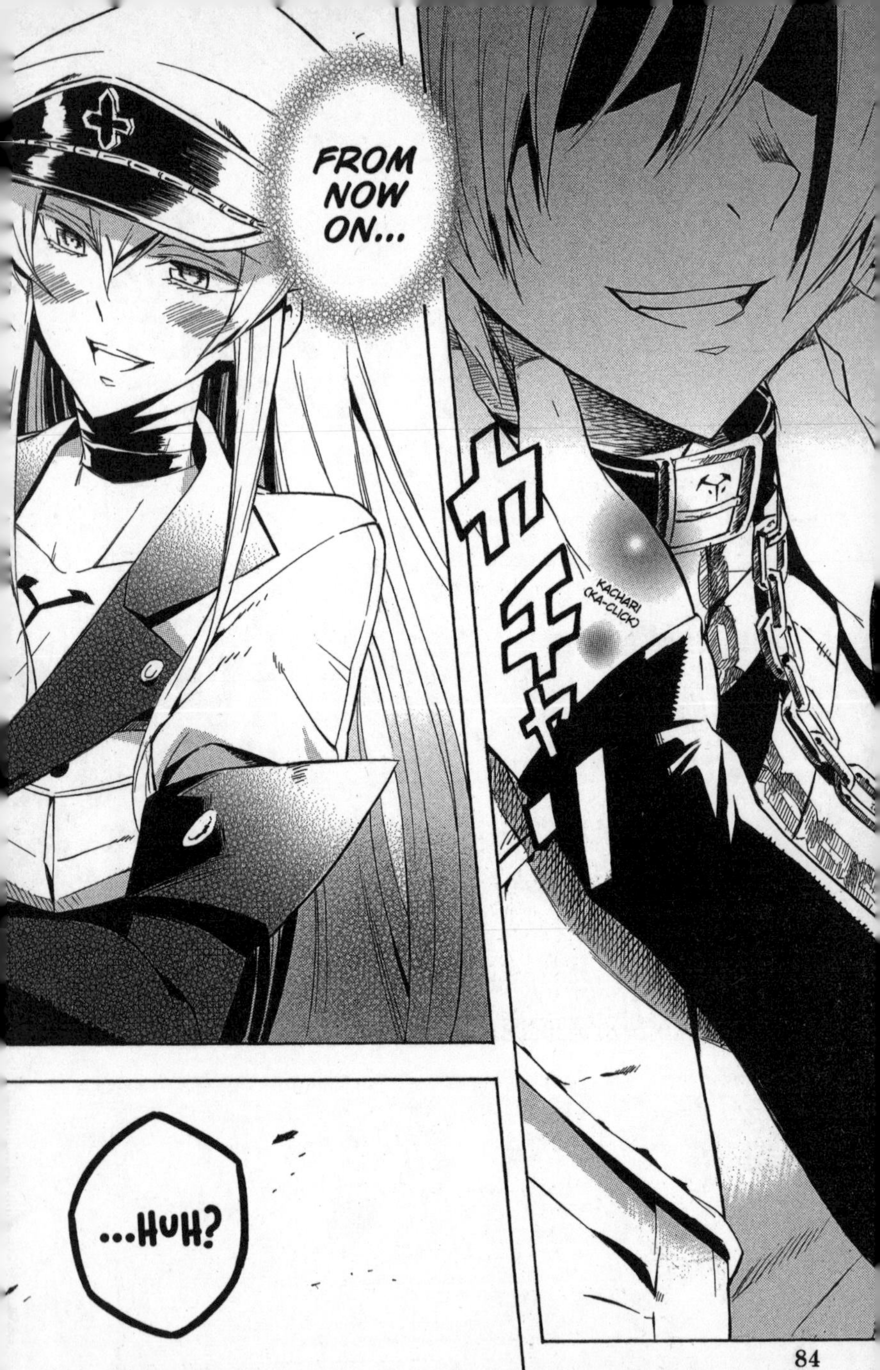
FROM NOW ON...
KACHARI (KA-CLICK)
...HUH?

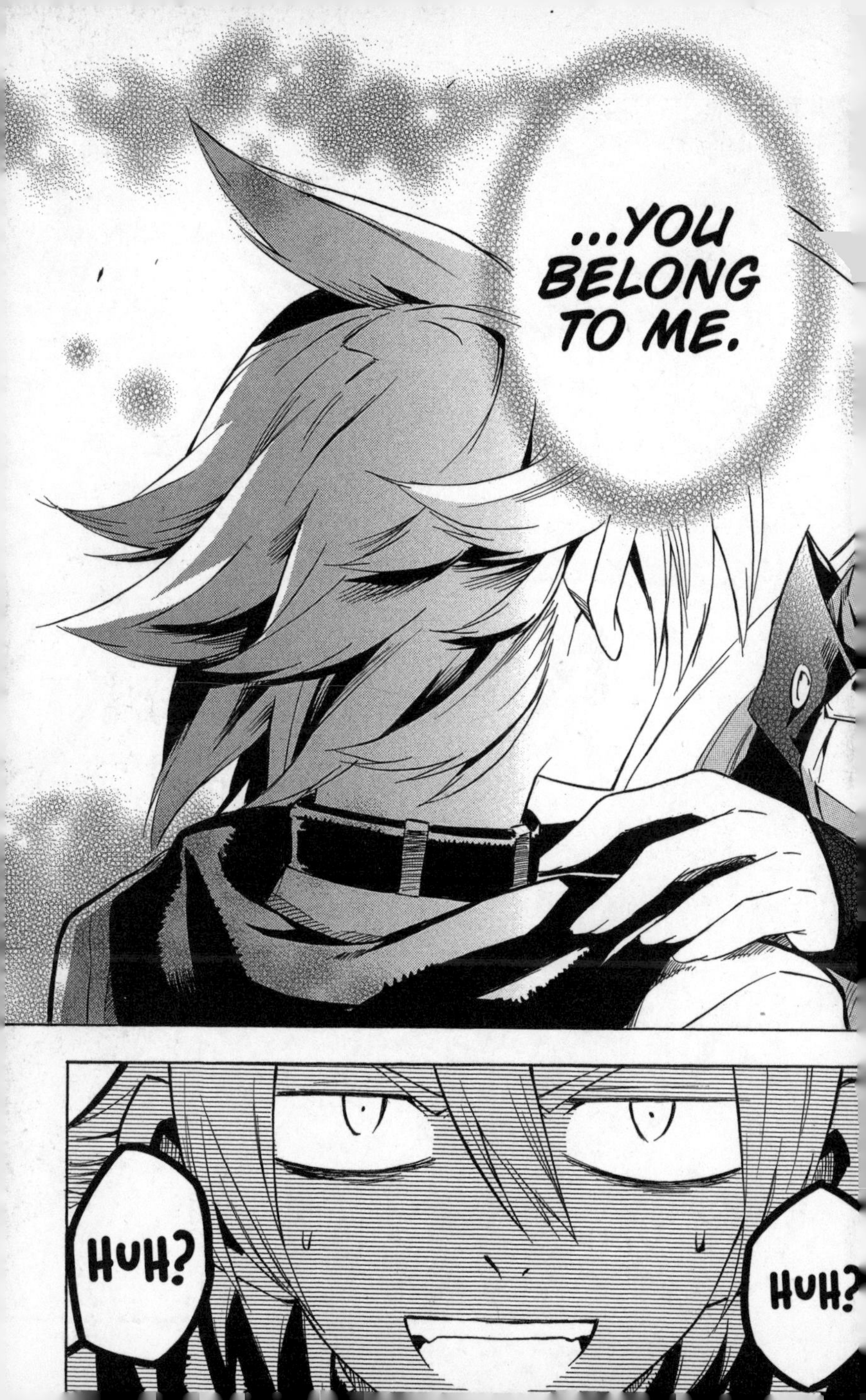
...YOU BELONG TO ME.
HUH?
HUH?

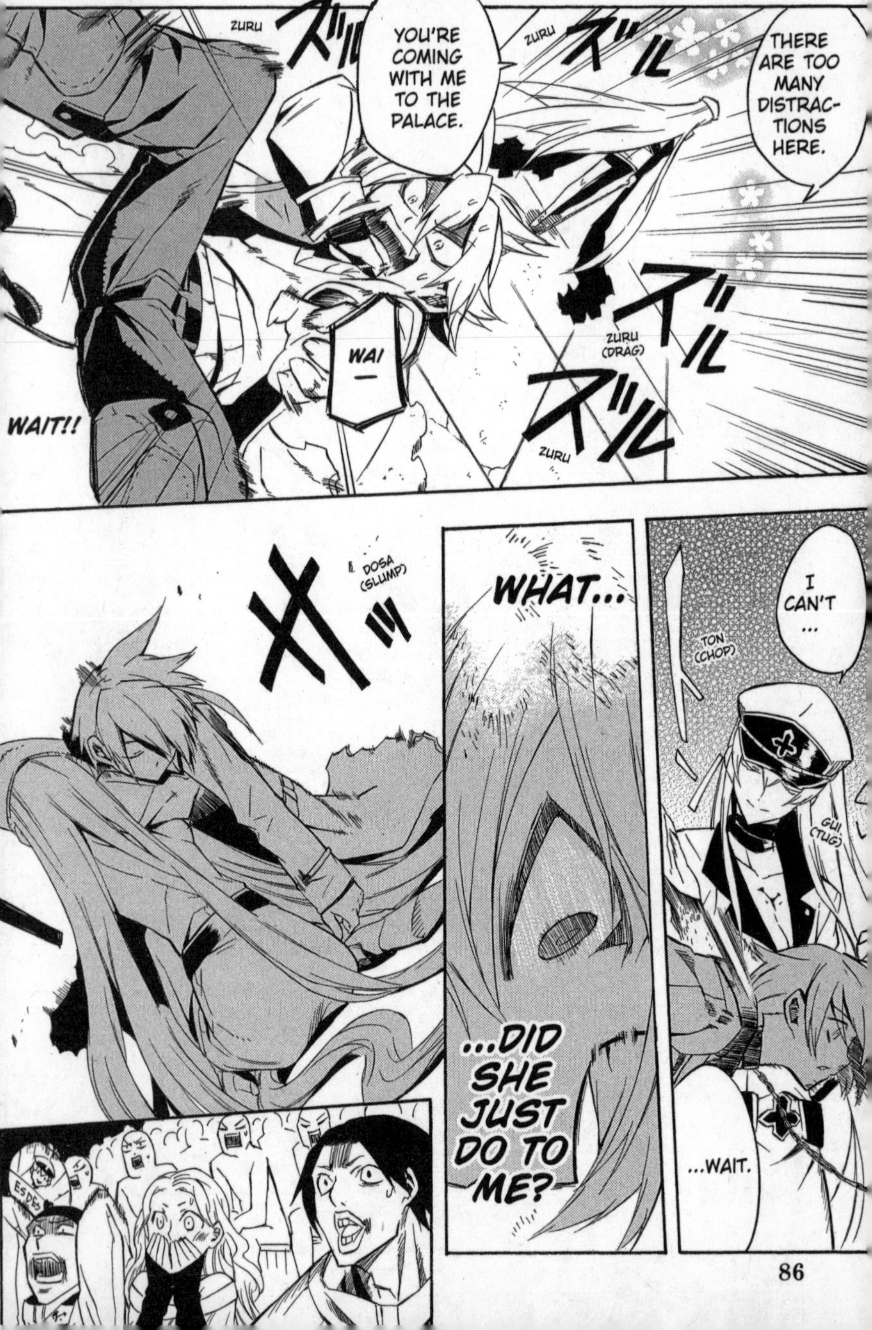
THERE ARE TOO MANY DISTRACTIONS HERE.
YOU'RE COMING WITH ME TO THE PALACE.
ZURU
ZURU
ZURU (DRAG)
ZURU
WAI—
WAIT!!
I CAN'T ...
TON (CHOP)
GUI (TUG)
...WAIT.
WHAT...
...DID SHE JUST DO TO ME?
DOSA (SLUMP)
ESDES

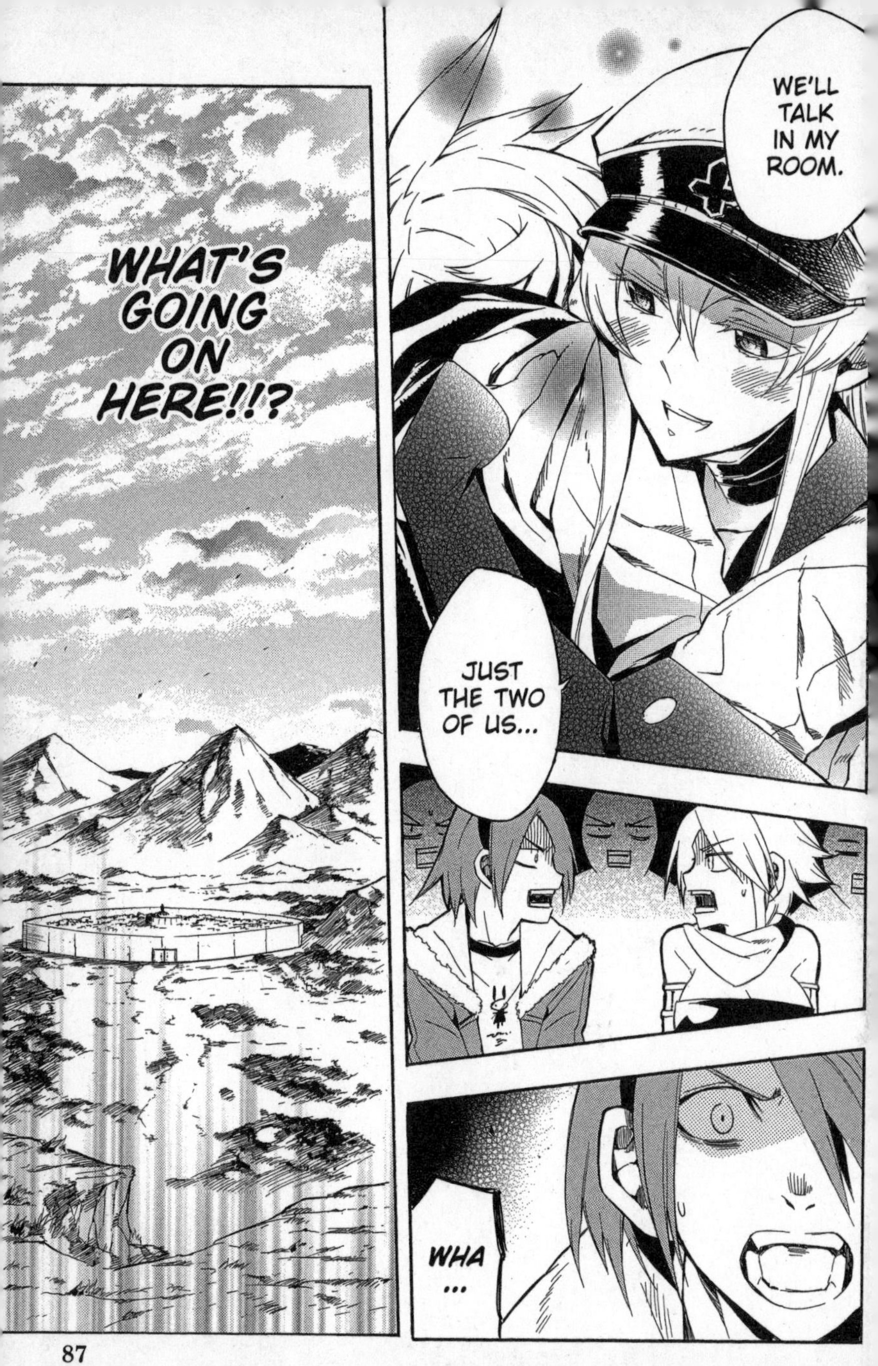
WE'LL TALK IN MY ROOM.
JUST THE TWO OF US...
WHA...
WHAT'S GOING ON HERE!!?

Akame ga KILL!
Rough Sketches 2

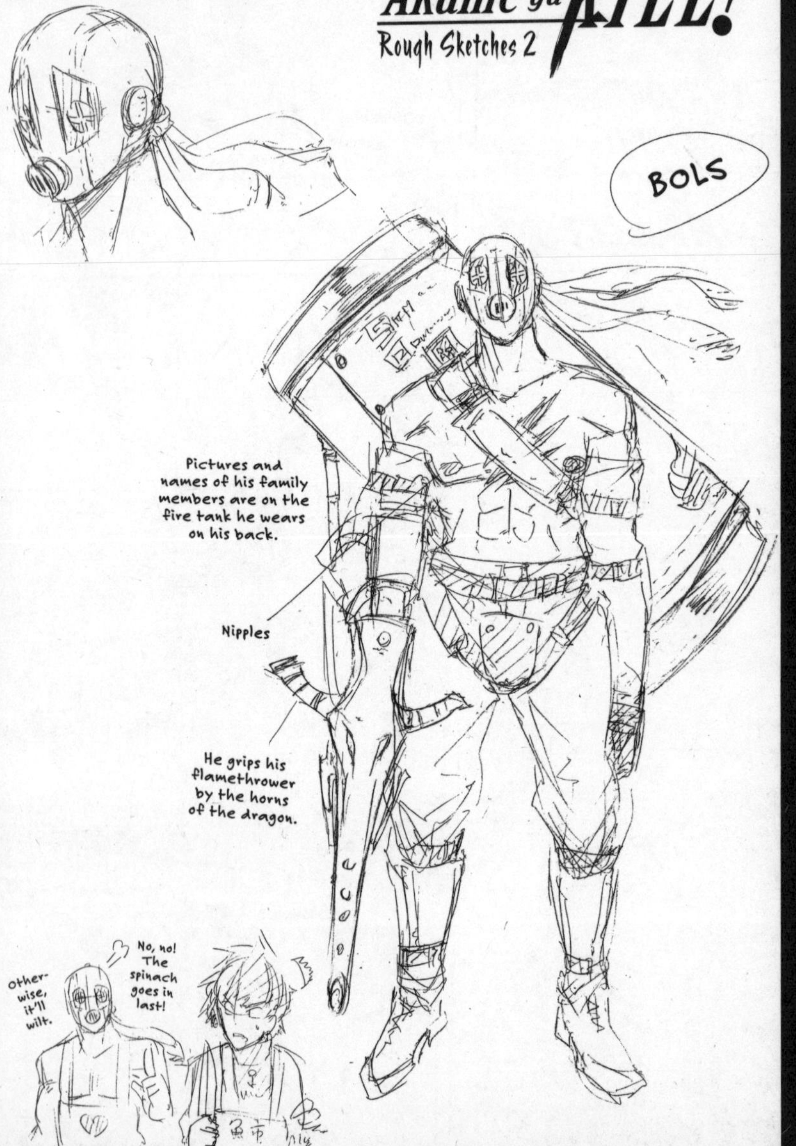
BOLS
Pictures and names of his family members are on the fire tank he wears on his back.
Nipples
He grips his flamethrower by the horns of the dragon.
Other-wise, it'll wilt.
No, no! The spinach goes in last!

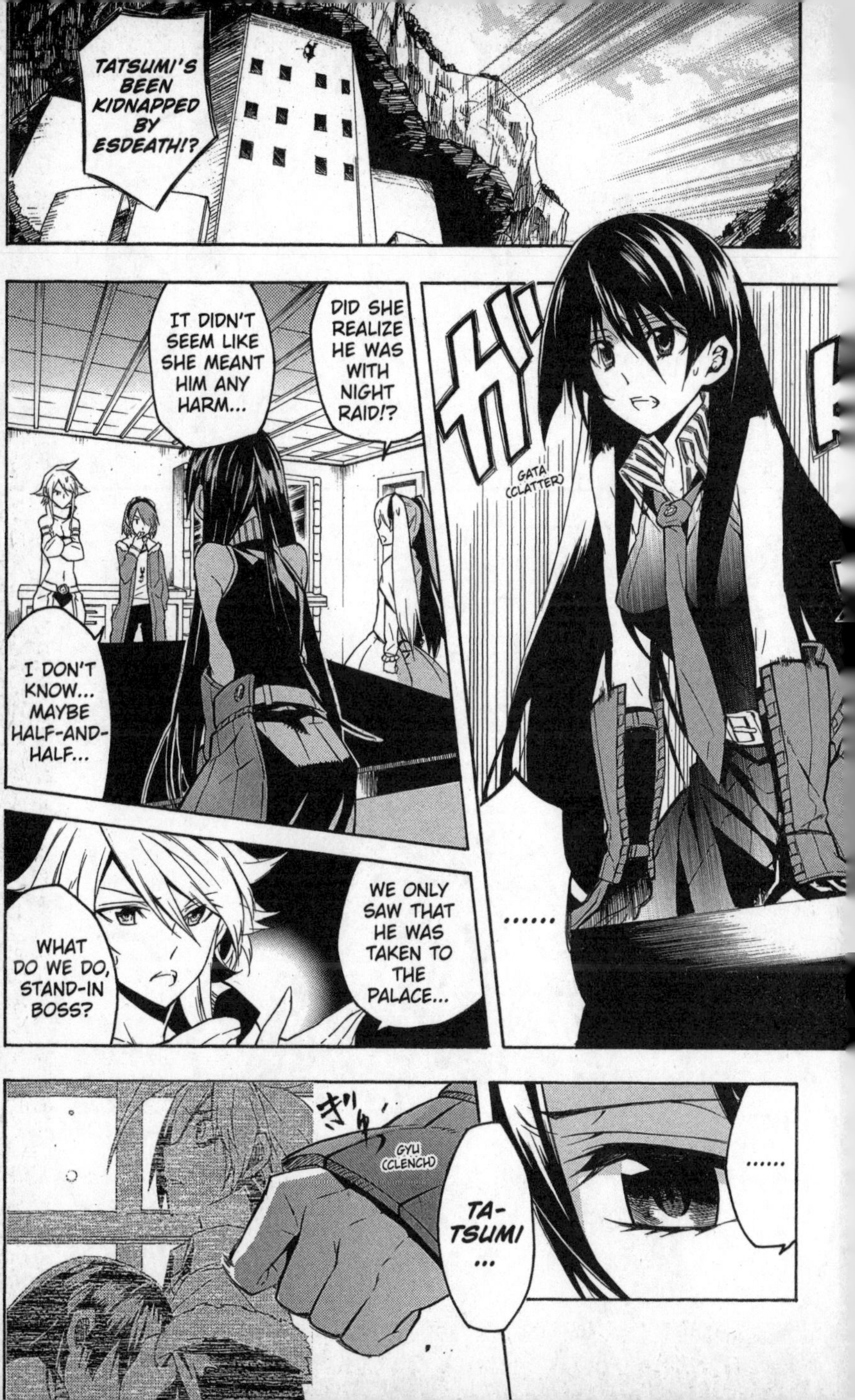
TATSUMI'S BEEN KIDNAPPED BY ESDEATH!?
GATA (CLATTER)
DID SHE REALIZE HE WAS WITH NIGHT RAID!?
IT DIDN'T SEEM LIKE SHE MEANT HIM ANY HARM...
I DON'T KNOW... MAYBE HALF-AND-HALF...
......
WE ONLY SAW THAT HE WAS TAKEN TO THE PALACE...
WHAT DO WE DO, STAND-IN BOSS?
......
TA-TSUMI...
GYU (CLENCH)

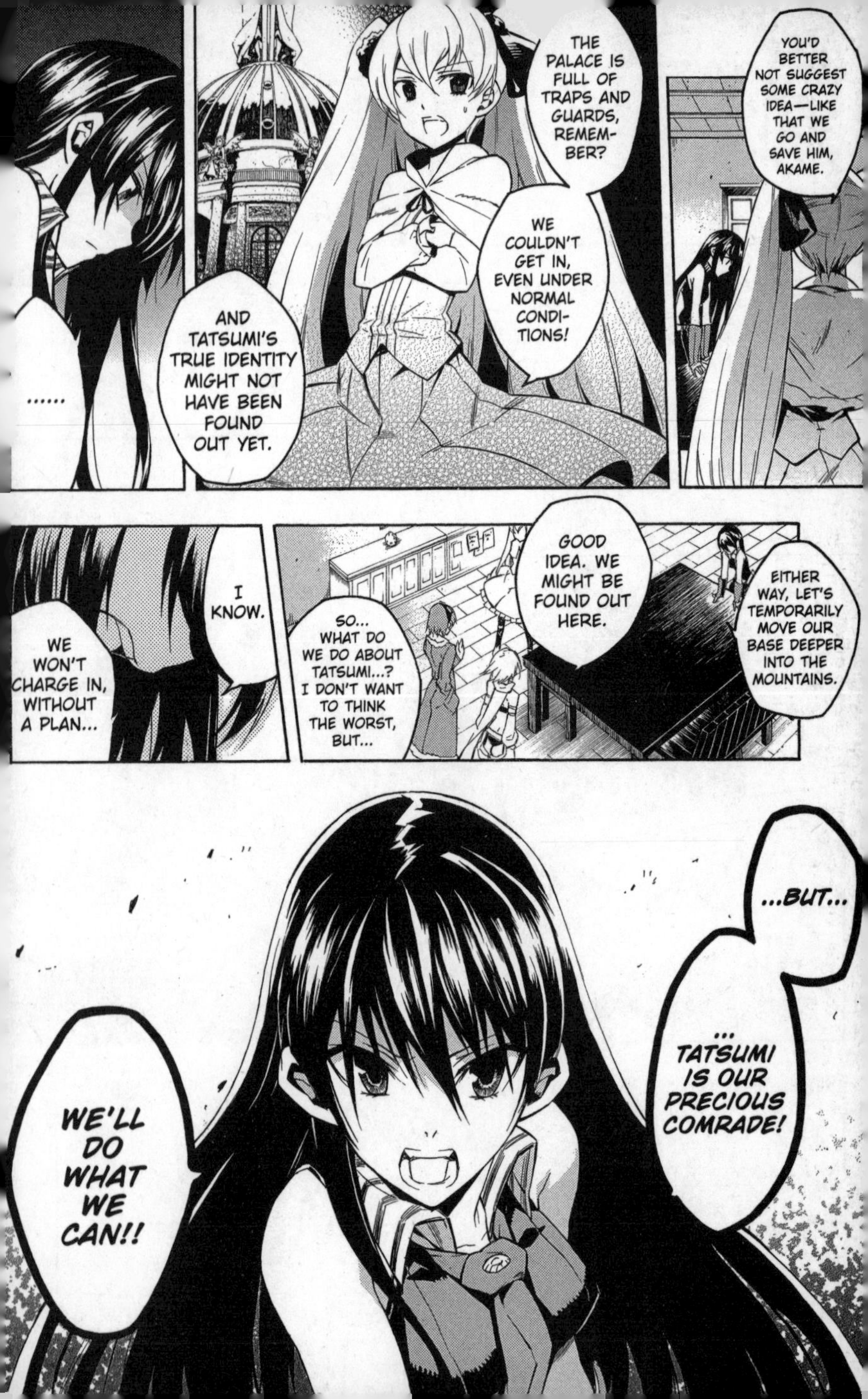
YOU'D BETTER NOT SUGGEST SOME CRAZY IDEA—LIKE THAT WE GO AND SAVE HIM, AKAME.
THE PALACE IS FULL OF TRAPS AND GUARDS, REMEMBER?
WE COULDN'T GET IN, EVEN UNDER NORMAL CONDITIONS!
AND TATSUMI'S TRUE IDENTITY MIGHT NOT HAVE BEEN FOUND OUT YET.
......
EITHER WAY, LET'S TEMPORARILY MOVE OUR BASE DEEPER INTO THE MOUNTAINS.
GOOD IDEA. WE MIGHT BE FOUND OUT HERE.
SO... WHAT DO WE DO ABOUT TATSUMI...? I DON'T WANT TO THINK THE WORST, BUT...
I KNOW.
WE WON'T CHARGE IN, WITHOUT A PLAN...
...BUT...
...TATSUMI IS OUR PRECIOUS COMRADE!
WE'LL DO WHAT WE CAN!!

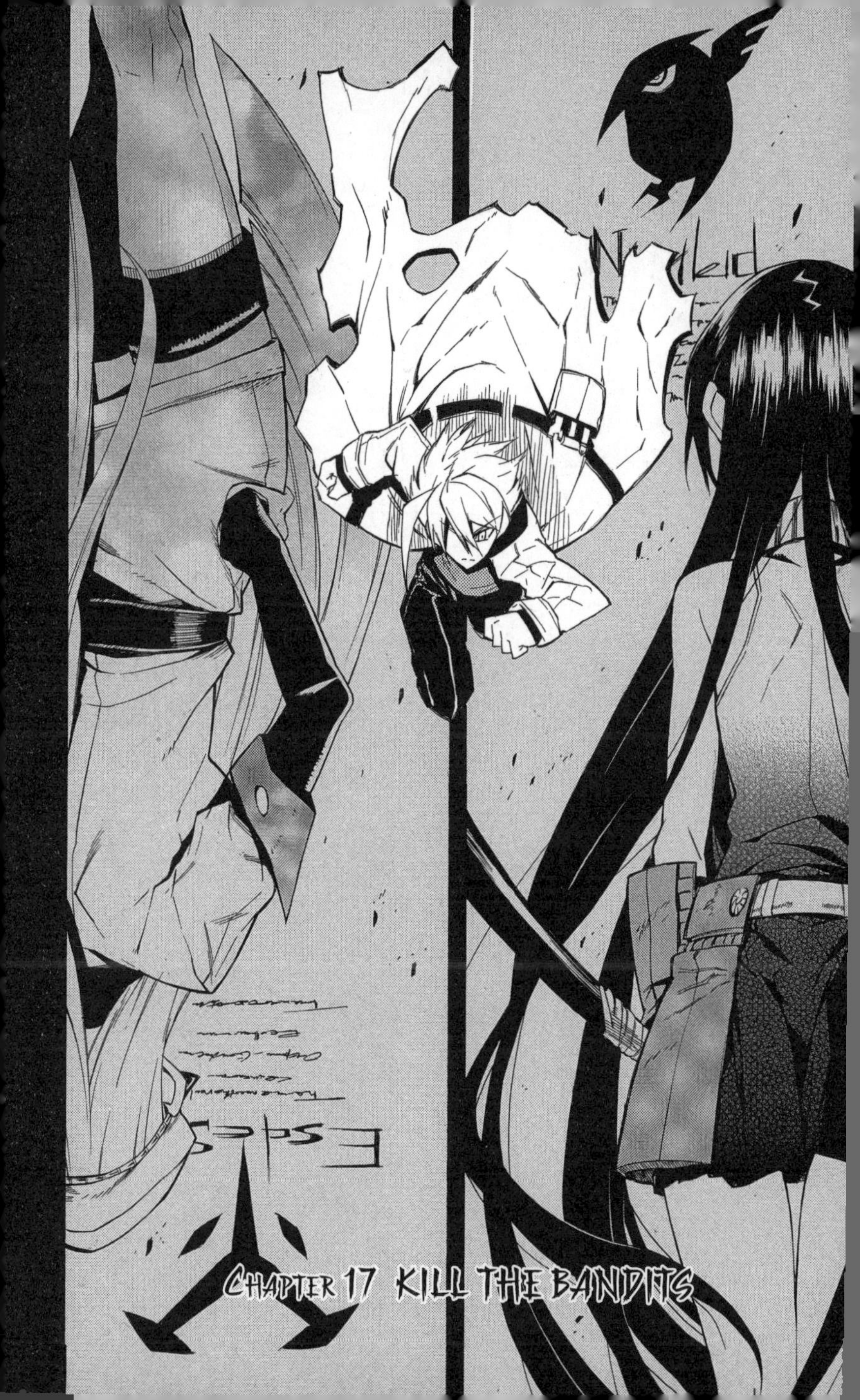
Chapter 17 Kill the Bandits

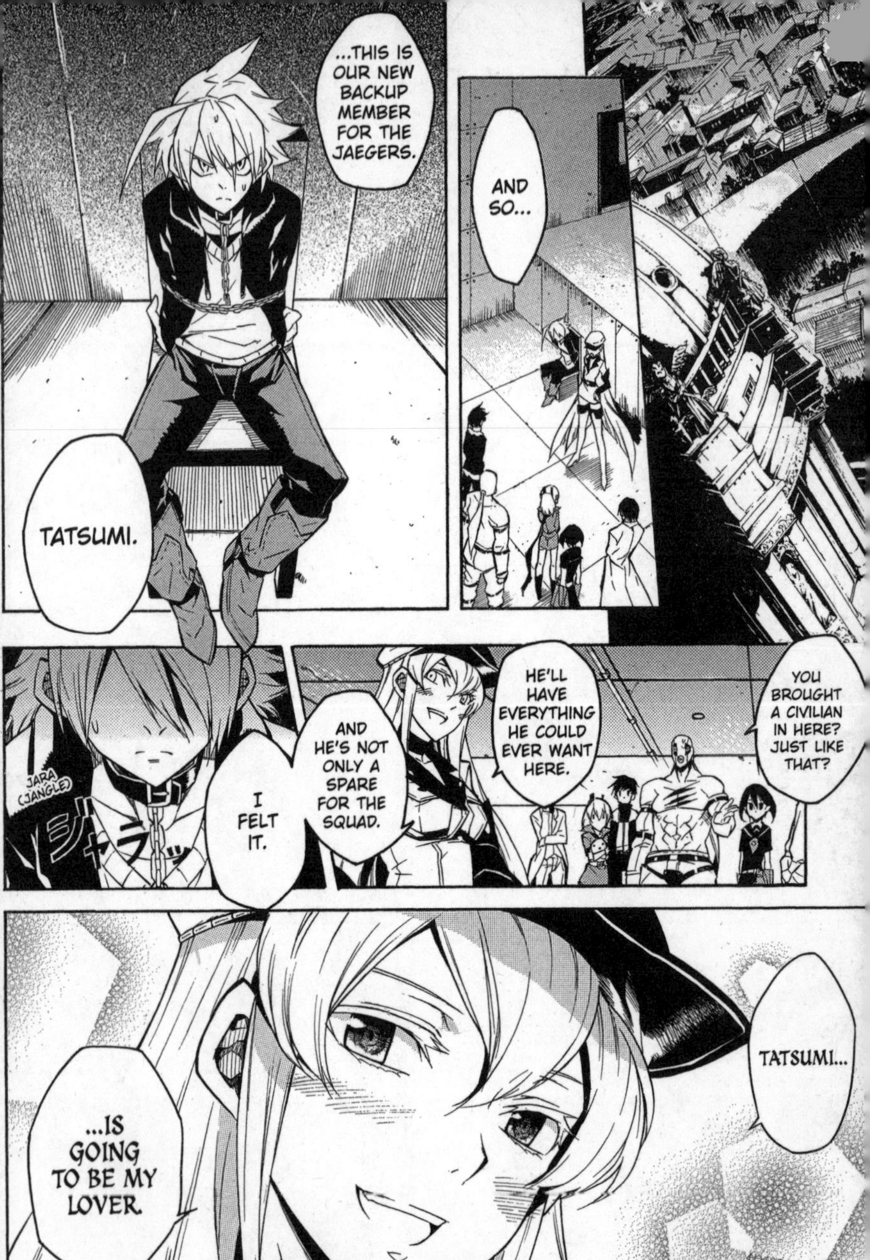
AND SO...
...THIS IS OUR NEW BACKUP MEMBER FOR THE JAEGERS.
TATSUMI.
YOU BROUGHT A CIVILIAN IN HERE? JUST LIKE THAT?
HE'LL HAVE EVERYTHING HE COULD EVER WANT HERE.
AND HE'S NOT ONLY A SPARE FOR THE SQUAD.
I FELT IT.
JARA (JANGLE)
TATSUMI...
...IS GOING TO BE MY LOVER.

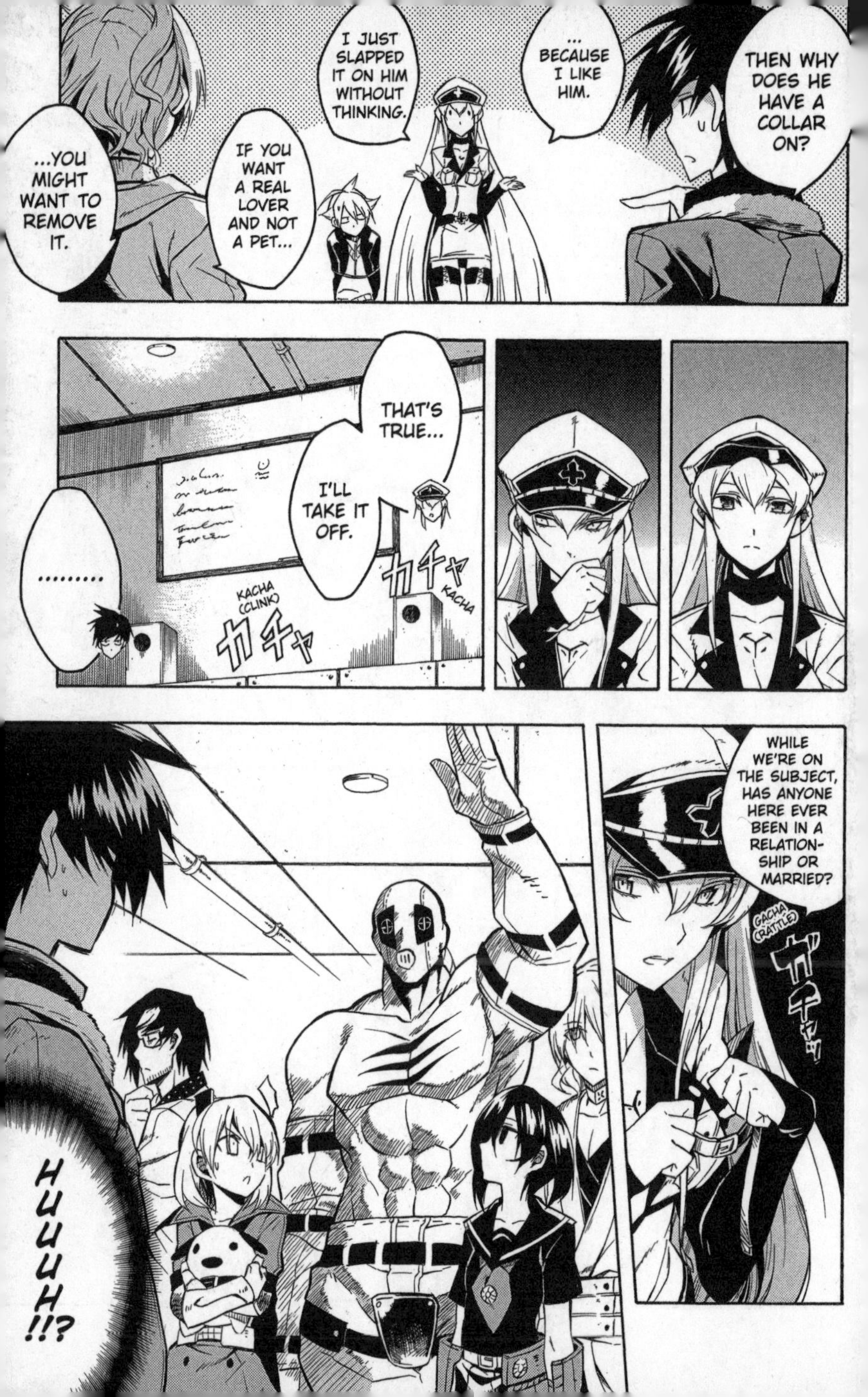
THEN WHY DOES HE HAVE A COLLAR ON?
... BECAUSE I LIKE HIM.
I JUST SLAPPED IT ON HIM WITHOUT THINKING.
IF YOU WANT A REAL LOVER AND NOT A PET...
...YOU MIGHT WANT TO REMOVE IT.
THAT'S TRUE...
I'LL TAKE IT OFF.
KACHA
KACHA (CLINK)
....
WHILE WE'RE ON THE SUBJECT, HAS ANYONE HERE EVER BEEN IN A RELATION-SHIP OR MARRIED?
GACHA (RATTLE)
HUUUUH!!?

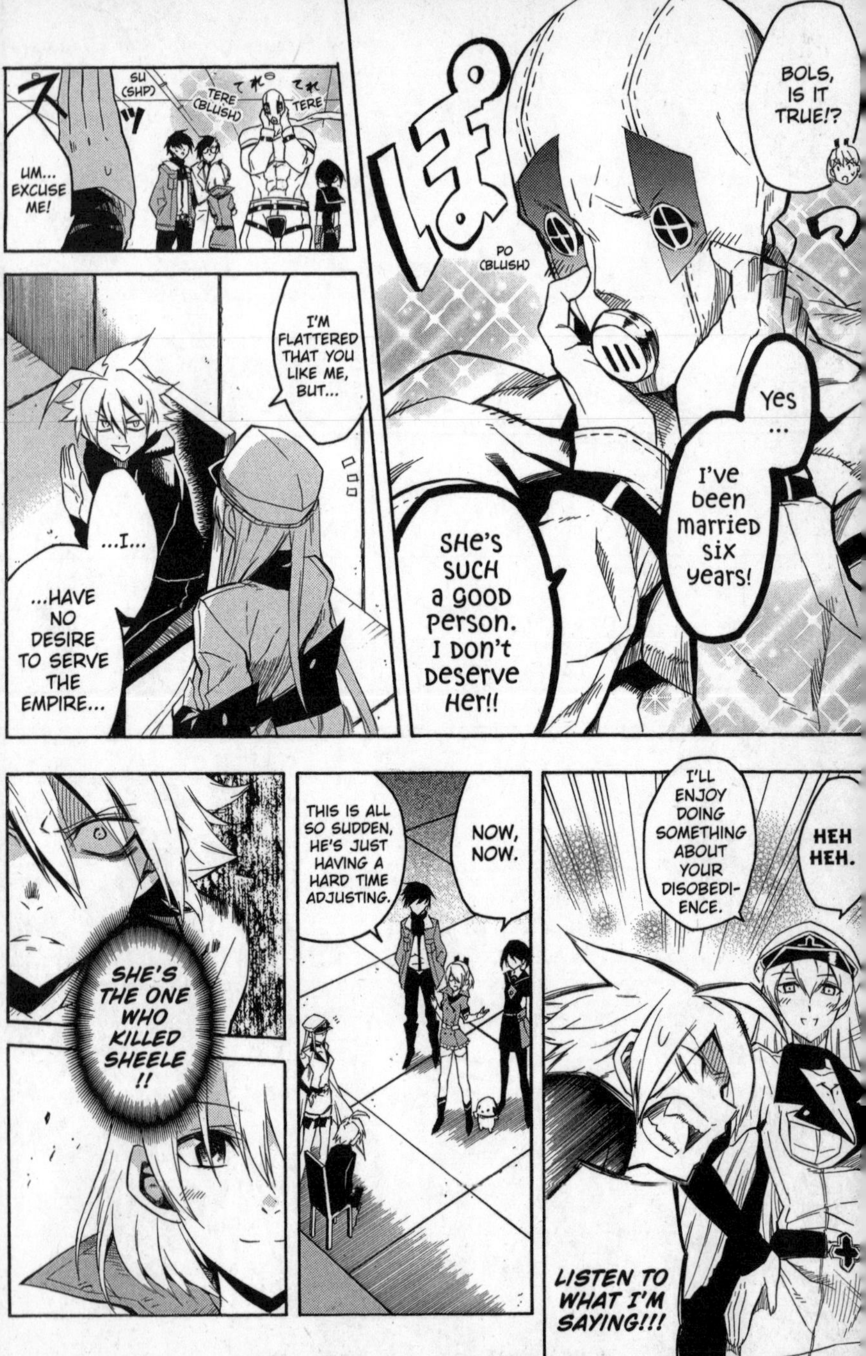
BOLS, IS IT TRUE!?
PO (BLUSH)
Yes... I've been married six years!
SHE's SUCH a good person. I don't deserve her!!
SU (SHP)
TERE (BLUSH)
TERE
UM... EXCUSE ME!
I'M FLATTERED THAT YOU LIKE ME, BUT...
...I...
...HAVE NO DESIRE TO SERVE THE EMPIRE...
HEH HEH.
I'LL ENJOY DOING SOMETHING ABOUT YOUR DISOBEDIENCE.
LISTEN TO WHAT I'M SAYING!!!
NOW, NOW.
THIS IS ALL SO SUDDEN, HE'S JUST HAVING A HARD TIME ADJUSTING.
SHE'S THE ONE WHO KILLED SHEELE!!

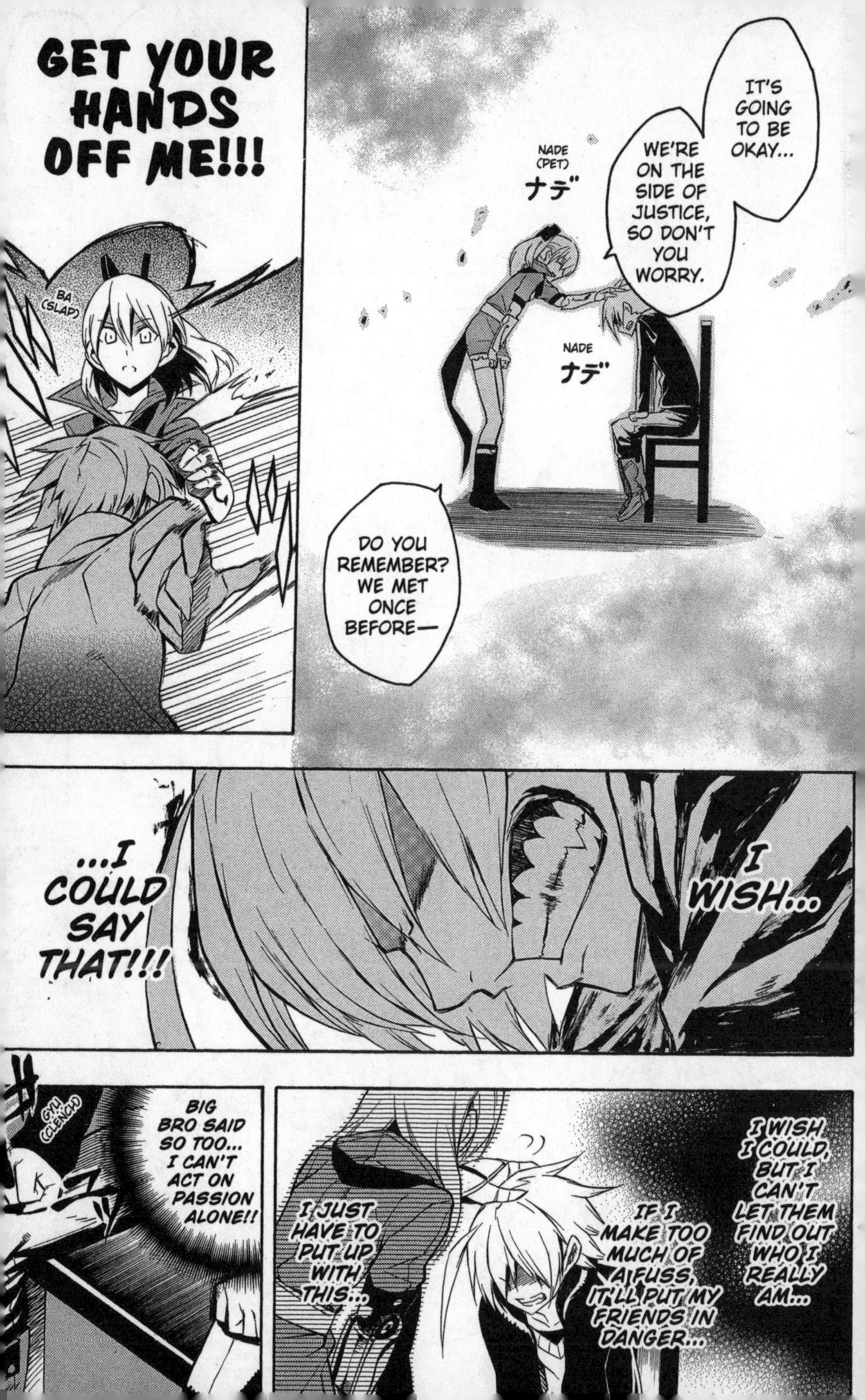
IT'S GOING TO BE OKAY...
WE'RE ON THE SIDE OF JUSTICE, SO DON'T YOU WORRY.
NADE (PET) ナデ
NADE ナデ
DO YOU REMEMBER? WE MET ONCE BEFORE—
GET YOUR HANDS OFF ME!!!
BA (SLAP)
I WISH...
...I COULD SAY THAT!!!
I WISH I COULD, BUT I CAN'T LET THEM FIND OUT WHO I REALLY AM...
IF I MAKE TOO MUCH OF A FUSS, IT'LL PUT MY FRIENDS IN DANGER...
I JUST HAVE TO PUT UP WITH THIS...
GYU (CLENCH)
BIG BRO SAID SO TOO... I CAN'T ACT ON PASSION ALONE!!

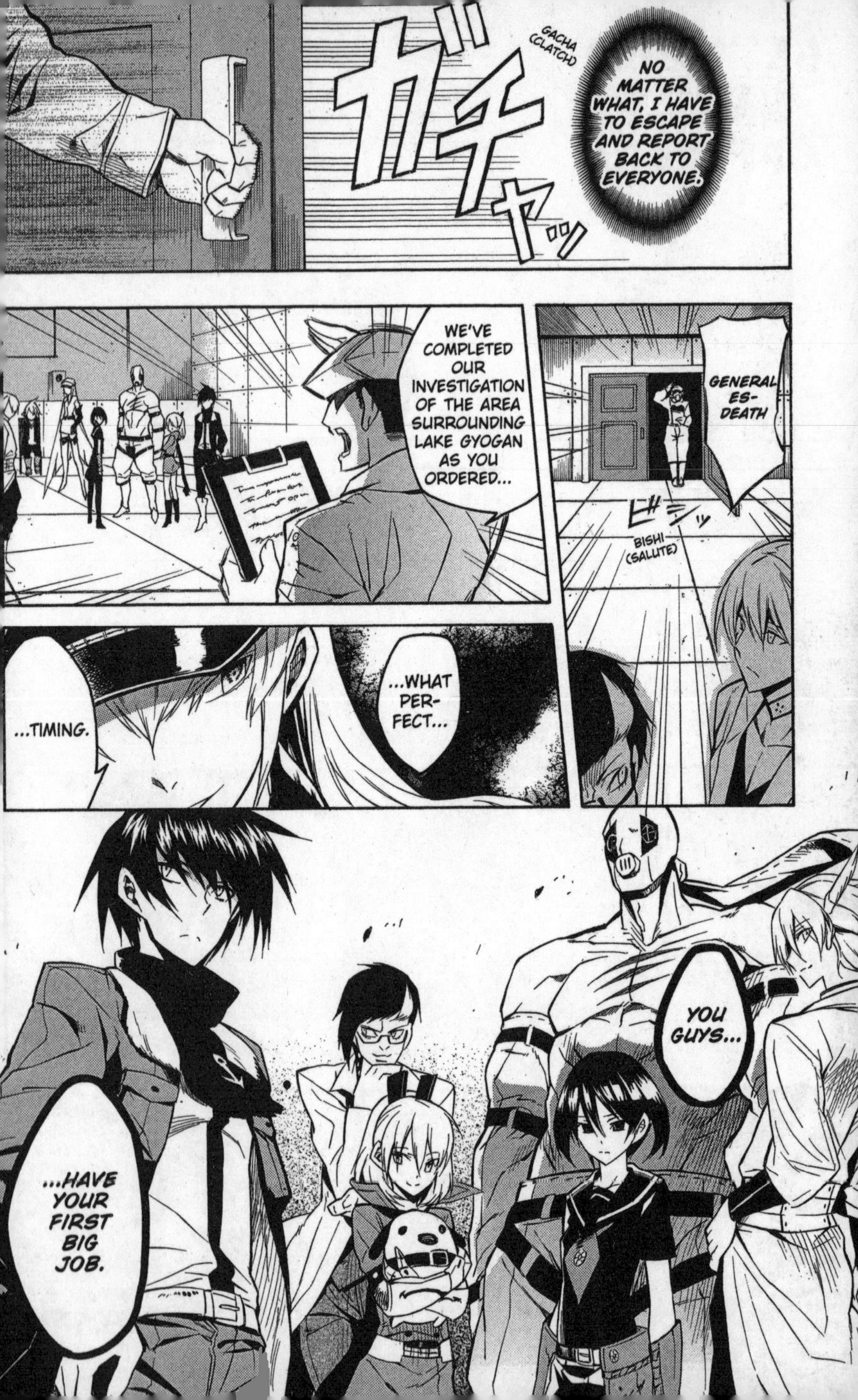
NO MATTER WHAT, I HAVE TO ESCAPE AND REPORT BACK TO EVERYONE.
GACHA (CLATCH)
GENERAL ES-DEATH
BISHI (SALUTE)
WE'VE COMPLETED OUR INVESTIGATION OF THE AREA SURROUNDING LAKE GYOGAN AS YOU ORDERED...
...WHAT PER-FECT...
...TIMING.
YOU GUYS...
...HAVE YOUR FIRST BIG JOB.

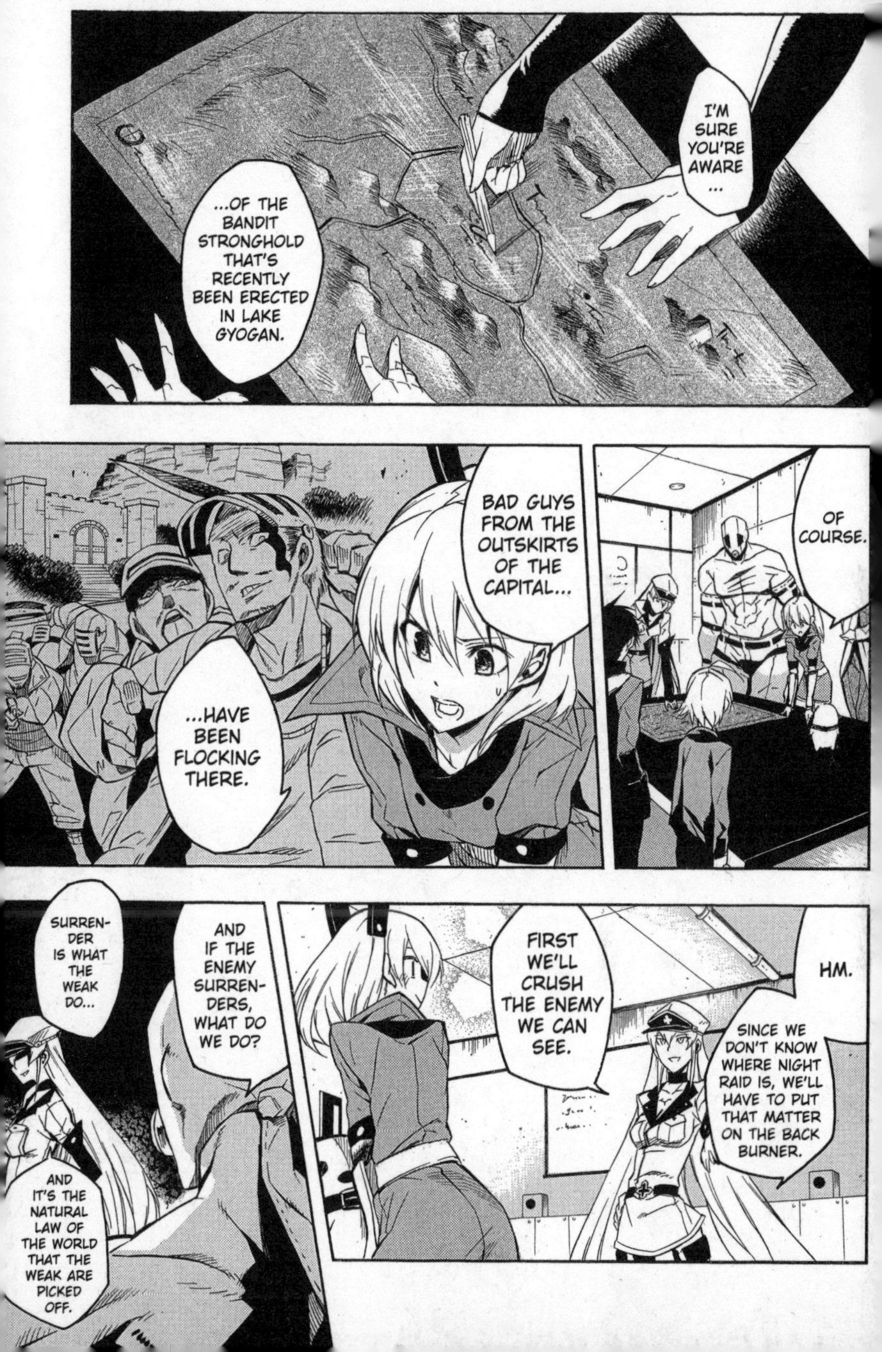
I'M SURE YOU'RE AWARE...
...OF THE BANDIT STRONGHOLD THAT'S RECENTLY BEEN ERECTED IN LAKE GYOGAN.
OF COURSE.
BAD GUYS FROM THE OUTSKIRTS OF THE CAPITAL...
...HAVE BEEN FLOCKING THERE.
HM.
SINCE WE DON'T KNOW WHERE NIGHT RAID IS, WE'LL HAVE TO PUT THAT MATTER ON THE BACK BURNER.
FIRST WE'LL CRUSH THE ENEMY WE CAN SEE.
AND IF THE ENEMY SURREN-DERS, WHAT DO WE DO?
SURREN-DER IS WHAT THE WEAK DO...
AND IT'S THE NATURAL LAW OF THE WORLD THAT THE WEAK ARE PICKED OFF.

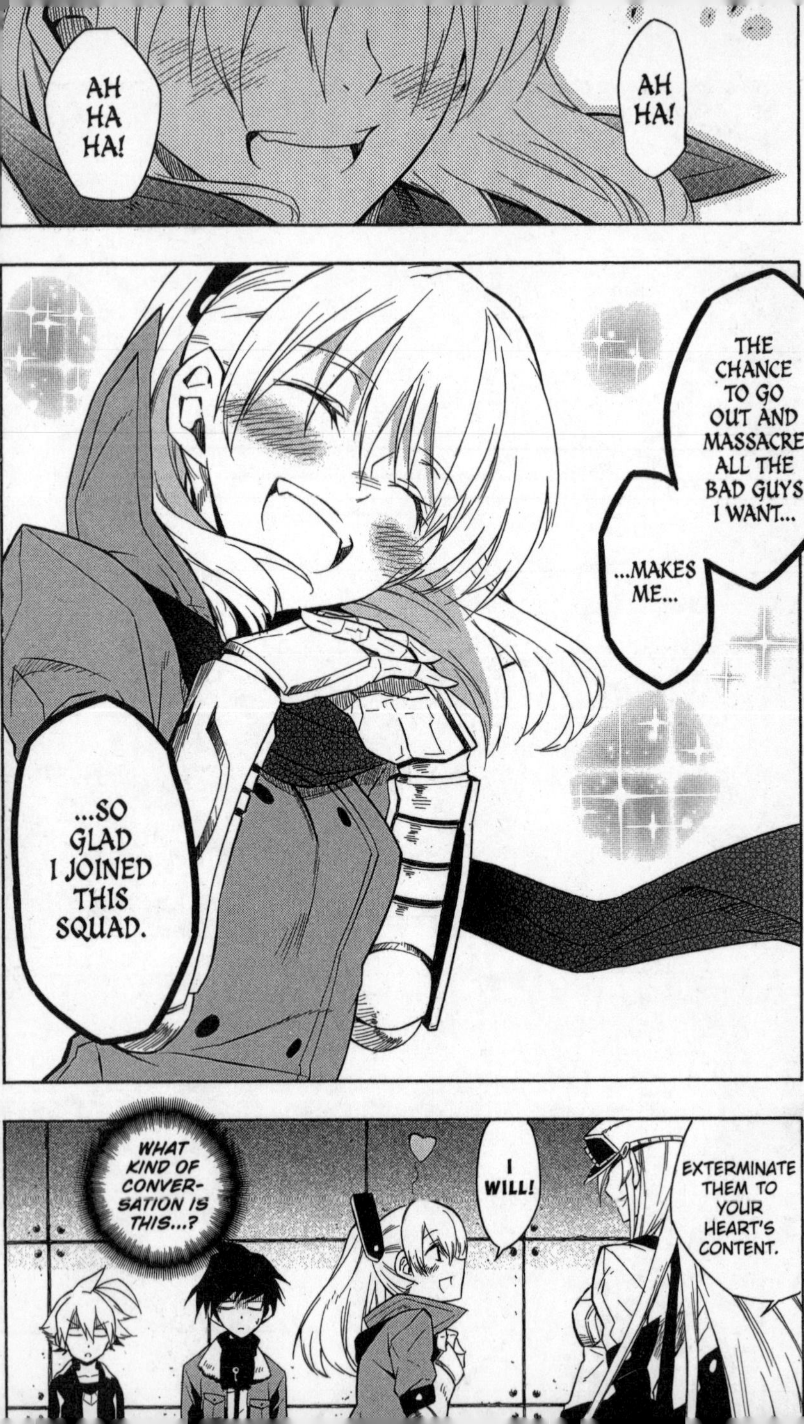
AH HA!
AH HA HA!
THE CHANCE TO GO OUT AND MASSACRE ALL THE BAD GUYS I WANT...
...MAKES ME...
...SO GLAD I JOINED THIS SQUAD.
EXTERMINATE THEM TO YOUR HEART'S CONTENT.
I WILL!
WHAT KIND OF CONVER-SATION IS THIS...?

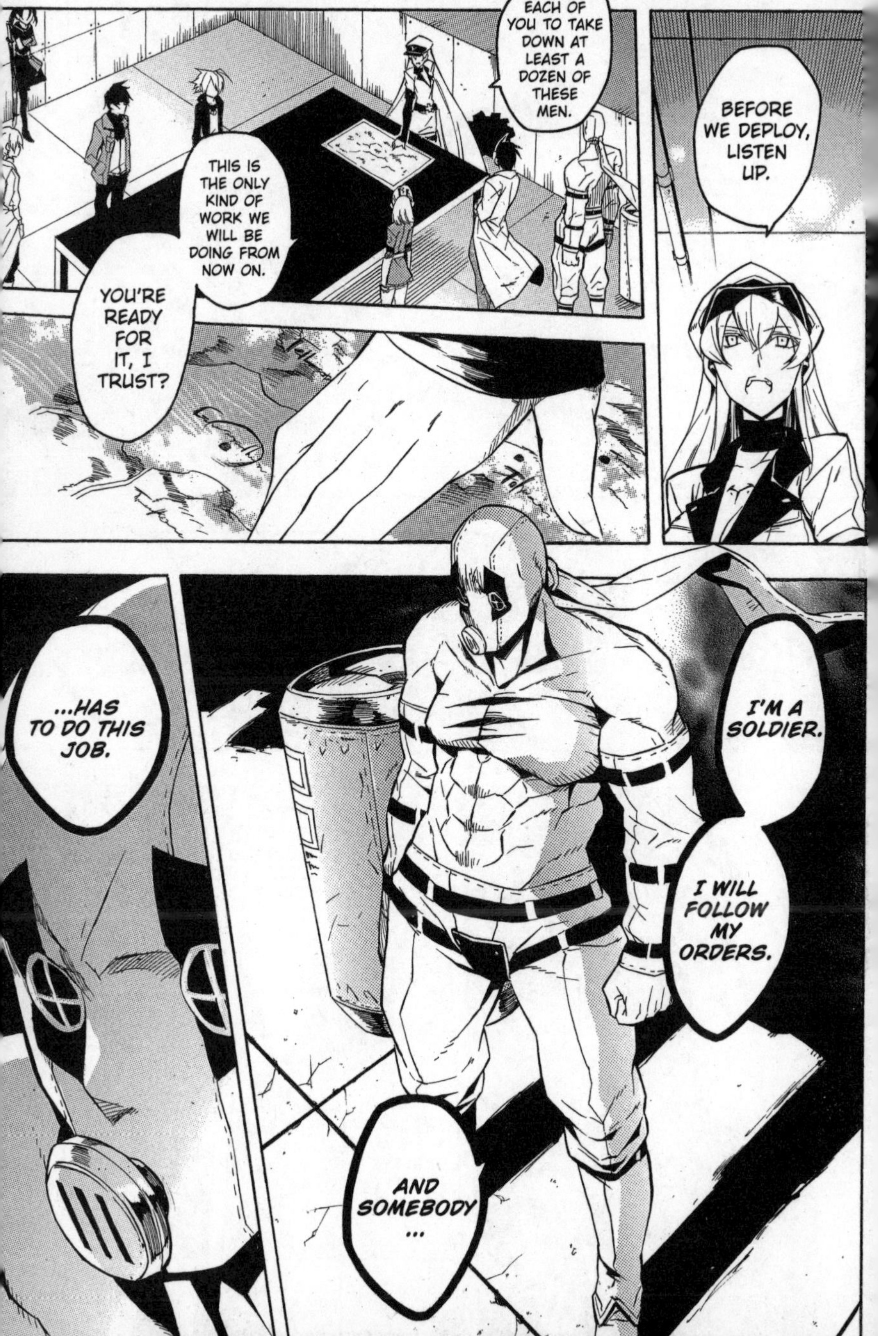
BEFORE WE DEPLOY, LISTEN UP.
I WANT EACH OF YOU TO TAKE DOWN AT LEAST A DOZEN OF THESE MEN.
THIS IS THE ONLY KIND OF WORK WE WILL BE DOING FROM NOW ON.
YOU'RE READY FOR IT, I TRUST?
I'M A SOLDIER.
I WILL FOLLOW MY ORDERS.
AND SOMEBODY ...
...HAS TO DO THIS JOB.

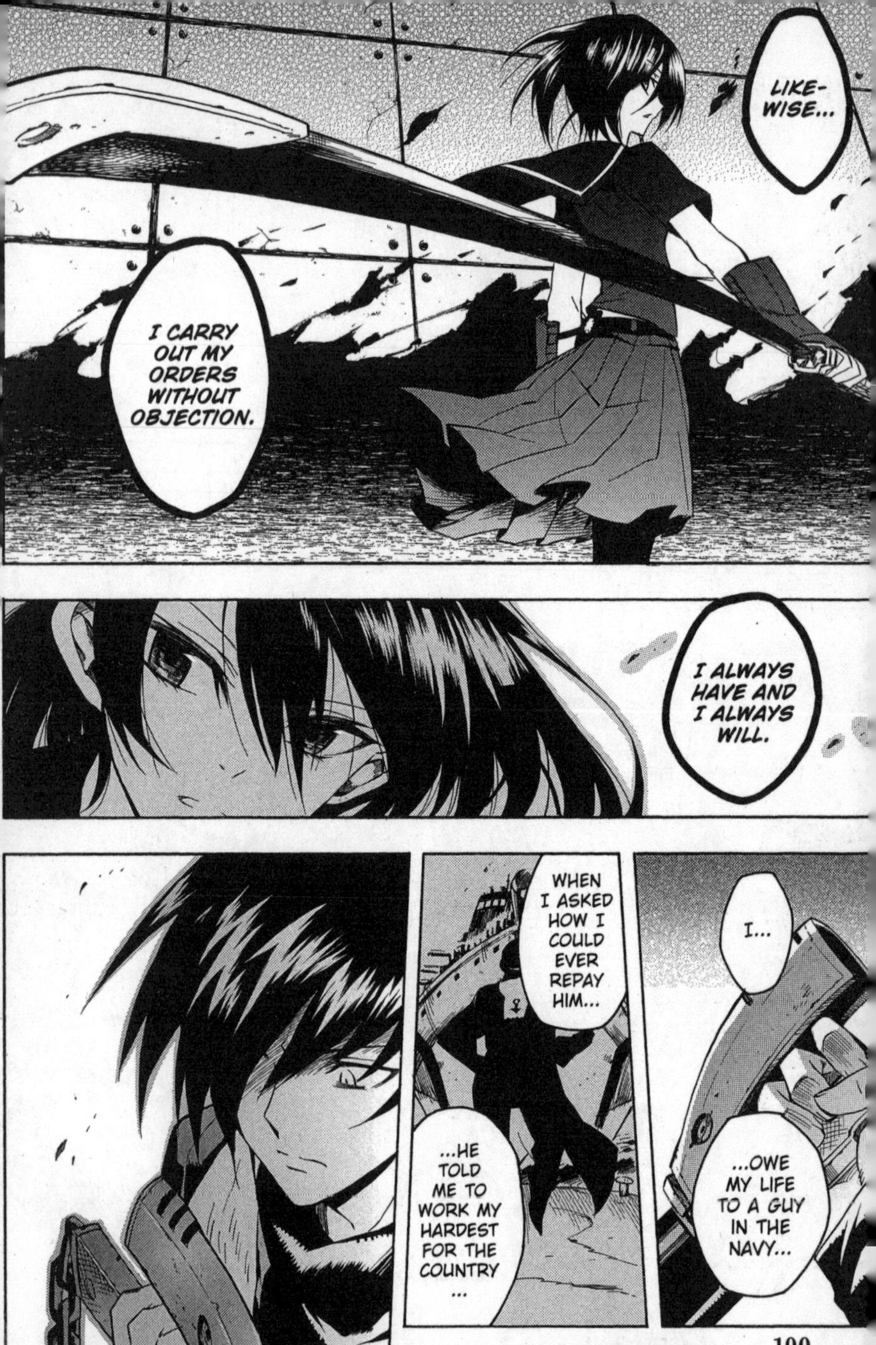
LIKE-WISE...
I CARRY OUT MY ORDERS WITHOUT OBJECTION.
I ALWAYS HAVE AND I ALWAYS WILL.
I...
...OWE MY LIFE TO A GUY IN THE NAVY...
WHEN I ASKED HOW I COULD EVER REPAY HIM...
...HE TOLD ME TO WORK MY HARDEST FOR THE COUNTRY ...

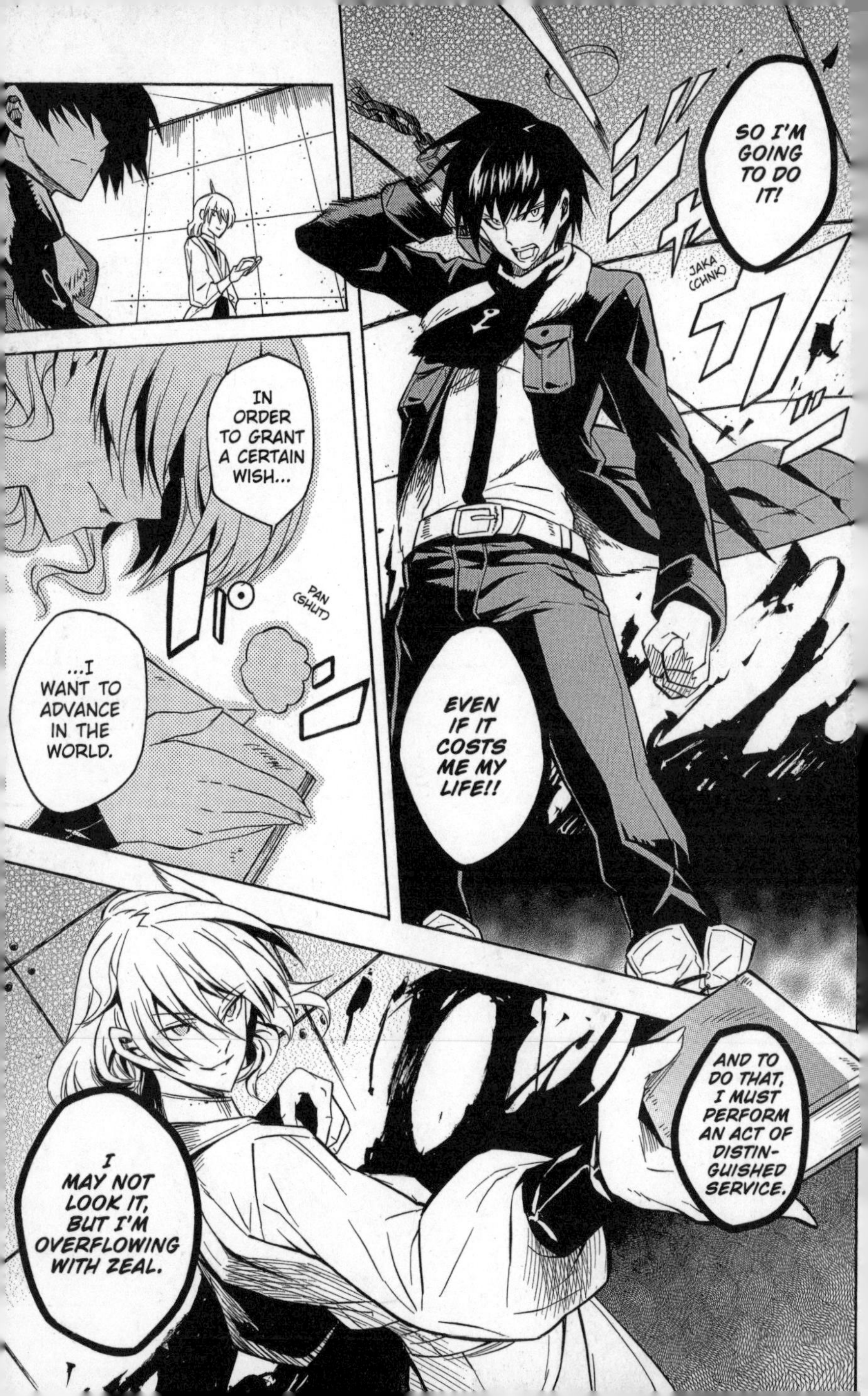

SO I'M GOING TO DO IT!
JAKA (CHNK)
EVEN IF IT COSTS ME MY LIFE!!
IN ORDER TO GRANT A CERTAIN WISH...
PAN (SHUT)
...I WANT TO ADVANCE IN THE WORLD.
AND TO DO THAT, I MUST PERFORM AN ACT OF DISTIN-GUISHED SERVICE.
I MAY NOT LOOK IT, BUT I'M OVERFLOWING WITH ZEAL.

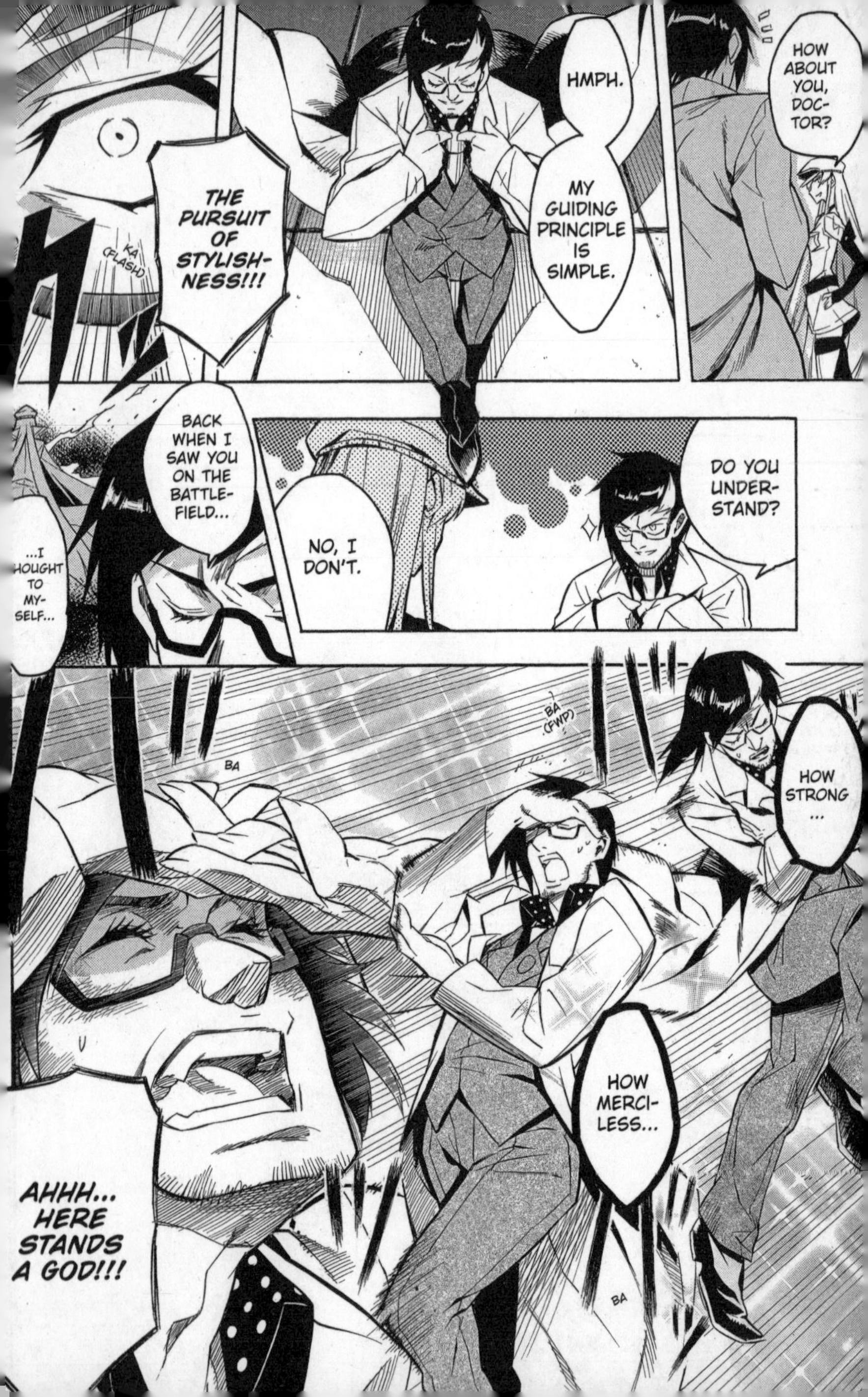
HOW ABOUT YOU, DOCTOR?
HMPH.
MY GUIDING PRINCIPLE IS SIMPLE.
THE PURSUIT OF STYLISHNESS!!!
KA (FLASH)
DO YOU UNDERSTAND?
NO, I DON'T.
BACK WHEN I SAW YOU ON THE BATTLEFIELD...
...I HOUGHT TO MYSELF...
BA (FWP)
BA
HOW STRONG...
HOW MERCILESS...
AHHH... HERE STANDS A GOD!!!
BA

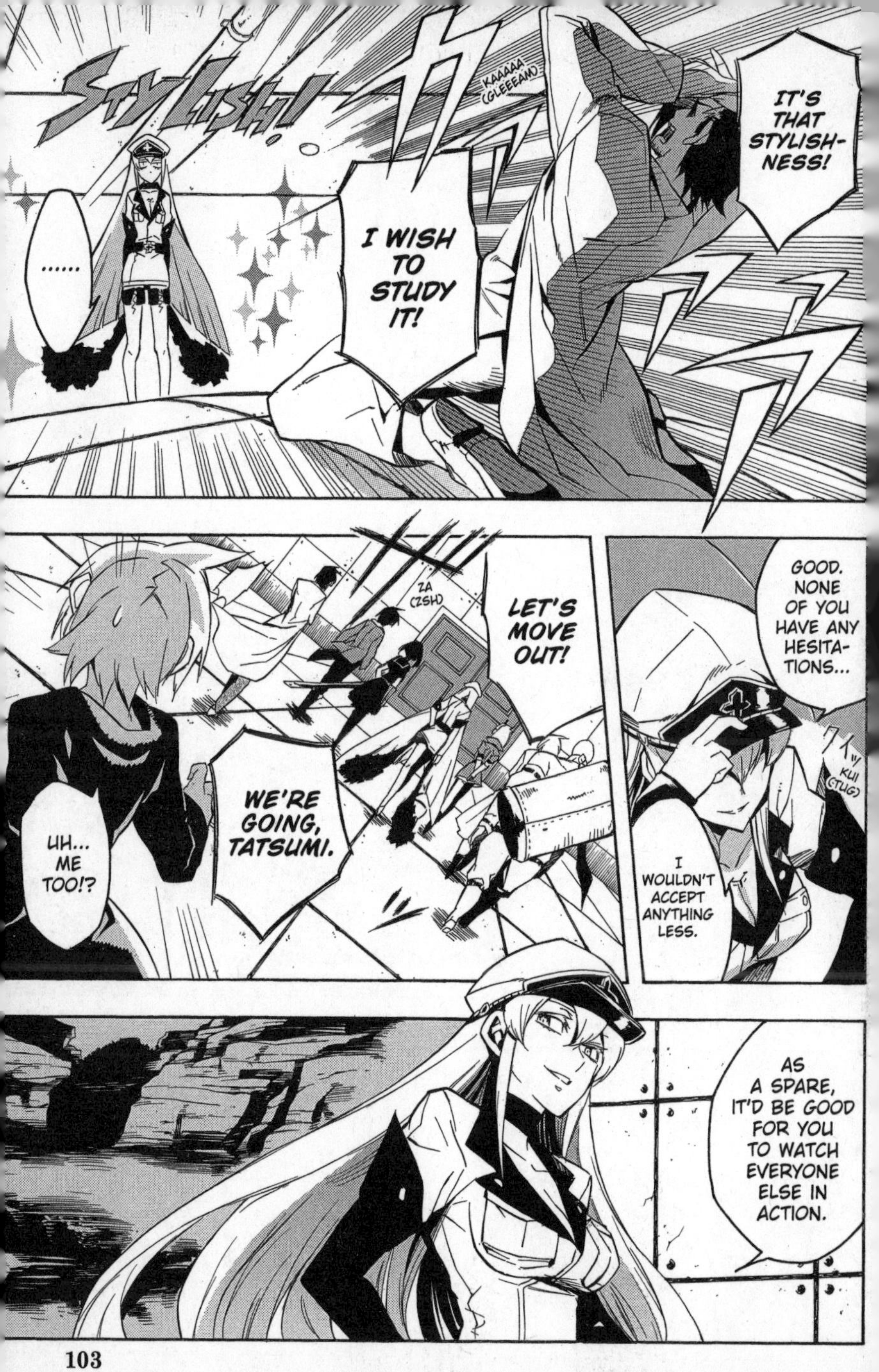
IT'S THAT STYLISH-NESS!
KAAAAA (GLEEEAN)
I WISH TO STUDY IT!
Stylish!!
......
GOOD. NONE OF YOU HAVE ANY HESITA-TIONS...
クイッ KUI (TUG)
I WOULDN'T ACCEPT ANYTHING LESS.
LET'S MOVE OUT!
ZA (ZSH)
WE'RE GOING, TATSUMI.
UH... ME TOO!?
AS A SPARE, IT'D BE GOOD FOR YOU TO WATCH EVERYONE ELSE IN ACTION.

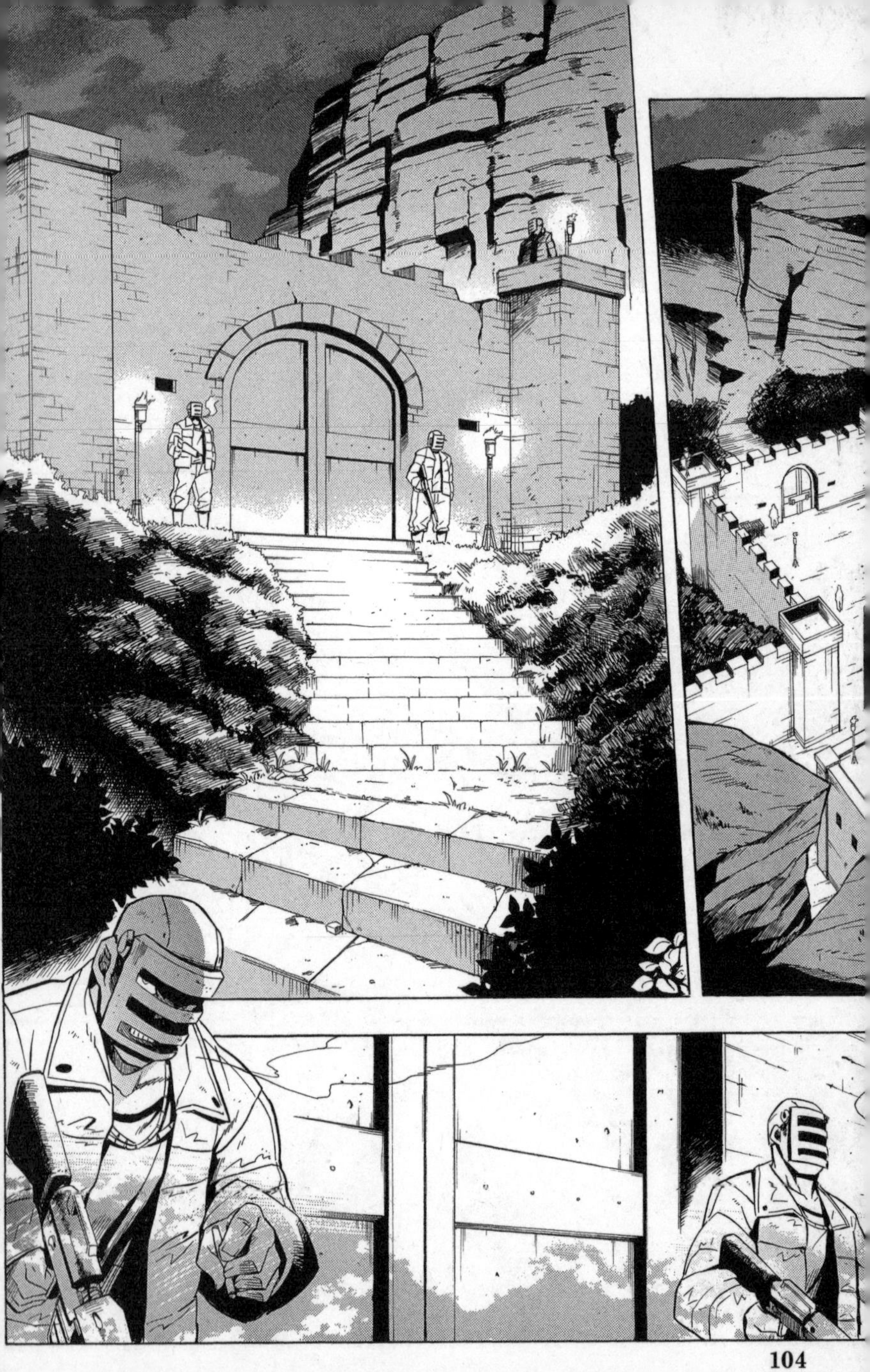

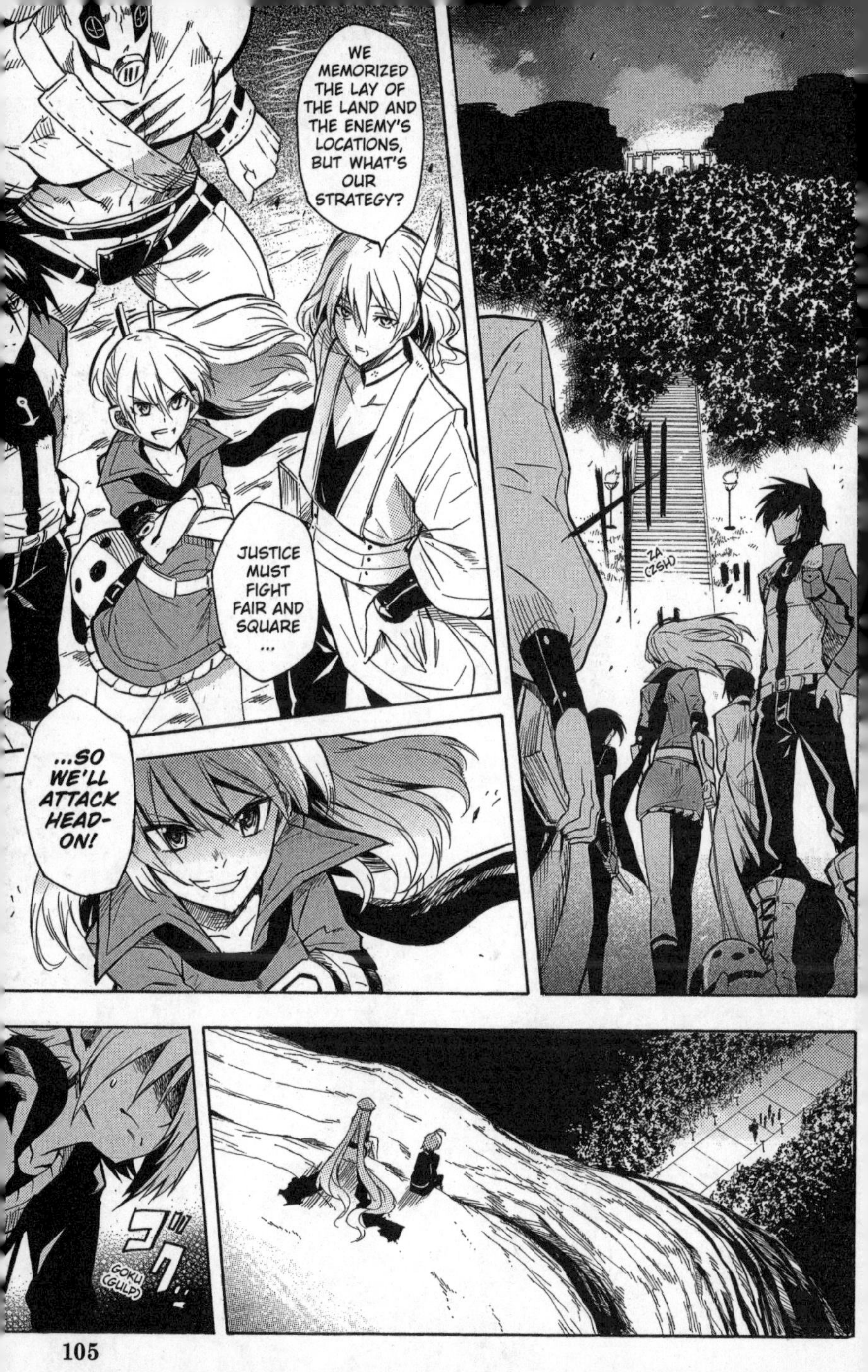
WE MEMORIZED THE LAY OF THE LAND AND THE ENEMY'S LOCATIONS, BUT WHAT'S OUR STRATEGY?
JUSTICE MUST FIGHT FAIR AND SQUARE ...
...SO WE'LL ATTACK HEAD-ON!
ZA (ZSH)
GOKU (GULP)

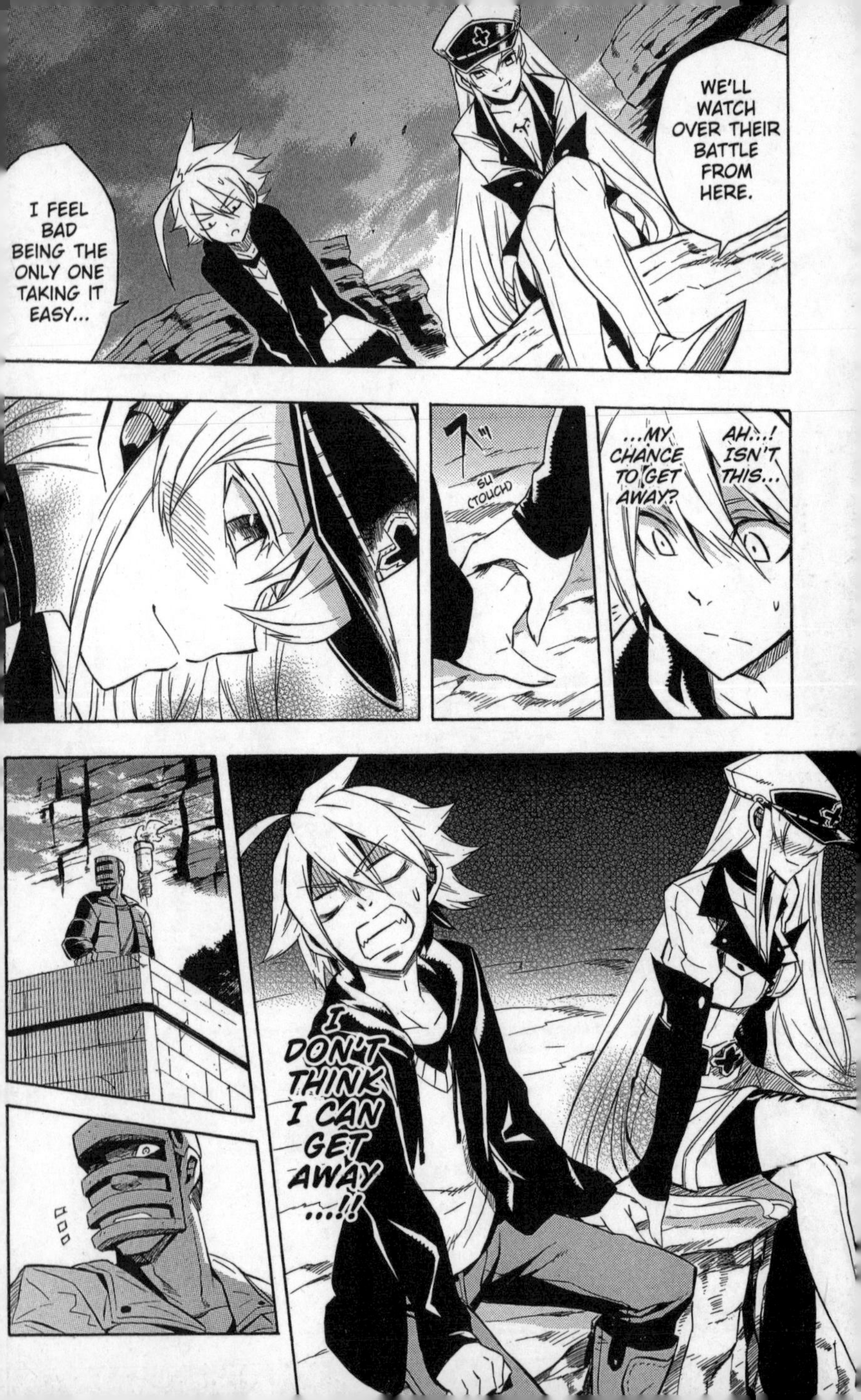
WE'LL WATCH OVER THEIR BATTLE FROM HERE.
I FEEL BAD BEING THE ONLY ONE TAKING IT EASY...
AH...! ISN'T THIS...
...MY CHANCE TO GET AWAY?
SU (TOUCH)
I DON'T THINK I CAN GET AWAY...!!

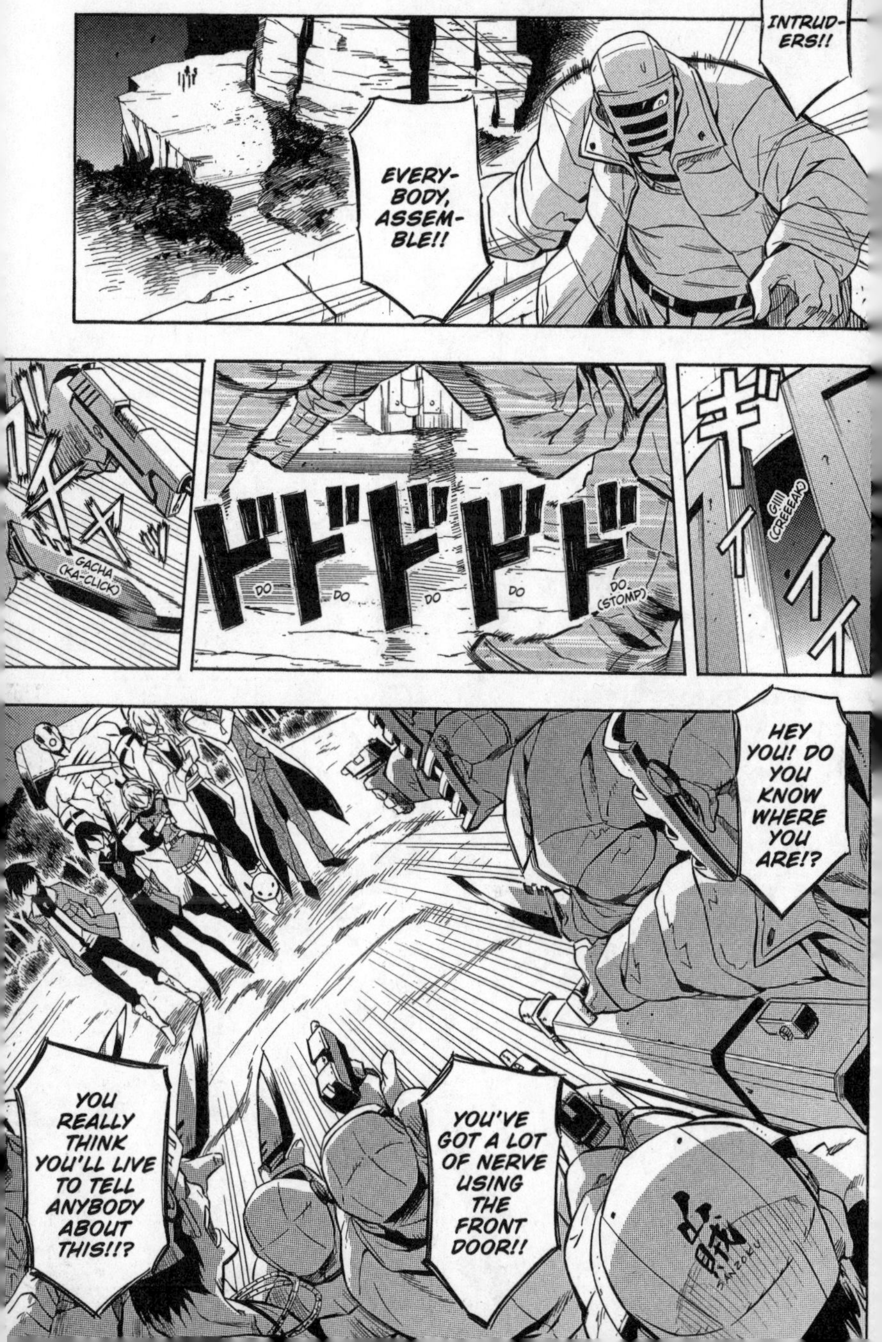
INTRUD-ERS!!
EVERY-BODY, ASSEMBLE!!
ギィィィ
GIIII (CREEEAK)
ドドドドド
DO DO DO DO DO (STOMP)
GACHA (KA-CLICK)
HEY YOU! DO YOU KNOW WHERE YOU ARE!?
YOU'VE GOT A LOT OF NERVE USING THE FRONT DOOR!!
YOU REALLY THINK YOU'LL LIVE TO TELL ANYBODY ABOUT THIS!!?
SANZOKU

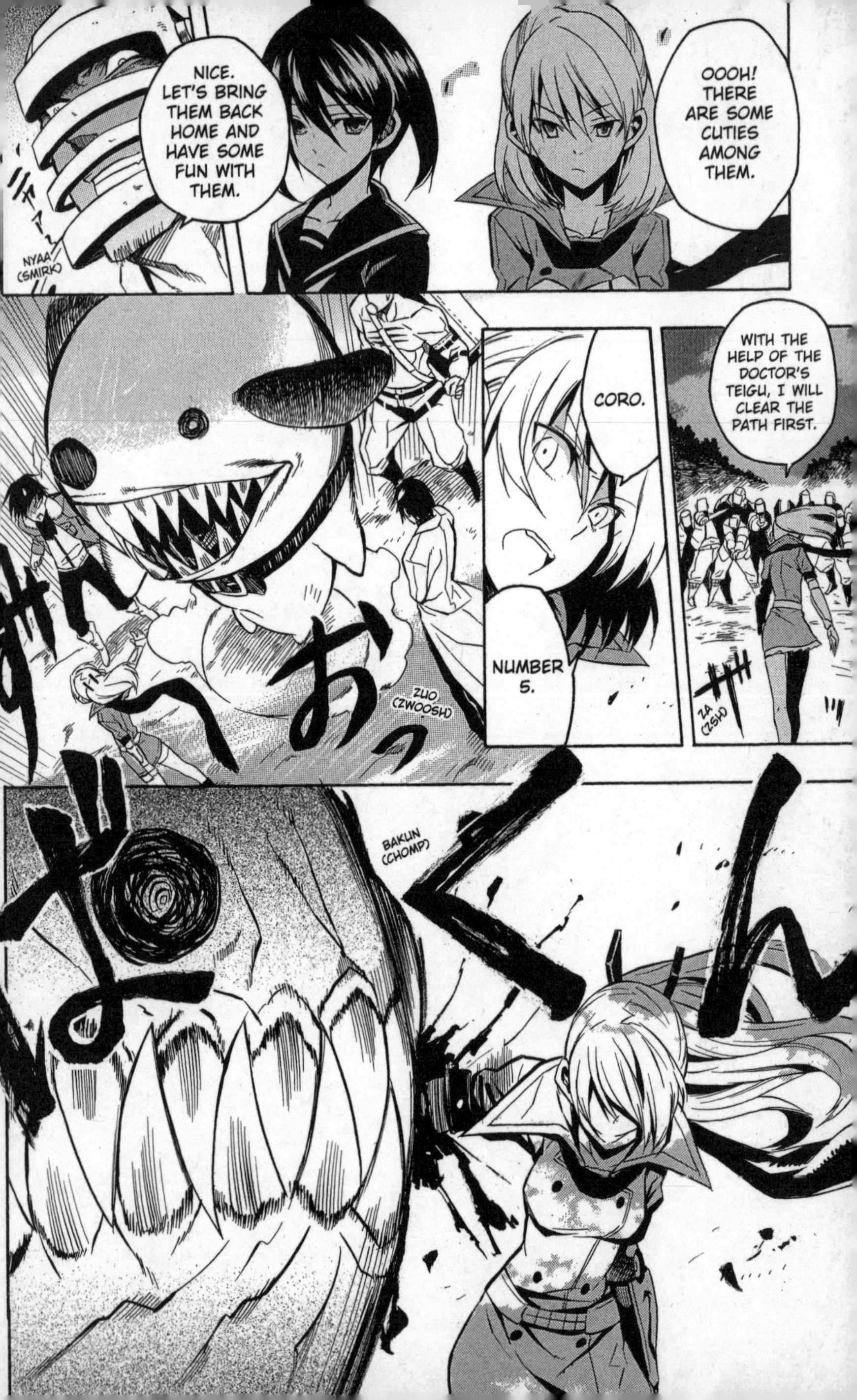
OOOH! THERE ARE SOME CUTIES AMONG THEM.
NICE. LET'S BRING THEM BACK HOME AND HAVE SOME FUN WITH THEM.
NYAA (SMIRK)
WITH THE HELP OF THE DOCTOR'S TEIGU, I WILL CLEAR THE PATH FIRST.
ZA (ZSH)
CORO.
NUMBER 5.
ZUO (ZWOOSH)
BAKUN (CHOMP)

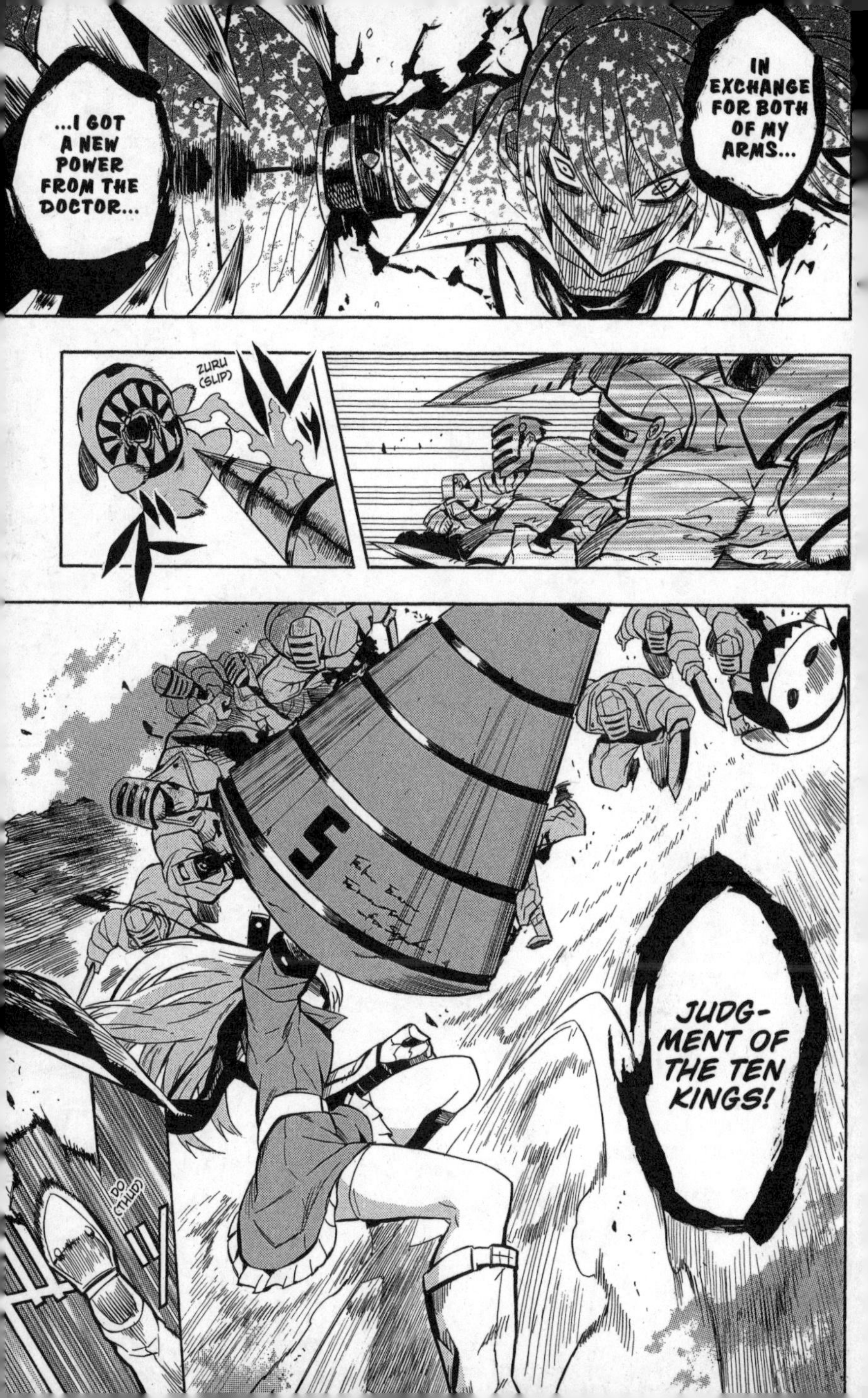

IN EXCHANGE FOR BOTH OF MY ARMS...
...I GOT A NEW POWER FROM THE DOCTOR...
ZURU (SLIP)
JUDG-MENT OF THE TEN KINGS!
DO (THUD)

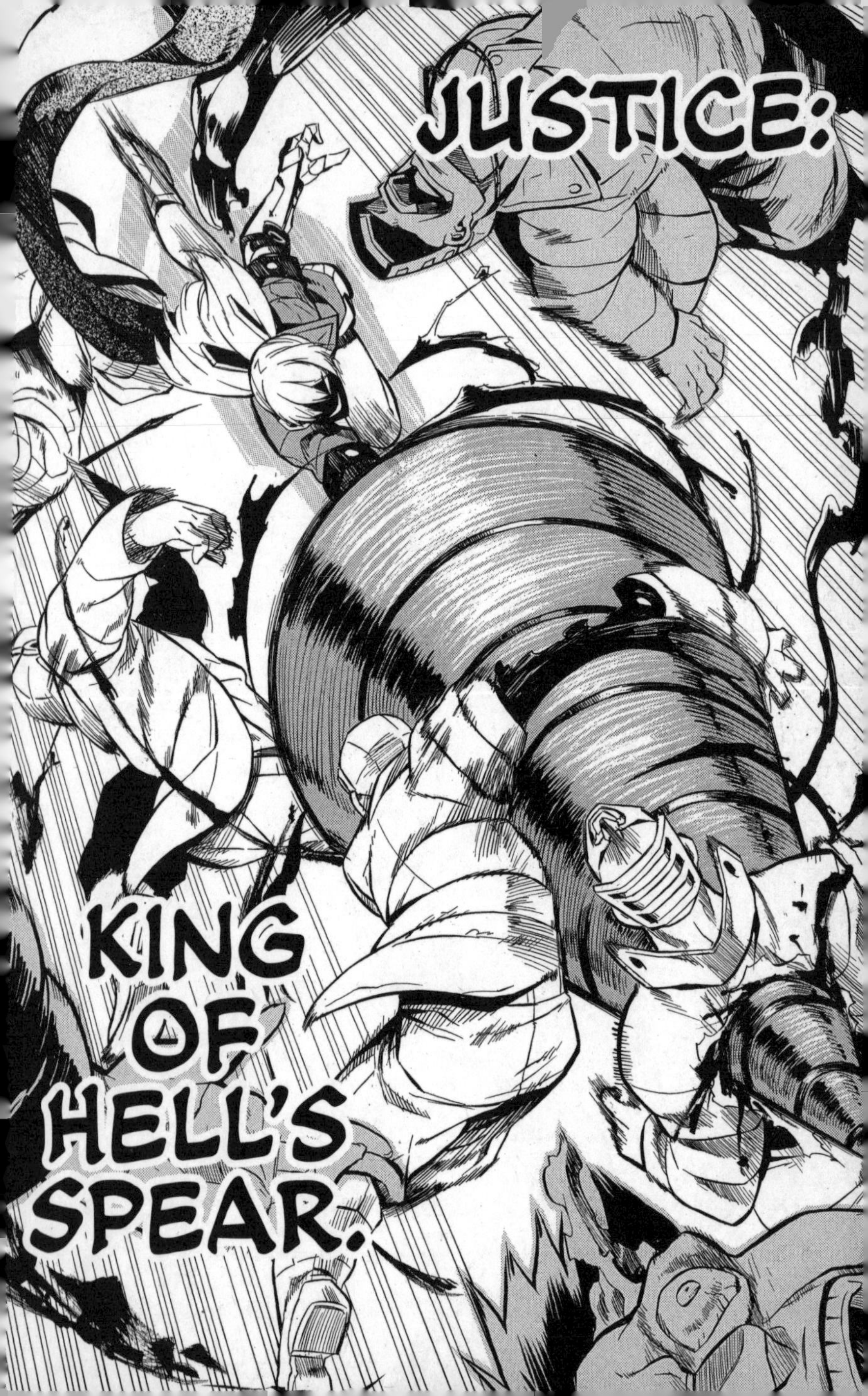
JUSTICE:
KING OF HELL'S SPEAR.

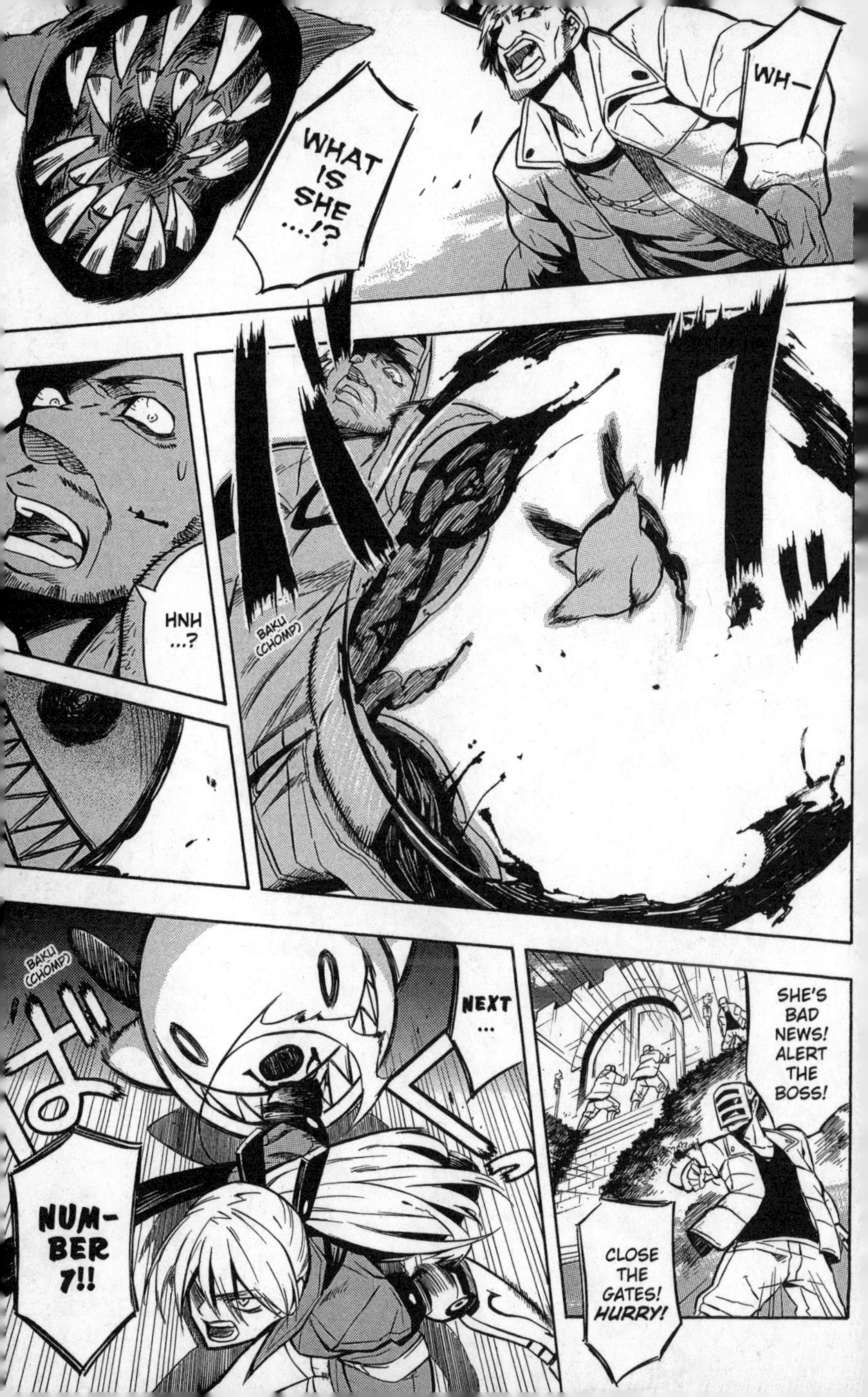
WH—
WHAT IS SHE ...!?
HNH ...?
BAKU (CHOMP)
SHE'S BAD NEWS! ALERT THE BOSS!
CLOSE THE GATES! *HURRY!*
NEXT ...
BAKU (CHOMP)
NUM-BER 7!!

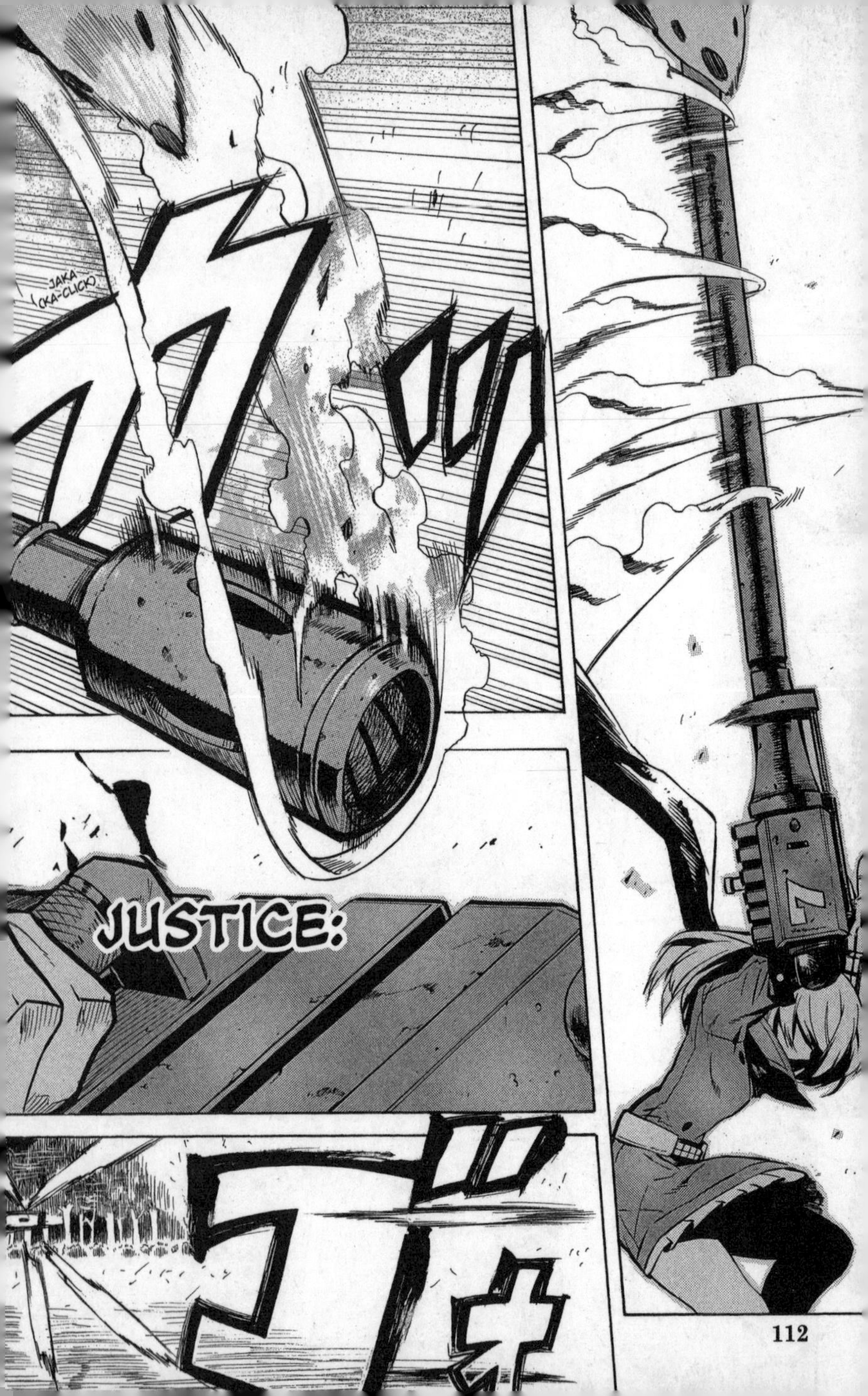
JAKA
(KA-CLICK)
JUSTICE:

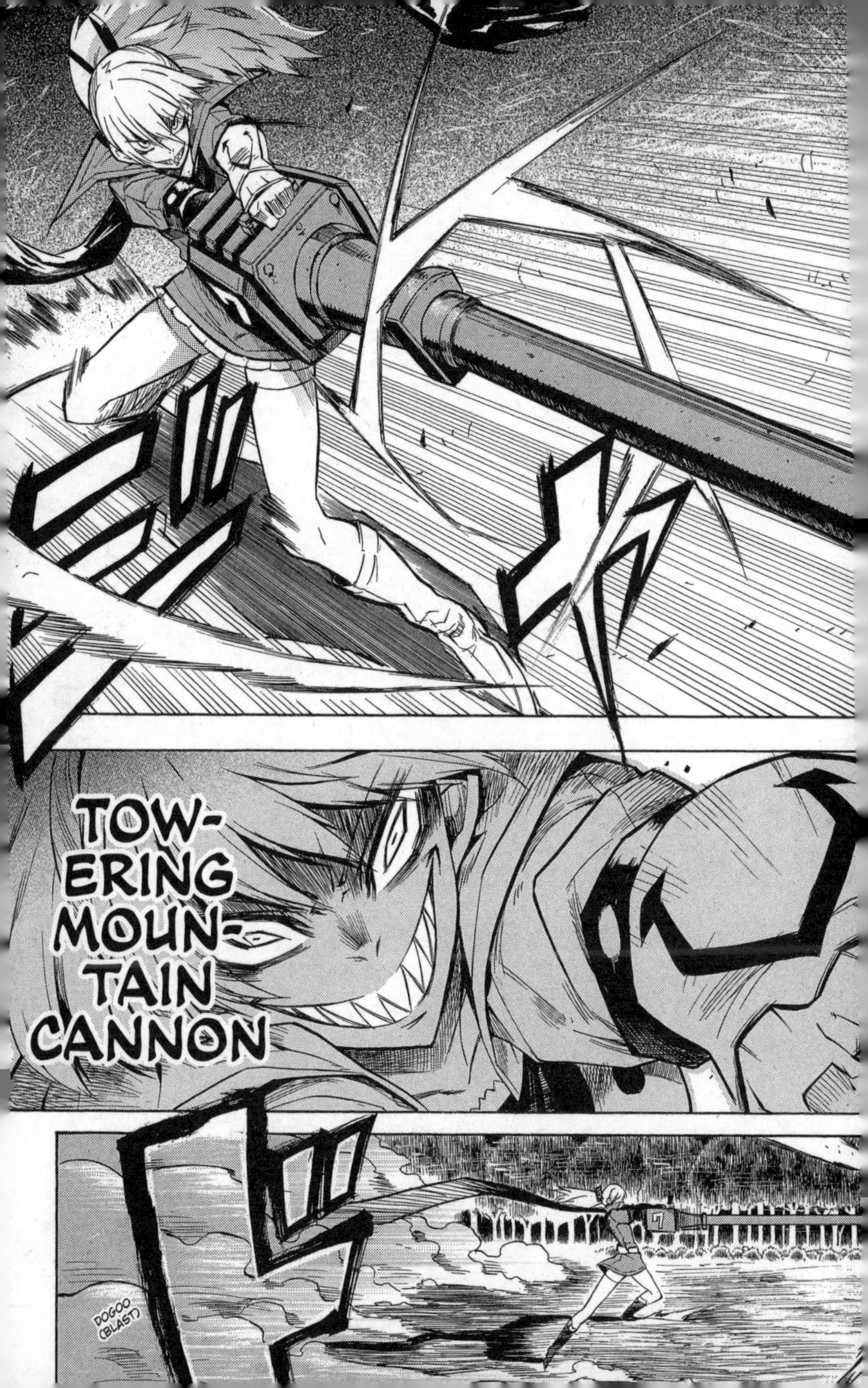
TOW-
ERING
MOUN-
TAIN
CANNON
DOGOO
(BLAST)

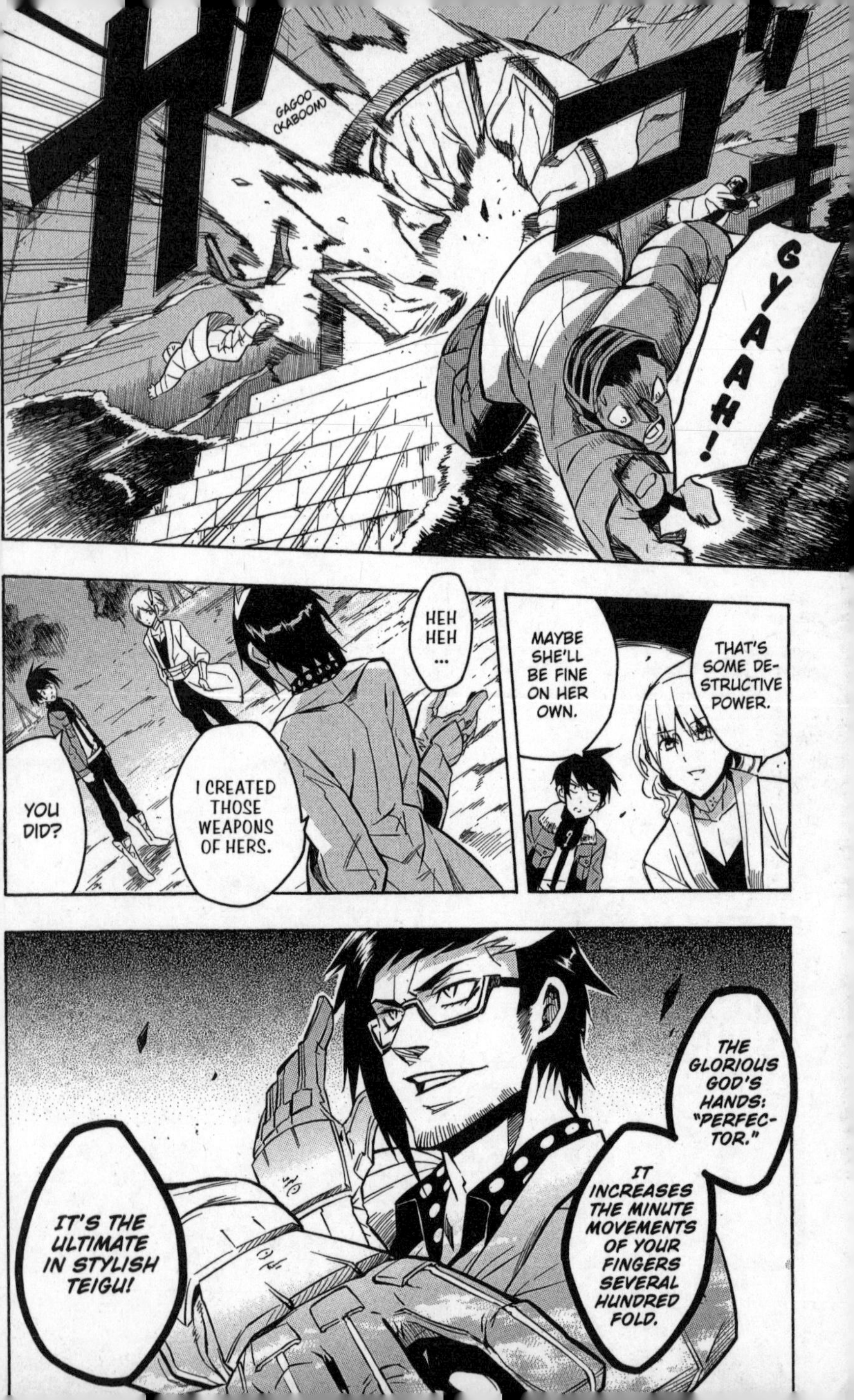
GAGOO (KABOOM)
GYAAH!
THAT'S SOME DE-STRUCTIVE POWER.
MAYBE SHE'LL BE FINE ON HER OWN.
HEH HEH ...
I CREATED THOSE WEAPONS OF HERS.
YOU DID?
THE GLORIOUS GOD'S HANDS: "PERFECTOR."
IT INCREASES THE MINUTE MOVEMENTS OF YOUR FINGERS SEVERAL HUNDRED FOLD.
IT'S THE ULTIMATE IN STYLISH TEIGU!

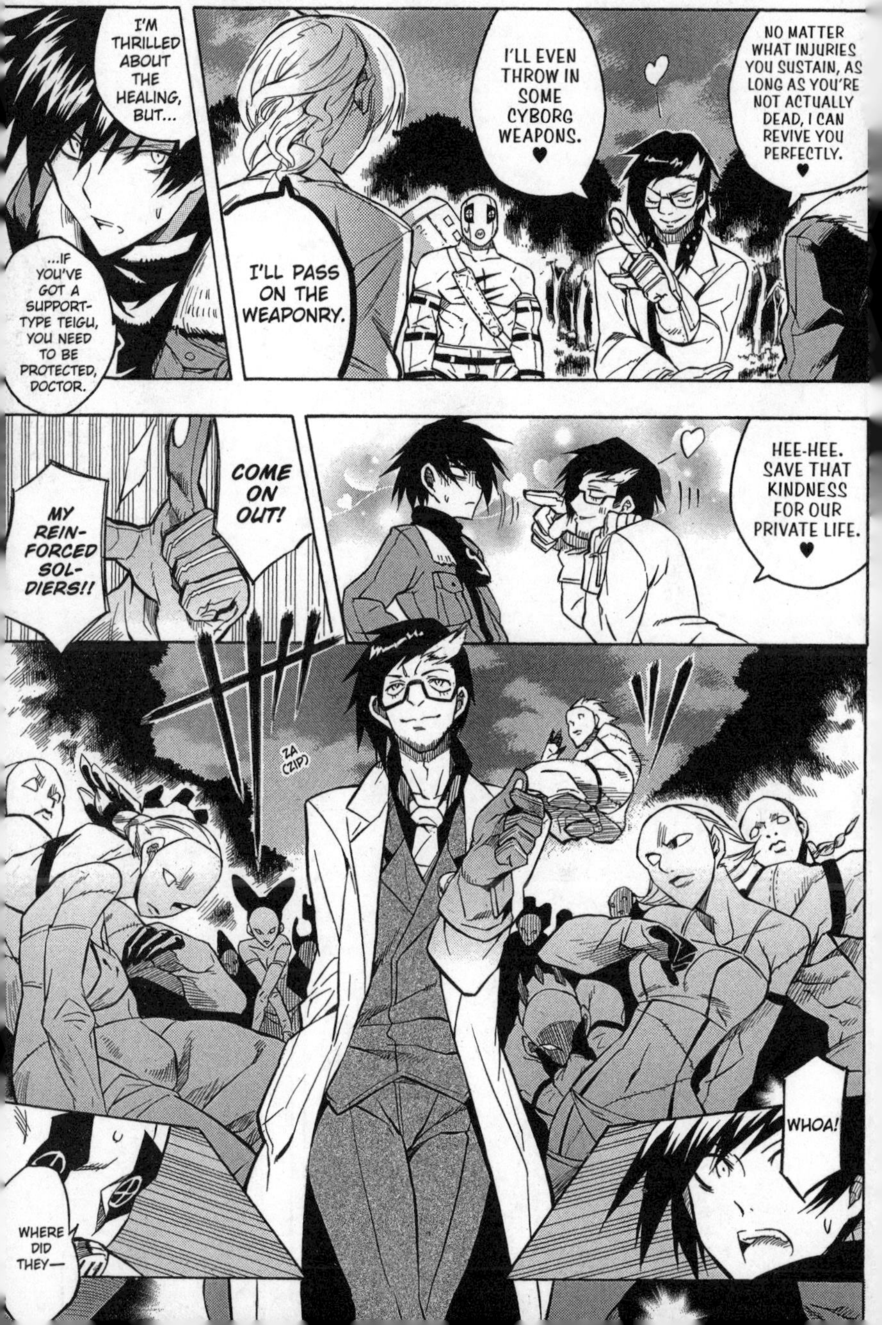
NO MATTER WHAT INJURIES YOU SUSTAIN, AS LONG AS YOU'RE NOT ACTUALLY DEAD, I CAN REVIVE YOU PERFECTLY. ♥
I'LL EVEN THROW IN SOME CYBORG WEAPONS. ♥
I'LL PASS ON THE WEAPONRY.
I'M THRILLED ABOUT THE HEALING, BUT...
...IF YOU'VE GOT A SUPPORT-TYPE TEIGU, YOU NEED TO BE PROTECTED, DOCTOR.
HEE-HEE. SAVE THAT KINDNESS FOR OUR PRIVATE LIFE. ♥
COME ON OUT!
MY REIN-FORCED SOL-DIERS!!
ZA (ZIP)
WHOA!
WHERE DID THEY—

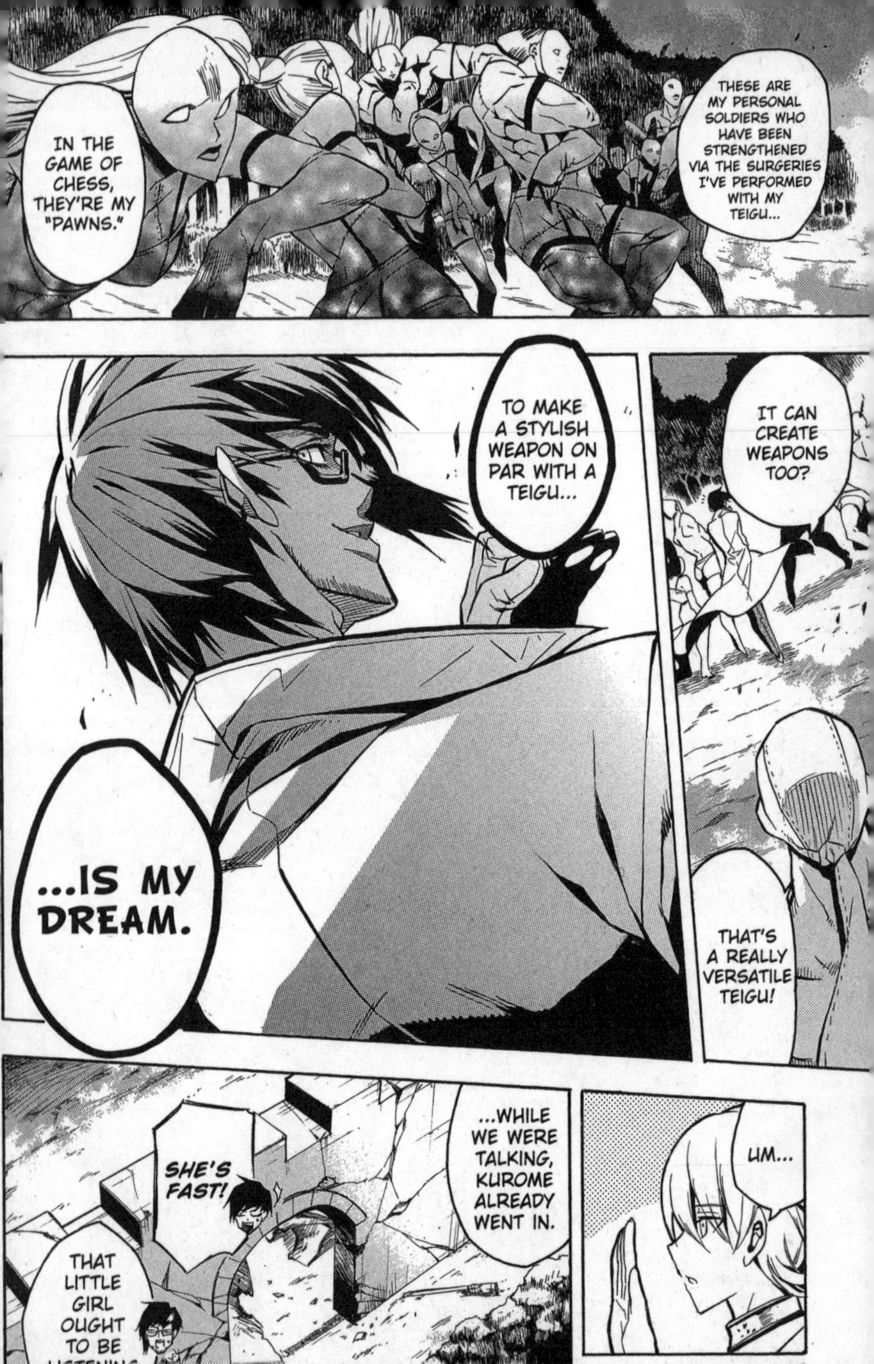
THESE ARE MY PERSONAL SOLDIERS WHO HAVE BEEN STRENGTHENED VIA THE SURGERIES I'VE PERFORMED WITH MY TEIGU...
IN THE GAME OF CHESS, THEY'RE MY "PAWNS."
IT CAN CREATE WEAPONS TOO?
THAT'S A REALLY VERSATILE TEIGU!
TO MAKE A STYLISH WEAPON ON PAR WITH A TEIGU...
...IS MY DREAM.
UM...
...WHILE WE WERE TALKING, KUROME ALREADY WENT IN.
SHE'S FAST!
THAT LITTLE GIRL OUGHT TO BE LISTENING TO ME.

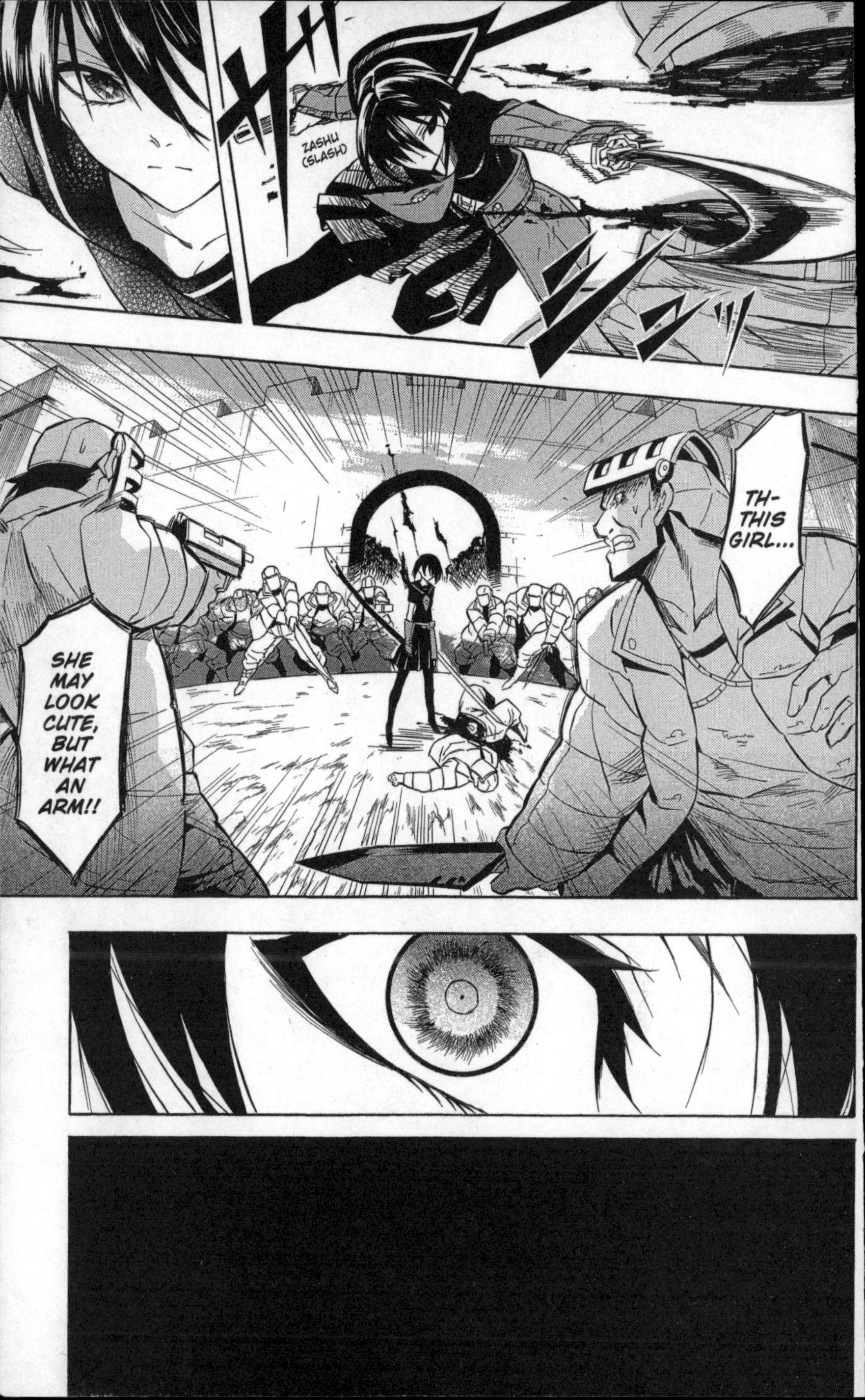
ZASHU (SLASH)
TH- THIS GIRL...
SHE MAY LOOK CUTE, BUT WHAT AN ARM!!

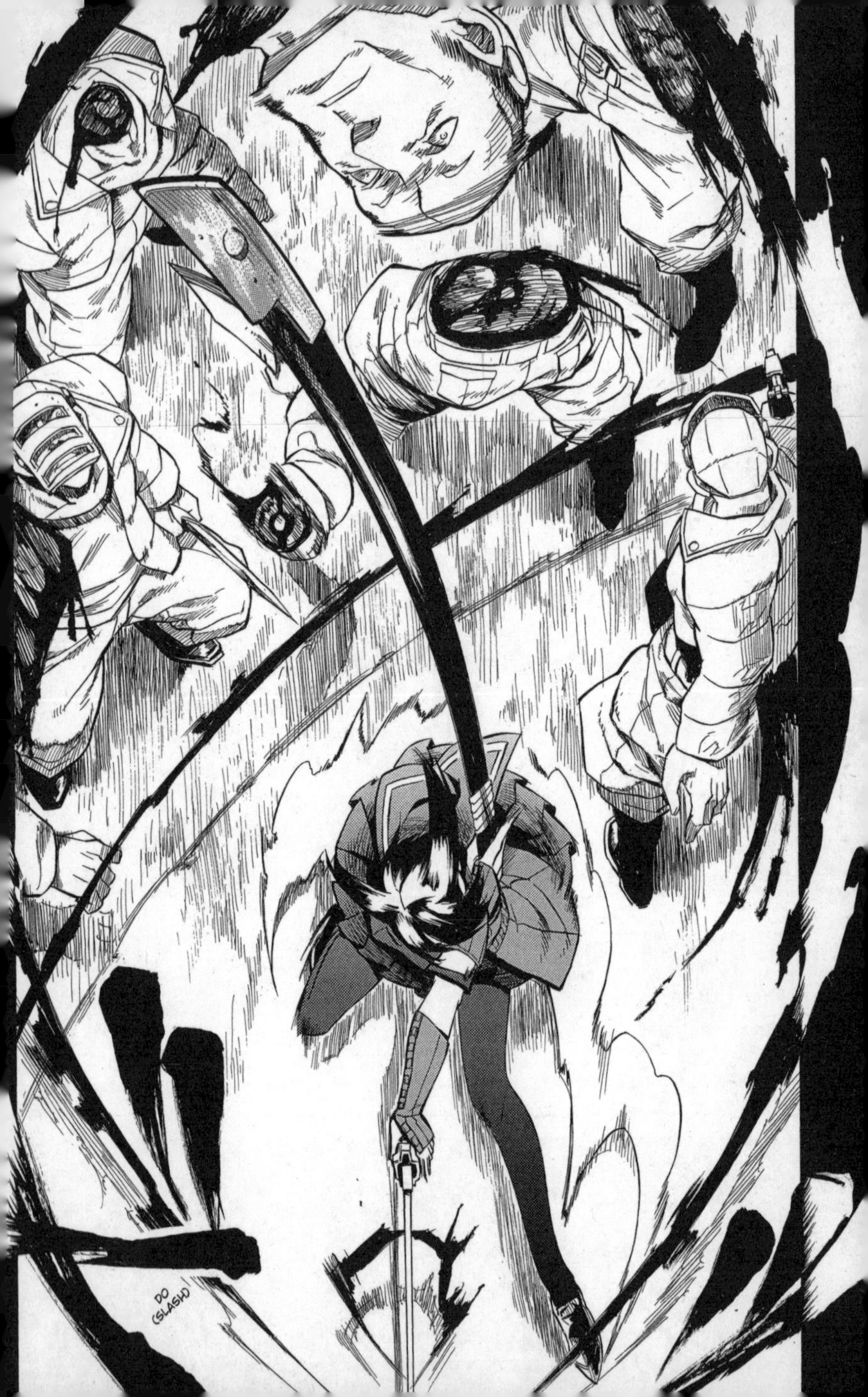
DO (SLASH)

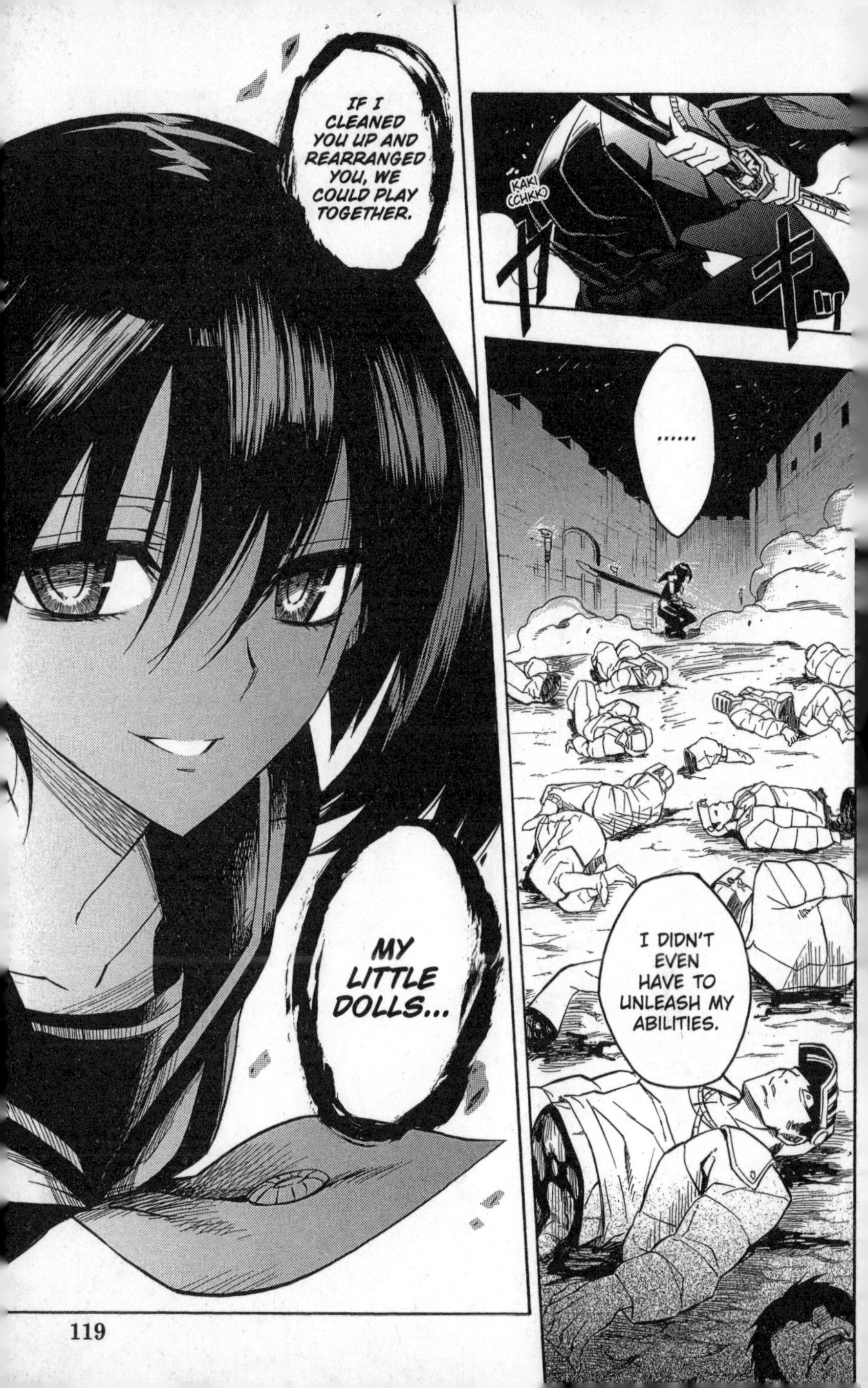
KAKI (CHKK)
......
I DIDN'T EVEN HAVE TO UNLEASH MY ABILITIES.
IF I CLEANED YOU UP AND REARRANGED YOU, WE COULD PLAY TOGETHER.
MY LITTLE DOLLS...

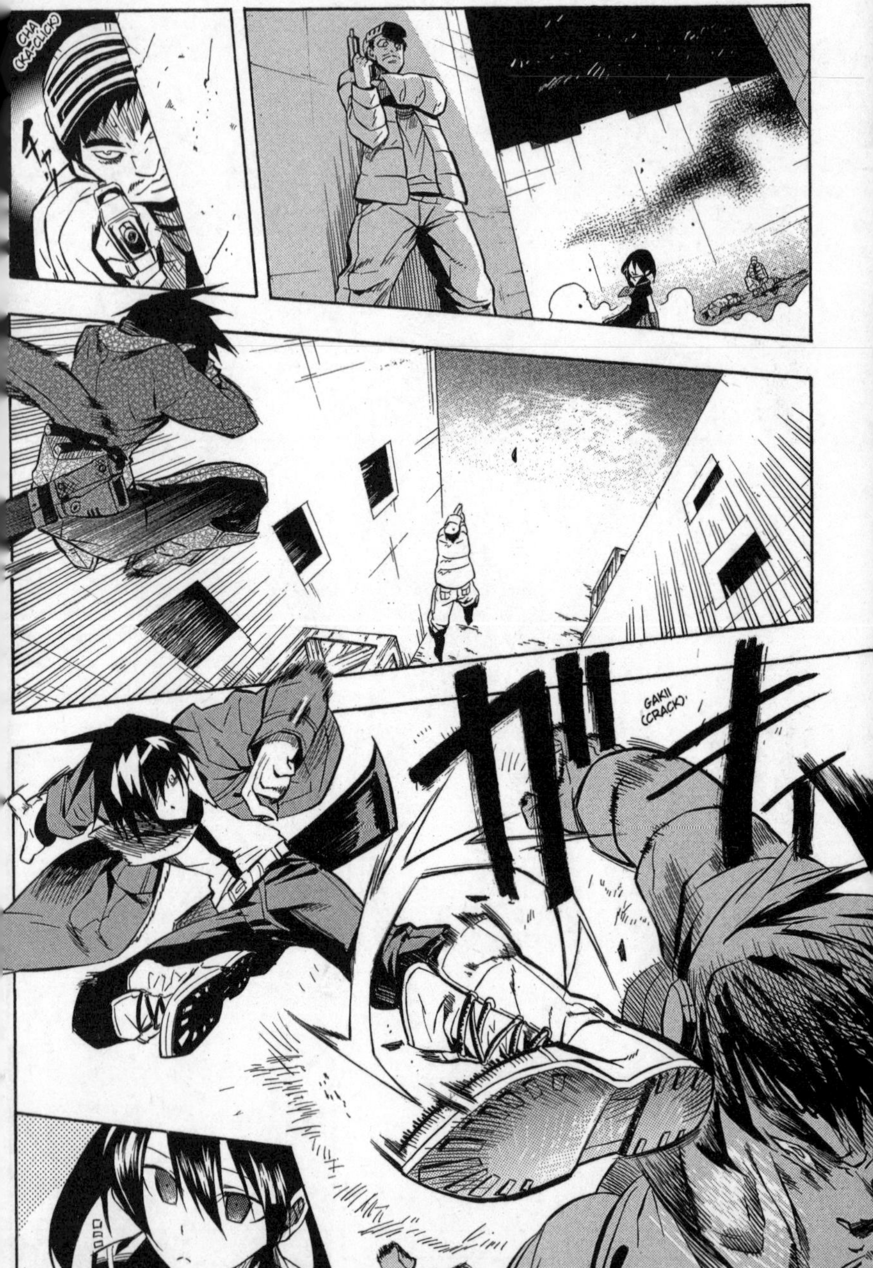
CHA (KA-CLICK)
GAKII (CRACK)

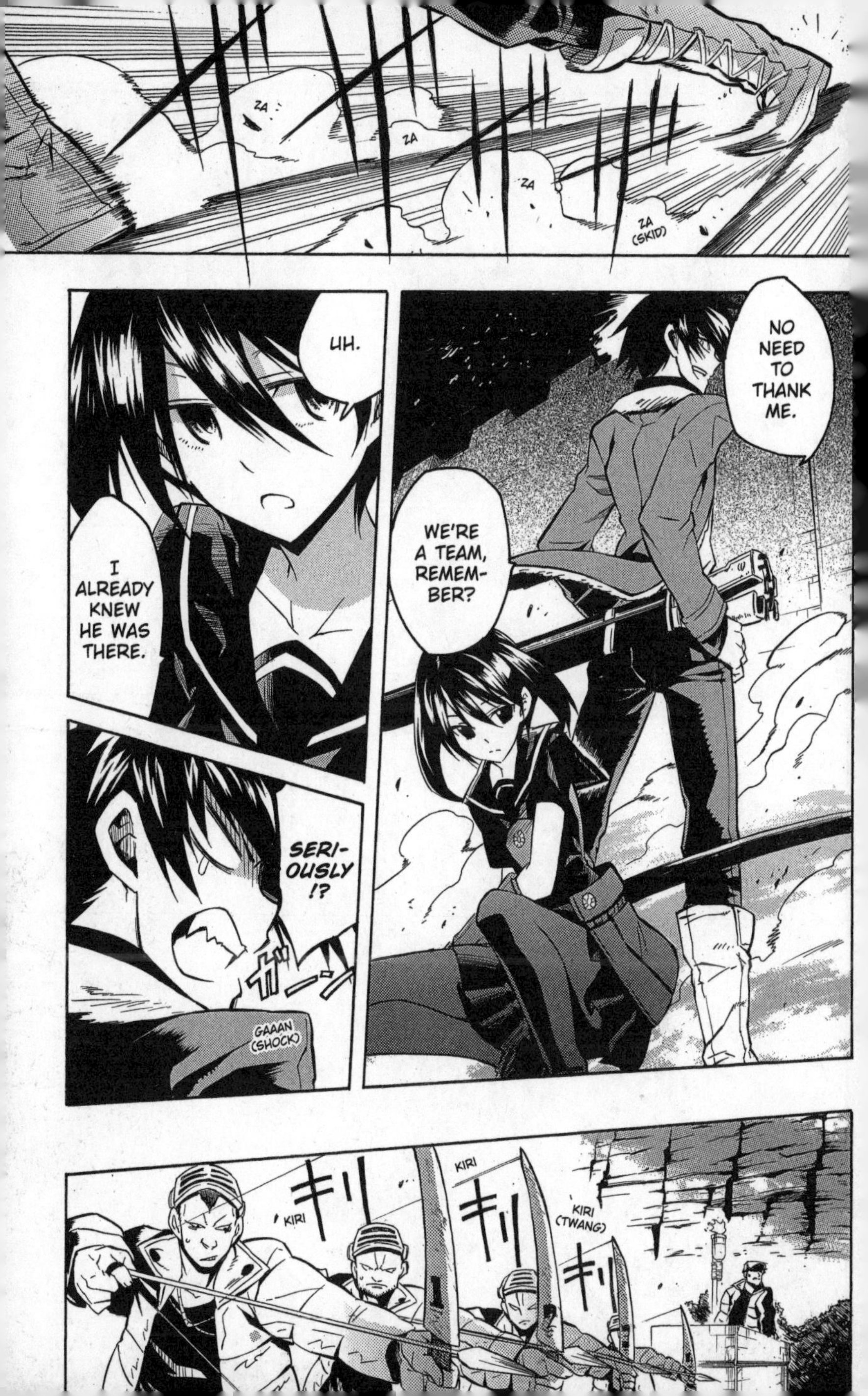
ZA
ZA
ZA
ZA (SKID)
NO NEED TO THANK ME.
WE'RE A TEAM, REMEMBER?
UH.
I ALREADY KNEW HE WAS THERE.
SERI-OUSLY!?
GAAAN (SHOCK)
KIRI
KIRI
KIRI (TWANG)

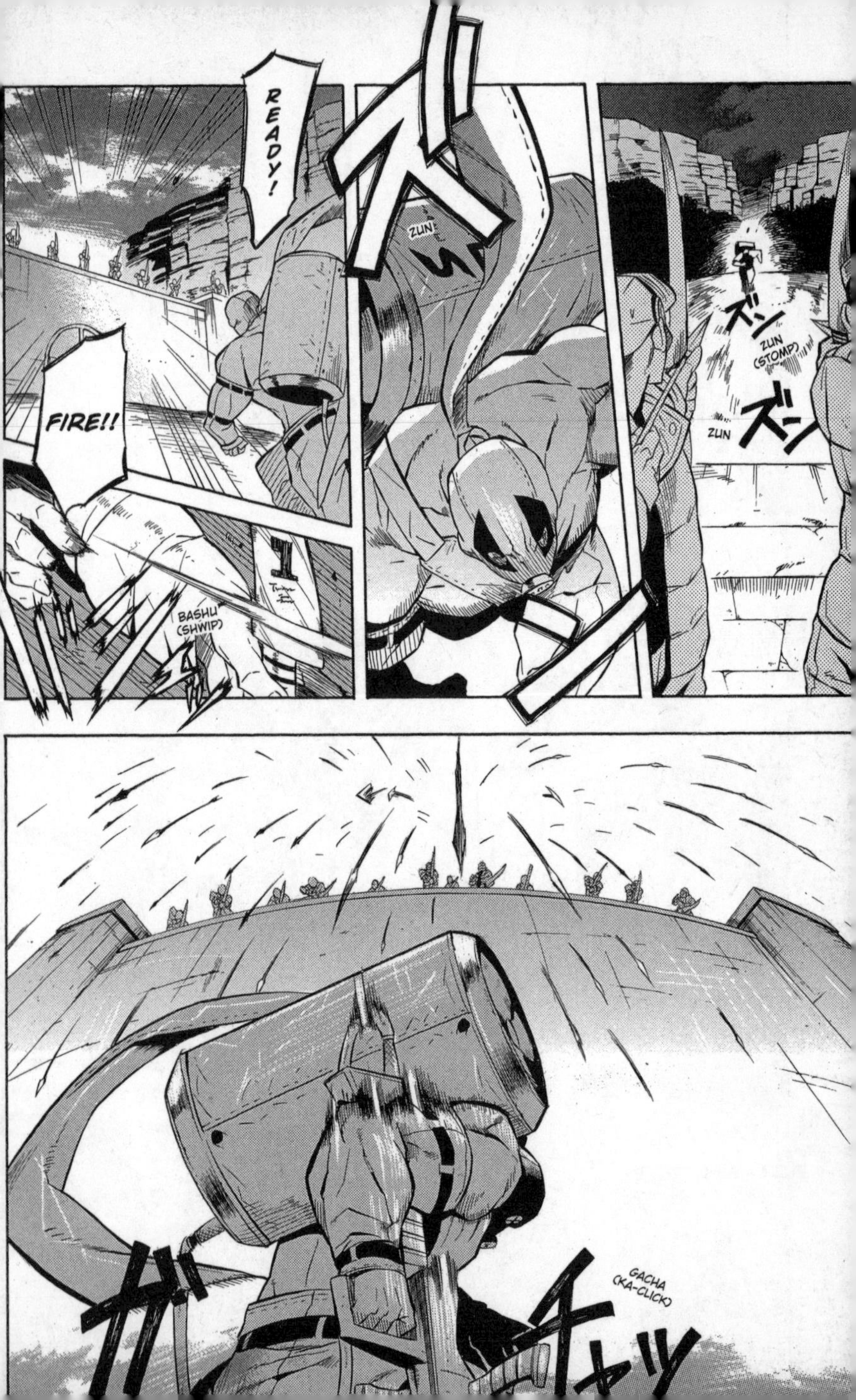
READY!
ズ
ZUN
ズン
ZUN (STOMP)
ズン
ZUN
FIRE!!
BASHU (SHWIP)
ガチャッ
GACHA (KA-CLICK)

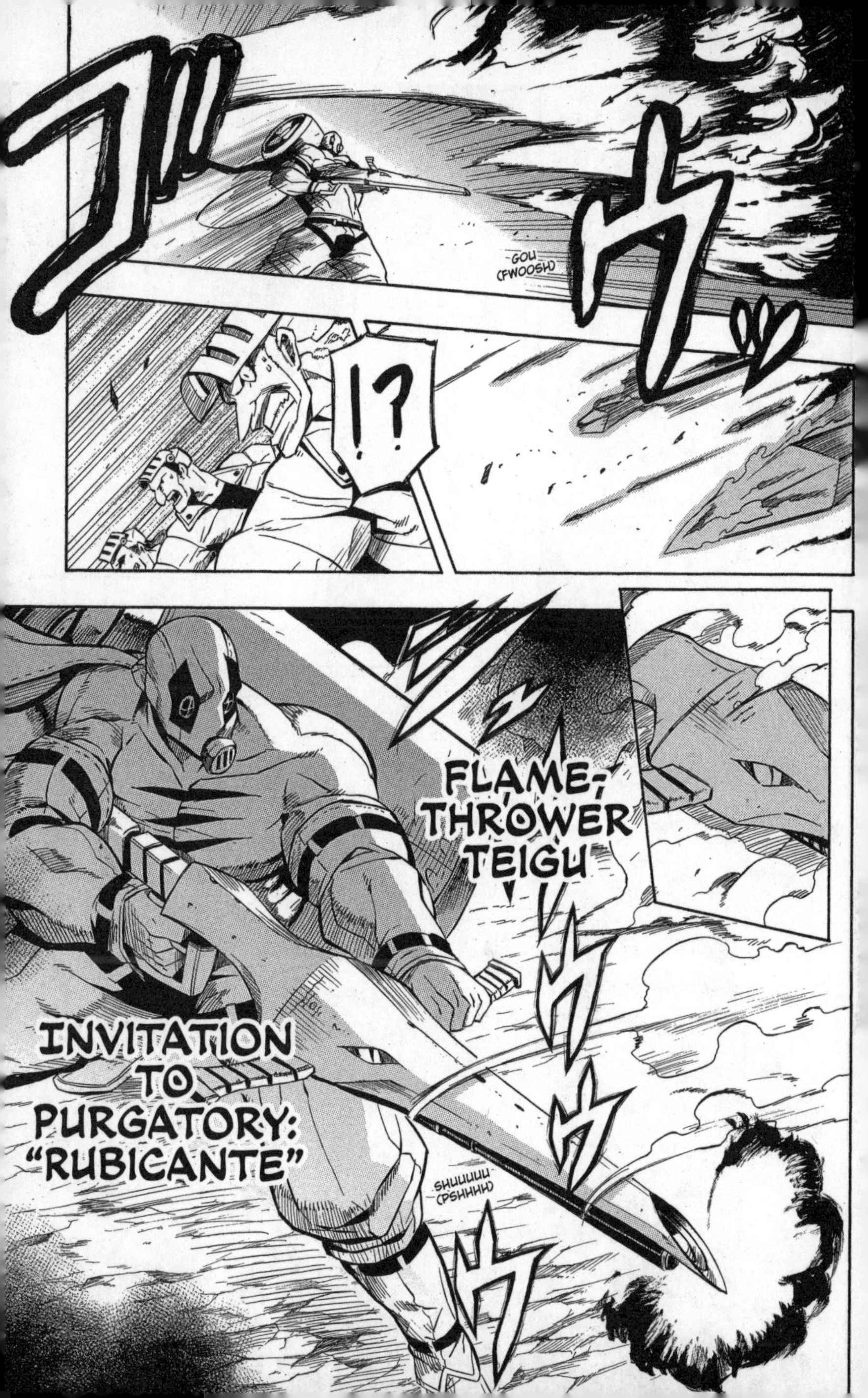
GOU
(FWOOSH)
!?
FLAME-THROWER TEIGU
INVITATION TO PURGATORY: "RUBICANTE"
SHUUUUU
(PSHHHH)

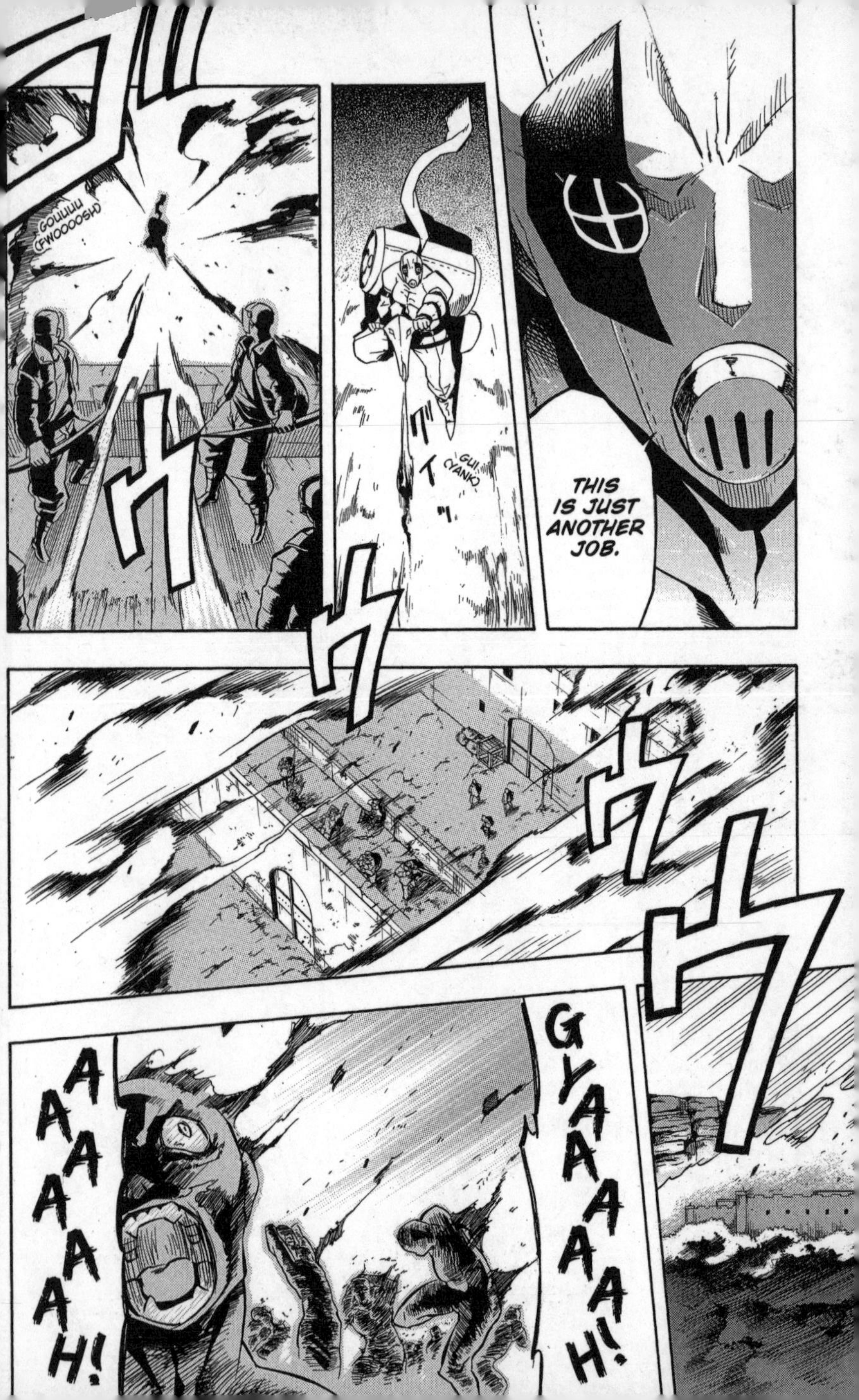
GOUUUU (FWOOOOSH)
GUI (YANK)
THIS IS JUST ANOTHER JOB.
GYAAAAAH!
AAAAAAH!

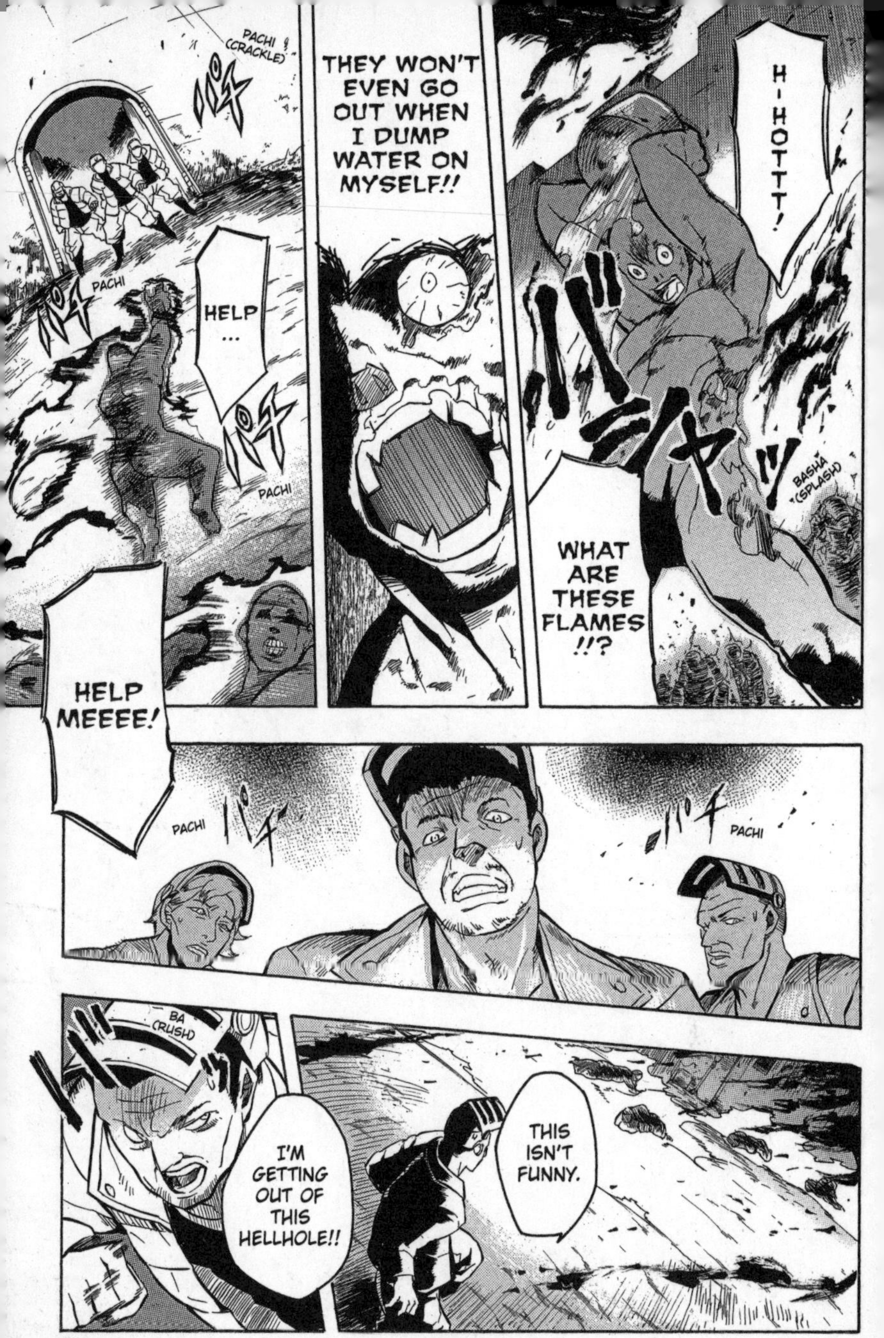

H-HOTTT!
BASHA (SPLASH)
WHAT ARE THESE FLAMES!!?
THEY WON'T EVEN GO OUT WHEN I DUMP WATER ON MYSELF!!
PACHI (CRACKLE)
PACHI
HELP...
PACHI
HELP MEEEE!
PACHI
PACHI
BA (RUSH)
THIS ISN'T FUNNY.
I'M GETTING OUT OF THIS HELLHOLE!!

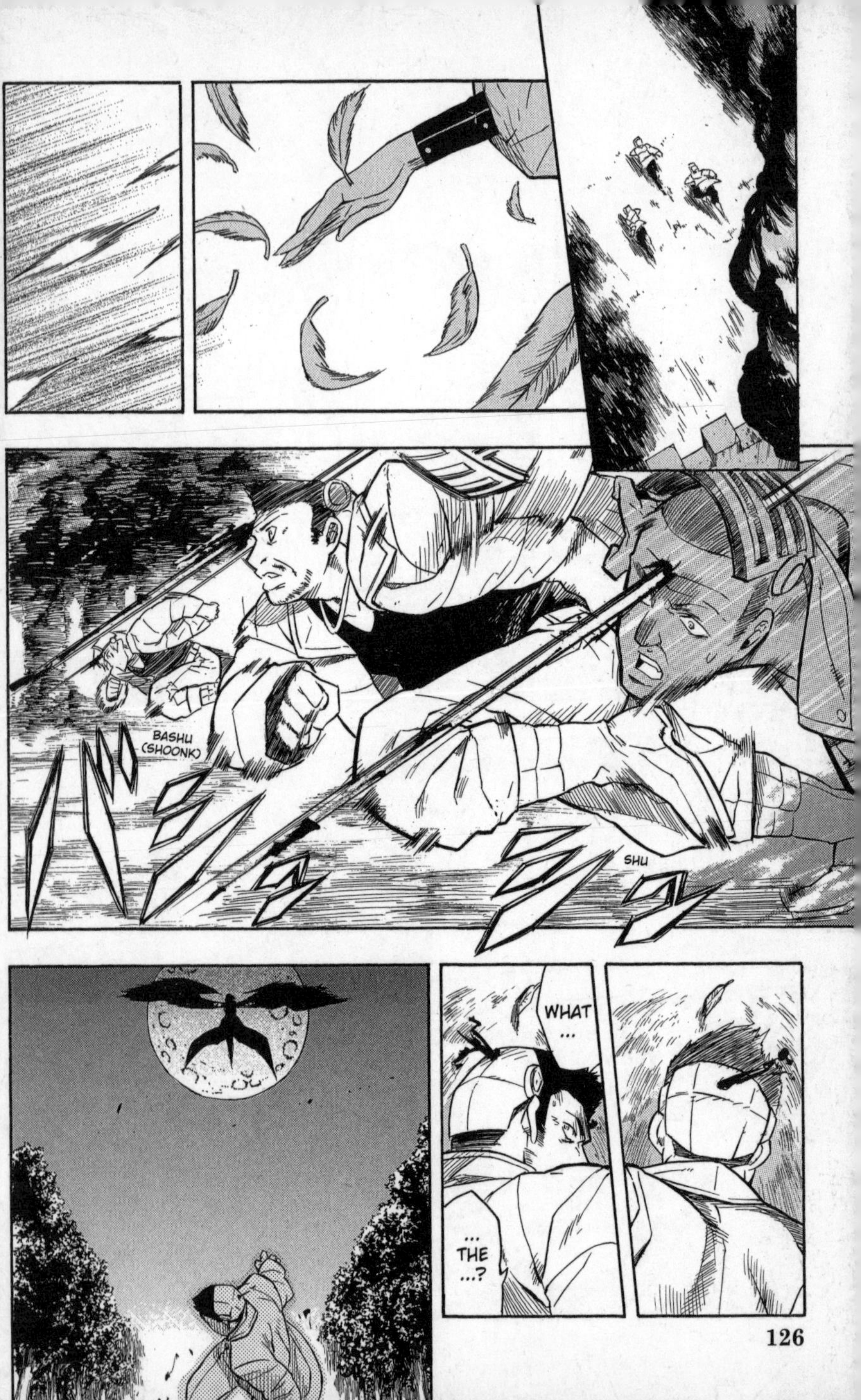
BASHU
(SHOONK)
SHU
WHAT
...
...
THE
...?

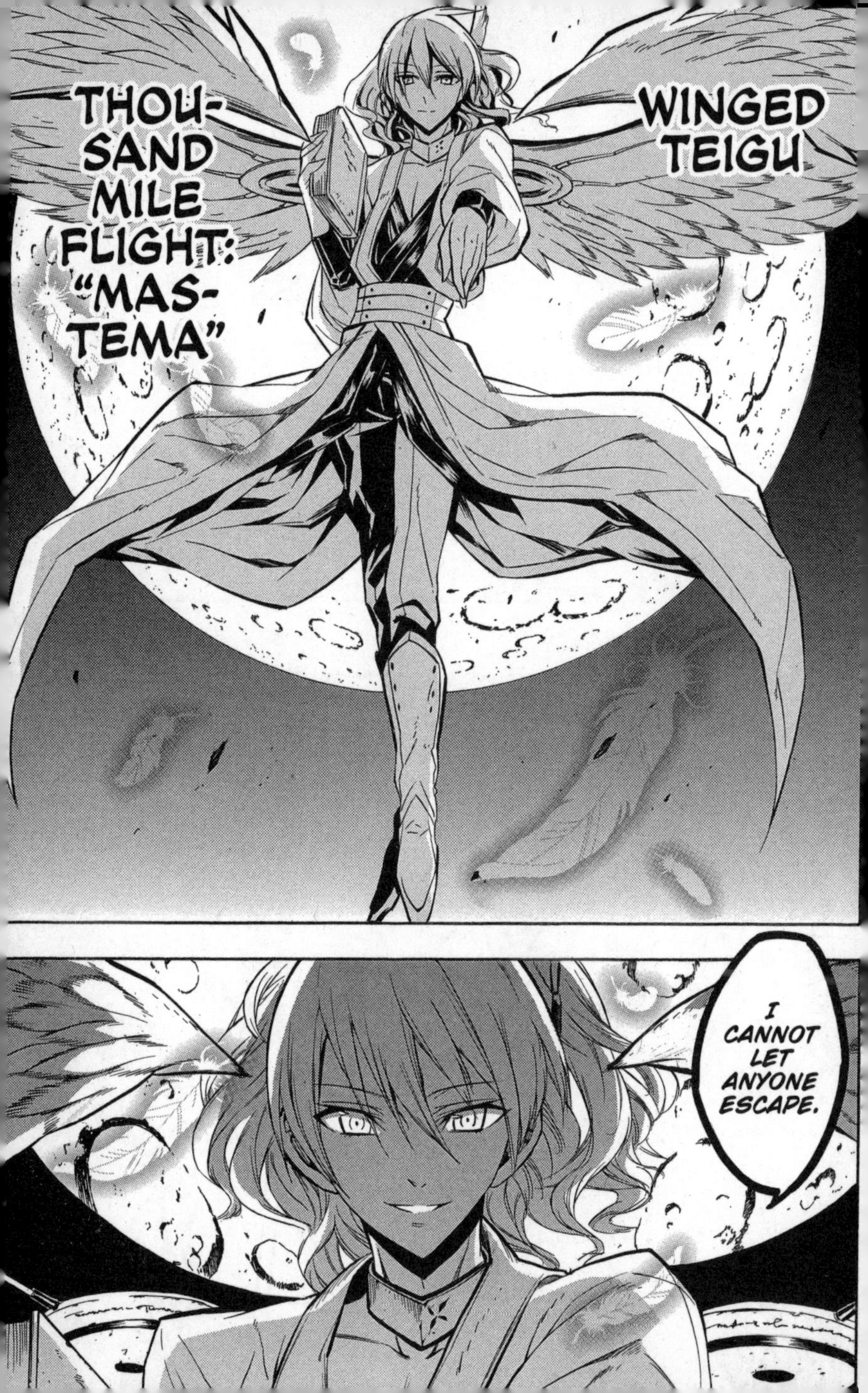
WINGED TEIGU
THOU-SAND MILE FLIGHT: "MAS-TEMA"
I CANNOT LET ANYONE ESCAPE.

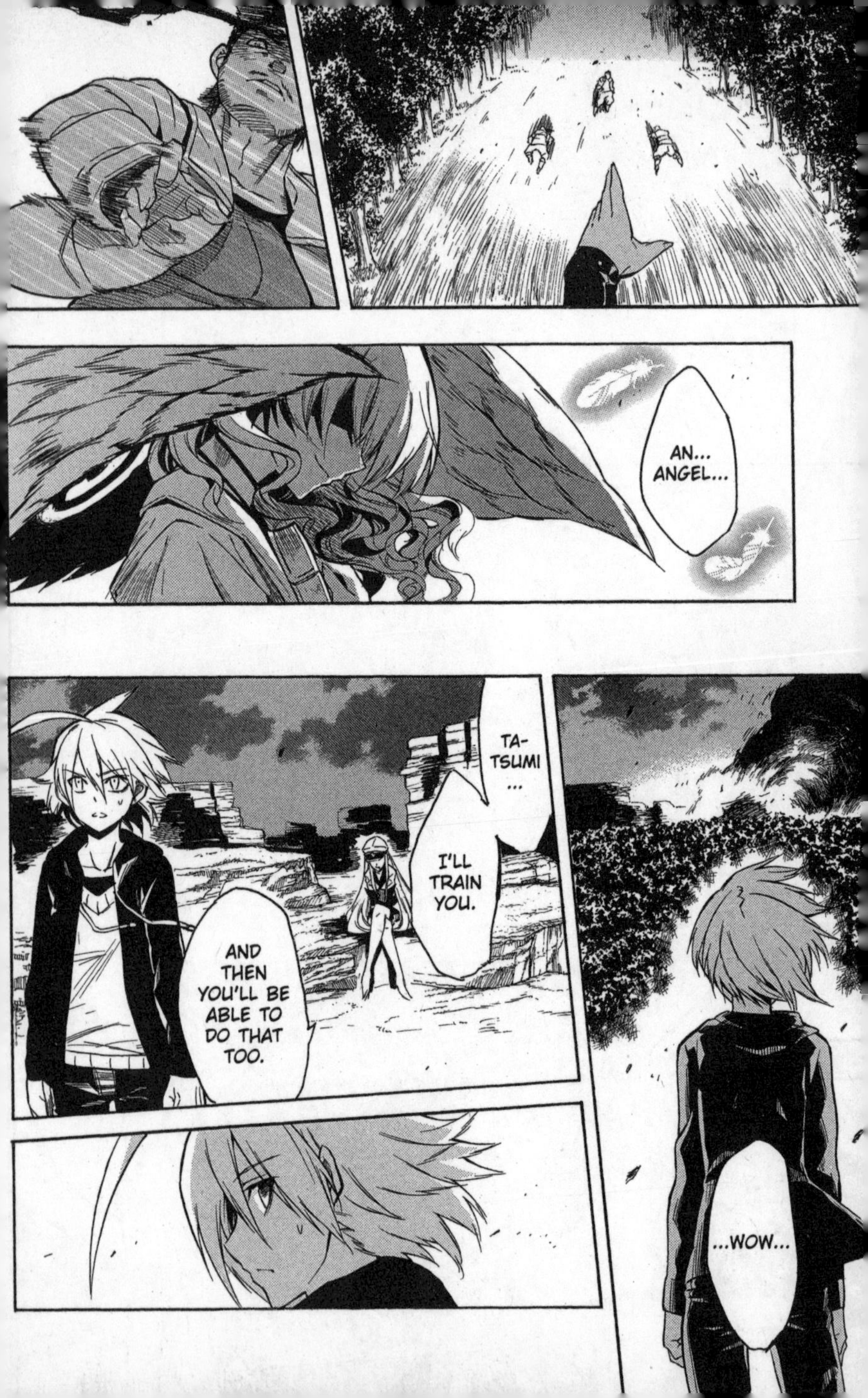
AN... ANGEL...
...WOW...
TA-TSUMI...
I'LL TRAIN YOU.
AND THEN YOU'LL BE ABLE TO DO THAT TOO.

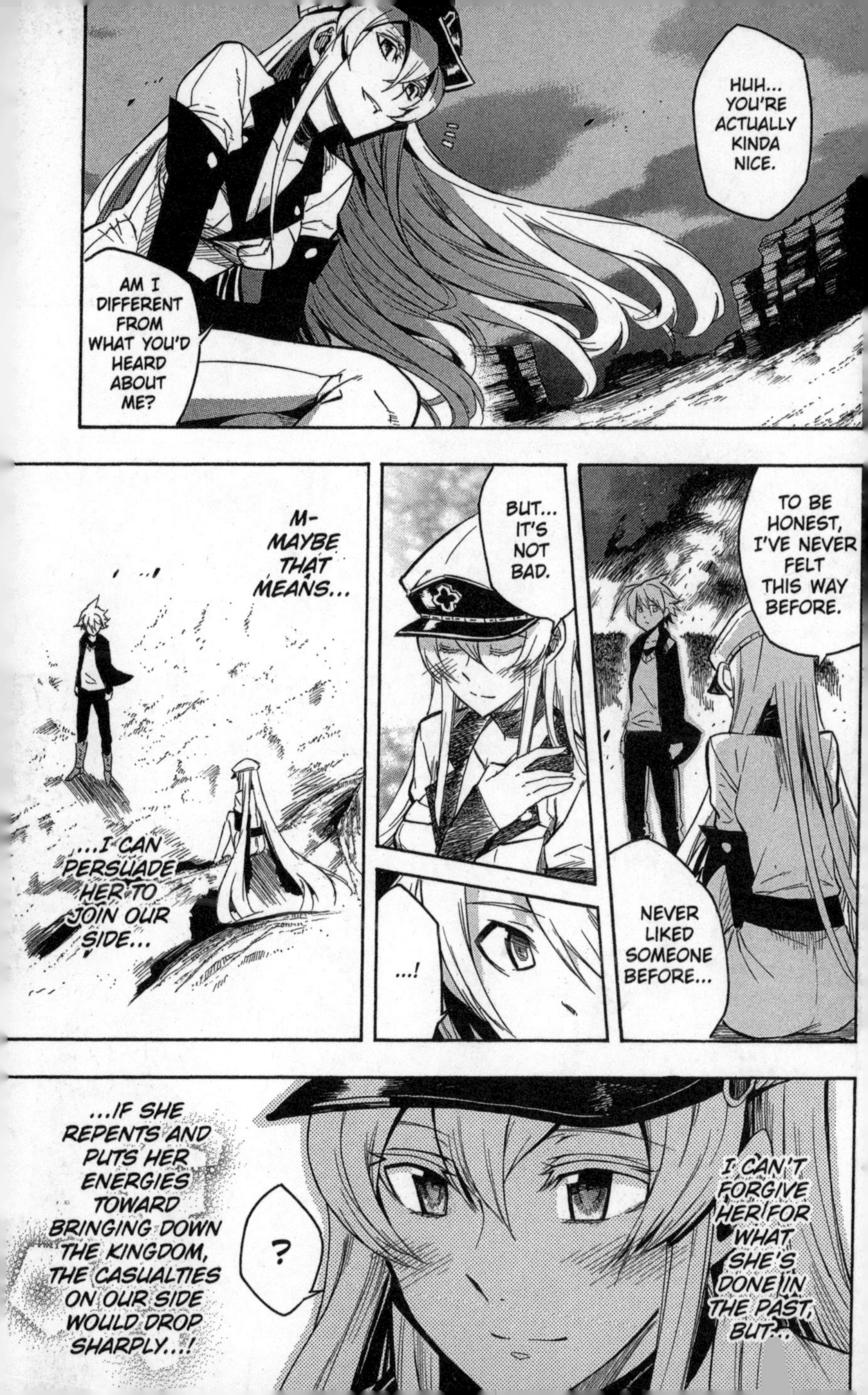
HUH... YOU'RE ACTUALLY KINDA NICE.
AM I DIFFERENT FROM WHAT YOU'D HEARD ABOUT ME?
TO BE HONEST, I'VE NEVER FELT THIS WAY BEFORE.
NEVER LIKED SOMEONE BEFORE...
BUT... IT'S NOT BAD.
...!
M-MAYBE THAT MEANS...
...I CAN PERSUADE HER TO JOIN OUR SIDE...
I CAN'T FORGIVE HER FOR WHAT SHE'S DONE IN THE PAST, BUT...
?
...IF SHE REPENTS AND PUTS HER ENERGIES TOWARD BRINGING DOWN THE KINGDOM, THE CASUALTIES ON OUR SIDE WOULD DROP SHARPLY...!

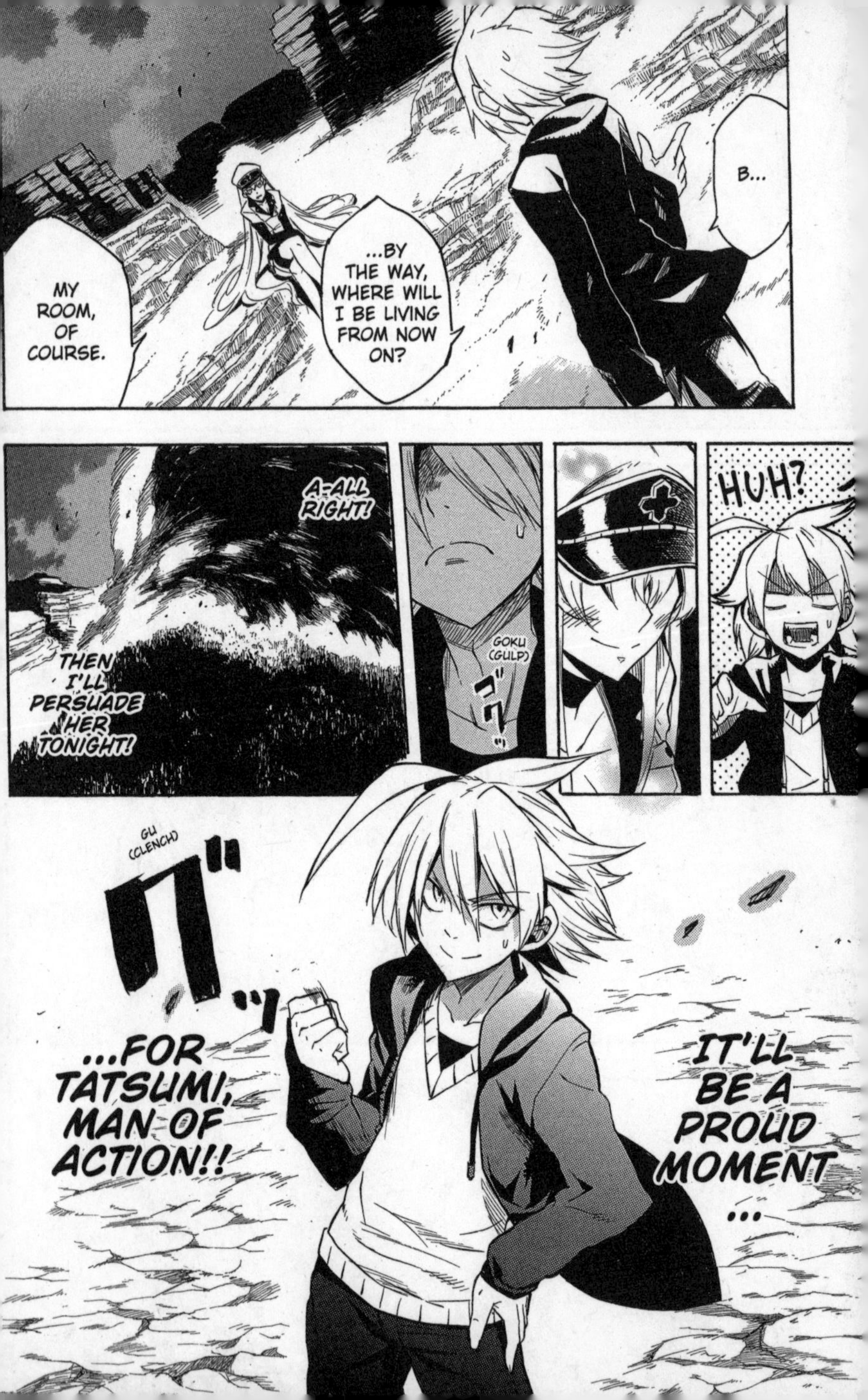
B...
...BY THE WAY, WHERE WILL I BE LIVING FROM NOW ON?
MY ROOM, OF COURSE.
HUH?
GOKU (GULP)
A-ALL RIGHT!
THEN I'LL PERSUADE HER TONIGHT!
GU (CLENCH)
IT'LL BE A PROUD MOMENT...
...FOR TATSUMI, MAN OF ACTION!!

Chapter 18 Kill the Seduction

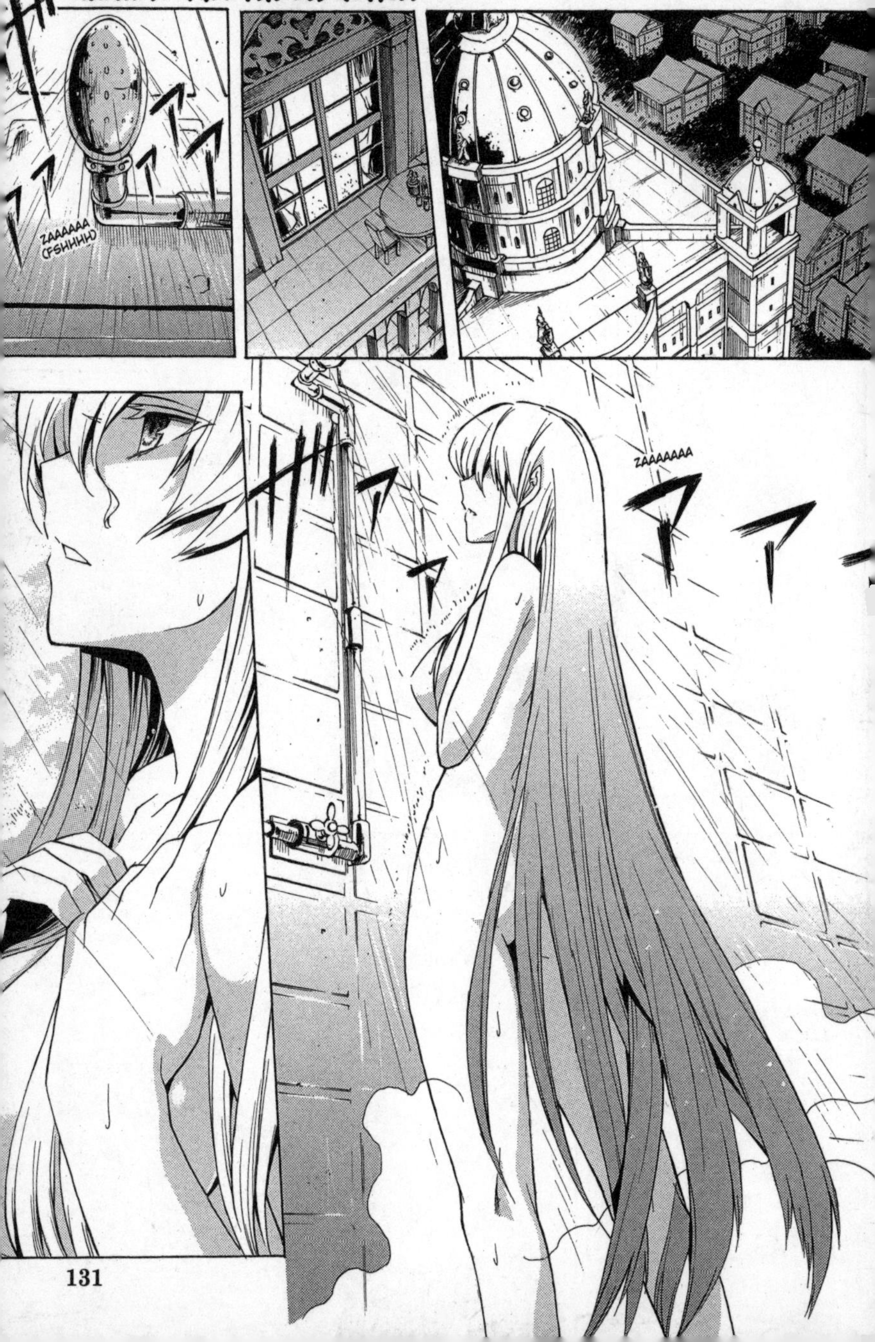
ZAAAAAA
(FSHHHH)
ZAAAAAAA

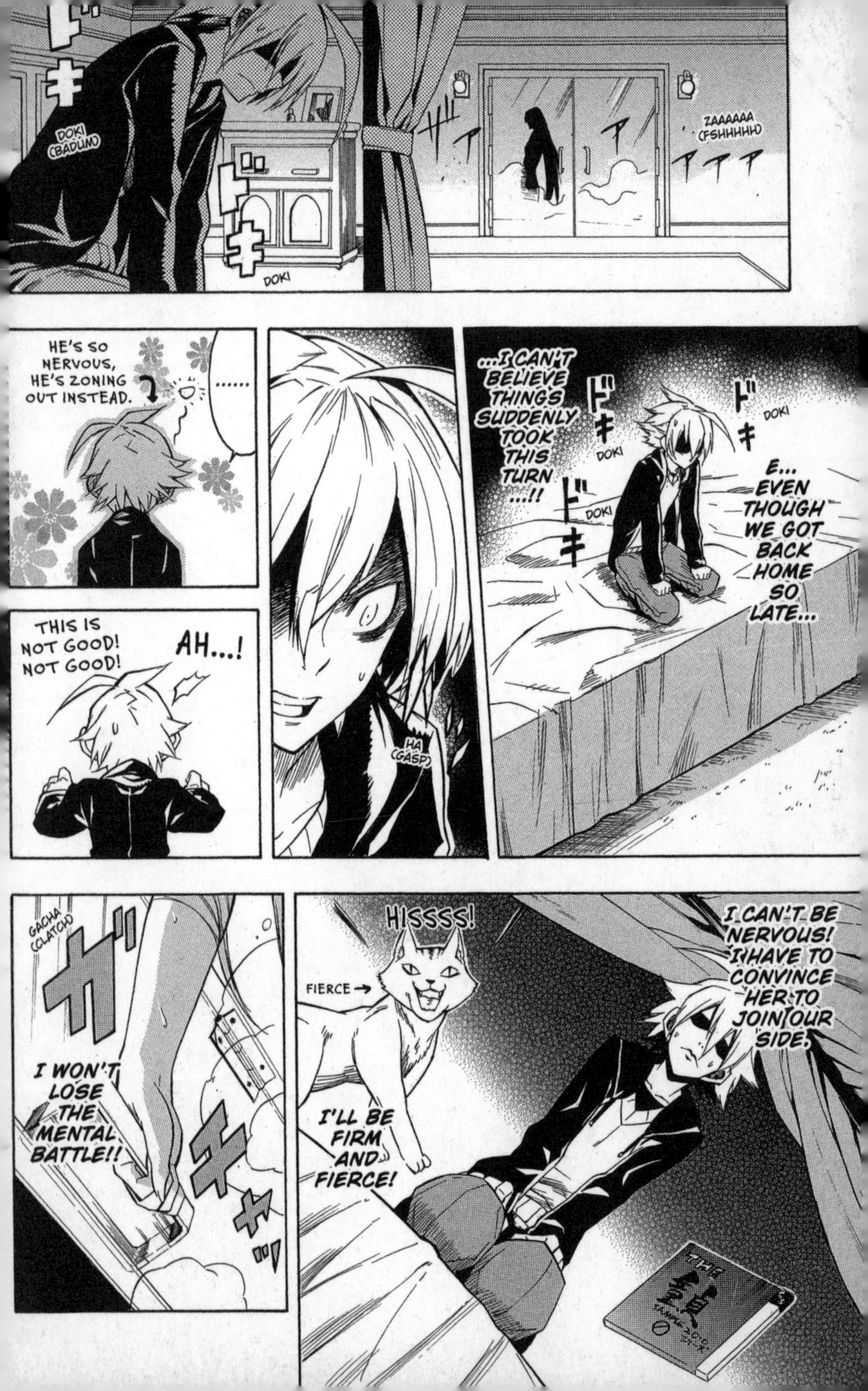
ZAAAAAA (FSHHHHH)
DOKI (BADUM)
DOKI
E... EVEN THOUGH WE GOT BACK HOME SO LATE...
DOKI
DOKI
DOKI
...I CAN'T BELIEVE THINGS SUDDENLY TOOK THIS TURN...!!
HA (GASP)
......
HE'S SO NERVOUS, HE'S ZONING OUT INSTEAD.
AH...!
THIS IS NOT GOOD! NOT GOOD!
I CAN'T BE NERVOUS! I HAVE TO CONVINCE HER TO JOIN OUR SIDE.
HISSSS!
FIERCE →
I'LL BE FIRM AND FIERCE!
GACHA (CLATCH)
I WON'T LOSE THE MENTAL BATTLE!!

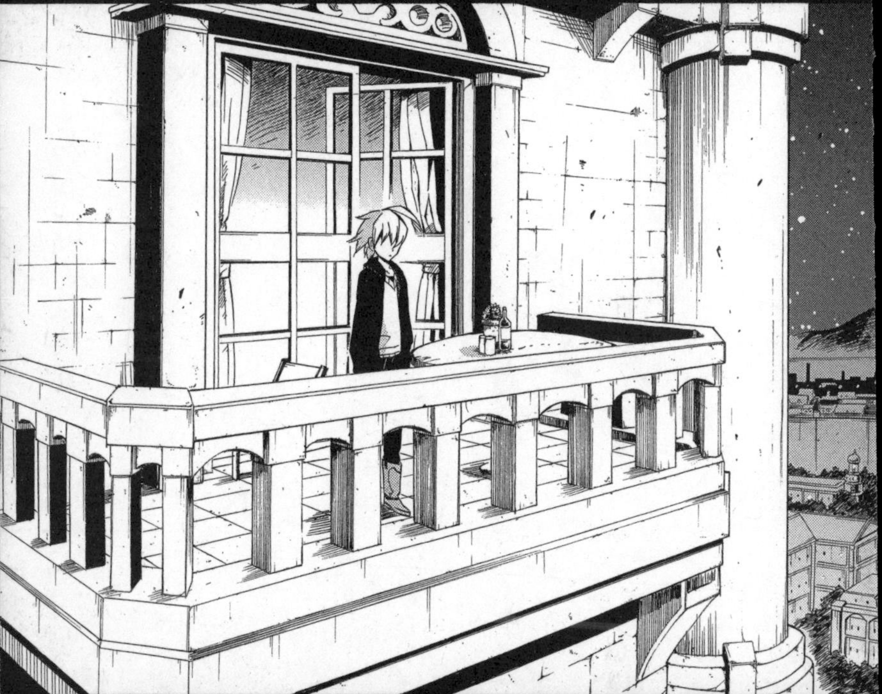

Chapter 18 KILL THE SEDUCTION

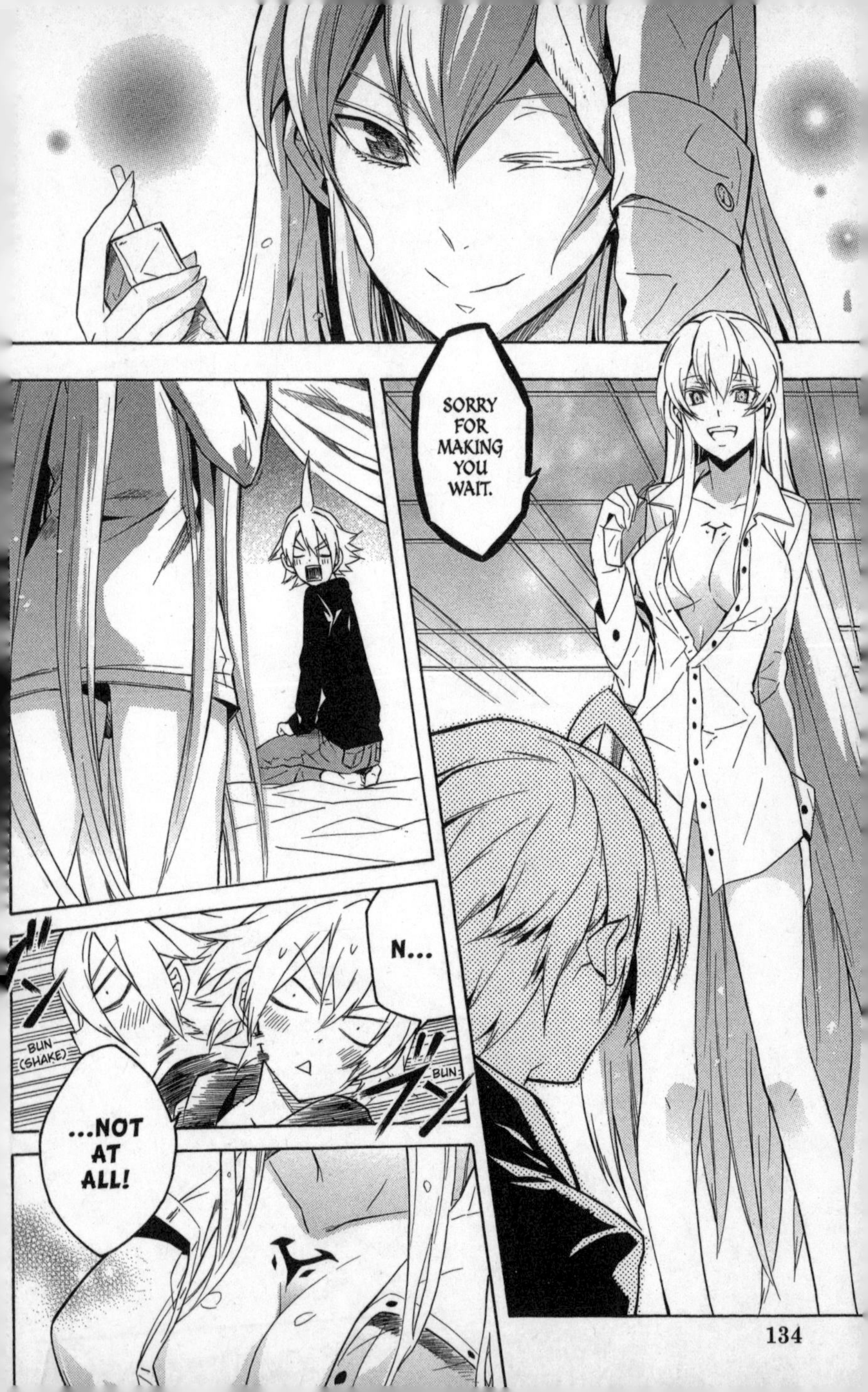
SORRY FOR MAKING YOU WAIT.
N...
BUN (SHAKE)
BUN
...NOT AT ALL!

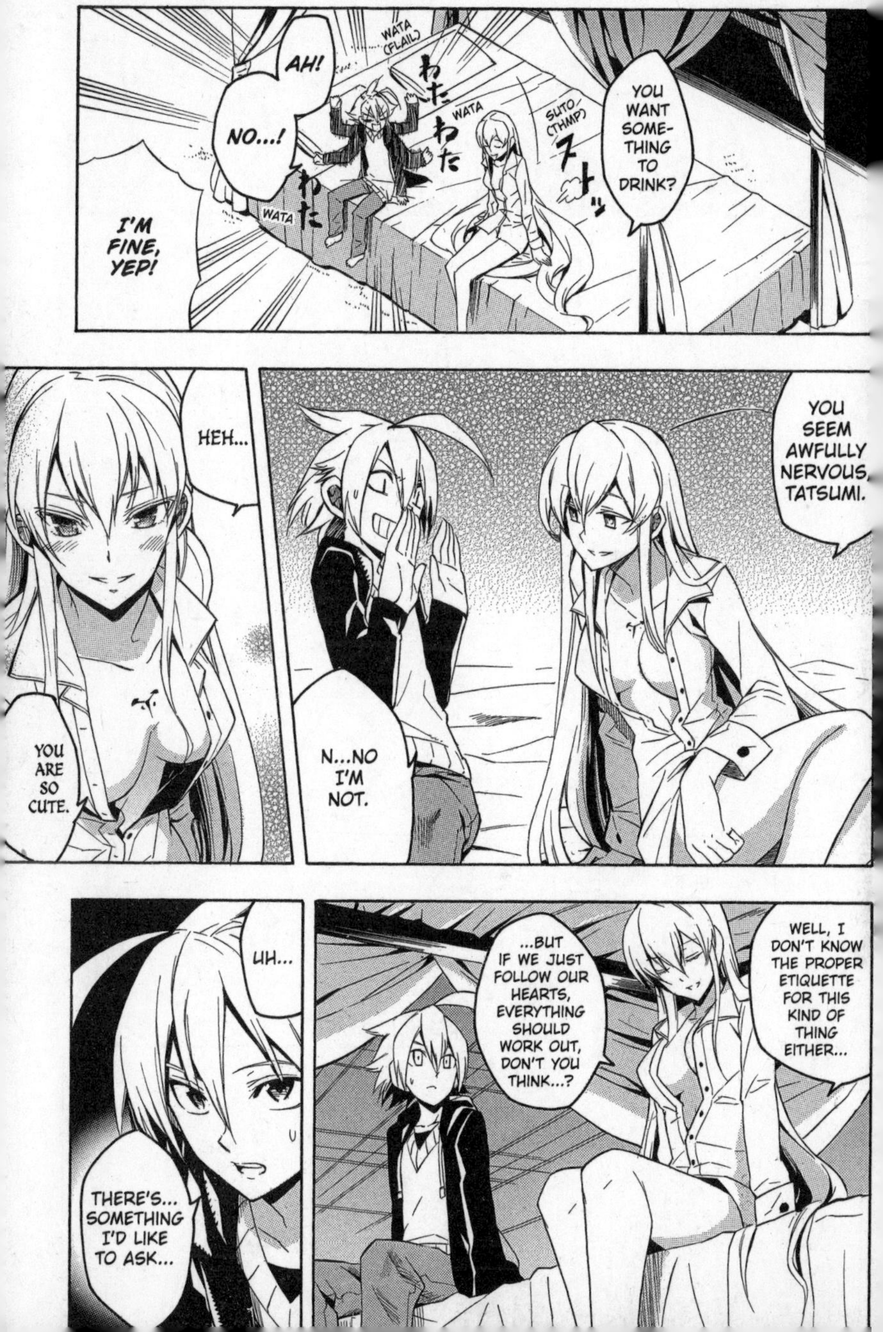
YOU WANT SOMETHING TO DRINK?
ストッ SUTO (THMP)
わた WATA (FLAIL)
わた WATA
わた WATA
AH!
NO...!
I'M FINE, YEP!
YOU SEEM AWFULLY NERVOUS, TATSUMI.
N...NO I'M NOT.
HEH...
YOU ARE SO CUTE.
WELL, I DON'T KNOW THE PROPER ETIQUETTE FOR THIS KIND OF THING EITHER...
...BUT IF WE JUST FOLLOW OUR HEARTS, EVERYTHING SHOULD WORK OUT, DON'T YOU THINK...?
UH...
THERE'S... SOMETHING I'D LIKE TO ASK...

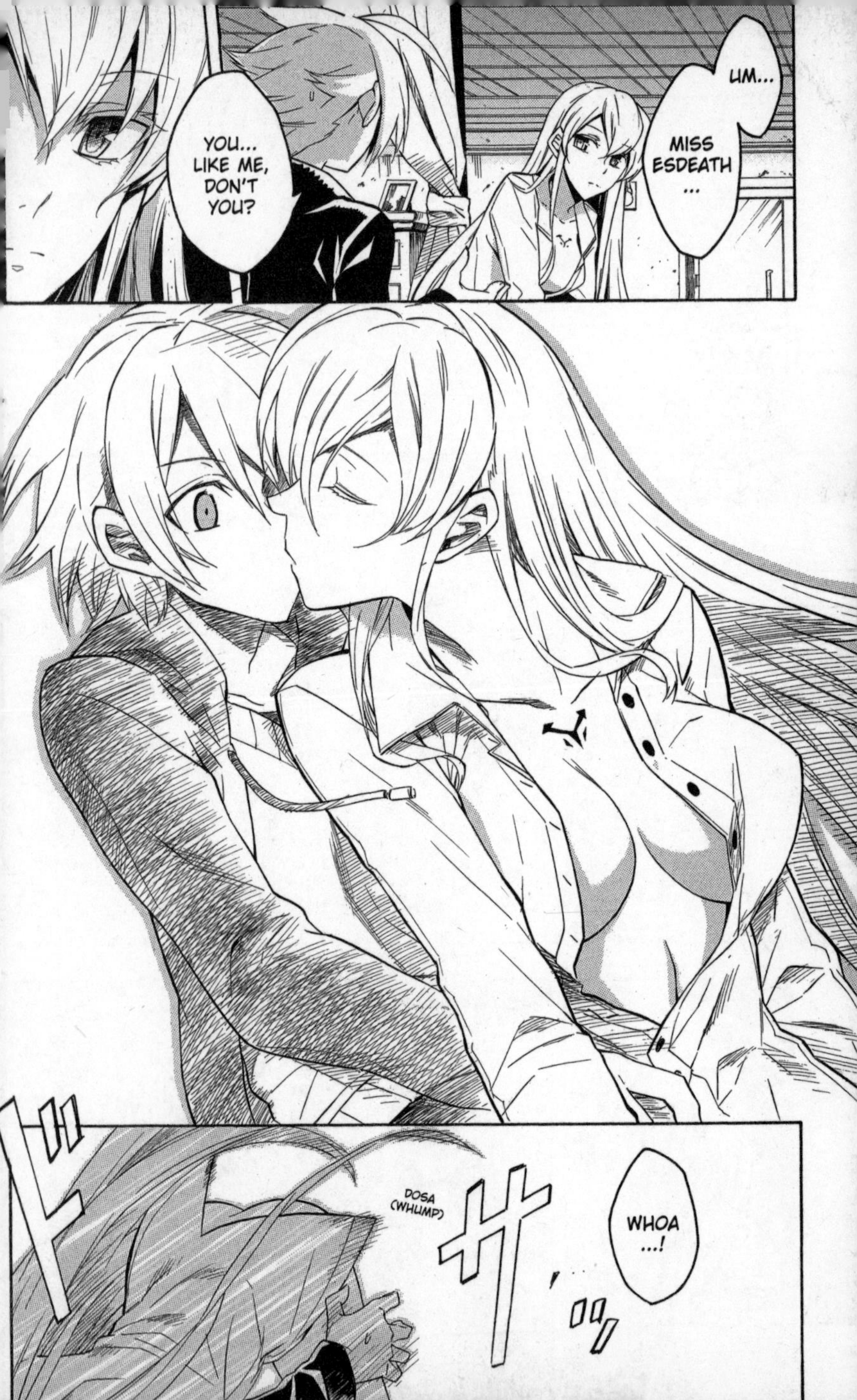
UM... MISS ESDEATH ...
YOU... LIKE ME, DON'T YOU?
WHOA ...!
DOSA (WHUMP)

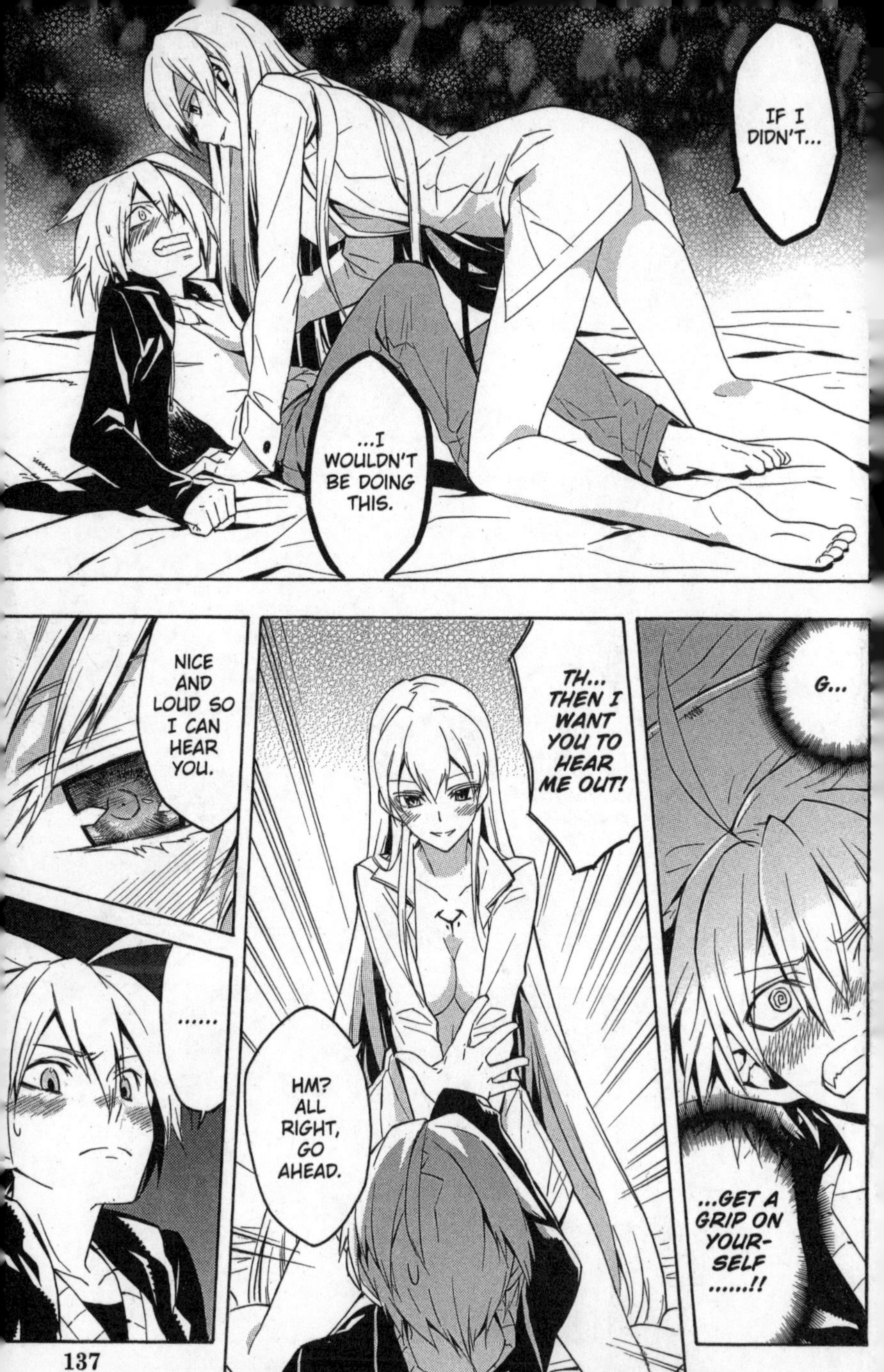
IF I DIDN'T...
...I WOULDN'T BE DOING THIS.
G...
...GET A GRIP ON YOURSELF ......!!
TH... THEN I WANT YOU TO HEAR ME OUT!
HM? ALL RIGHT, GO AHEAD.
NICE AND LOUD SO I CAN HEAR YOU.
......

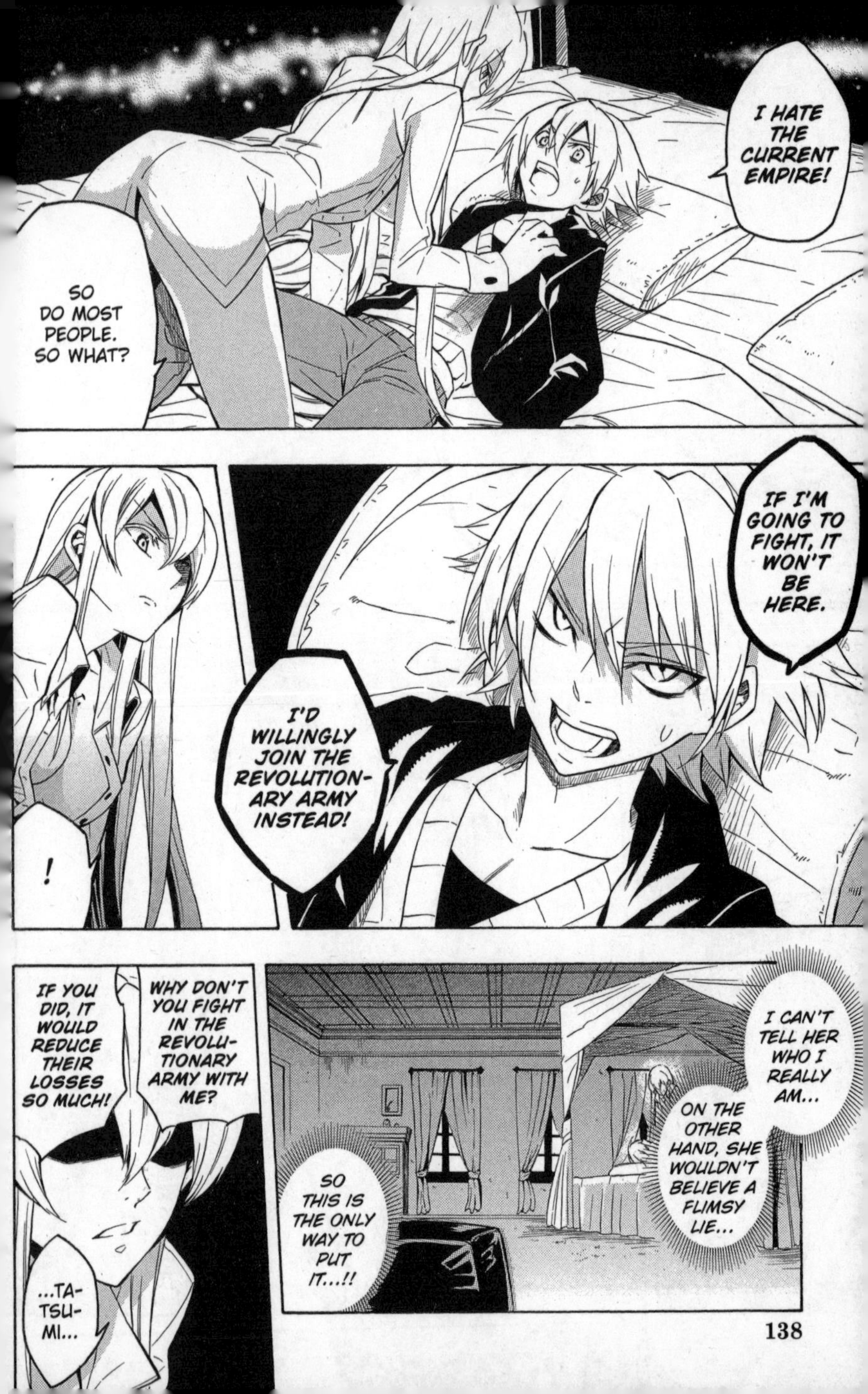
I HATE THE CURRENT EMPIRE!
SO DO MOST PEOPLE. SO WHAT?
IF I'M GOING TO FIGHT, IT WON'T BE HERE.
I'D WILLINGLY JOIN THE REVOLUTIONARY ARMY INSTEAD!
!
I CAN'T TELL HER WHO I REALLY AM...
ON THE OTHER HAND, SHE WOULDN'T BELIEVE A FLIMSY LIE...
SO THIS IS THE ONLY WAY TO PUT IT...!!
WHY DON'T YOU FIGHT IN THE REVOLUTIONARY ARMY WITH ME?
IF YOU DID, IT WOULD REDUCE THEIR LOSSES SO MUCH!
...TA-TSU-MI...

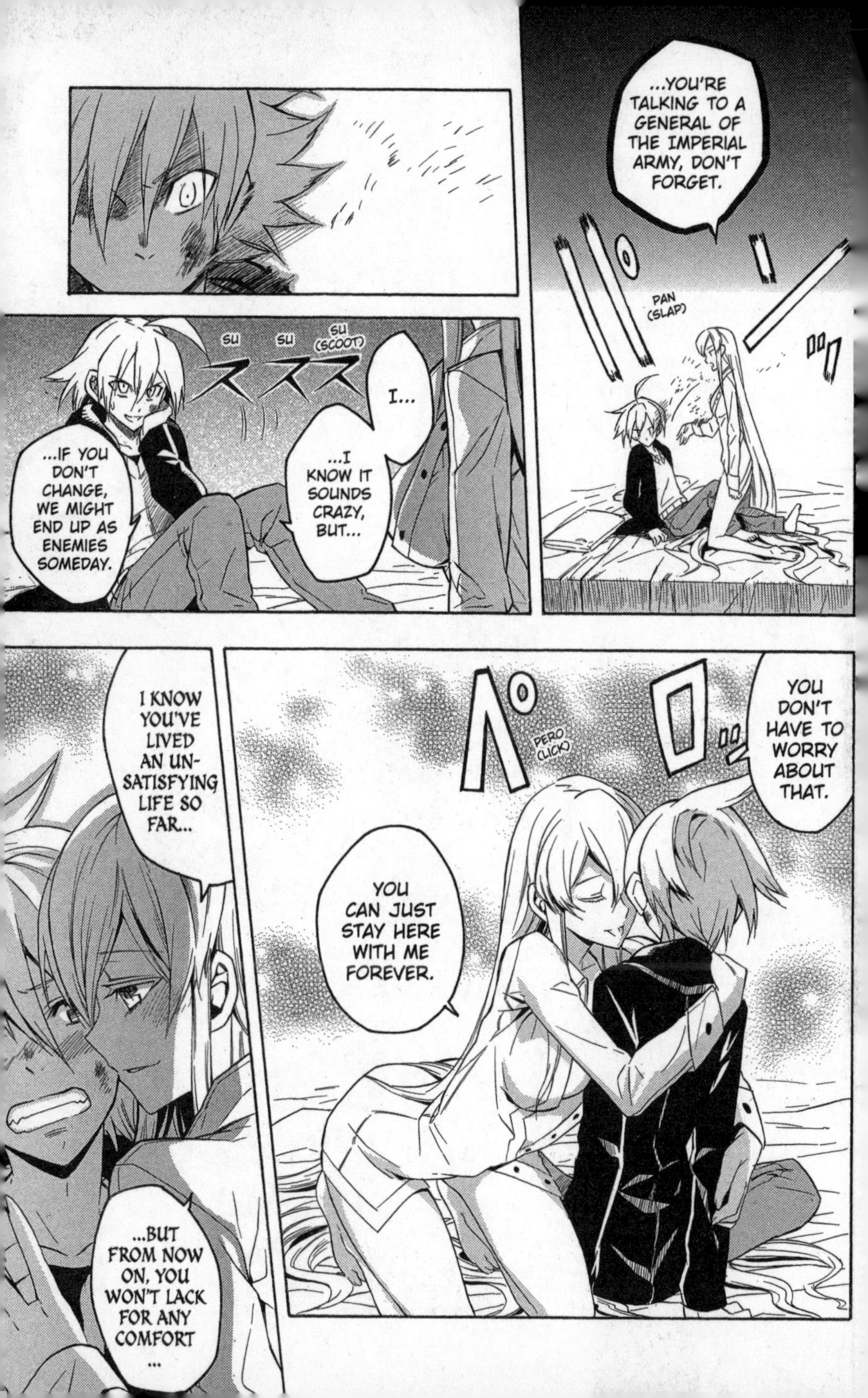

SU SU SU (SCOOT)
I...
...I KNOW IT SOUNDS CRAZY, BUT...
...IF YOU DON'T CHANGE, WE MIGHT END UP AS ENEMIES SOMEDAY.
...YOU'RE TALKING TO A GENERAL OF THE IMPERIAL ARMY, DON'T FORGET.
PAN (SLAP)
YOU DON'T HAVE TO WORRY ABOUT THAT.
PERO (LICK)
YOU CAN JUST STAY HERE WITH ME FOREVER.
I KNOW YOU'VE LIVED AN UN-SATISFYING LIFE SO FAR...
...BUT FROM NOW ON, YOU WON'T LACK FOR ANY COMFORT ...

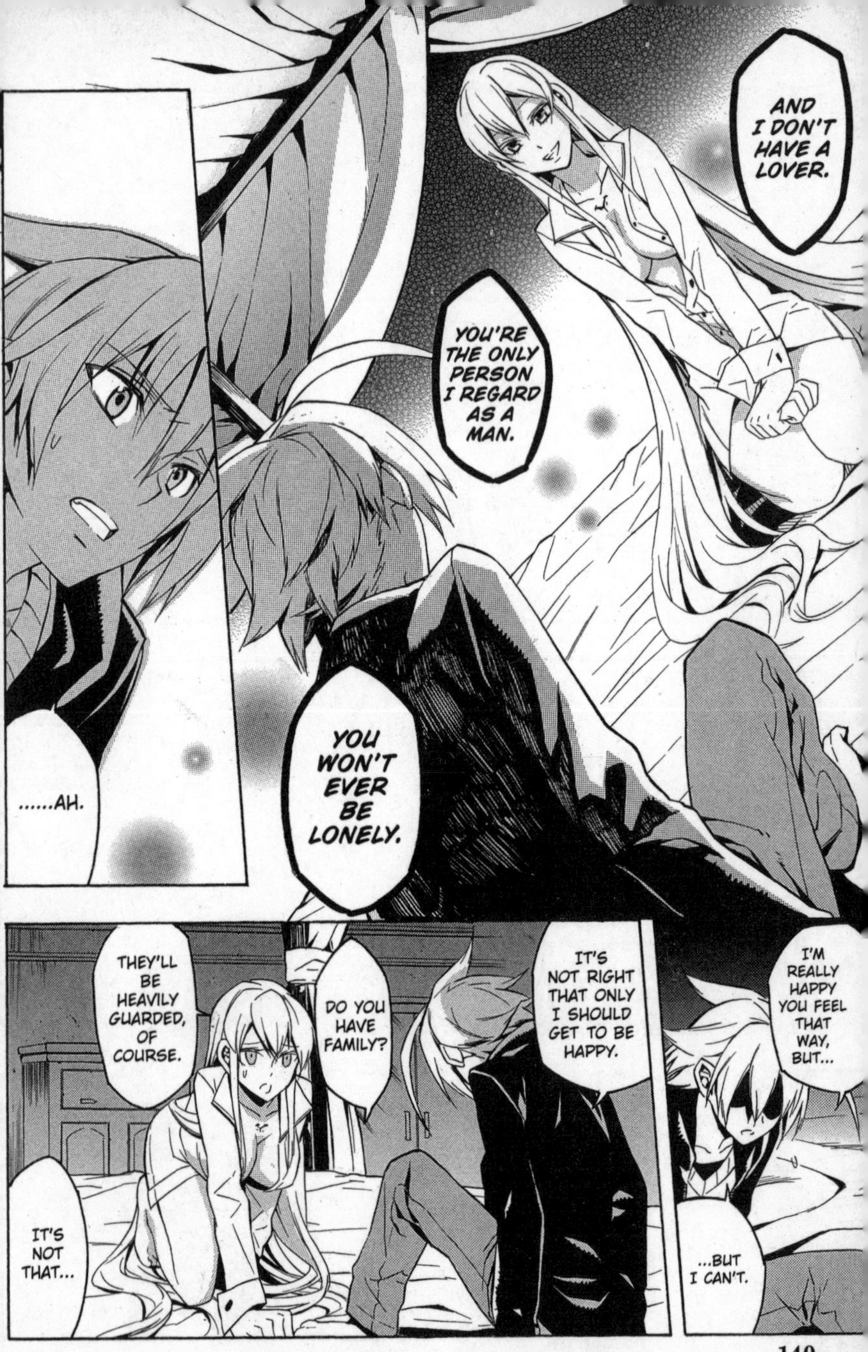
AND I DON'T HAVE A LOVER.
YOU'RE THE ONLY PERSON I REGARD AS A MAN.
YOU WON'T EVER BE LONELY.
......AH.
I'M REALLY HAPPY YOU FEEL THAT WAY, BUT...
...BUT I CAN'T.
IT'S NOT RIGHT THAT ONLY I SHOULD GET TO BE HAPPY.
DO YOU HAVE FAMILY?
THEY'LL BE HEAVILY GUARDED, OF COURSE.
IT'S NOT THAT...

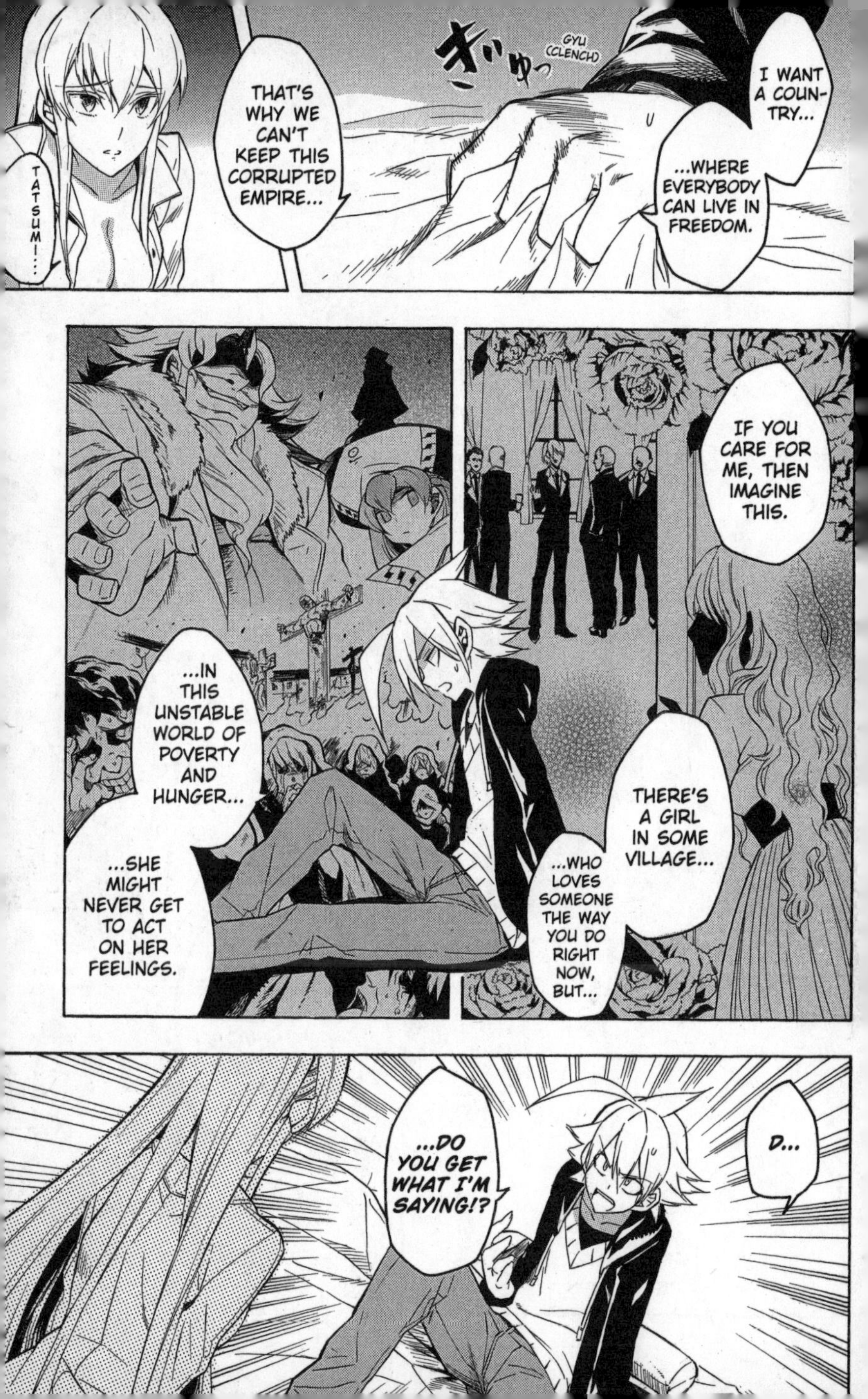
I WANT A COUNTRY...
...WHERE EVERYBODY CAN LIVE IN FREEDOM.
ぎゅっ
GYU (CLENCH)
THAT'S WHY WE CAN'T KEEP THIS CORRUPTED EMPIRE...
TATSUMI...
IF YOU CARE FOR ME, THEN IMAGINE THIS.
THERE'S A GIRL IN SOME VILLAGE...
...WHO LOVES SOMEONE THE WAY YOU DO RIGHT NOW, BUT...
...IN THIS UNSTABLE WORLD OF POVERTY AND HUNGER...
...SHE MIGHT NEVER GET TO ACT ON HER FEELINGS.
D...
...DO YOU GET WHAT I'M SAYING!?

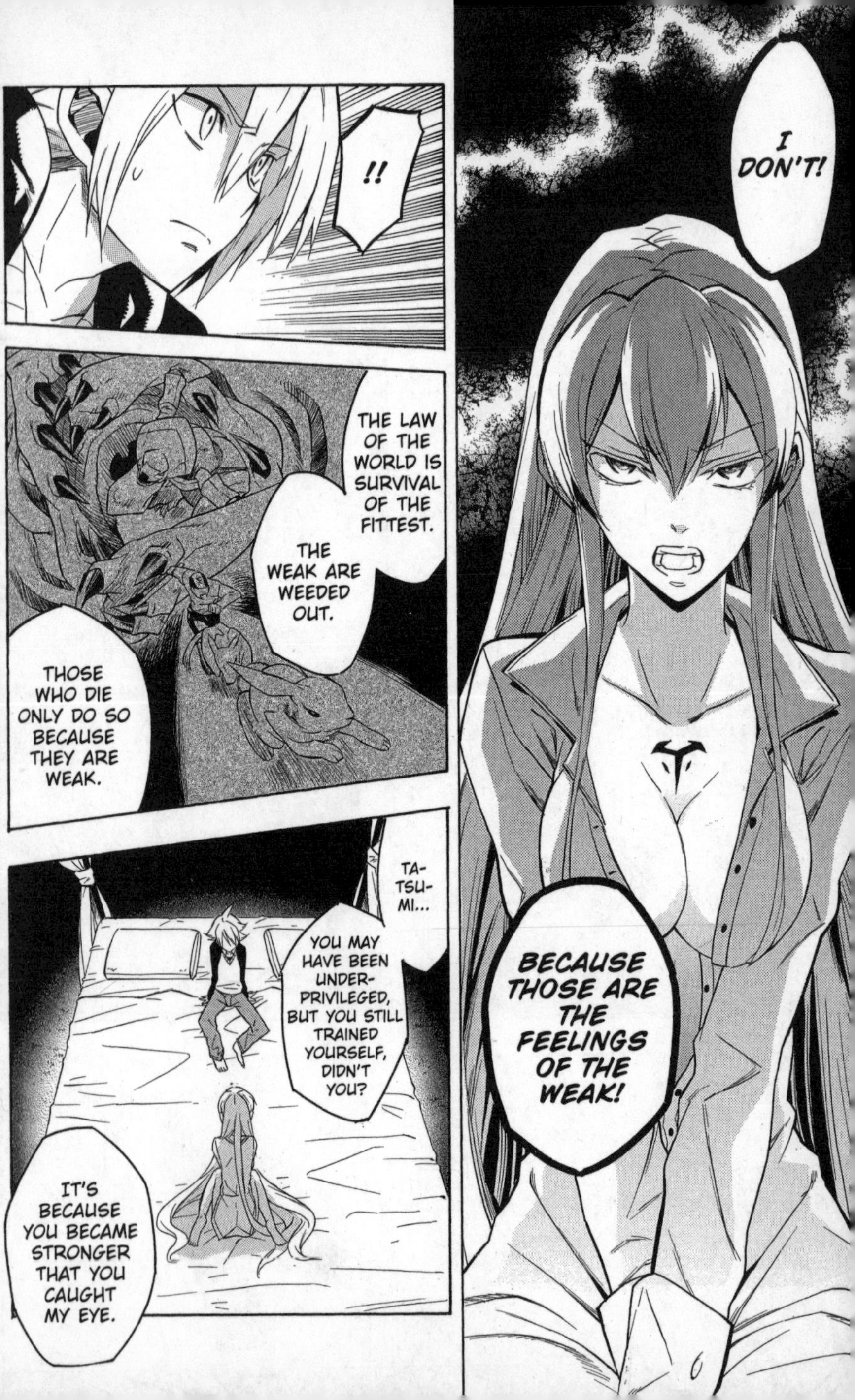

I DON'T!
BECAUSE THOSE ARE THE FEELINGS OF THE WEAK!
!!
THE LAW OF THE WORLD IS SURVIVAL OF THE FITTEST.
THE WEAK ARE WEEDED OUT.
THOSE WHO DIE ONLY DO SO BECAUSE THEY ARE WEAK.
TA-TSU-MI...
YOU MAY HAVE BEEN UNDER-PRIVILEGED, BUT YOU STILL TRAINED YOURSELF, DIDN'T YOU?
IT'S BECAUSE YOU BECAME STRONGER THAT YOU CAUGHT MY EYE.

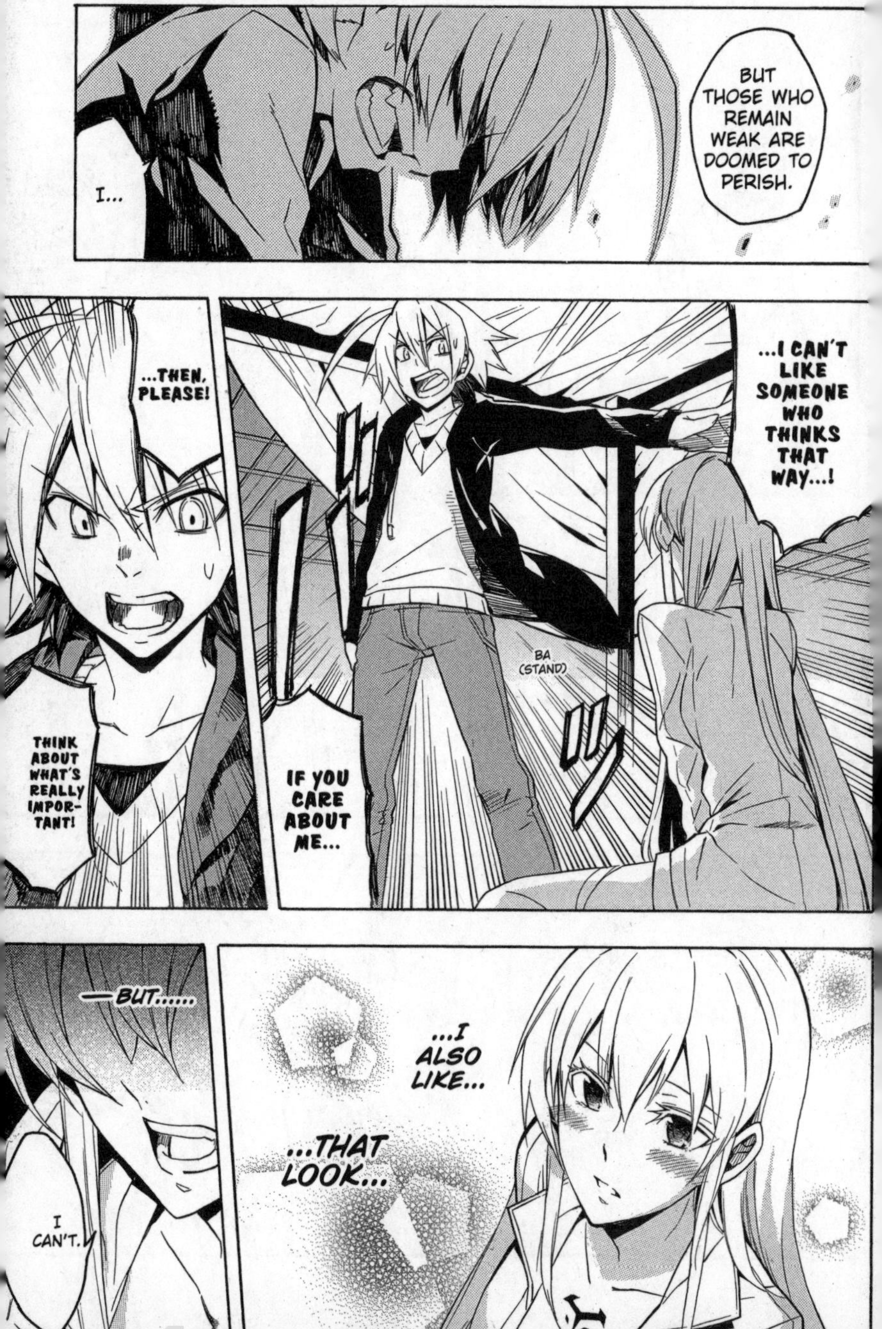
BUT THOSE WHO REMAIN WEAK ARE DOOMED TO PERISH.
I...
...I CAN'T LIKE SOMEONE WHO THINKS THAT WAY...!
BA (STAND)
IF YOU CARE ABOUT ME...
...THEN, PLEASE!
THINK ABOUT WHAT'S REALLY IMPORTANT!
...I ALSO LIKE...
...THAT LOOK...
—BUT......
I CAN'T.

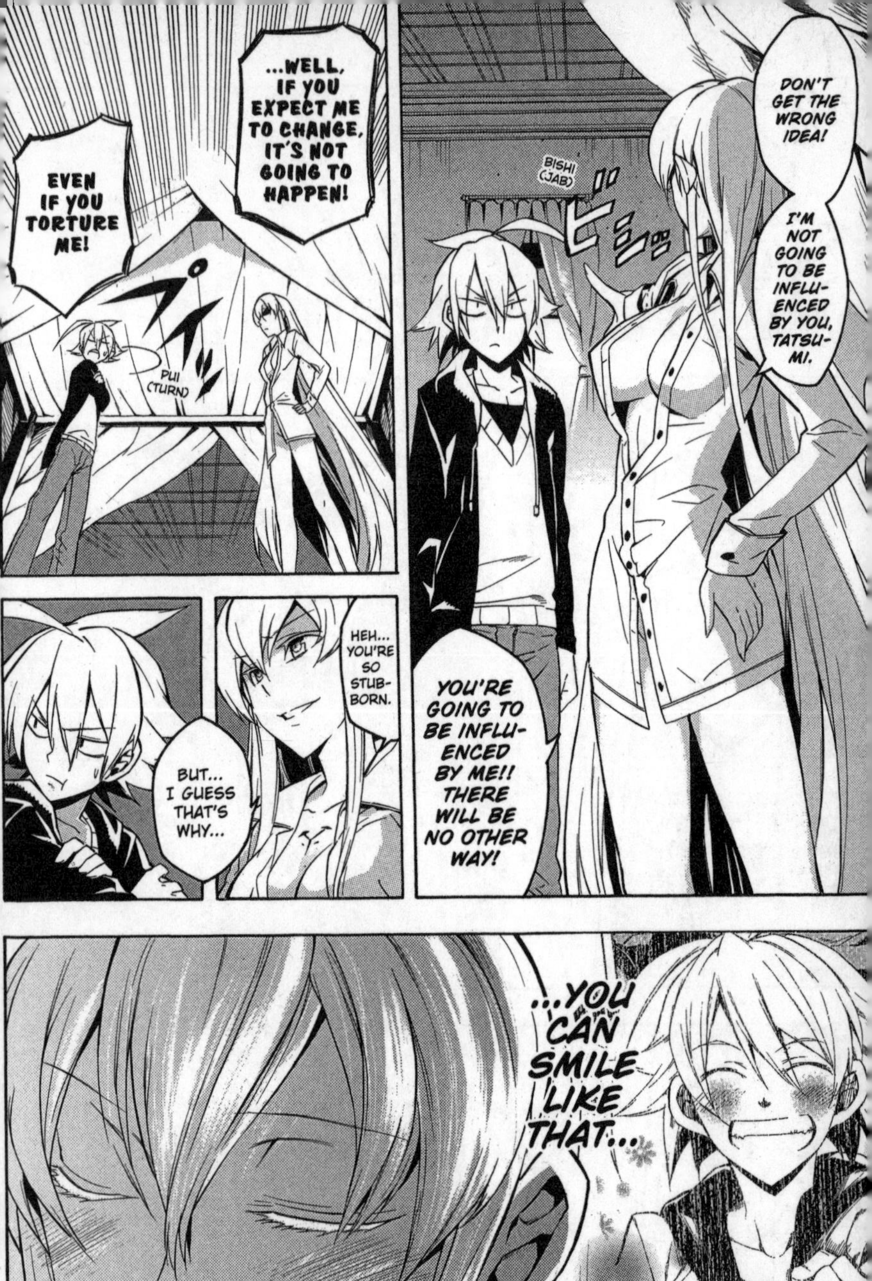
DON'T GET THE WRONG IDEA!
I'M NOT GOING TO BE INFLUENCED BY YOU, TATSUMI.
BISHI (JAB)
YOU'RE GOING TO BE INFLUENCED BY ME!! THERE WILL BE NO OTHER WAY!
...WELL, IF YOU EXPECT ME TO CHANGE, IT'S NOT GOING TO HAPPEN!
EVEN IF YOU TORTURE ME!
PUI (TURN)
HEH... YOU'RE SO STUBBORN.
BUT... I GUESS THAT'S WHY...
...YOU CAN SMILE LIKE THAT...

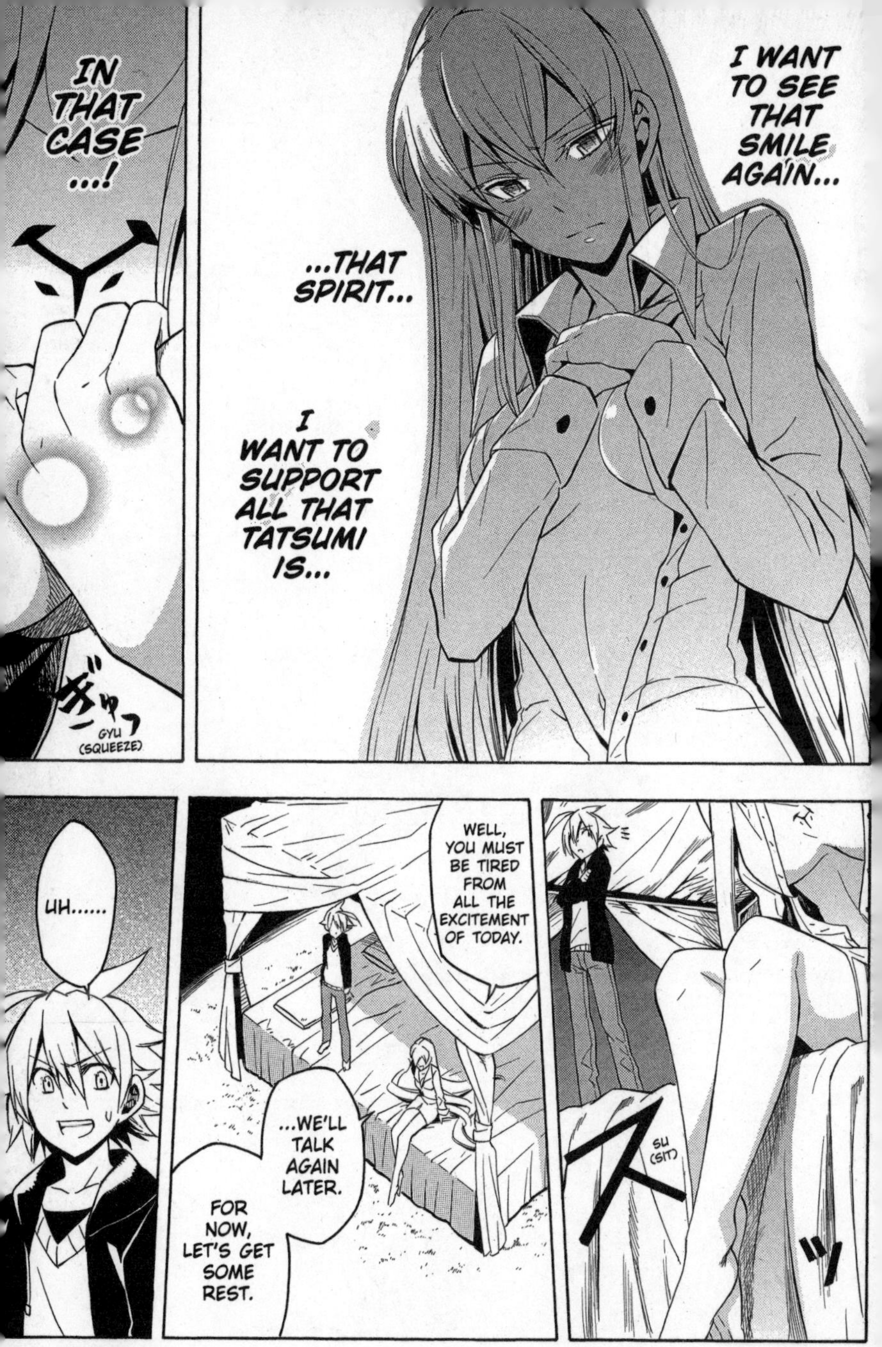
I WANT TO SEE THAT SMILE AGAIN...
...THAT SPIRIT...
I WANT TO SUPPORT ALL THAT TATSUMI IS...
IN THAT CASE ...!
GYU (SQUEEZE)
SU (SIT)
WELL, YOU MUST BE TIRED FROM ALL THE EXCITEMENT OF TODAY.
...WE'LL TALK AGAIN LATER.
FOR NOW, LET'S GET SOME REST.
UH......

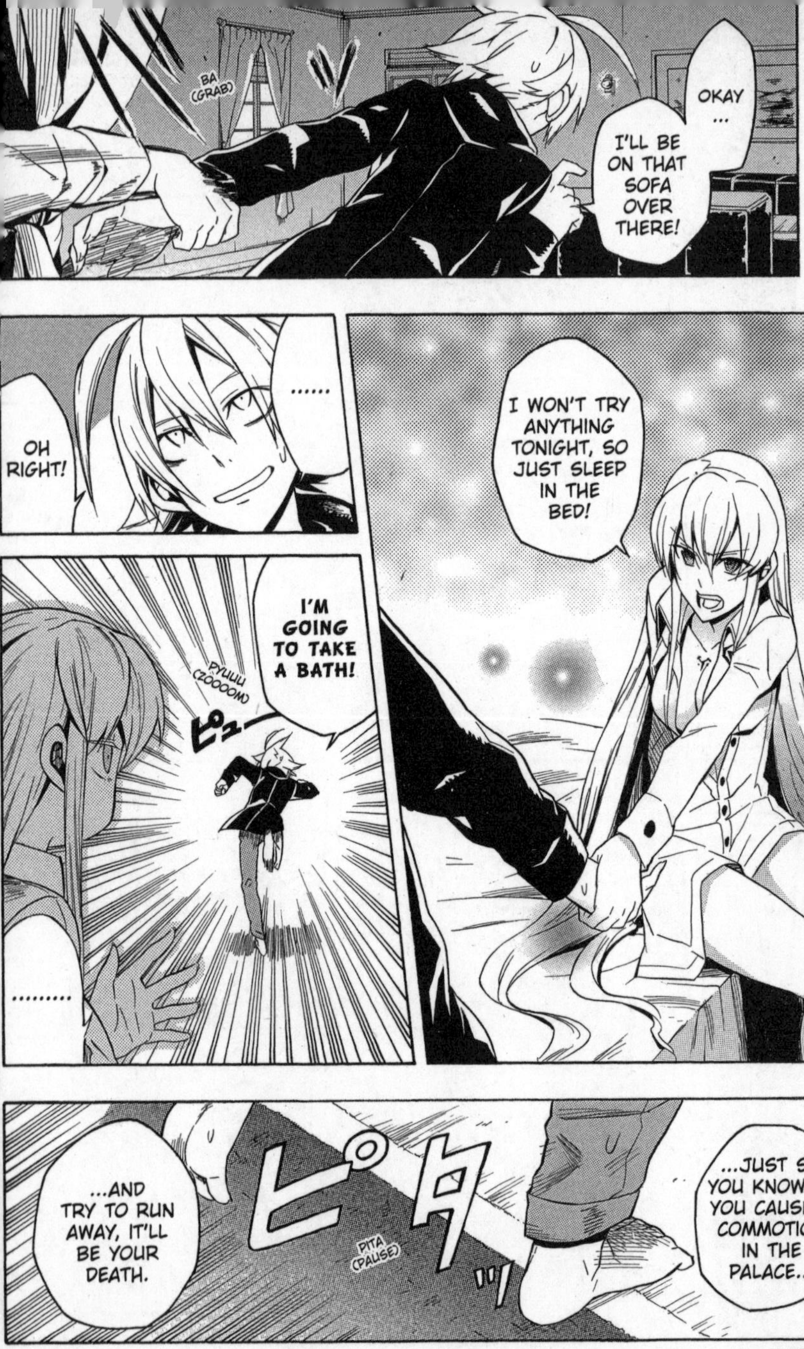
OKAY ...
I'LL BE ON THAT SOFA OVER THERE!
BA (GRAB)
I WON'T TRY ANYTHING TONIGHT, SO JUST SLEEP IN THE BED!
......
OH RIGHT!
I'M GOING TO TAKE A BATH!
PYUUU (ZOOOOM)
....
...JUST SO YOU KNOW, IF YOU CAUSE A COMMOTION IN THE PALACE...
PITA (PAUSE)
...AND TRY TO RUN AWAY, IT'LL BE YOUR DEATH.

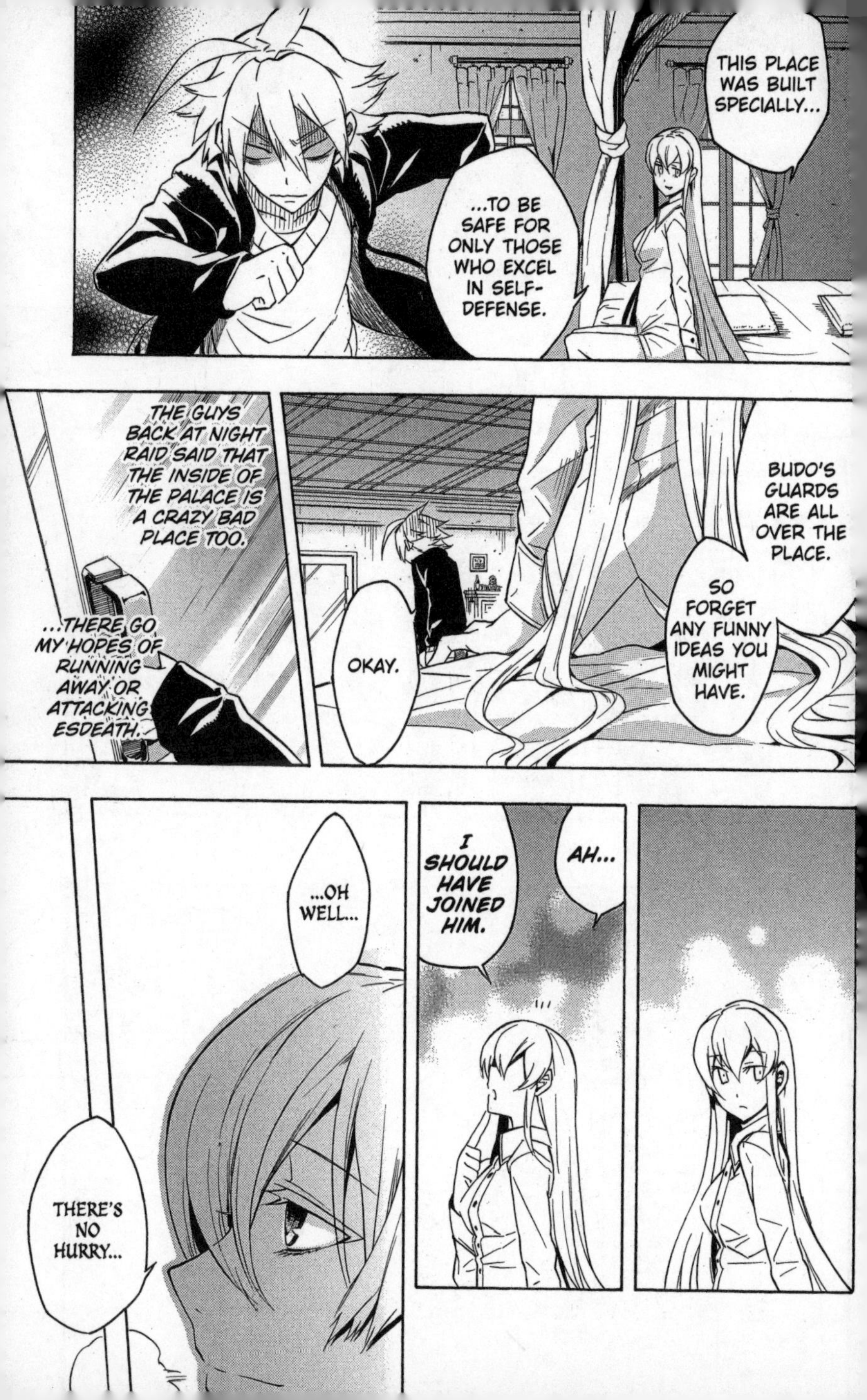
THIS PLACE WAS BUILT SPECIALLY...
...TO BE SAFE FOR ONLY THOSE WHO EXCEL IN SELF-DEFENSE.
BUDO'S GUARDS ARE ALL OVER THE PLACE.
SO FORGET ANY FUNNY IDEAS YOU MIGHT HAVE.
OKAY.
THE GUYS BACK AT NIGHT RAID SAID THAT THE INSIDE OF THE PALACE IS A CRAZY BAD PLACE TOO.
...THERE GO MY HOPES OF RUNNING AWAY OR ATTACKING ESDEATH.
AH...
I SHOULD HAVE JOINED HIM.
...OH WELL...
THERE'S NO HURRY...

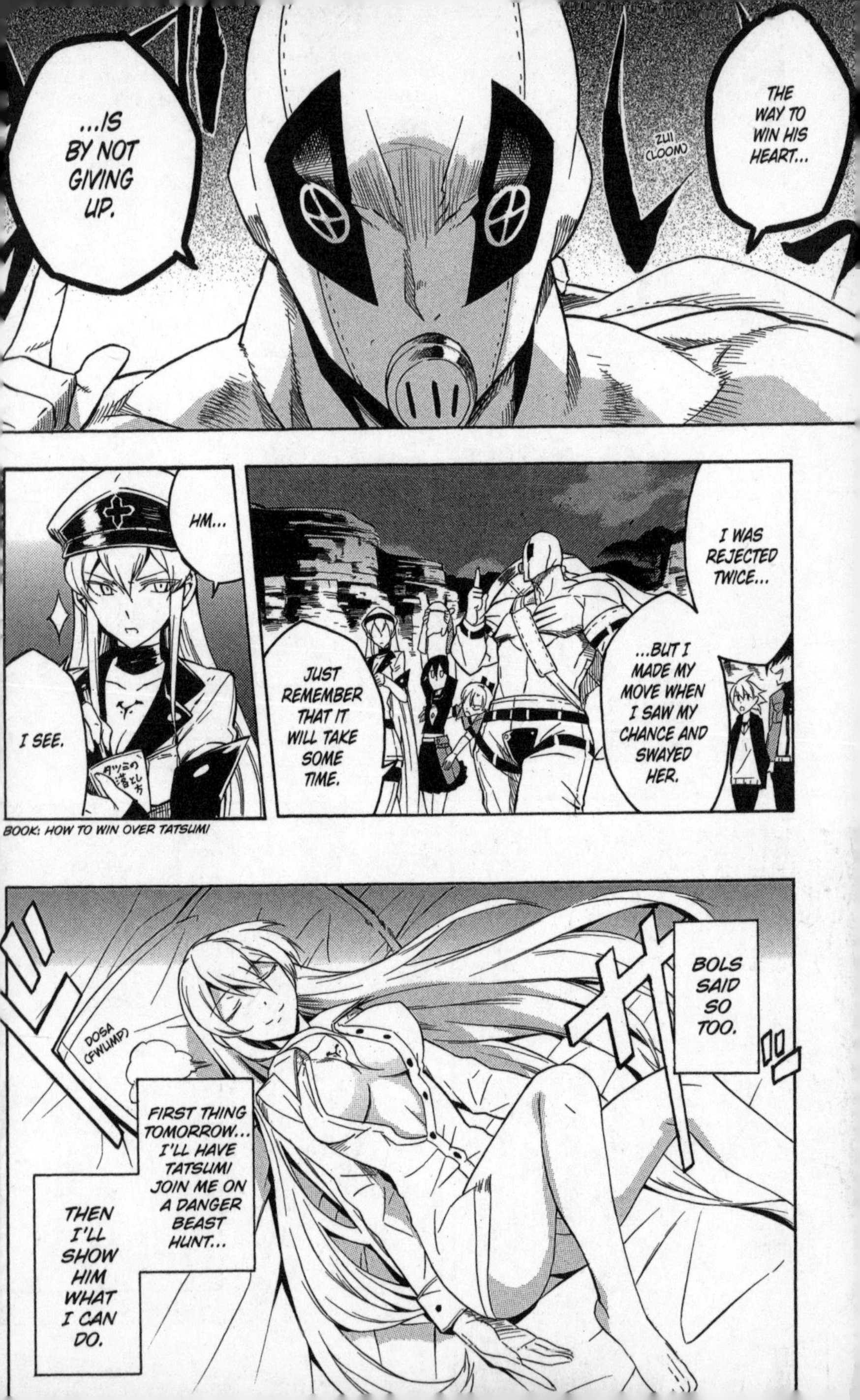
THE WAY TO WIN HIS HEART...
ZUI (LOOM)
...IS BY NOT GIVING UP.
I WAS REJECTED TWICE...
...BUT I MADE MY MOVE WHEN I SAW MY CHANCE AND SWAYED HER.
JUST REMEMBER THAT IT WILL TAKE SOME TIME.
HM...
I SEE.
BOOK: HOW TO WIN OVER TATSUMI
BOLS SAID SO TOO.
DOSA (FWUMP)
FIRST THING TOMORROW... I'LL HAVE TATSUMI JOIN ME ON A DANGER BEAST HUNT...
THEN I'LL SHOW HIM WHAT I CAN DO.

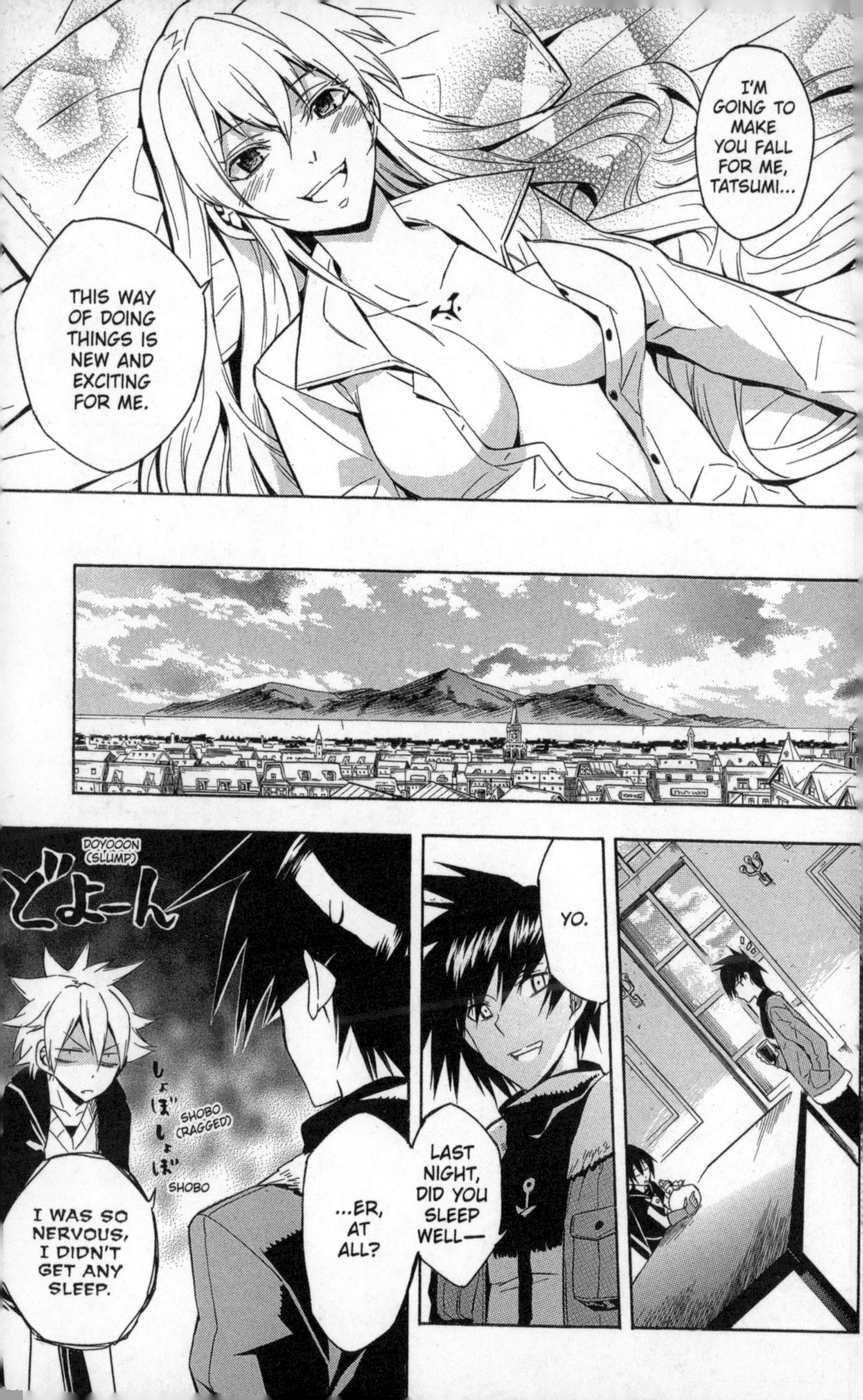
I'M GOING TO MAKE YOU FALL FOR ME, TATSUMI...
THIS WAY OF DOING THINGS IS NEW AND EXCITING FOR ME.
YO.
LAST NIGHT, DID YOU SLEEP WELL—
...ER, AT ALL?
どよーん
DOYOOON (SLUMP)
しょぼしょぼ
SHOBO (RAGGED)
SHOBO
I WAS SO NERVOUS, I DIDN'T GET ANY SLEEP.

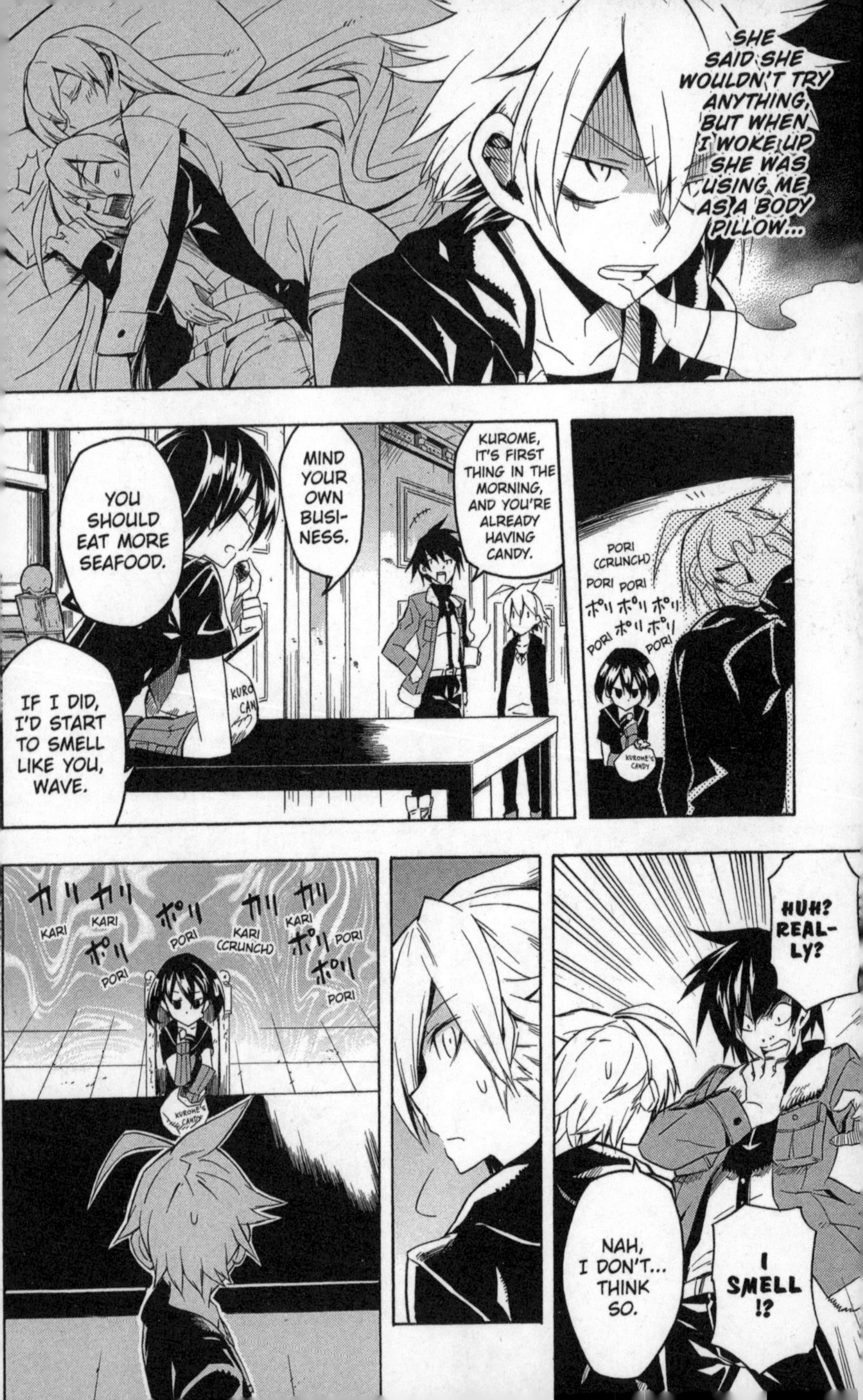

SHE SAID SHE WOULDN'T TRY ANYTHING, BUT WHEN I WOKE UP SHE WAS USING ME AS A BODY PILLOW...
PORI (CRUNCH)
PORI PORI
ポリポリポリ
PORI
ポリポリ
PORI
KUROME'S CANDY
KUROME, IT'S FIRST THING IN THE MORNING, AND YOU'RE ALREADY HAVING CANDY.
MIND YOUR OWN BUSI-NESS.
YOU SHOULD EAT MORE SEAFOOD.
KURO CAN
IF I DID, I'D START TO SMELL LIKE YOU, WAVE.
HUH? REAL-LY?
I SMELL!?
NAH, I DON'T... THINK SO.
カリカリ
KARI
KARI
ポリ
PORI
カリ
KARI (CRUNCH)
ガリ
KARI
ポリ
PORI
ポリ
PORI
ポリ
PORI
KUROME'S CANDY

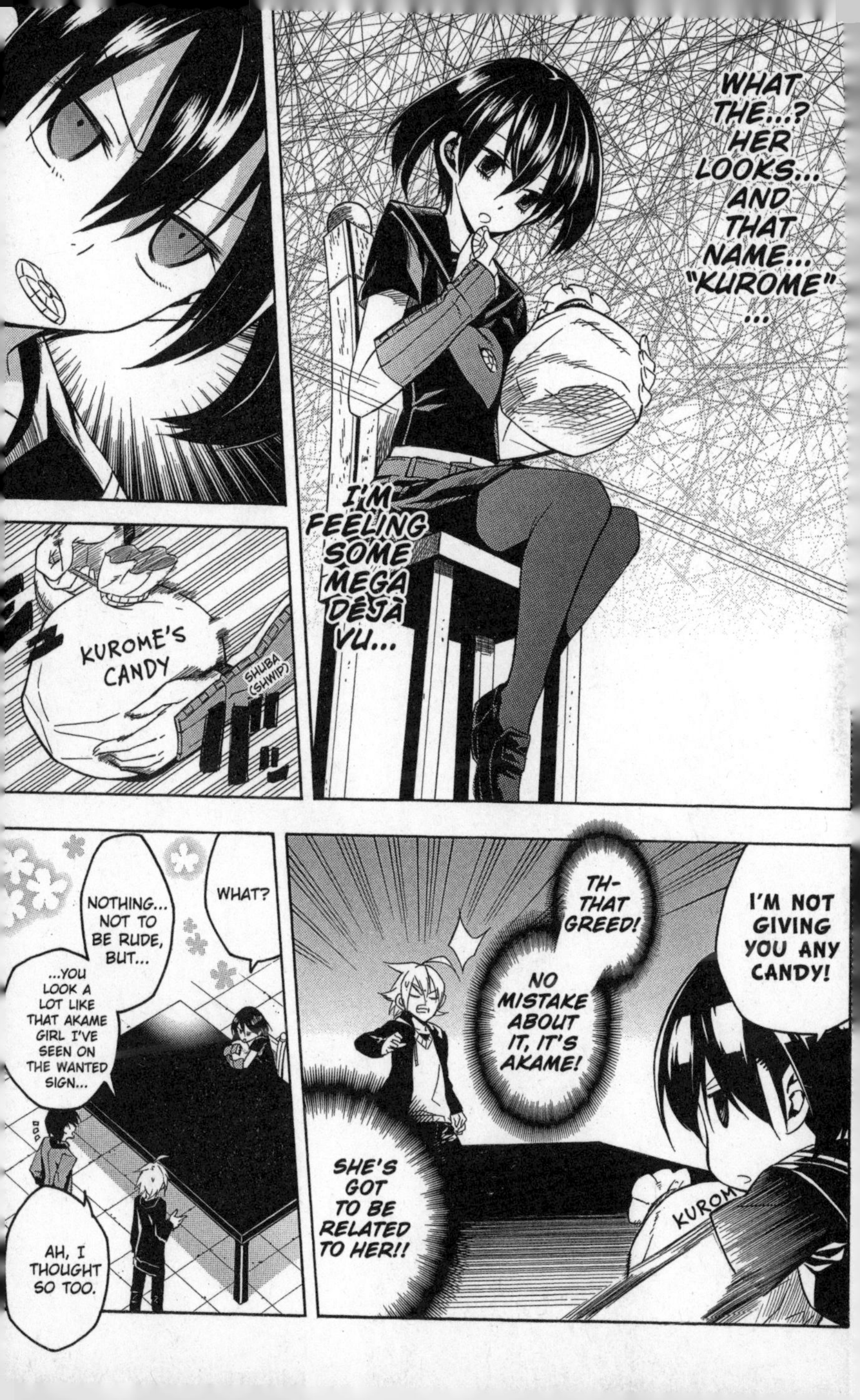
WHAT THE...? HER LOOKS... AND THAT NAME... "KUROME"...
I'M FEELING SOME MEGA DÉJÀ VU...
KUROME'S CANDY
SHUBA (SHWIP)
I'M NOT GIVING YOU ANY CANDY!
KUROM
TH-THAT GREED!
NO MISTAKE ABOUT IT, IT'S AKAME!
SHE'S GOT TO BE RELATED TO HER!!
WHAT?
NOTHING... NOT TO BE RUDE, BUT...
...YOU LOOK A LOT LIKE THAT AKAME GIRL I'VE SEEN ON THE WANTED SIGN...
AH, I THOUGHT SO TOO.

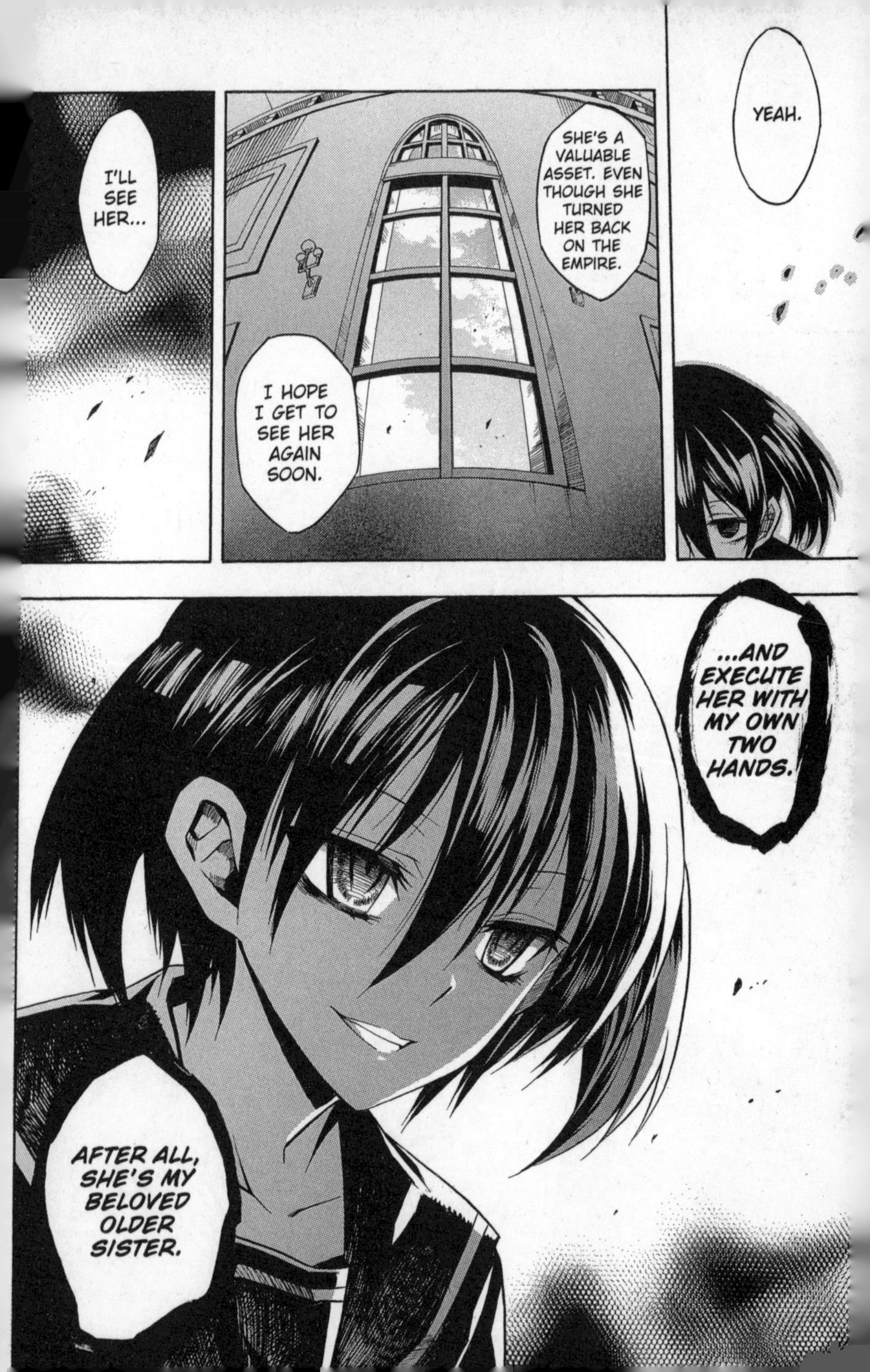
YEAH.
SHE'S A VALUABLE ASSET. EVEN THOUGH SHE TURNED HER BACK ON THE EMPIRE.
I HOPE I GET TO SEE HER AGAIN SOON.
I'LL SEE HER...
...AND EXECUTE HER WITH MY OWN TWO HANDS.
AFTER ALL, SHE'S MY BELOVED OLDER SISTER.

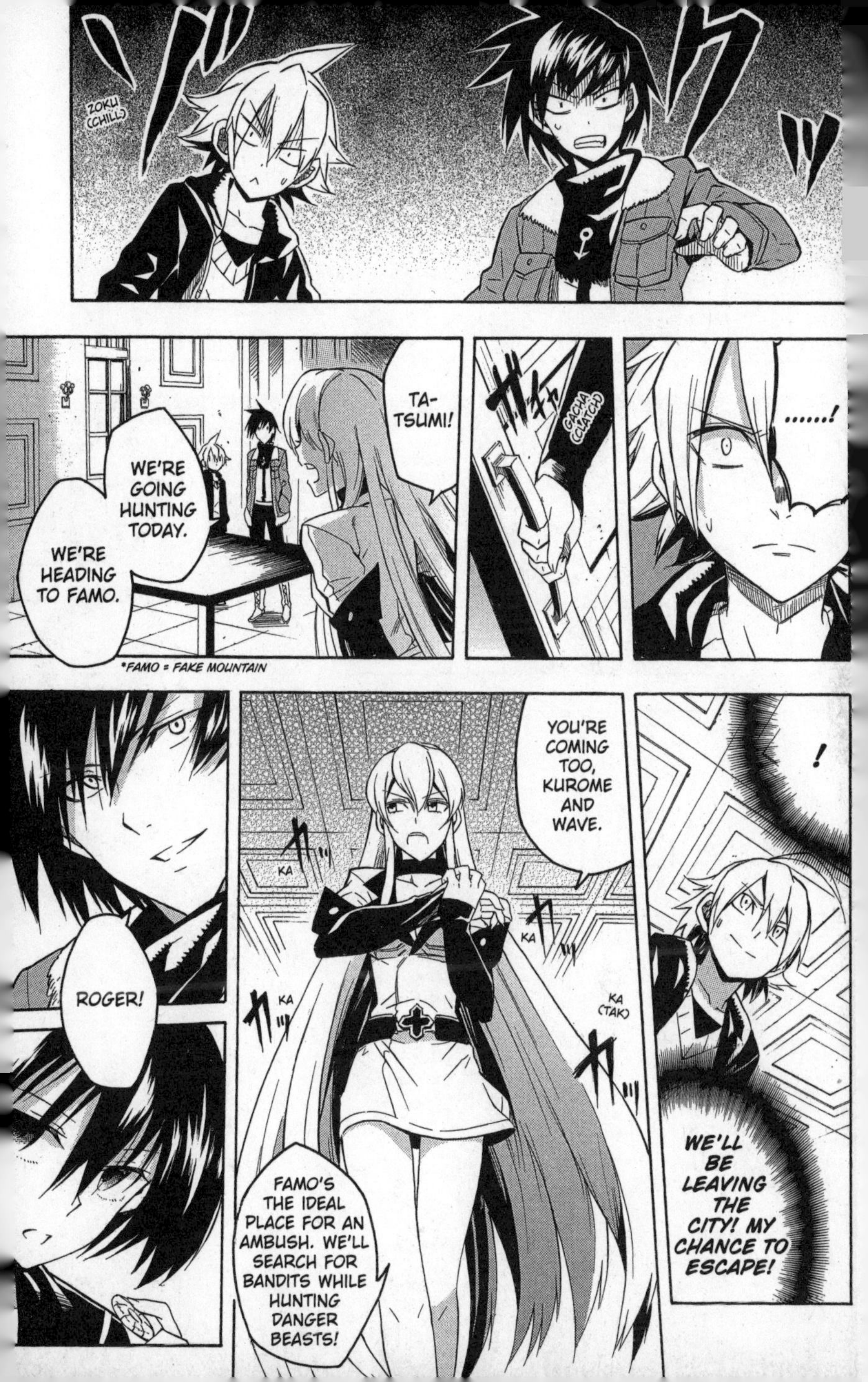
ZOKU (CHILL)
TA-TSUMI!
WE'RE GOING HUNTING TODAY.
WE'RE HEADING TO FAMO.
GACHA (CLATCH)
......!
*FAMO = FAKE MOUNTAIN
!
WE'LL BE LEAVING THE CITY! MY CHANCE TO ESCAPE!
YOU'RE COMING TOO, KUROME AND WAVE.
KA
KA
KA (TAK)
KA
FAMO'S THE IDEAL PLACE FOR AN AMBUSH. WE'LL SEARCH FOR BANDITS WHILE HUNTING DANGER BEASTS!
ROGER!

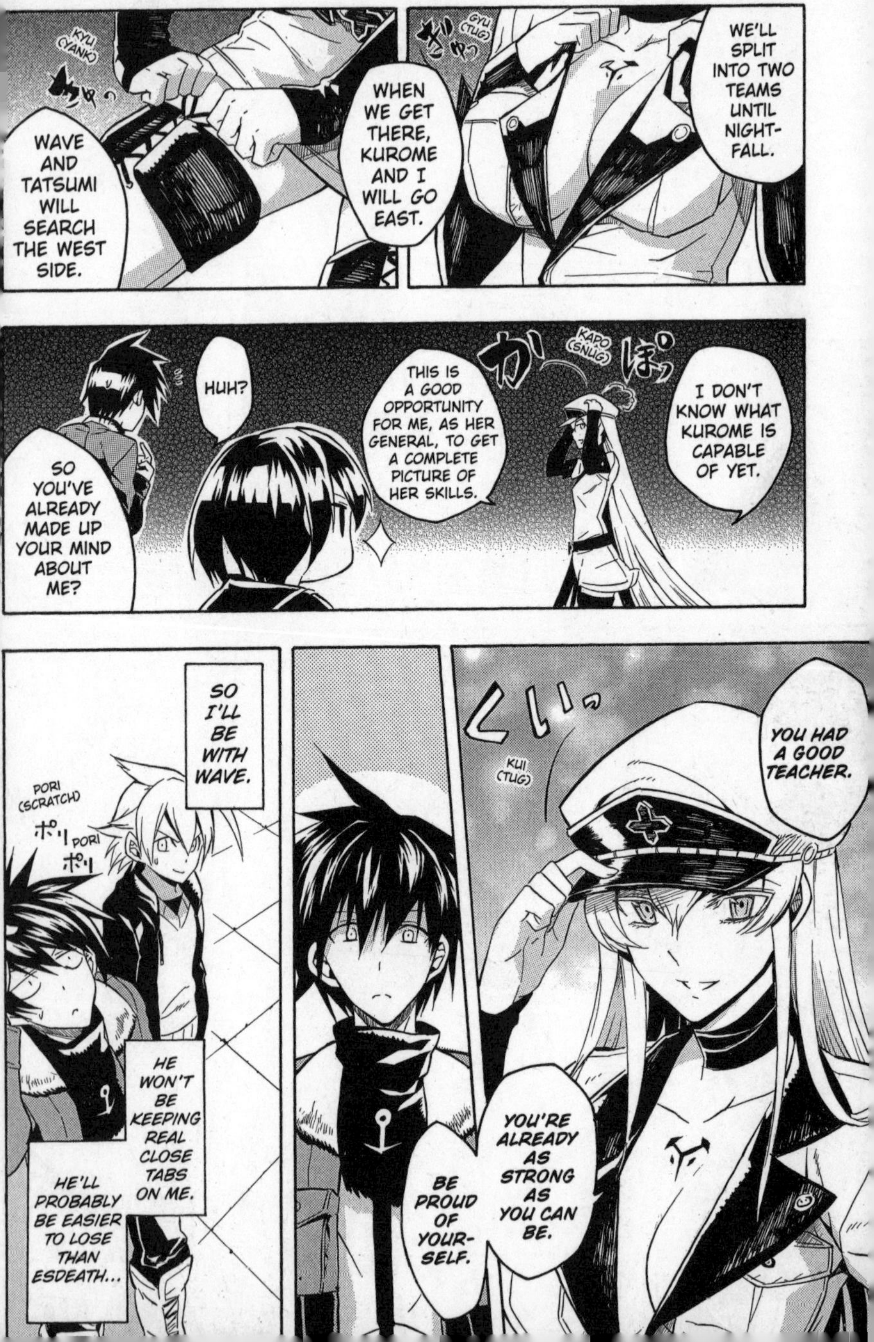
GYU (TUG)
WE'LL SPLIT INTO TWO TEAMS UNTIL NIGHT-FALL.
WHEN WE GET THERE, KUROME AND I WILL GO EAST.
KYU (YANK)
WAVE AND TATSUMI WILL SEARCH THE WEST SIDE.
KAPO (SNUG)
I DON'T KNOW WHAT KUROME IS CAPABLE OF YET.
THIS IS A GOOD OPPORTUNITY FOR ME, AS HER GENERAL, TO GET A COMPLETE PICTURE OF HER SKILLS.
HUH?
SO YOU'VE ALREADY MADE UP YOUR MIND ABOUT ME?
YOU HAD A GOOD TEACHER.
KUI (TUG)
YOU'RE ALREADY AS STRONG AS YOU CAN BE.
BE PROUD OF YOUR-SELF.
SO I'LL BE WITH WAVE.
PORI (SCRATCH)
PORI
HE WON'T BE KEEPING REAL CLOSE TABS ON ME.
HE'LL PROBABLY BE EASIER TO LOSE THAN ESDEATH...

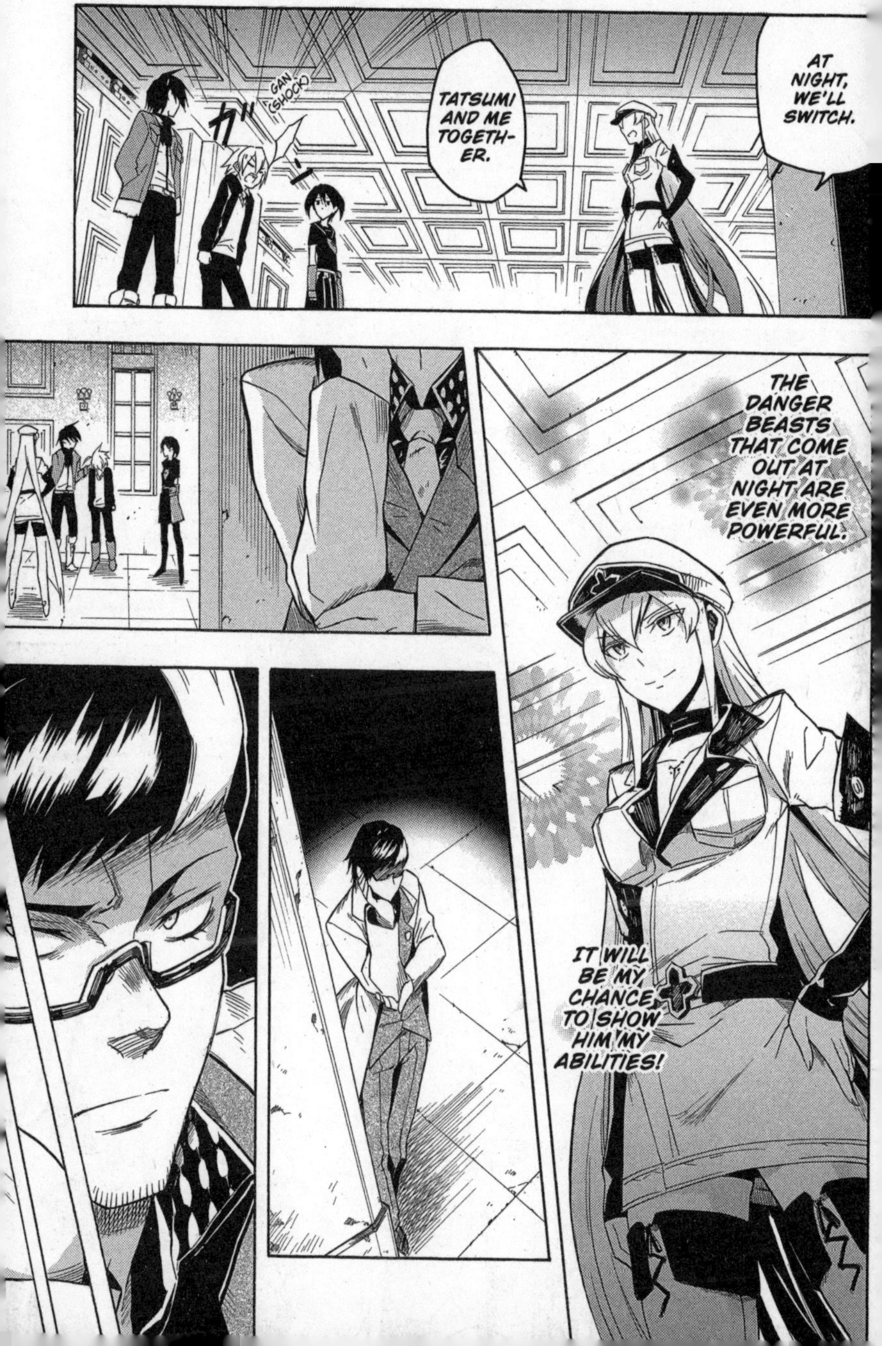

AT NIGHT, WE'LL SWITCH.
TATSUMI AND ME TOGETH-ER.
GAN (SHOCK)
THE DANGER BEASTS THAT COME OUT AT NIGHT ARE EVEN MORE POWERFUL.
IT WILL BE MY CHANCE TO SHOW HIM MY ABILITIES!

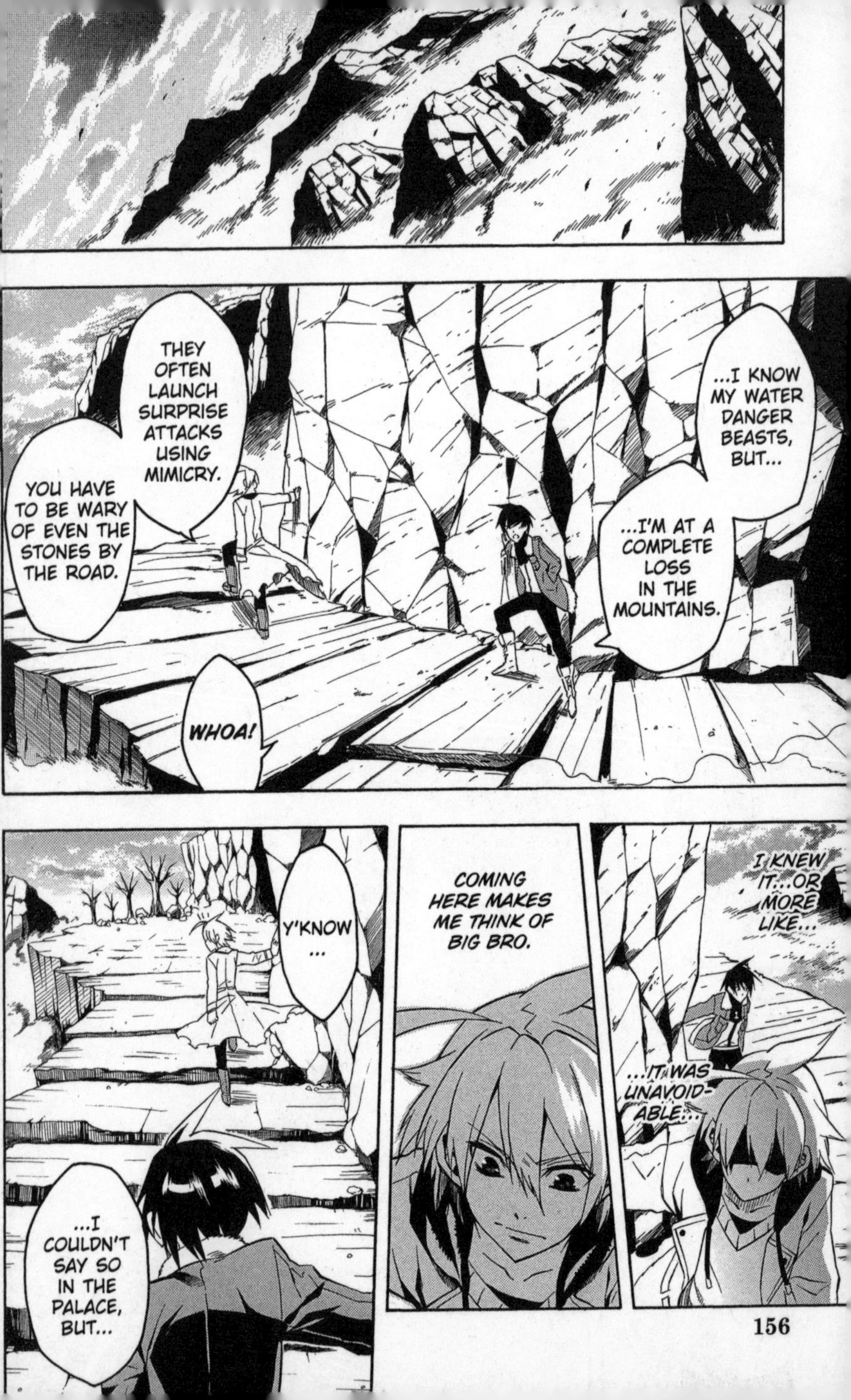
...I KNOW MY WATER DANGER BEASTS, BUT...
...I'M AT A COMPLETE LOSS IN THE MOUNTAINS.
THEY OFTEN LAUNCH SURPRISE ATTACKS USING MIMICRY.
YOU HAVE TO BE WARY OF EVEN THE STONES BY THE ROAD.
WHOA!
I KNEW IT...OR MORE LIKE...
...IT WAS UNAVOIDABLE...
COMING HERE MAKES ME THINK OF BIG BRO.
Y'KNOW...
...I COULDN'T SAY SO IN THE PALACE, BUT...

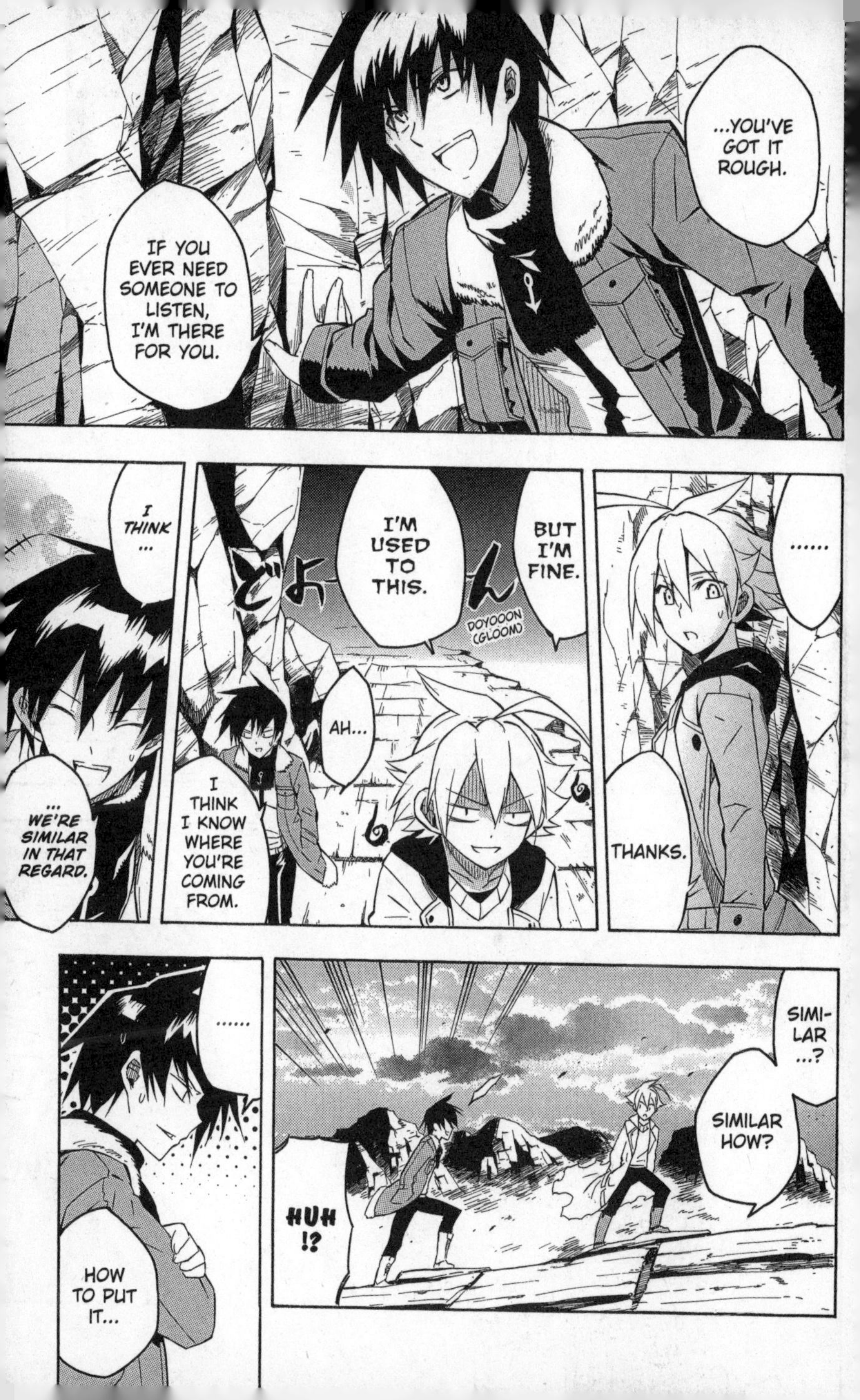

...YOU'VE GOT IT ROUGH.
IF YOU EVER NEED SOMEONE TO LISTEN, I'M THERE FOR YOU.
......
THANKS.
BUT I'M FINE.
I'M USED TO THIS.
どよん
DOYOOON (GLOOM)
AH...
I THINK I KNOW WHERE YOU'RE COMING FROM.
I THINK ...
... WE'RE SIMILAR IN THAT REGARD.
SIMI-LAR ...?
SIMILAR HOW?
HUH !?
......
HOW TO PUT IT...

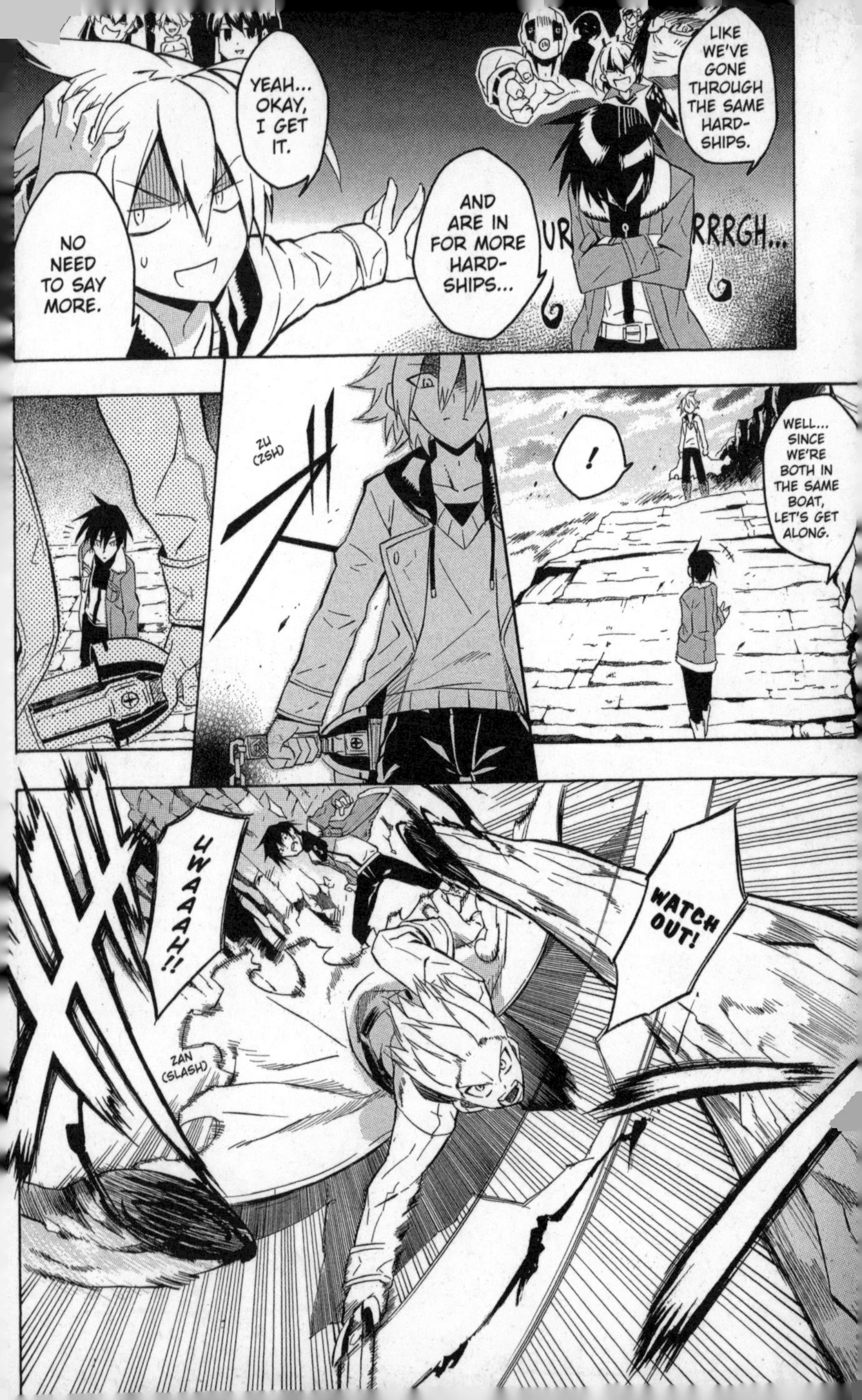
LIKE WE'VE GONE THROUGH THE SAME HARD-SHIPS.
AND ARE IN FOR MORE HARD-SHIPS...
UR RRRGH...
YEAH... OKAY, I GET IT.
NO NEED TO SAY MORE.
WELL... SINCE WE'RE BOTH IN THE SAME BOAT, LET'S GET ALONG.
!
ZU (ZSH)
WATCH OUT!
UWAAAAH!!
ZAN (SLASH)

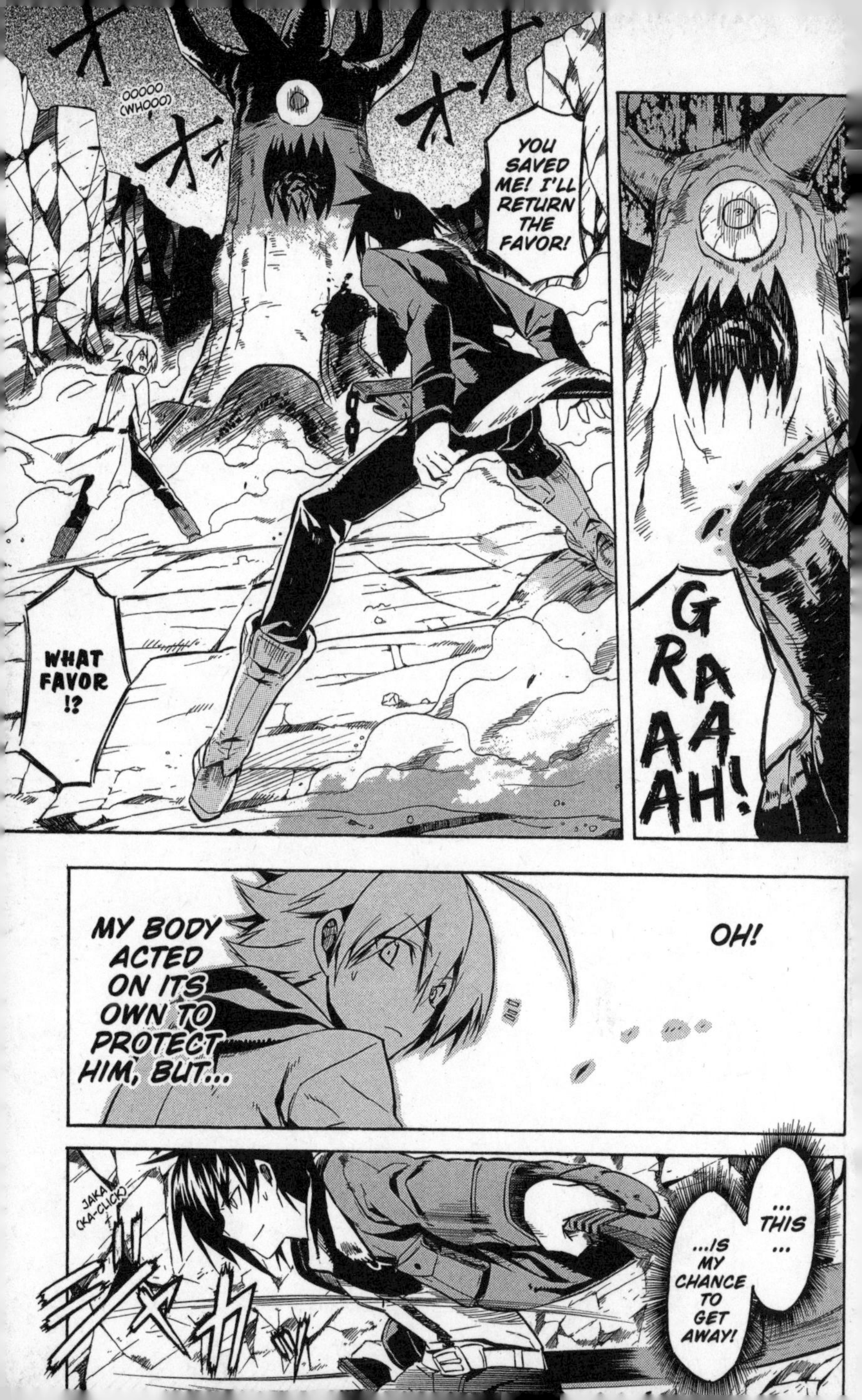
YOU SAVED ME! I'LL RETURN THE FAVOR!
OOOOO (WHOOO)
WHAT FAVOR !?
GRAAAAH!
OH!
MY BODY ACTED ON ITS OWN TO PROTECT HIM, BUT...
... THIS ...
...IS MY CHANCE TO GET AWAY!
JAKA (KA-CLICK)

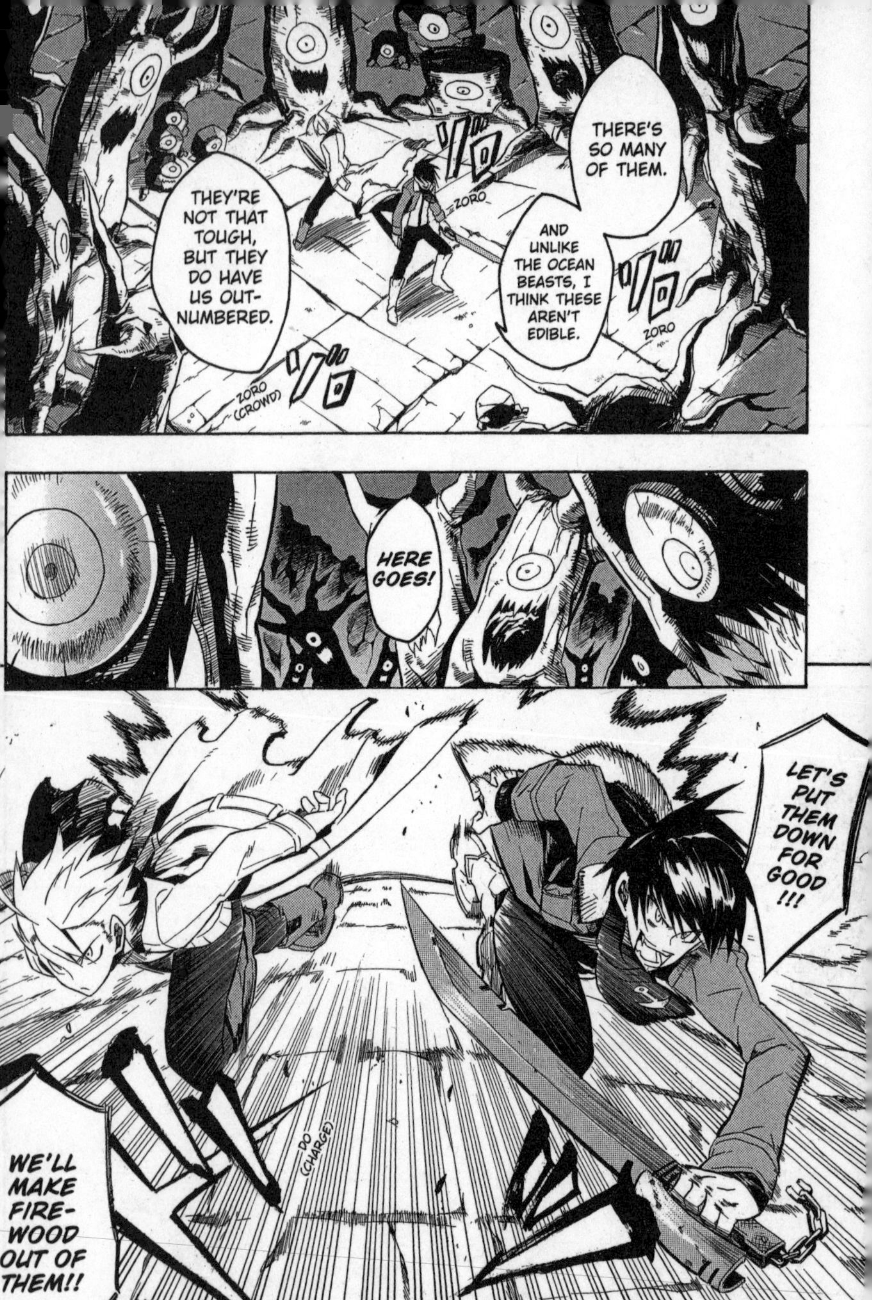
THERE'S SO MANY OF THEM.
ZORO
THEY'RE NOT THAT TOUGH, BUT THEY DO HAVE US OUT-NUMBERED.
AND UNLIKE THE OCEAN BEASTS, I THINK THESE AREN'T EDIBLE.
ZORO
ZORO (CROWD)
HERE GOES!
LET'S PUT THEM DOWN FOR GOOD!!!
WE'LL MAKE FIRE-WOOD OUT OF THEM!!
DO (CHARGE)

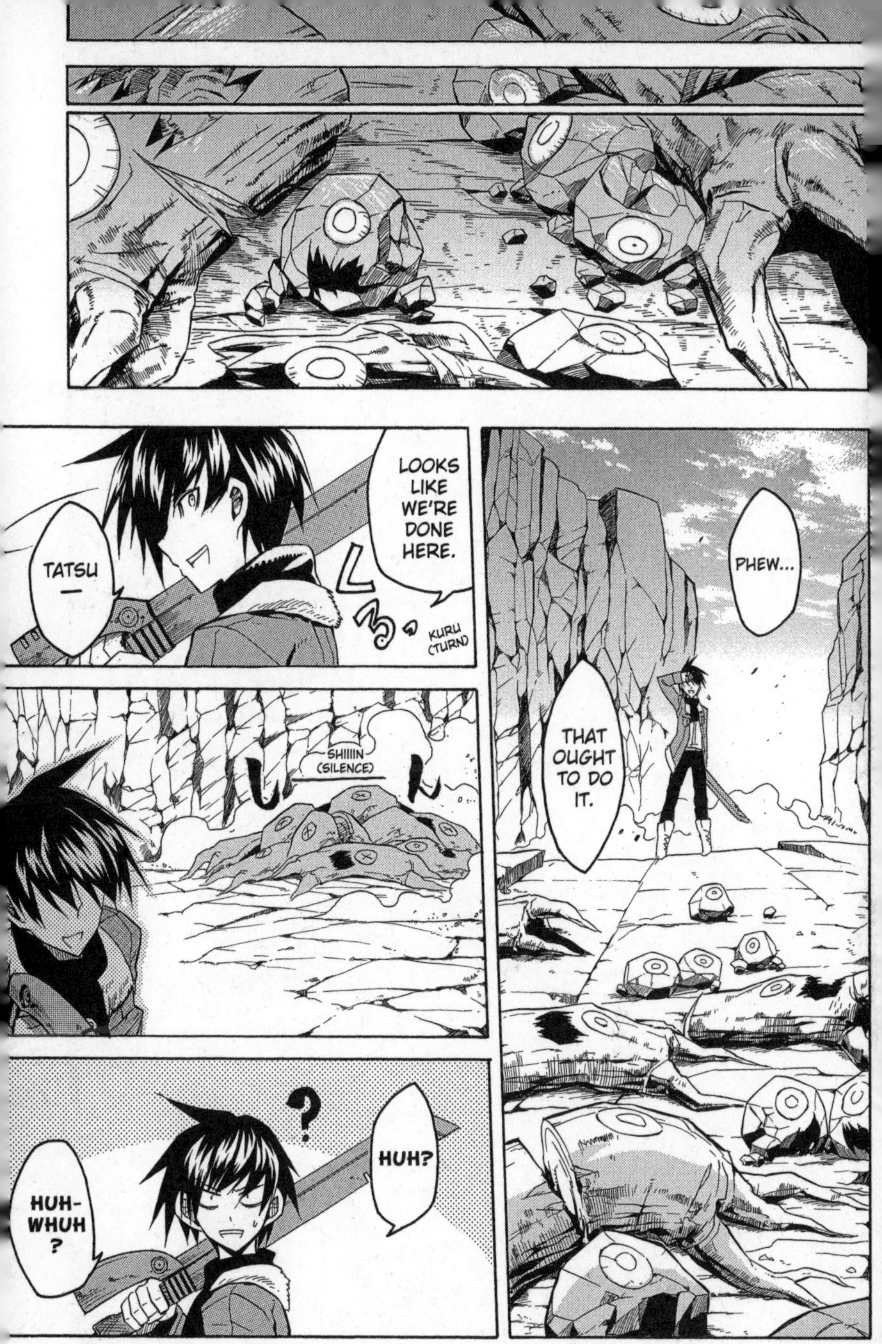

PHEW...
THAT OUGHT TO DO IT.
LOOKS LIKE WE'RE DONE HERE.
KURU (TURN)
TATSU—
SHIIIIN (SILENCE)
HUH?
HUH-WHUH?

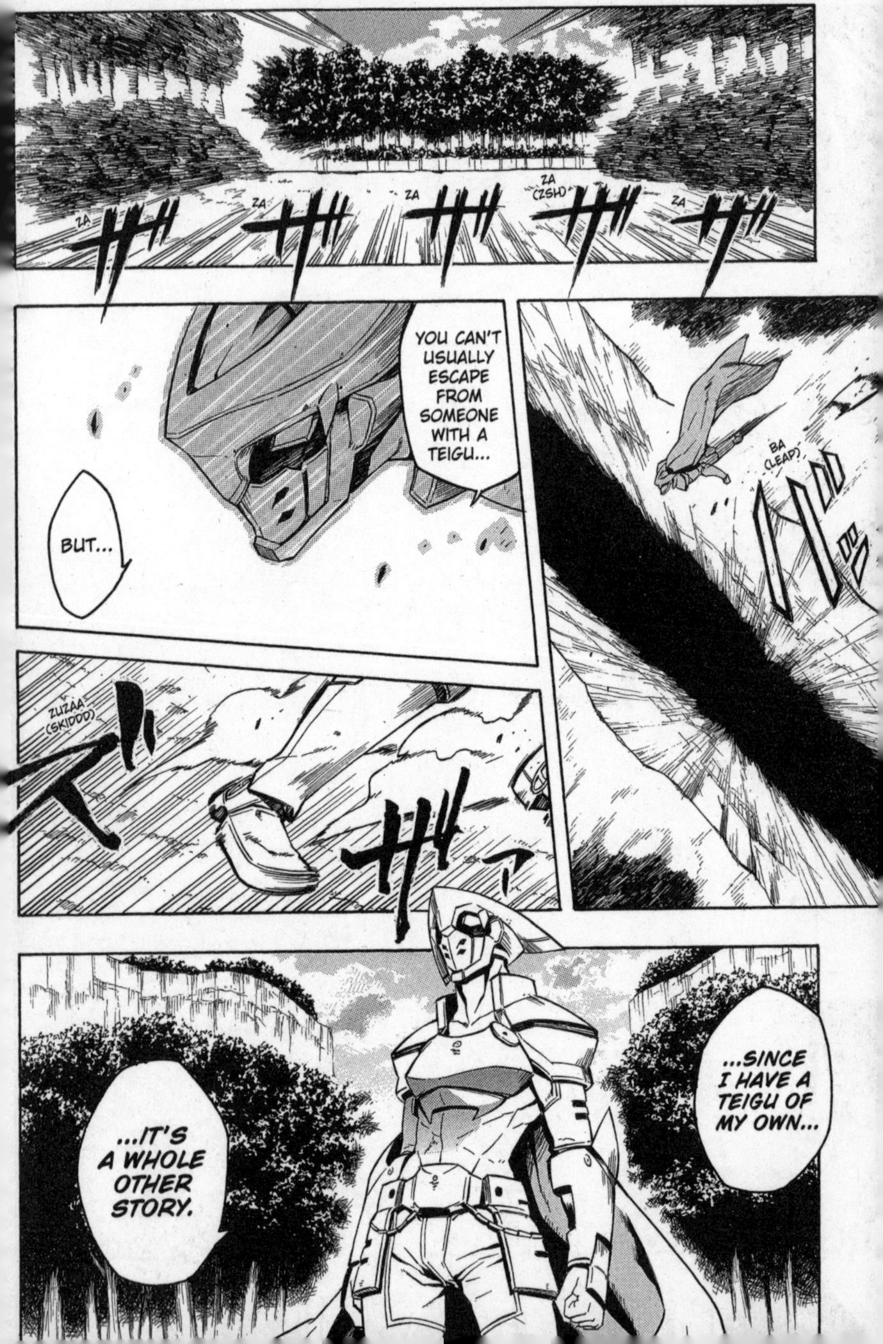
ZA
ZA
ZA
ZA
(ZSH)
ZA
YOU CAN'T USUALLY ESCAPE FROM SOMEONE WITH A TEIGU...
BA
(LEAP)
BUT...
ZUZAA
(SKIDDD)
...SINCE I HAVE A TEIGU OF MY OWN...
...IT'S A WHOLE OTHER STORY.

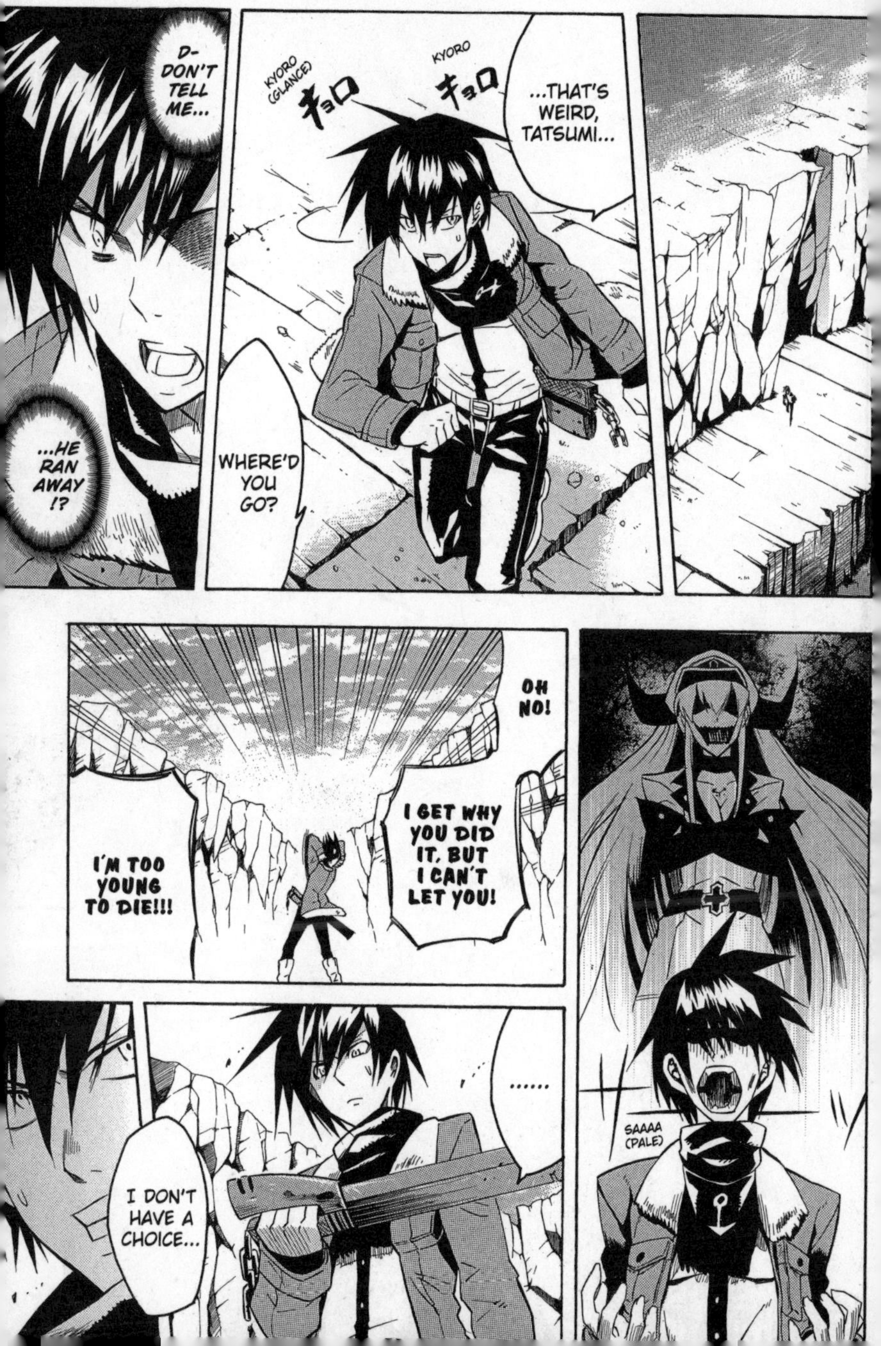
...THAT'S WEIRD, TATSUMI...
KYORO
キョロ
KYORO (GLANCE)
キョロ
WHERE'D YOU GO?
D-DON'T TELL ME...
...HE RAN AWAY!?
SAAAA (PALE)
OH NO!
I GET WHY YOU DID IT, BUT I CAN'T LET YOU!
I'M TOO YOUNG TO DIE!!!
......
I DON'T HAVE A CHOICE...

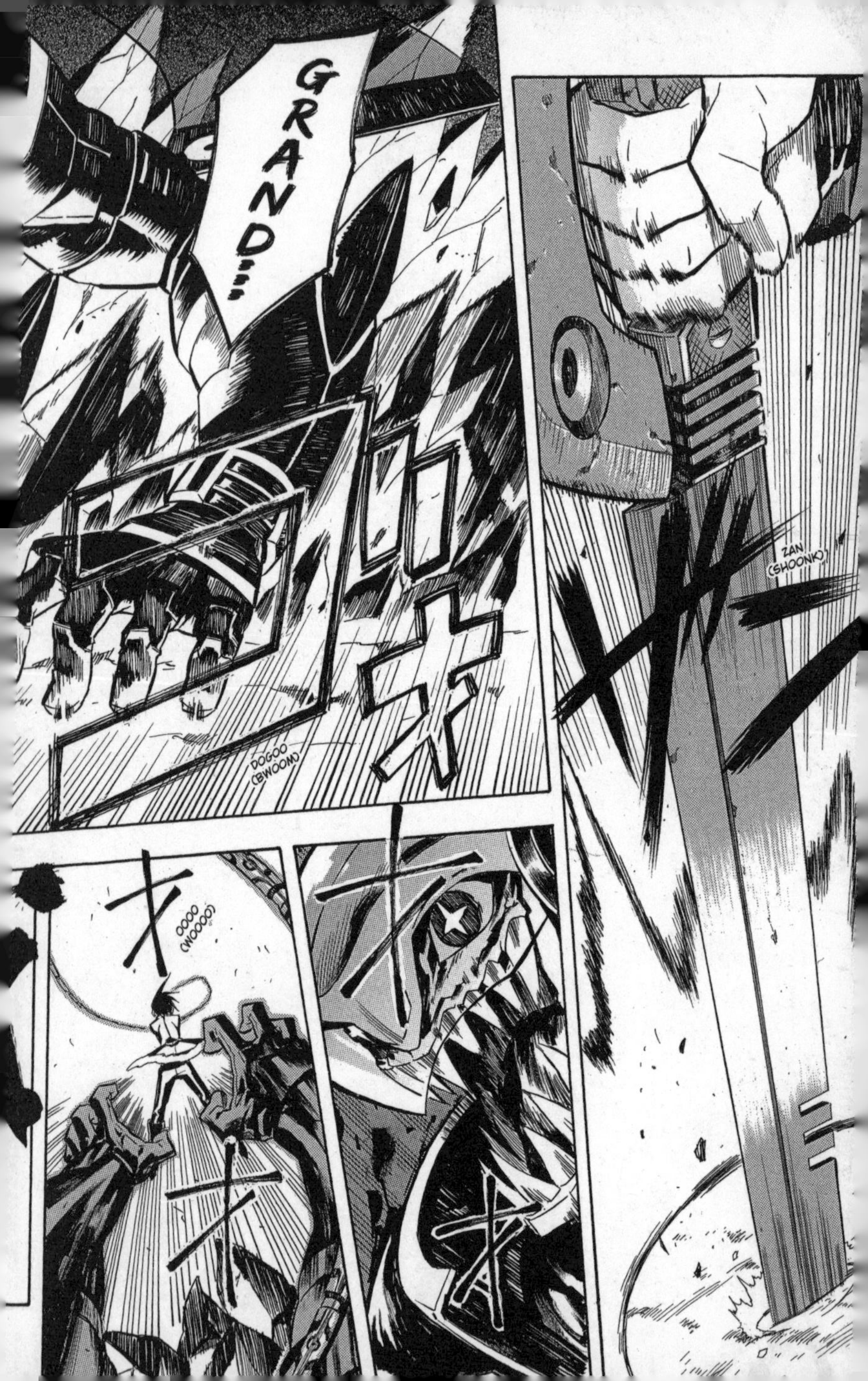
ZAN (SHOONK)
GRAND...!!
DOGOO (BWOOM)
OOOO (WOOOO)

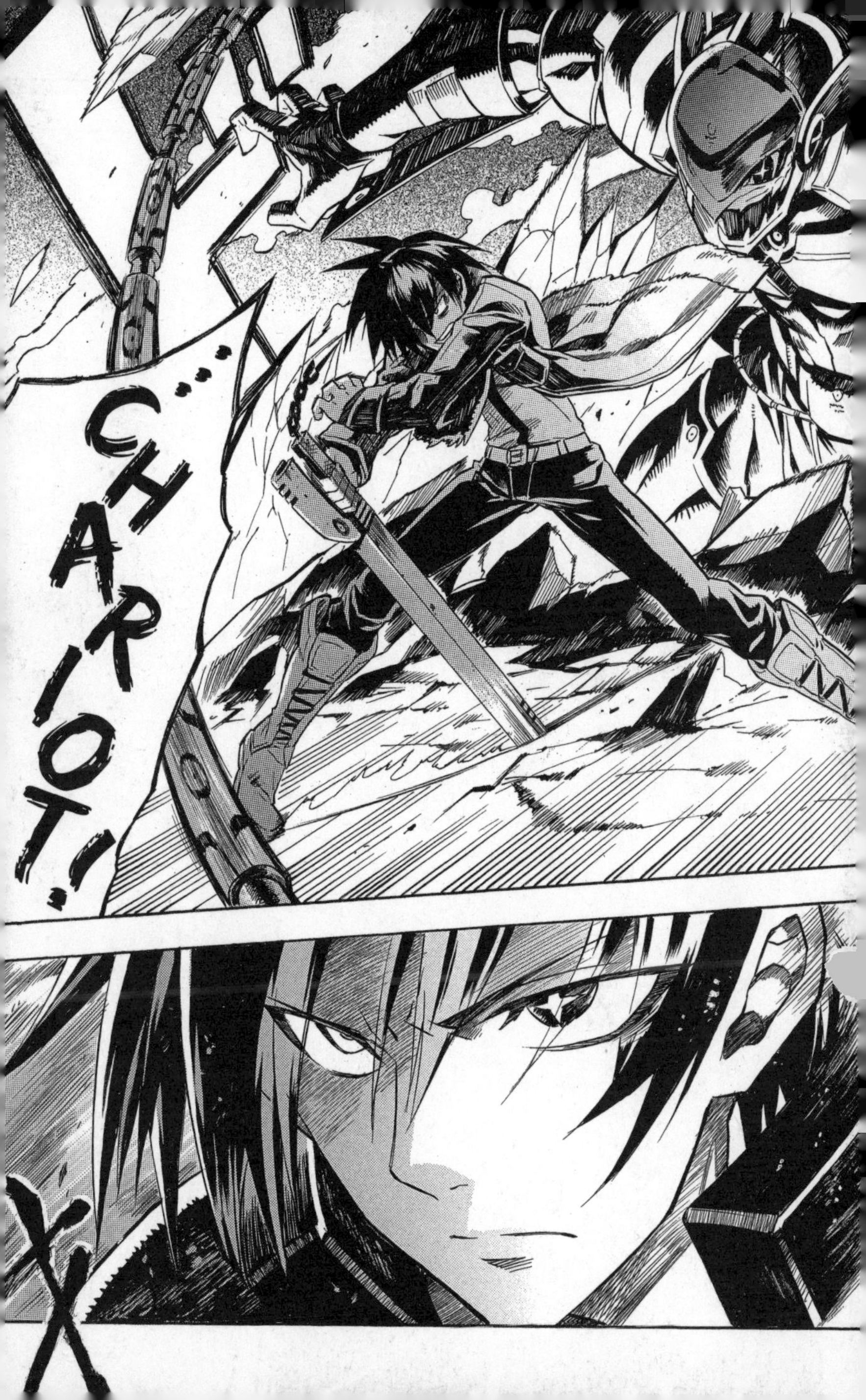
...
CHARIOT!!

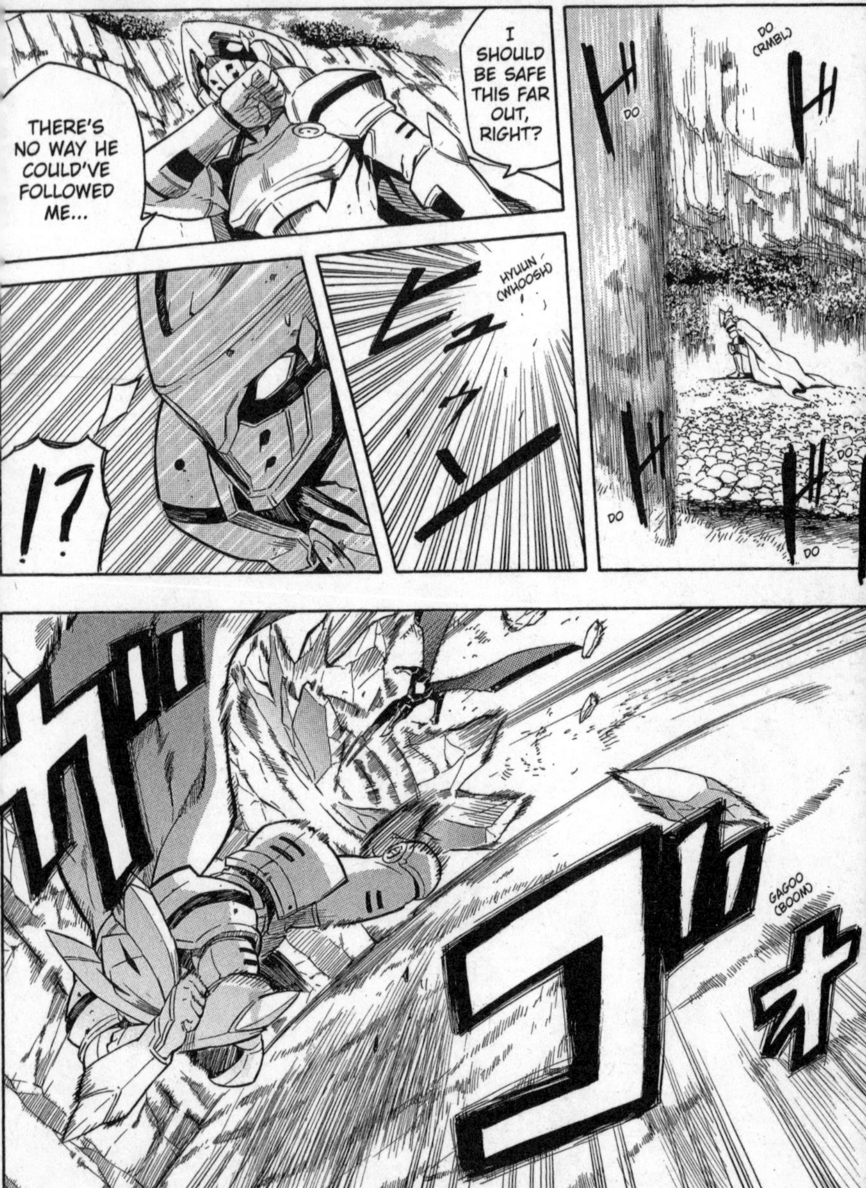
DO (RMBL)
DO
DO
DO
DO
I SHOULD BE SAFE THIS FAR OUT, RIGHT?
THERE'S NO WAY HE COULD'VE FOLLOWED ME...
HYUUN (WHOOSH)
!?
GAGOO (BOOM)

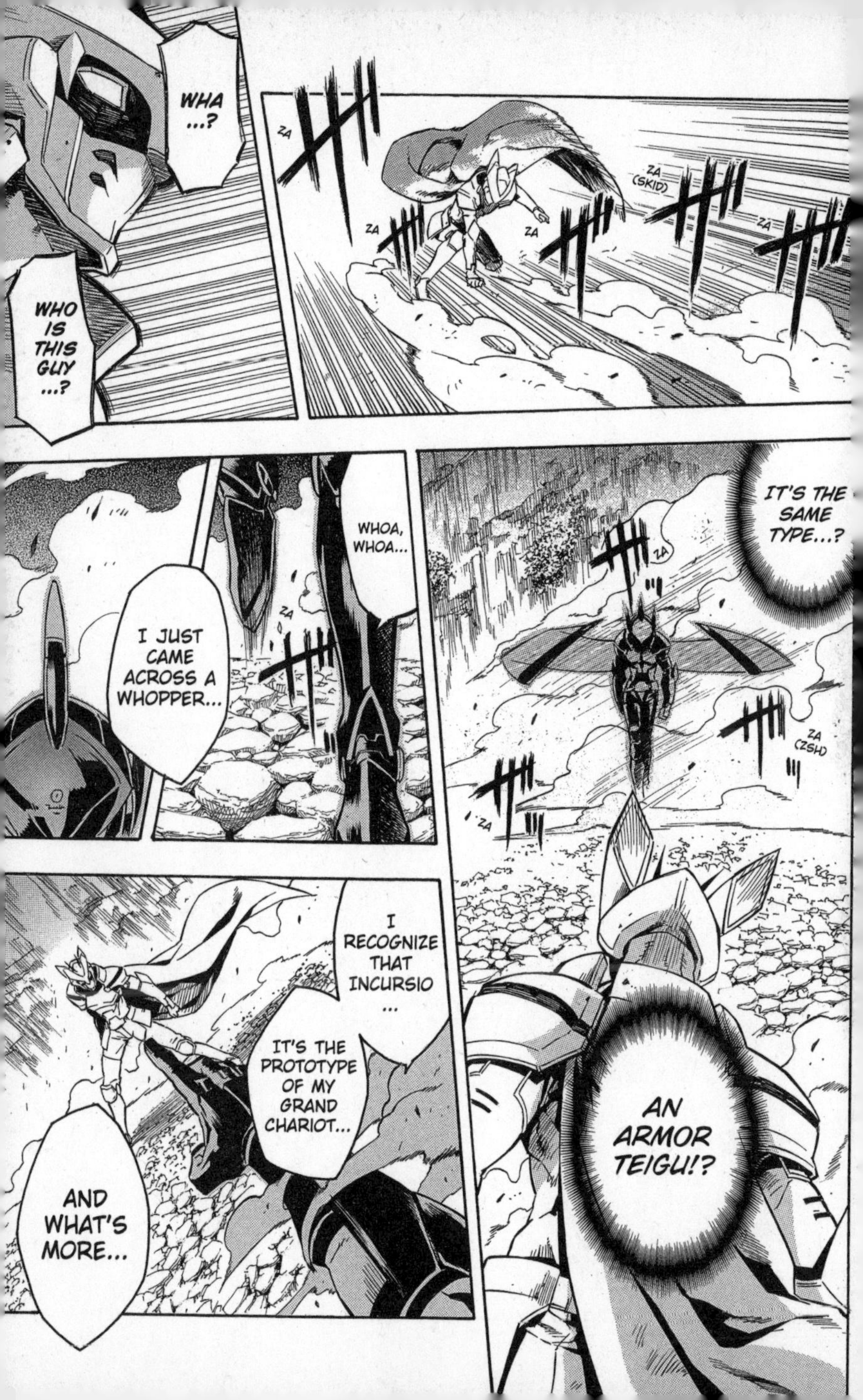
ZA
ZA
ZA
ZA (SKID)
ZA
WHA ...?
WHO IS THIS GUY ...?
IT'S THE SAME TYPE...?
ZA
ZA (ZSH)
ZA
WHOA, WHOA...
ZA
I JUST CAME ACROSS A WHOPPER...
AN ARMOR TEIGU!?
I RECOGNIZE THAT INCURSIO ...
IT'S THE PROTOTYPE OF MY GRAND CHARIOT...
AND WHAT'S MORE...

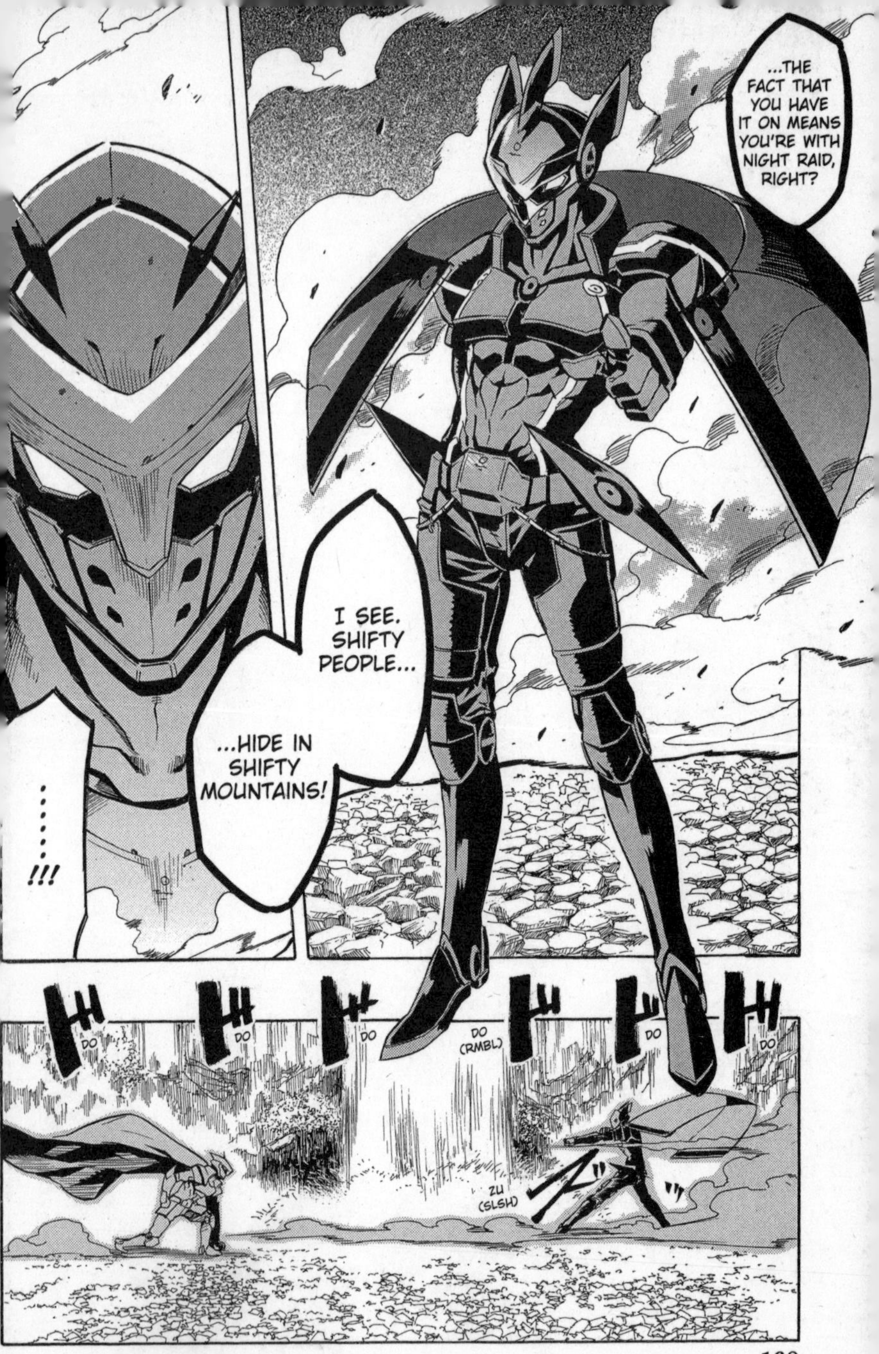
...THE FACT THAT YOU HAVE IT ON MEANS YOU'RE WITH NIGHT RAID, RIGHT?
I SEE. SHIFTY PEOPLE...
...HIDE IN SHIFTY MOUNTAINS!
......!!!
DO
DO
DO
DO (RMBL)
DO
DO
ZU (SLSH)

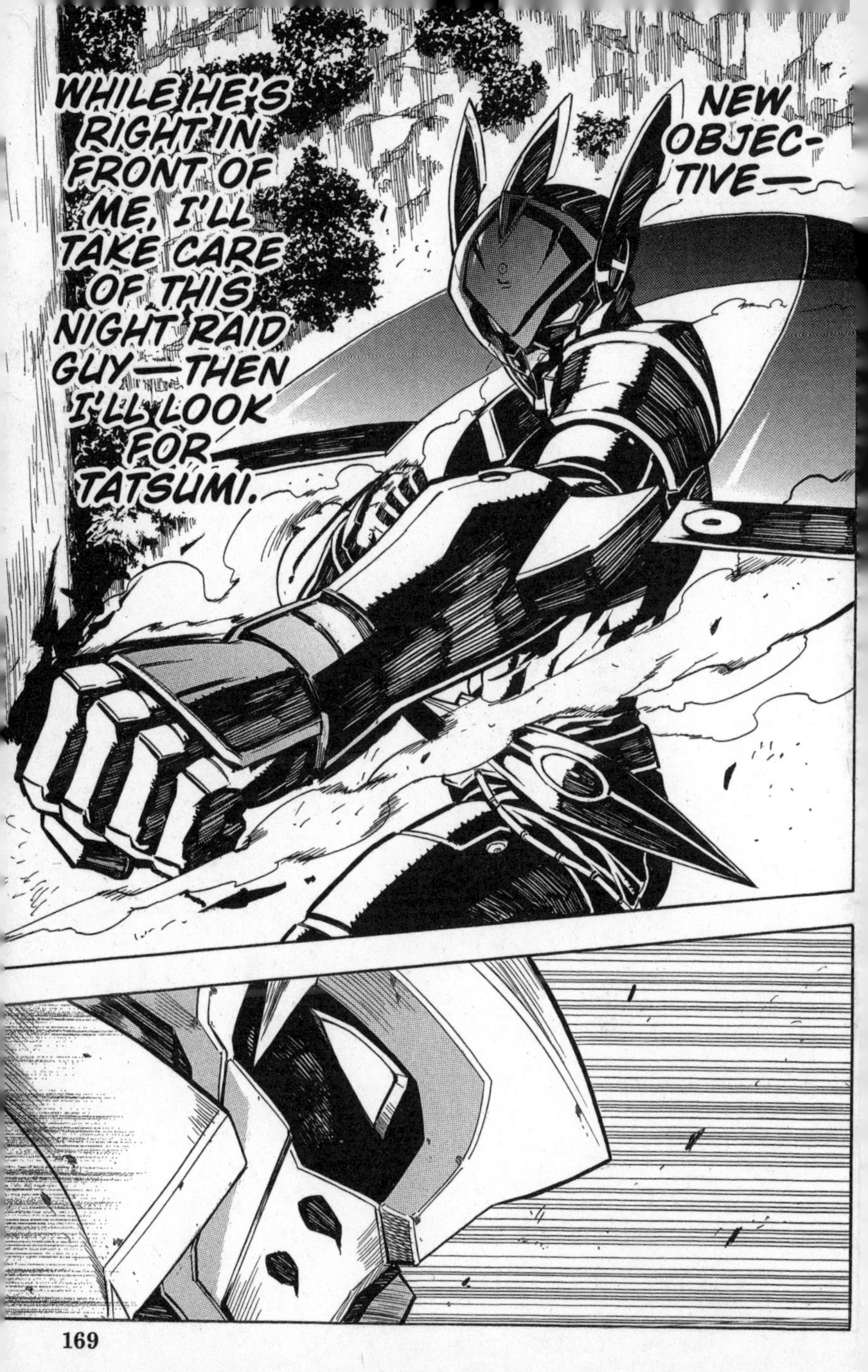
NEW OBJEC- TIVE—
WHILE HE'S RIGHT IN FRONT OF ME, I'LL TAKE CARE OF THIS NIGHT RAID GUY—THEN I'LL LOOK FOR TATSUMI.

Akame ga KILL!
Rough Sketches 3

GRAND CHARIOT

Since Incursio was its prototype, it's a little more streamlined than Incursio.

The helmet mask is transparent and will be left clear. Or could possibly use a tone on it.

Film Parts:
In place of Incursio's cape, Grand Chariot is clad in a phantasmagoric defensive film. Also gradient toned.

Unlike Incursio, it has a chain.

Silvery

Has more armor parts than Incursio.

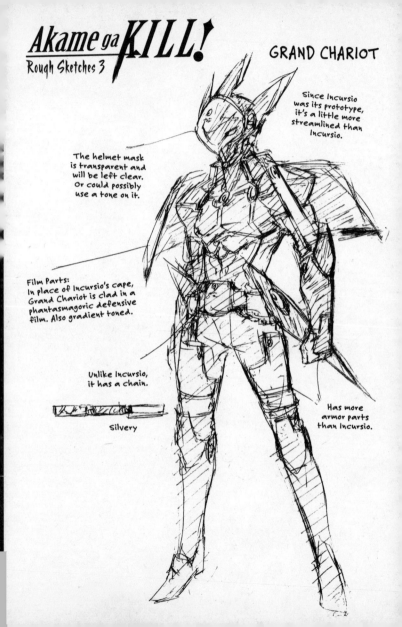

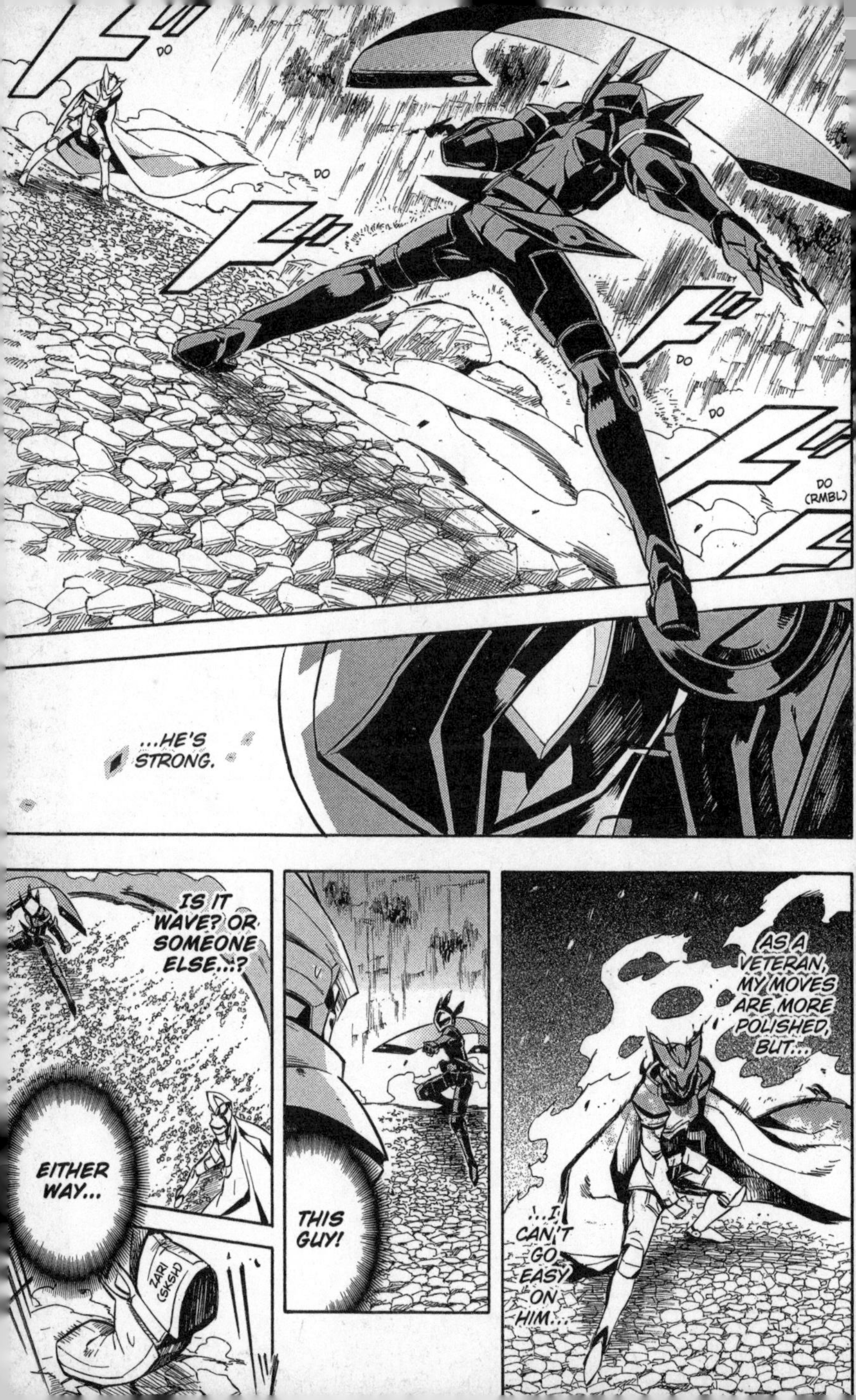

DO
DO
DO
DO
DO
(RMBL)
...HE'S STRONG.
IS IT WAVE? OR SOMEONE ELSE...?
EITHER WAY...
ZARI (SKSH)
THIS GUY!
AS A VETERAN, MY MOVES ARE MORE POLISHED, BUT...
...I CAN'T GO EASY ON HIM...

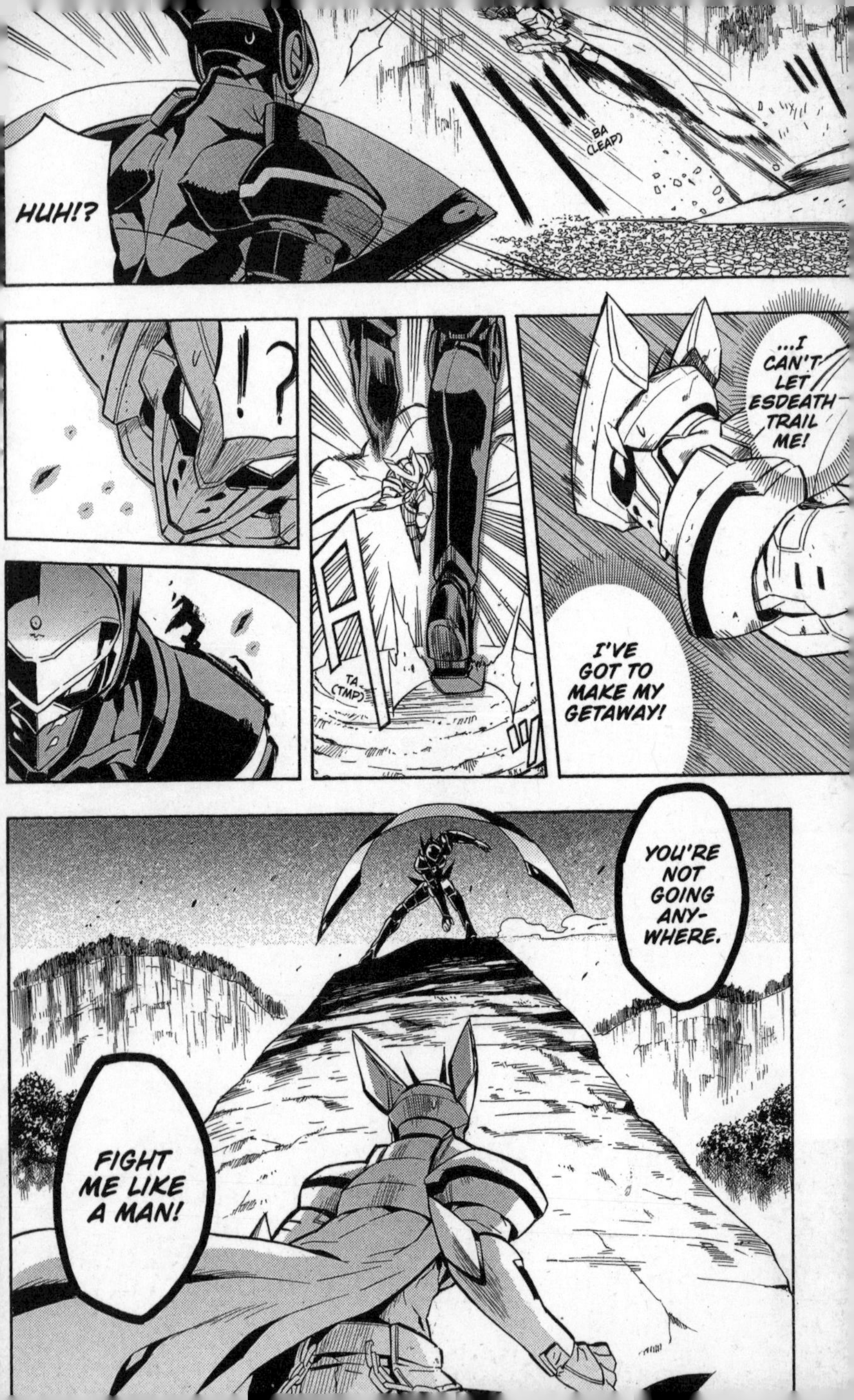
BA (LEAP)
HUH!?
...I CAN'T LET ESDEATH TRAIL ME!
I'VE GOT TO MAKE MY GETAWAY!
TA (TMP)
!?
YOU'RE NOT GOING ANY-WHERE.
FIGHT ME LIKE A MAN!

CHAPTER 19 KILL THE DANGER

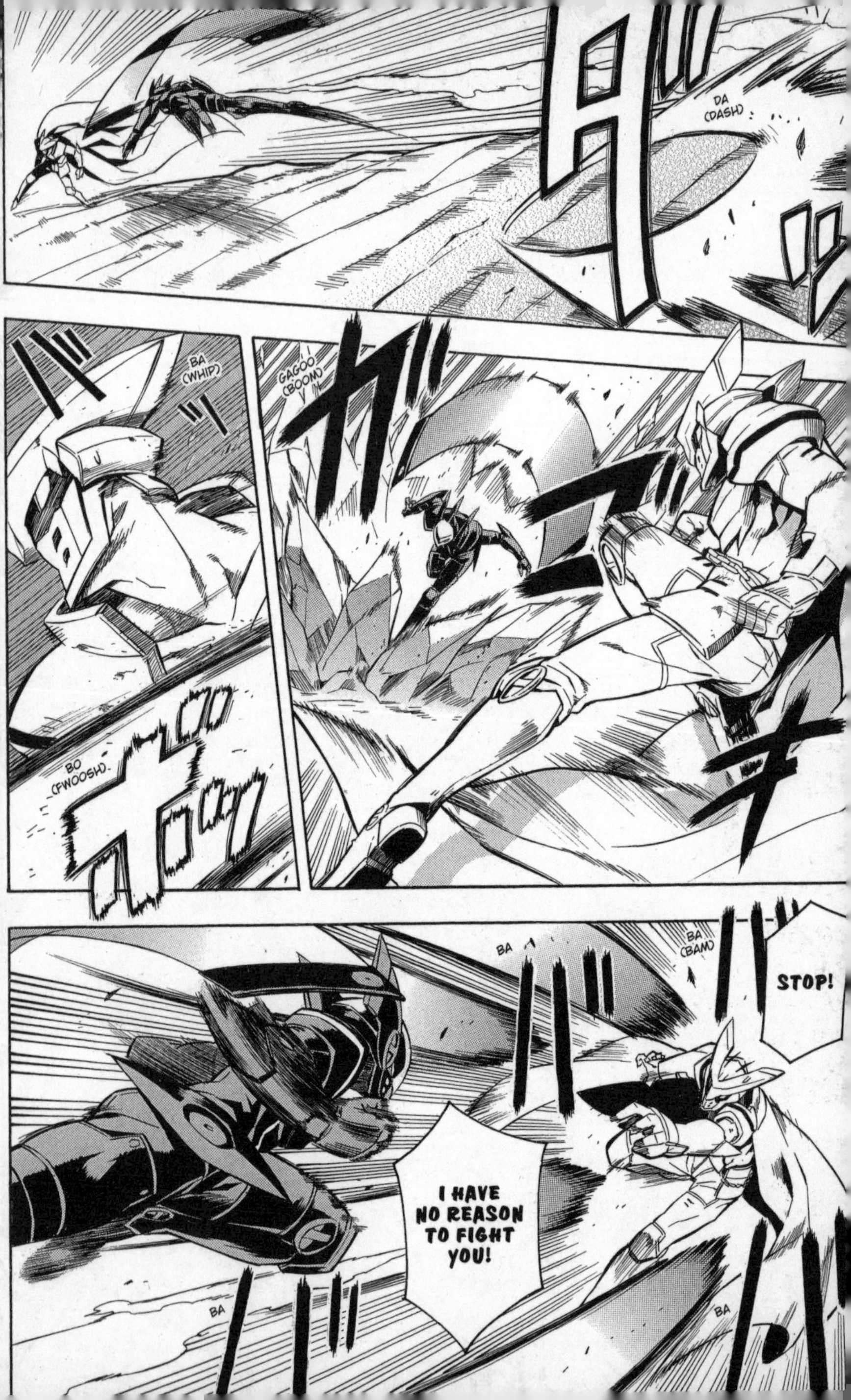
DA (DASH)
GAGOO (BOOM)
BA (WHIP)
BO (FWOOSH)
STOP!
BA
BA (BAM)
I HAVE NO REASON TO FIGHT YOU!
BA
BA

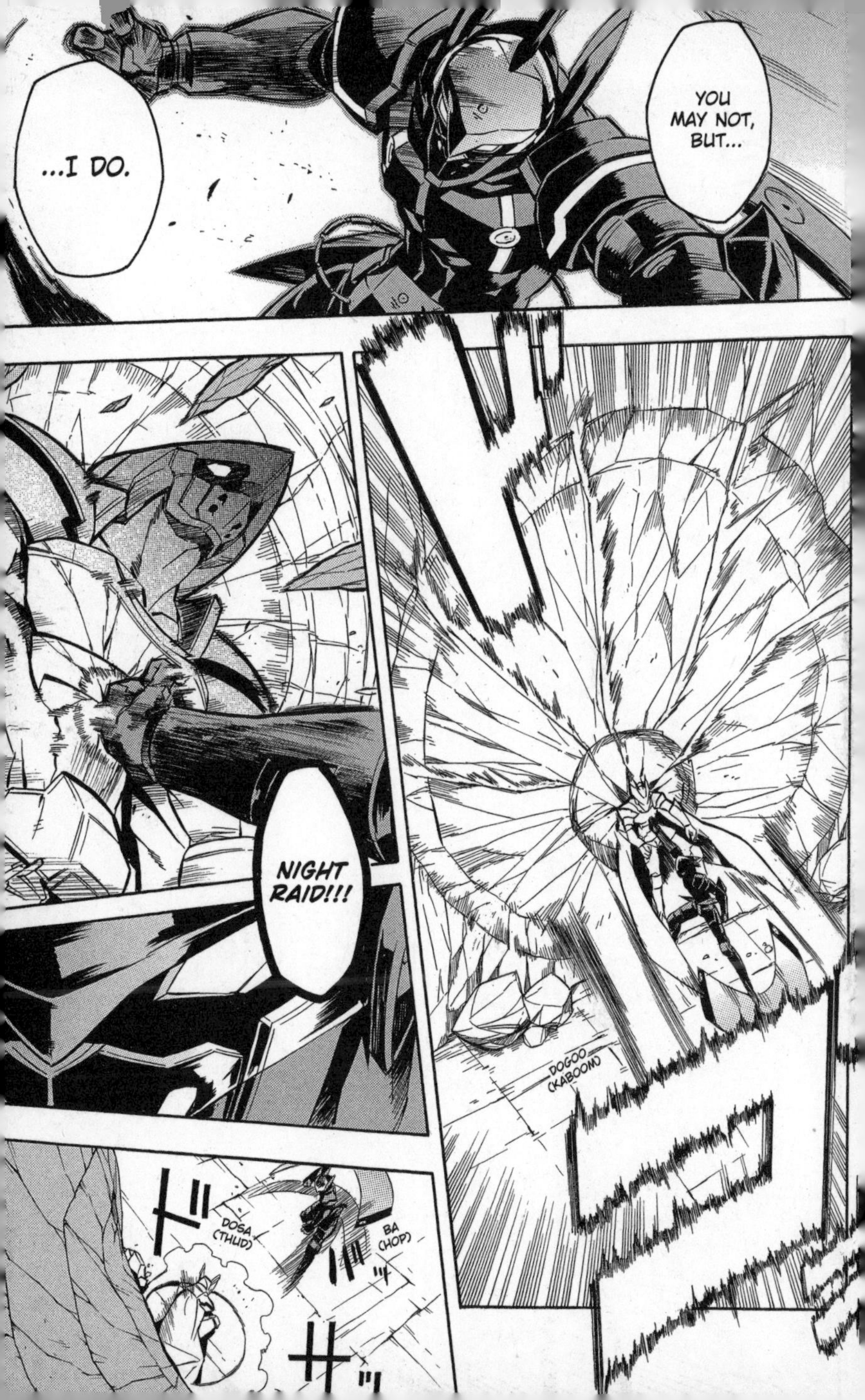
YOU MAY NOT, BUT...
...I DO.
DOGOO (KABOOM)
NIGHT RAID!!!
BA (HOP)
DOSA (THUD)

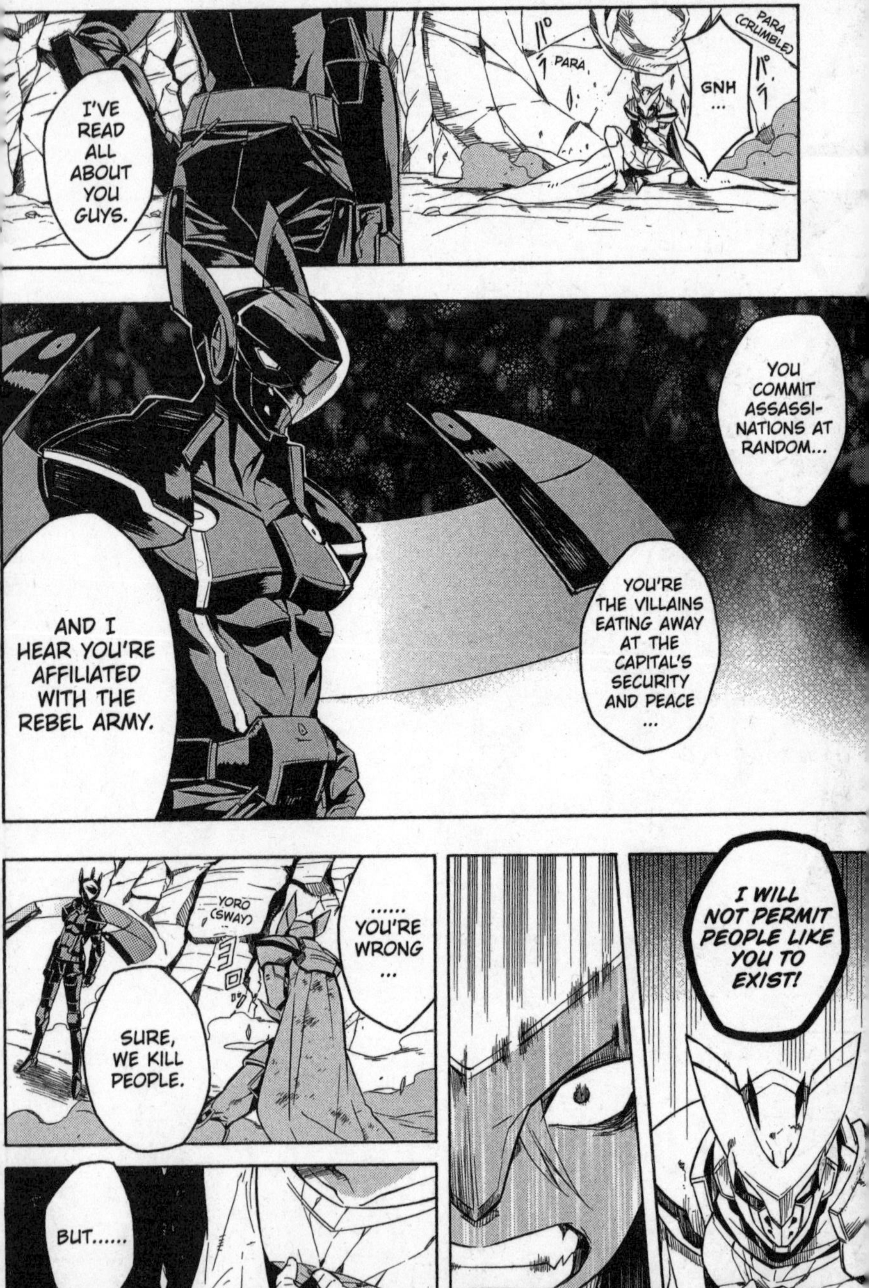
PARA (CRUMBLE)
PARA
GNH ...
I'VE READ ALL ABOUT YOU GUYS.
YOU COMMIT ASSASSI-NATIONS AT RANDOM...
YOU'RE THE VILLAINS EATING AWAY AT THE CAPITAL'S SECURITY AND PEACE ...
AND I HEAR YOU'RE AFFILIATED WITH THE REBEL ARMY.
I WILL NOT PERMIT PEOPLE LIKE YOU TO EXIST!
...... YOU'RE WRONG ...
YORO (SWAY)
SURE, WE KILL PEOPLE.
BUT......

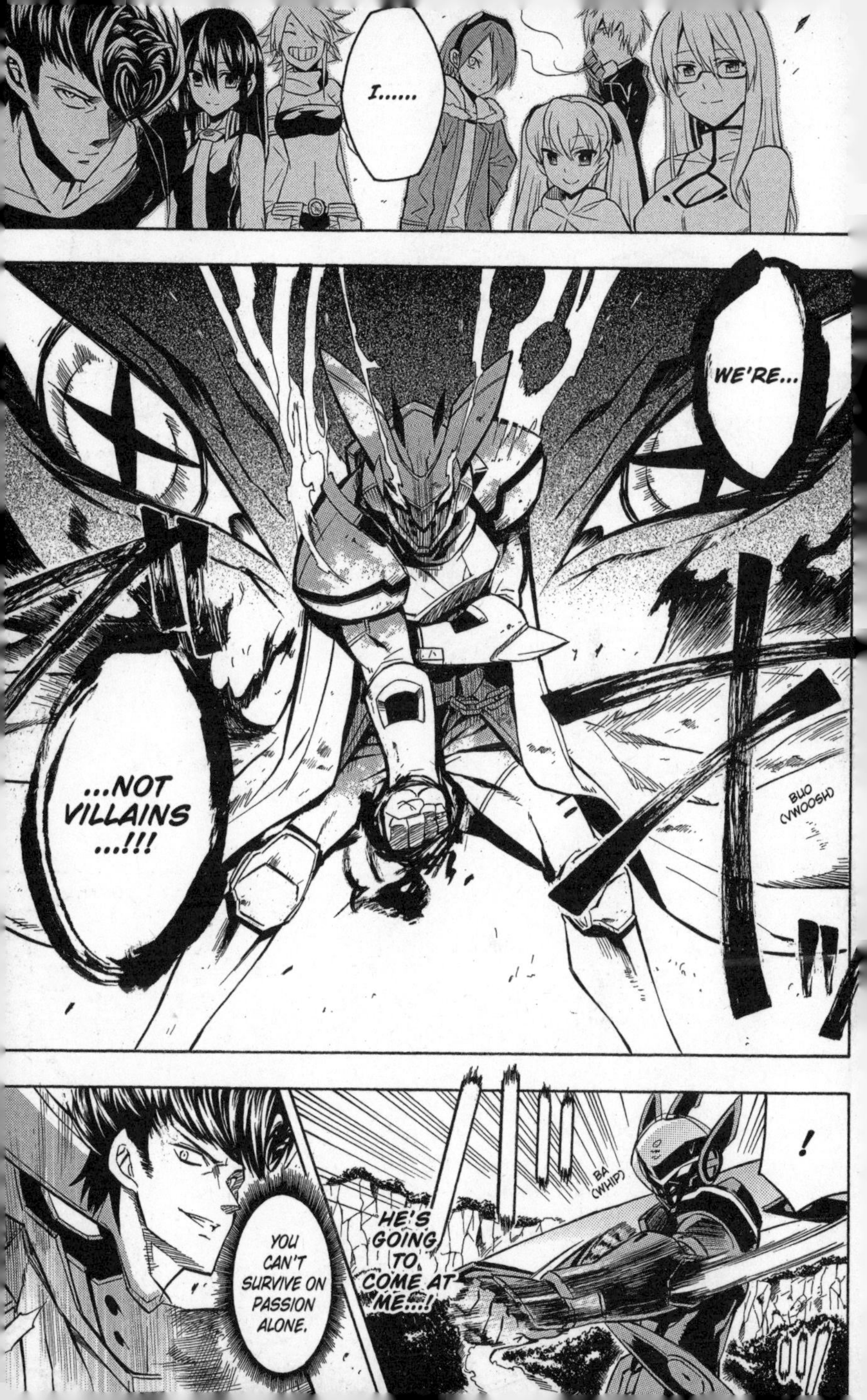
I......
WE'RE...
...NOT VILLAINS ...!!!
BUO (VWOOSH)
BA (WHIP)
HE'S GOING TO COME AT ME...!
YOU CAN'T SURVIVE ON PASSION ALONE.

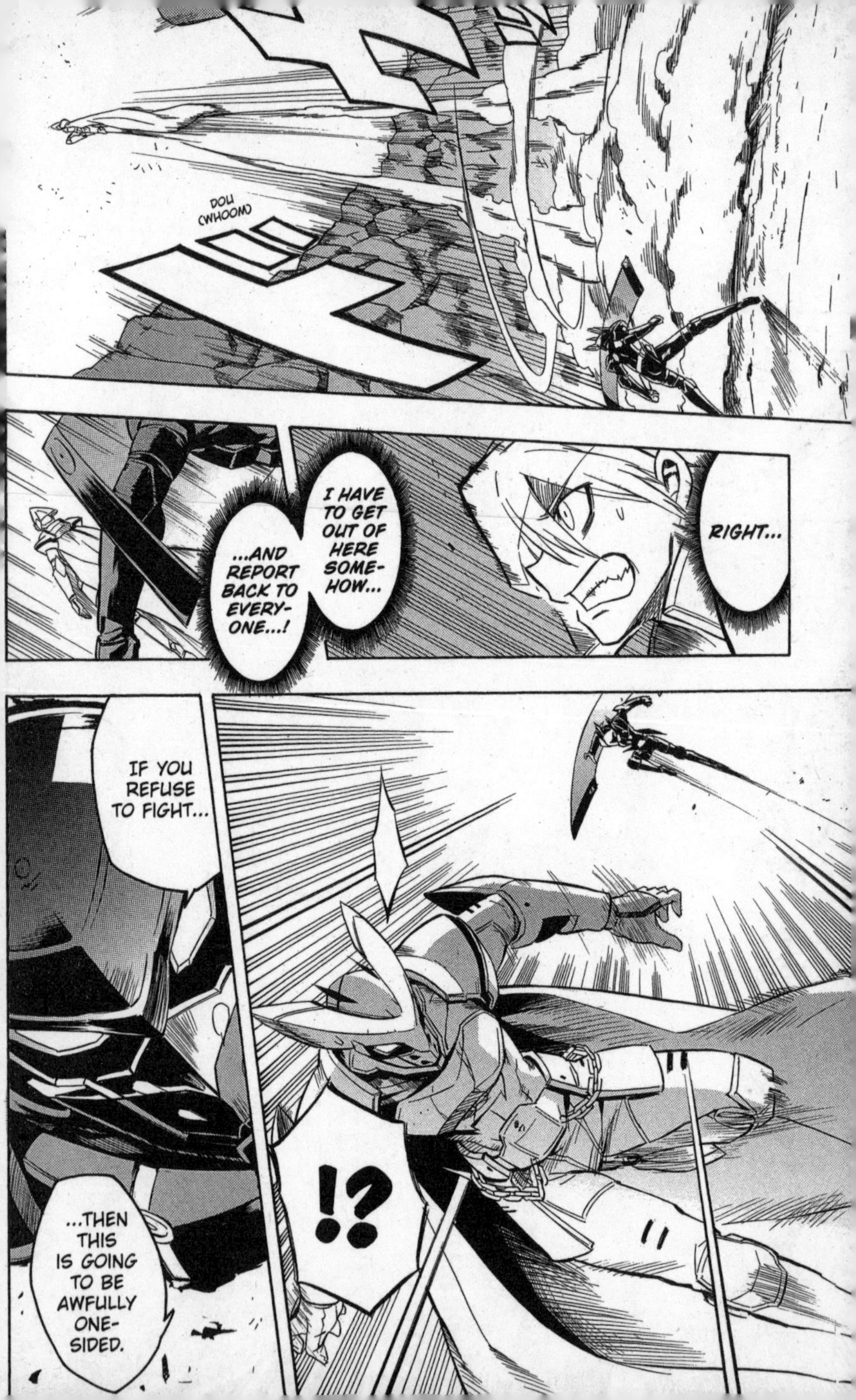
DOU (WHOOM)
RIGHT...
I HAVE TO GET OUT OF HERE SOME-HOW...
...AND REPORT BACK TO EVERY-ONE...!
IF YOU REFUSE TO FIGHT...
!?
...THEN THIS IS GOING TO BE AWFULLY ONE-SIDED.

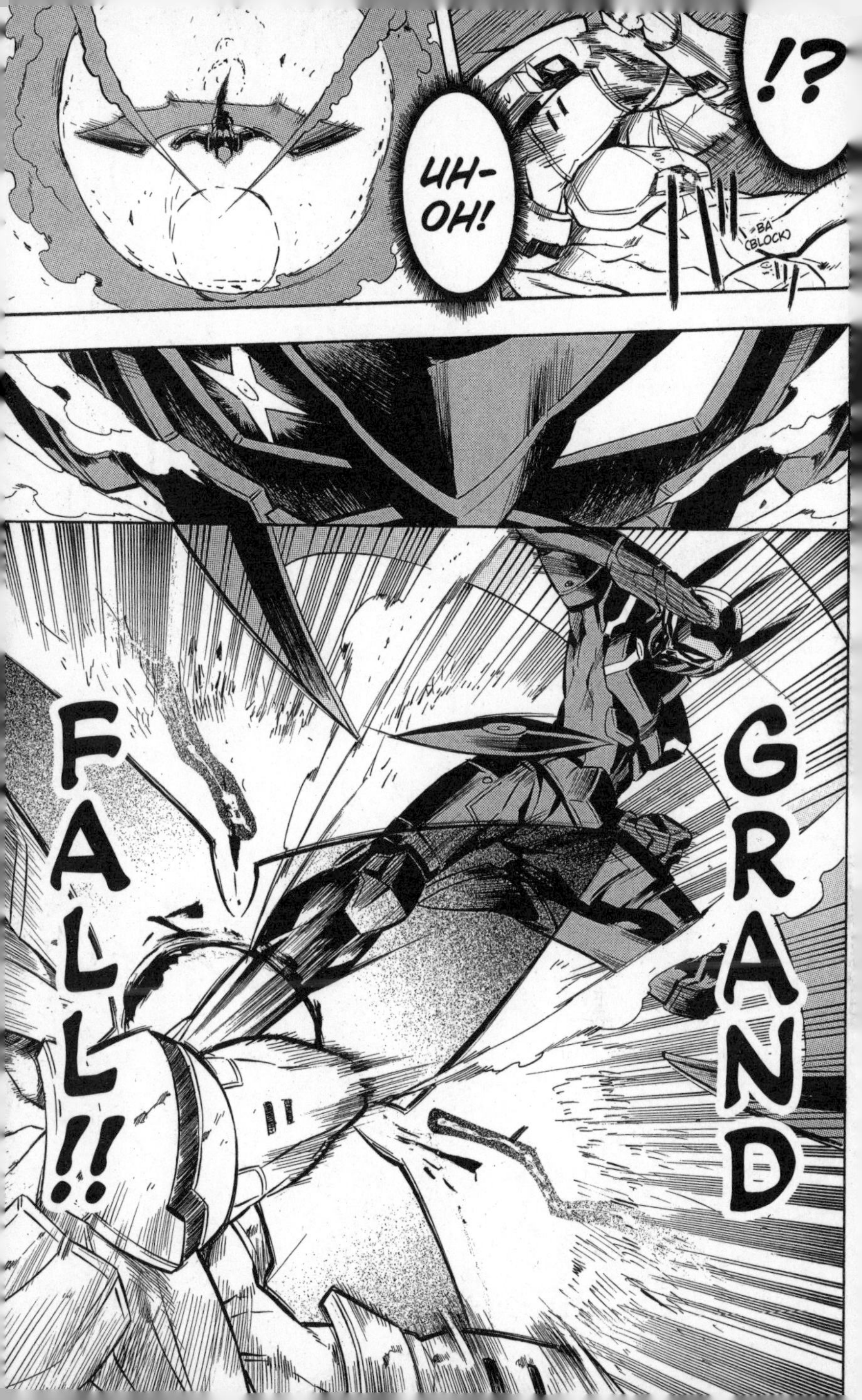
!?
UH-OH!
BA (BLOCK)
GRAND
FALL!!

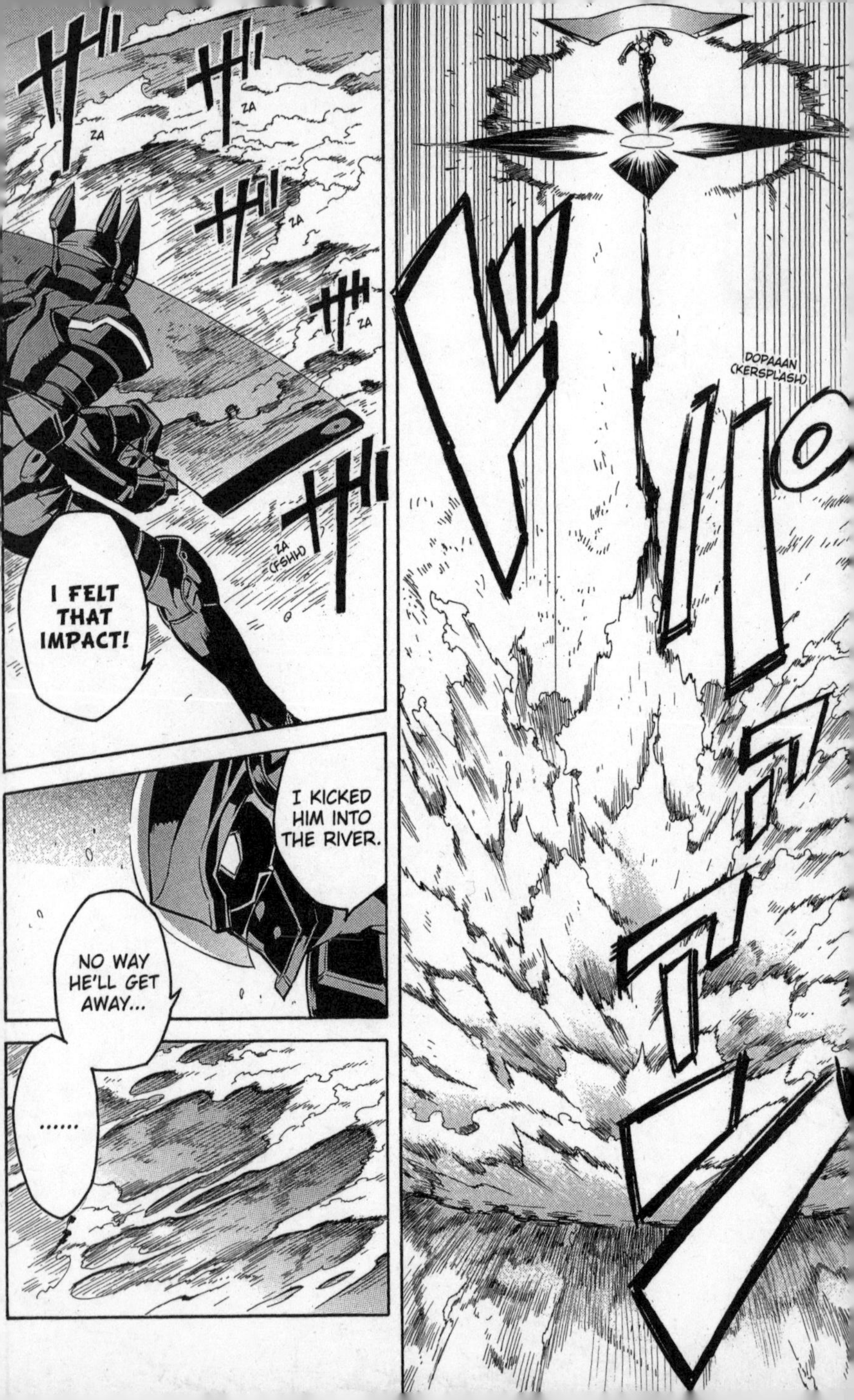
DOPAAAN (KERSPLASH)
ZA
ZA
ZA
ZA
ZA (FSHH)
I FELT THAT IMPACT!
I KICKED HIM INTO THE RIVER.
NO WAY HE'LL GET AWAY...
......

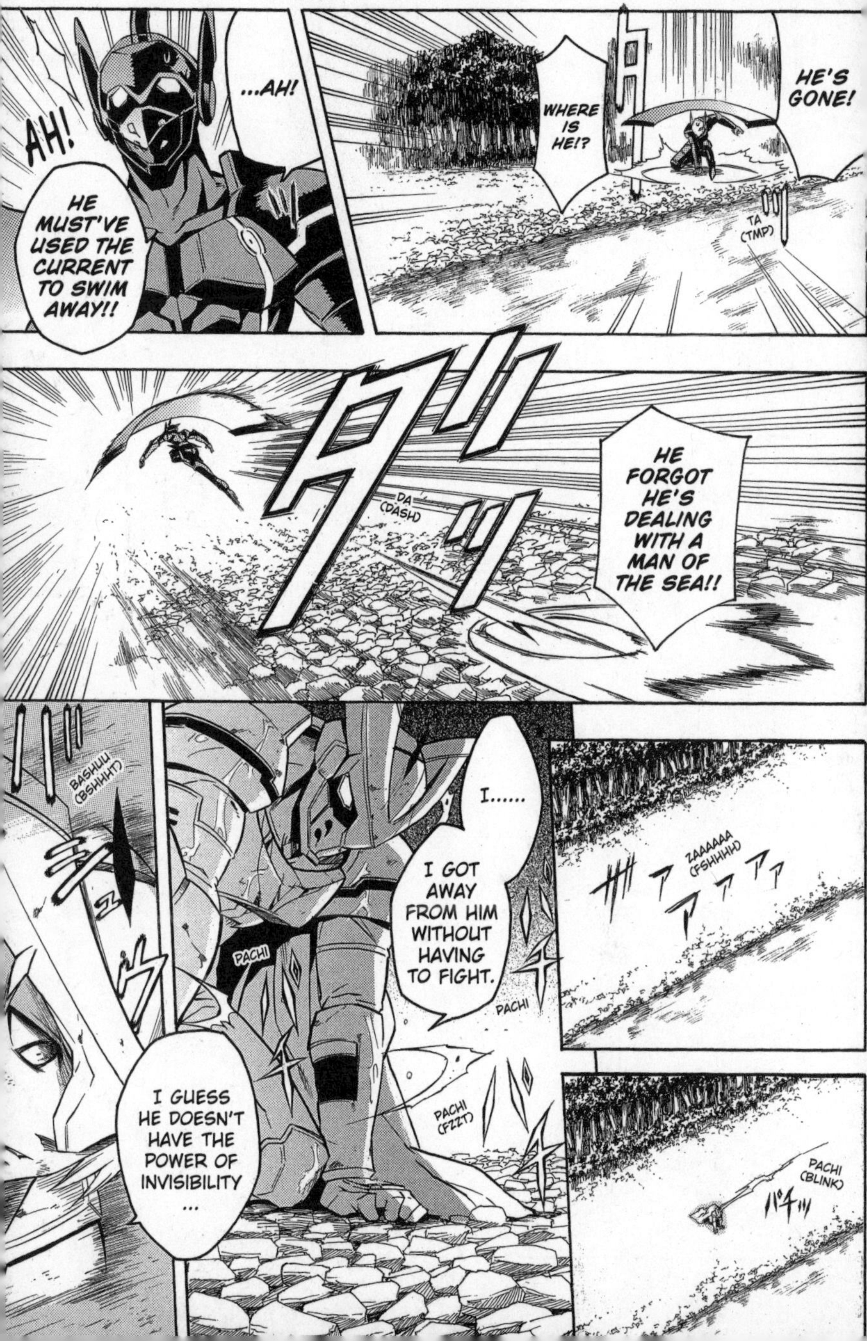

HE'S GONE!
WHERE IS HE!?
TA (TMP)
...AH!
AH!
HE MUST'VE USED THE CURRENT TO SWIM AWAY!!
DA (DASH)
HE FORGOT HE'S DEALING WITH A MAN OF THE SEA!!
ZAAAAAA (FSHHHH)
PACHI (BLINK)
I......
I GOT AWAY FROM HIM WITHOUT HAVING TO FIGHT.
PACHI
PACHI
PACHI (FZZT)
BASHUU (BSHHHT)
I GUESS HE DOESN'T HAVE THE POWER OF INVISIBILITY ...

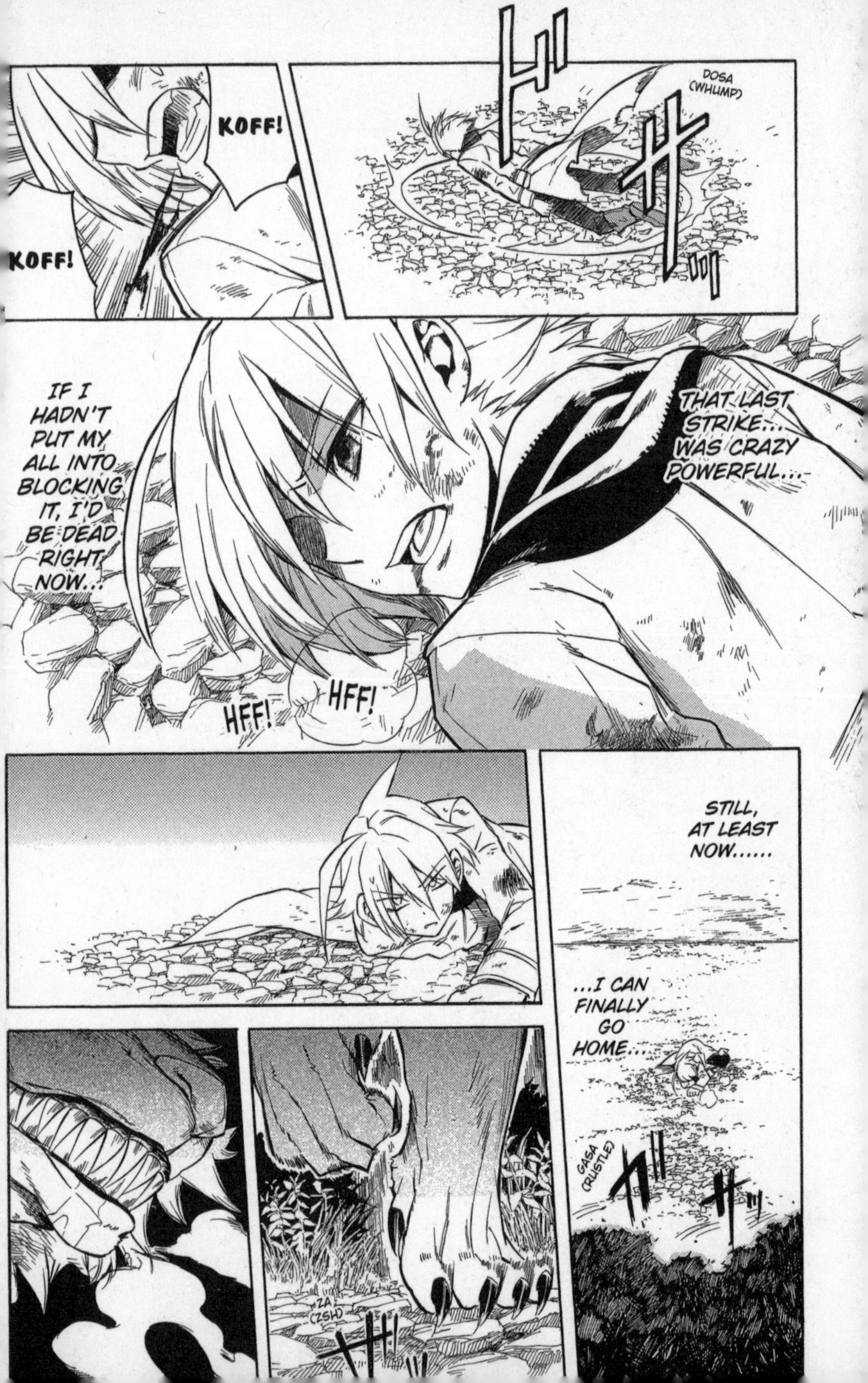
DOSA (WHUMP)
KOFF!
KOFF!
THAT LAST STRIKE... WAS CRAZY POWERFUL...
IF I HADN'T PUT MY ALL INTO BLOCKING IT, I'D BE DEAD RIGHT NOW...
HFF!
HFF!
STILL, AT LEAST NOW......
...I CAN FINALLY GO HOME...
GASA (RUSTLE)
ZA (ZSH)

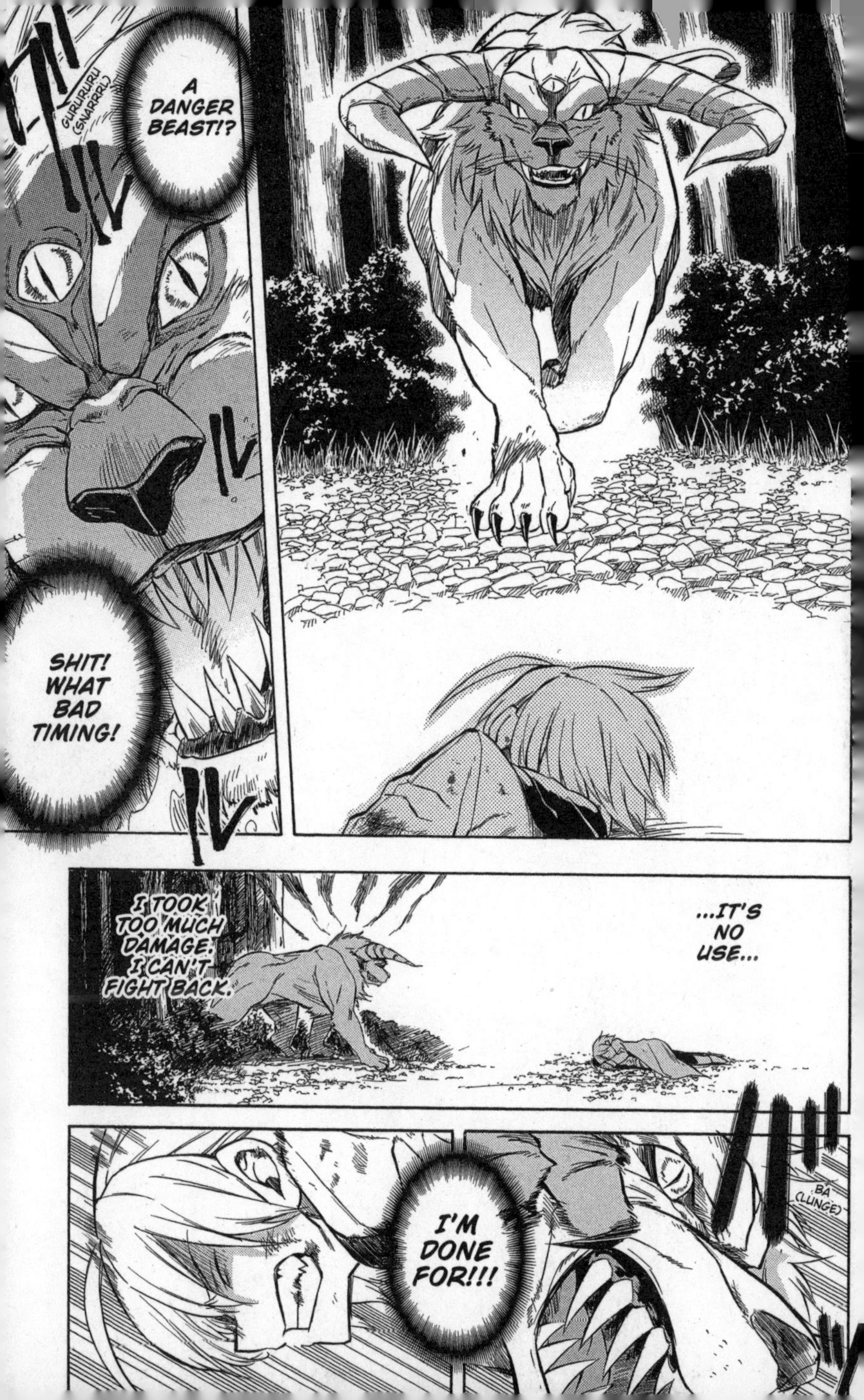
GURURURU (SNARRRL)
A DANGER BEAST!?
SHIT! WHAT BAD TIMING!
...IT'S NO USE...
I TOOK TOO MUCH DAMAGE. I CAN'T FIGHT BACK.
BA (LUNGE)
I'M DONE FOR!!!

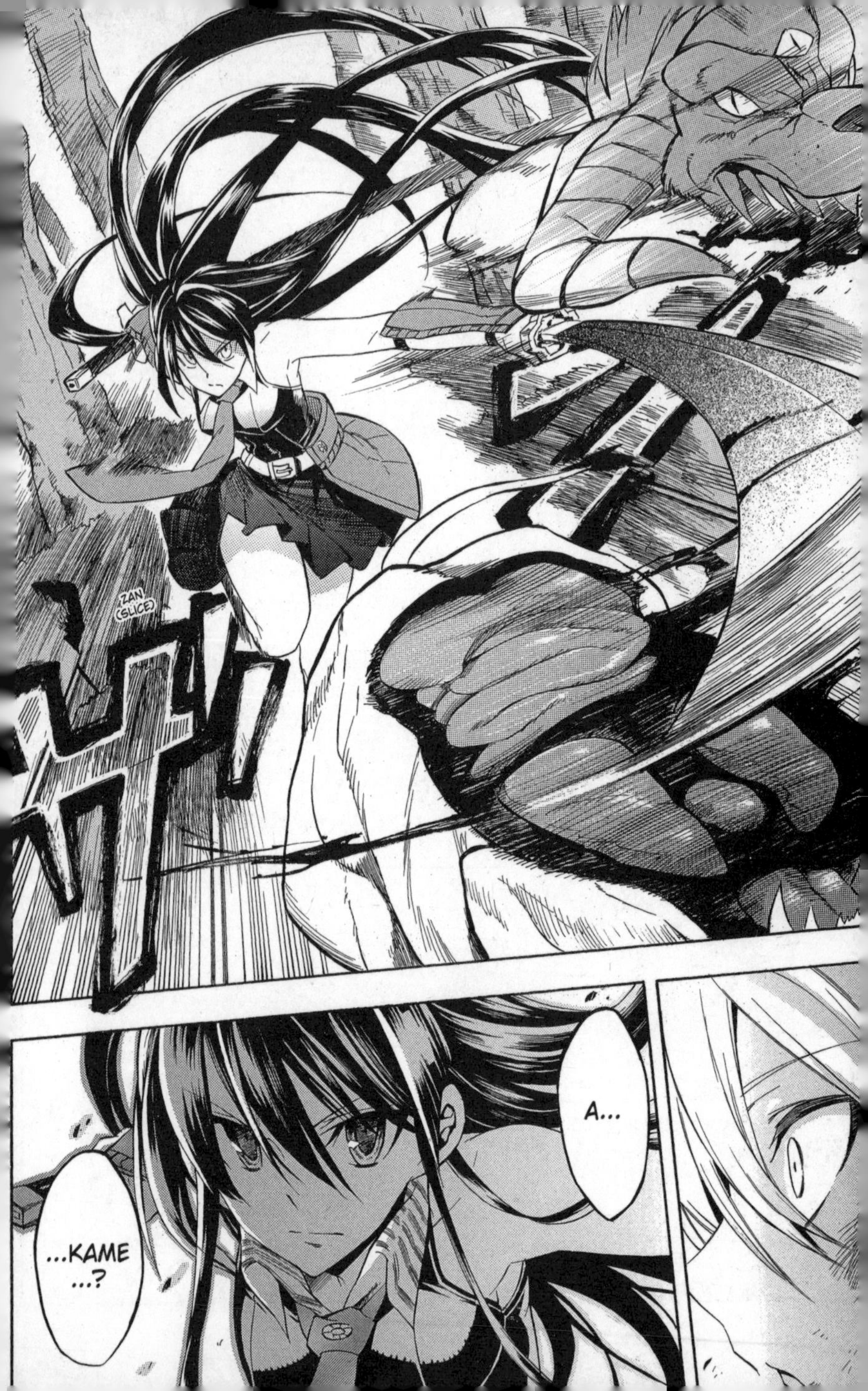
ZAN (SLICE)
A...
...KAME ...?

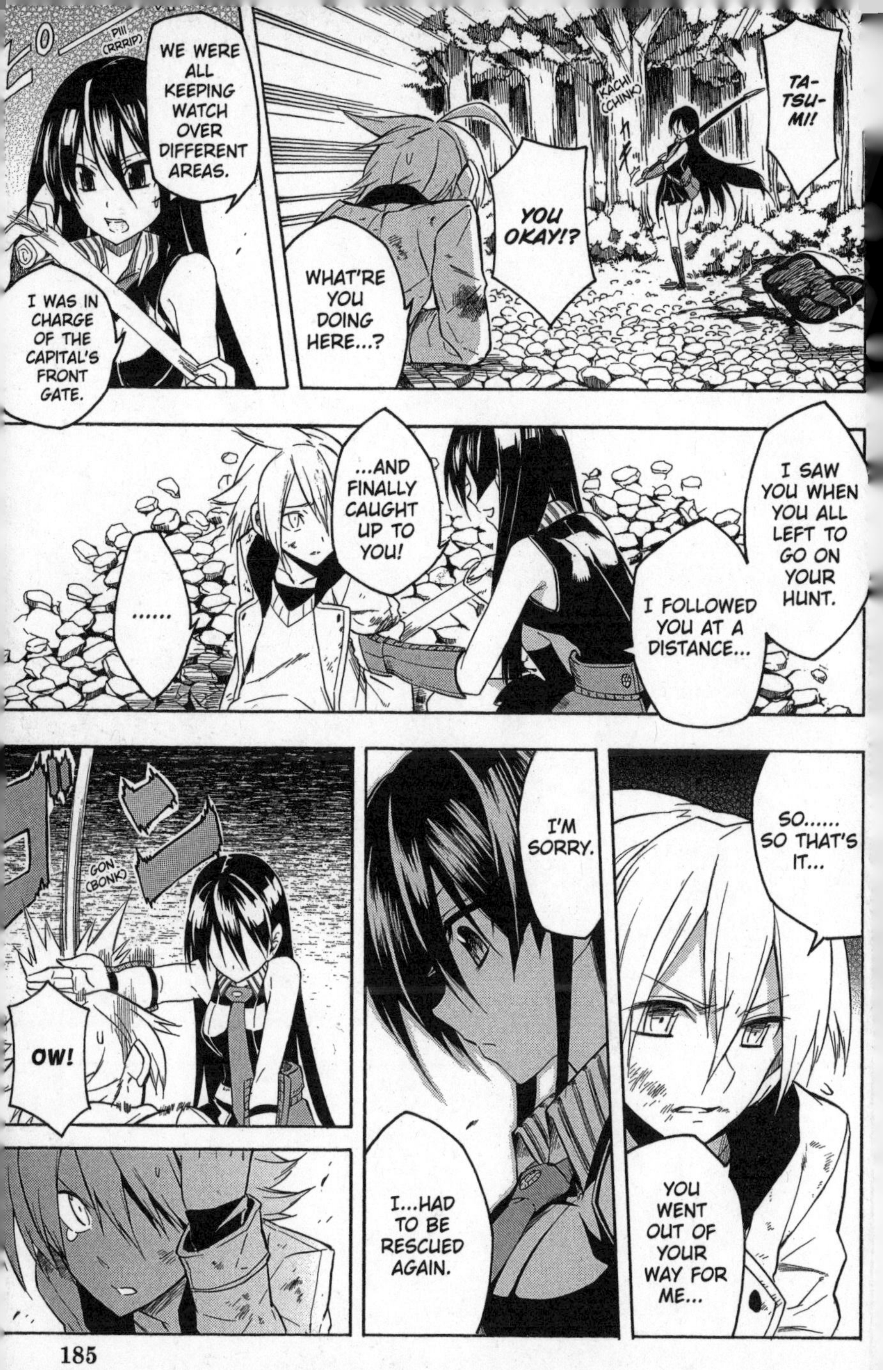
TA-TSU-MI!
KACHI (CHINK)
YOU OKAY!?
WHAT'RE YOU DOING HERE...?
PIII (RRRIP)
WE WERE ALL KEEPING WATCH OVER DIFFERENT AREAS.
I WAS IN CHARGE OF THE CAPITAL'S FRONT GATE.
I SAW YOU WHEN YOU ALL LEFT TO GO ON YOUR HUNT.
I FOLLOWED YOU AT A DISTANCE...
...AND FINALLY CAUGHT UP TO YOU!
......
SO...... SO THAT'S IT...
YOU WENT OUT OF YOUR WAY FOR ME...
I'M SORRY.
I...HAD TO BE RESCUED AGAIN.
GON (BONK)
OW!

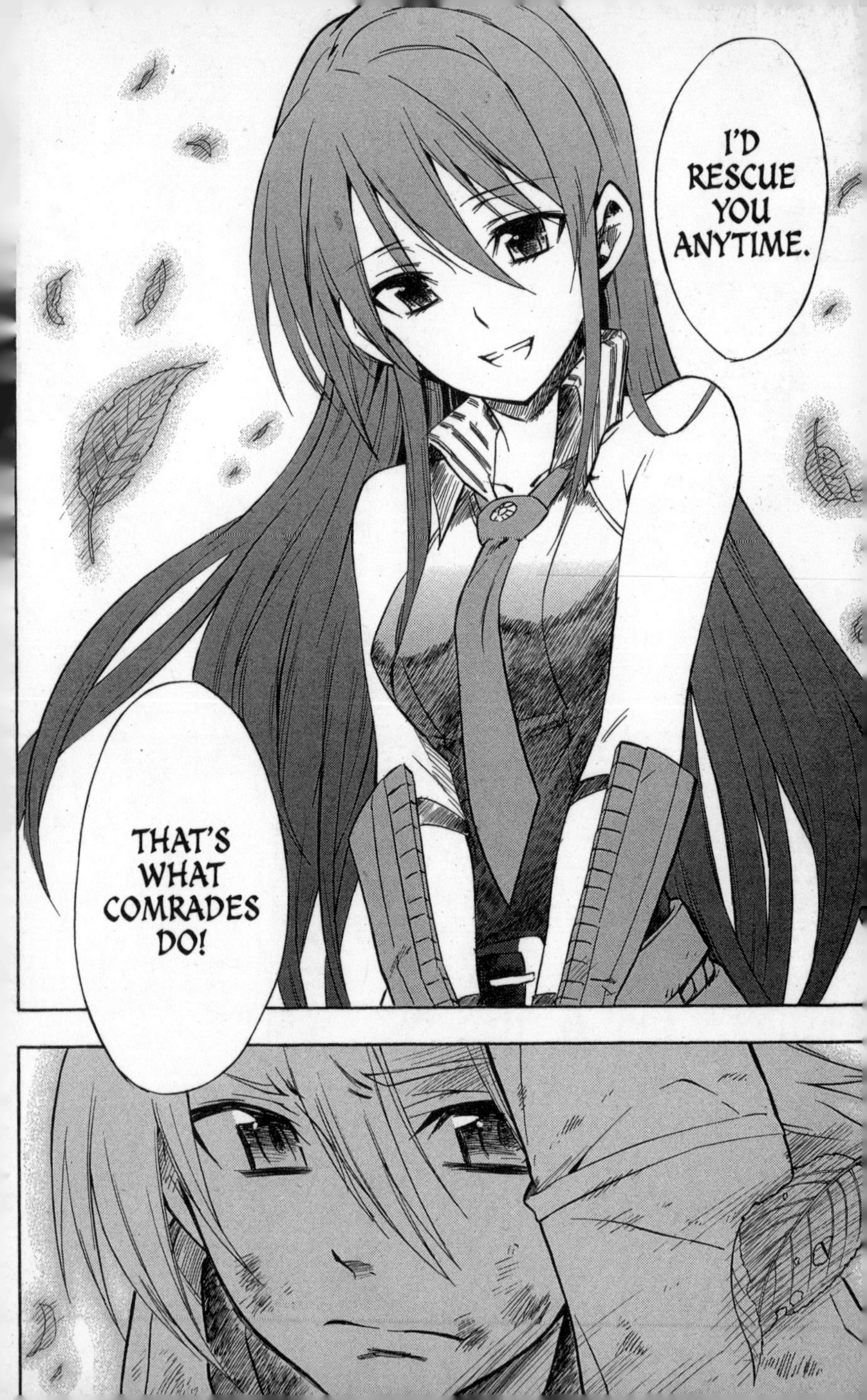
I'D RESCUE YOU ANYTIME.
THAT'S WHAT COMRADES DO!

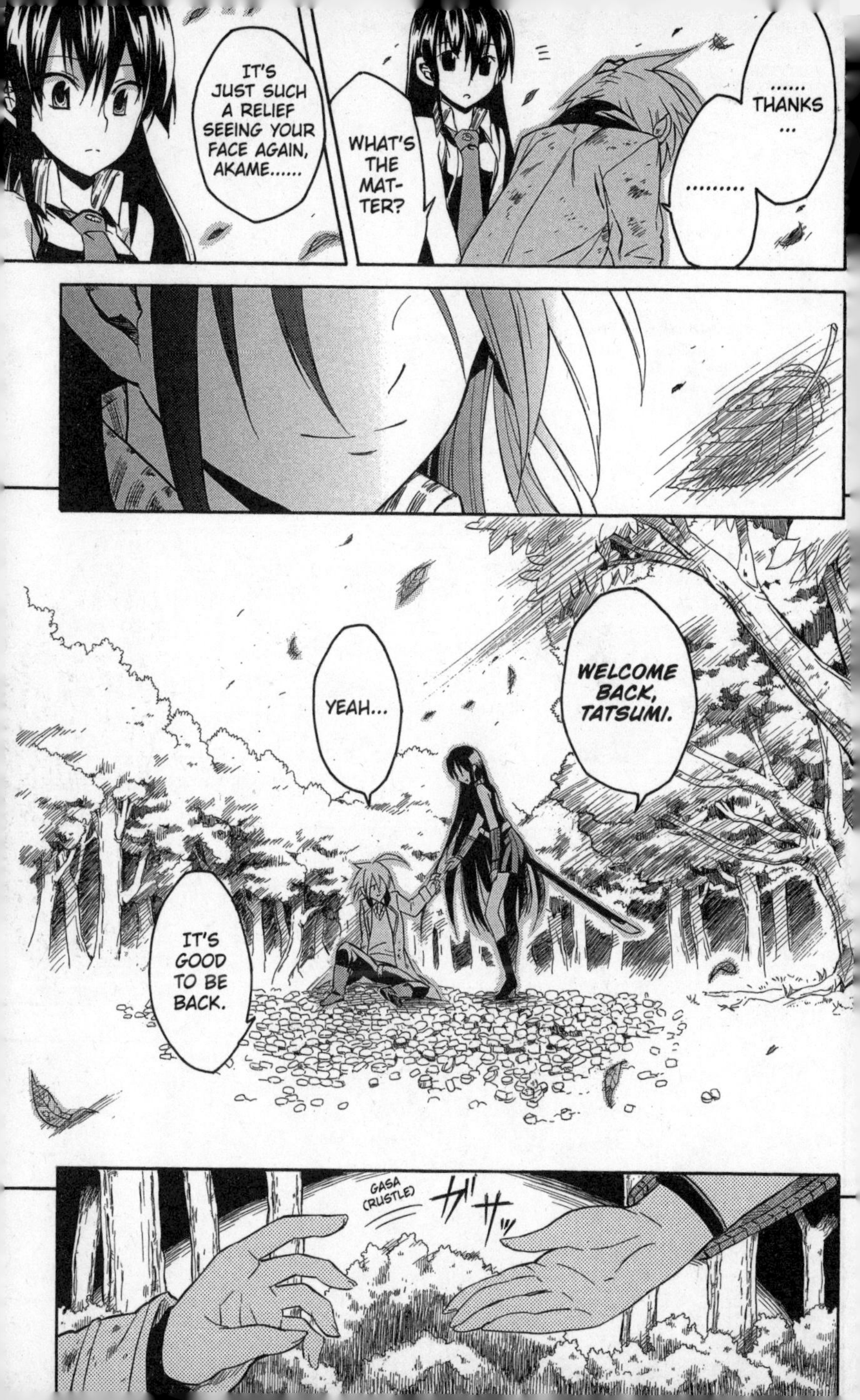

......THANKS ...
....
WHAT'S THE MAT-TER?
IT'S JUST SUCH A RELIEF SEEING YOUR FACE AGAIN, AKAME......
WELCOME BACK, TATSUMI.
YEAH...
IT'S GOOD TO BE BACK.
GASA (RUSTLE)

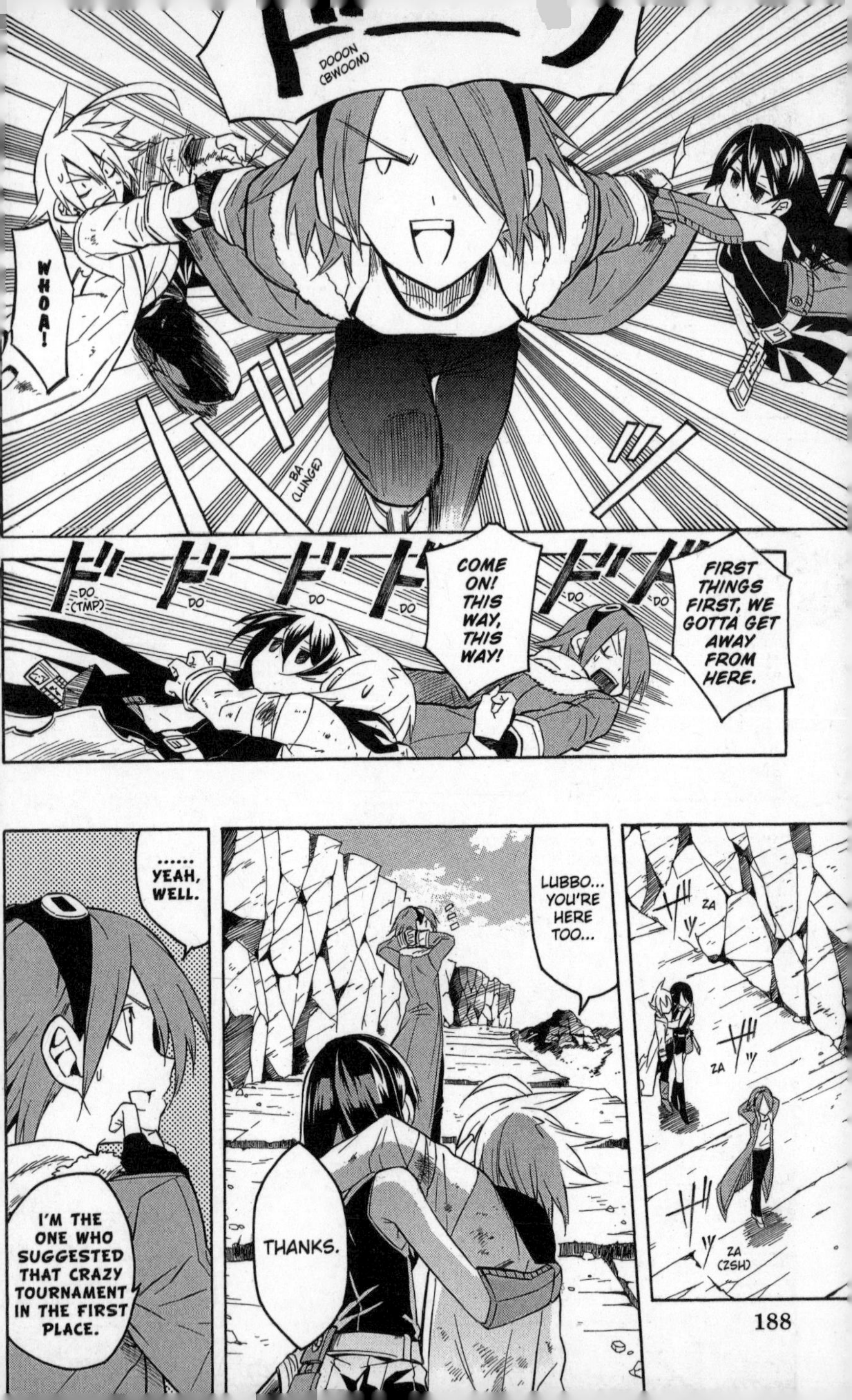
DOOON (BWOOM)
WHOA!
BA (LUNGE)
FIRST THINGS FIRST, WE GOTTA GET AWAY FROM HERE.
COME ON! THIS WAY, THIS WAY!
DO DO DO DO DO DO (TMP)
ZA ZA ZA (ZSH)
LUBBO... YOU'RE HERE TOO...
THANKS.
...... YEAH, WELL.
I'M THE ONE WHO SUGGESTED THAT CRAZY TOURNAMENT IN THE FIRST PLACE.

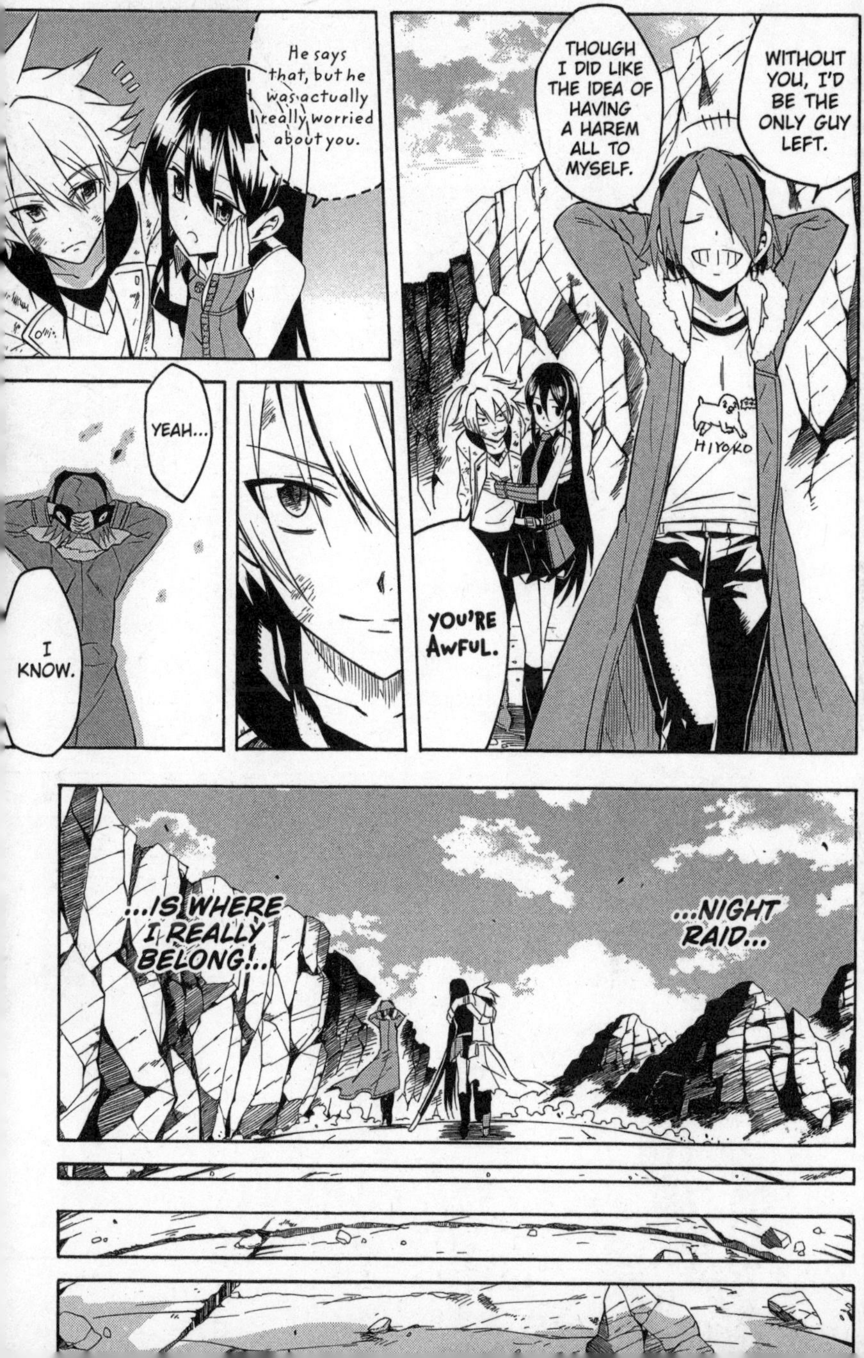
WITHOUT YOU, I'D BE THE ONLY GUY LEFT.
THOUGH I DID LIKE THE IDEA OF HAVING A HAREM ALL TO MYSELF.
He says that, but he was actually really worried about you.
HIYOKO
YOU'RE AWFUL.
YEAH...
I KNOW.
...NIGHT RAID...
...IS WHERE I REALLY BELONG!...

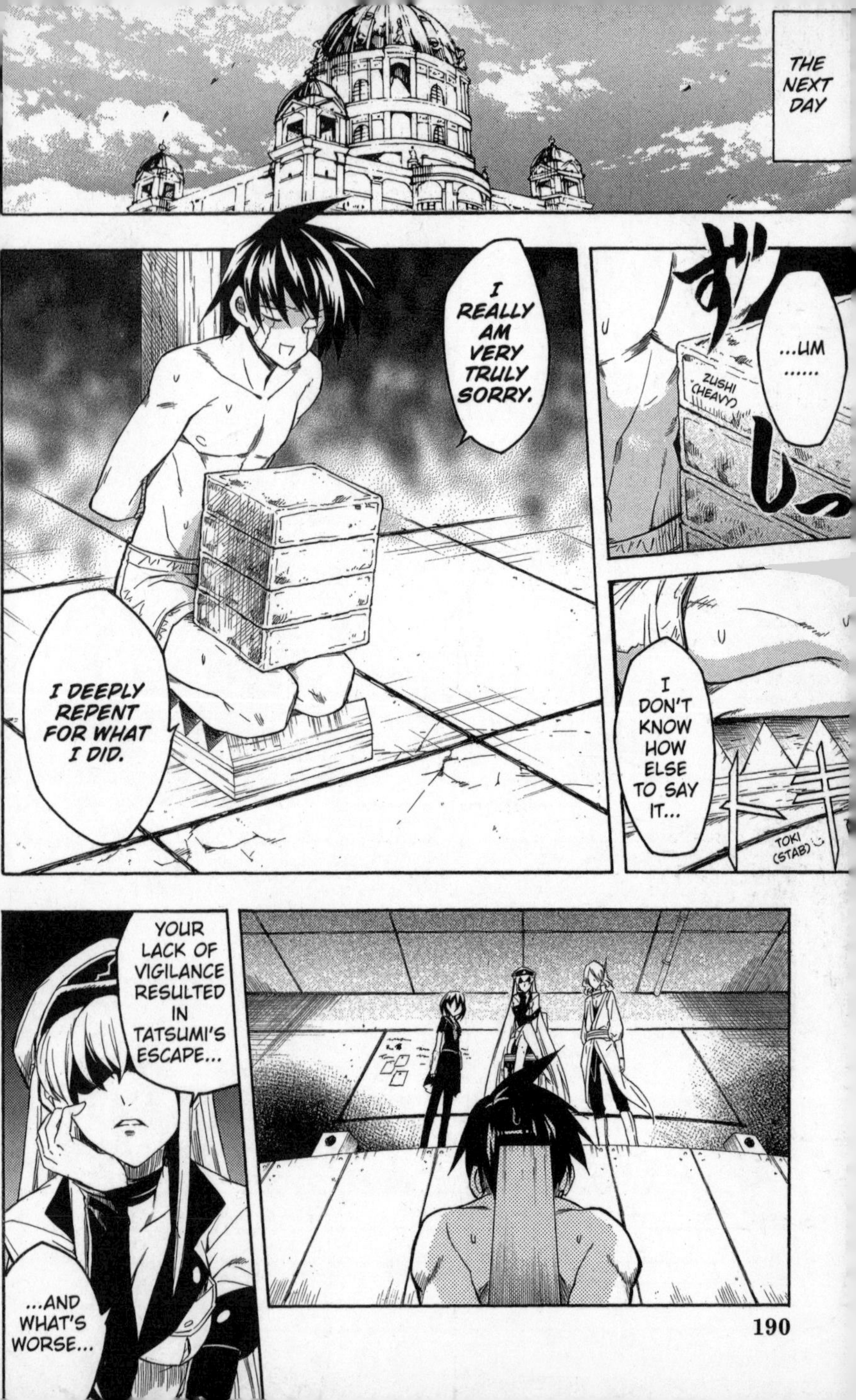
THE NEXT DAY
ずしっ
ZUSHI (HEAVY)
...UM ......
I DON'T KNOW HOW ELSE TO SAY IT...
TOKI (STAB)
I REALLY AM VERY TRULY SORRY.
I DEEPLY REPENT FOR WHAT I DID.
YOUR LACK OF VIGILANCE RESULTED IN TATSUMI'S ESCAPE...
...AND WHAT'S WORSE...

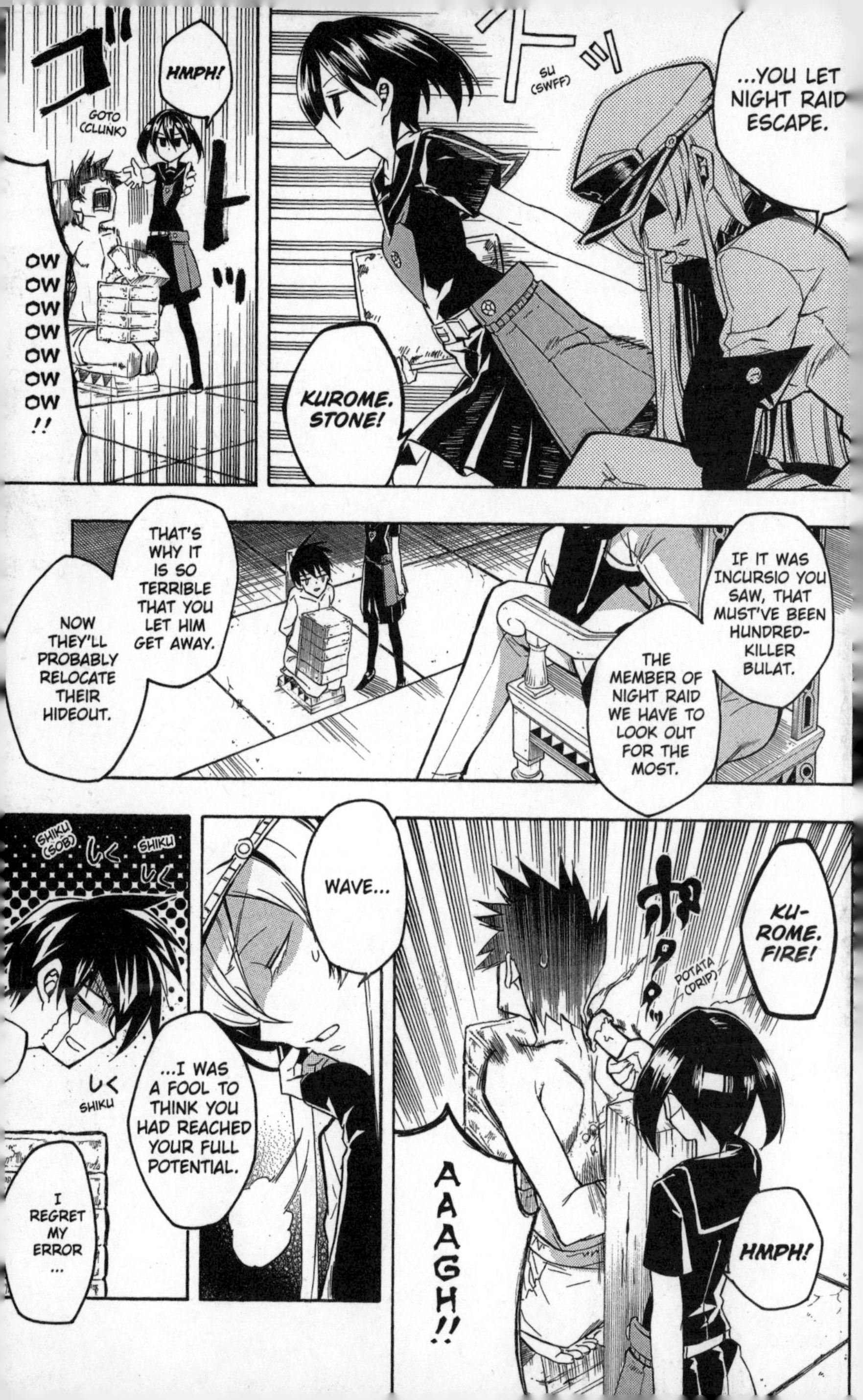
SU (SWFF)
...YOU LET NIGHT RAID ESCAPE.
KUROME. STONE!
HMPH!
GOTO (CLUNK)
OW OW OW OW OW OW OW !!
IF IT WAS INCURSIO YOU SAW, THAT MUST'VE BEEN HUNDRED-KILLER BULAT.
THE MEMBER OF NIGHT RAID WE HAVE TO LOOK OUT FOR THE MOST.
THAT'S WHY IT IS SO TERRIBLE THAT YOU LET HIM GET AWAY.
NOW THEY'LL PROBABLY RELOCATE THEIR HIDEOUT.
KU-ROME. FIRE!
POTATA (DRIP)
HMPH!
AAAGH!!
WAVE...
...I WAS A FOOL TO THINK YOU HAD REACHED YOUR FULL POTENTIAL.
SHIKU (SOB)
SHIKU
SHIKU
I REGRET MY ERROR...

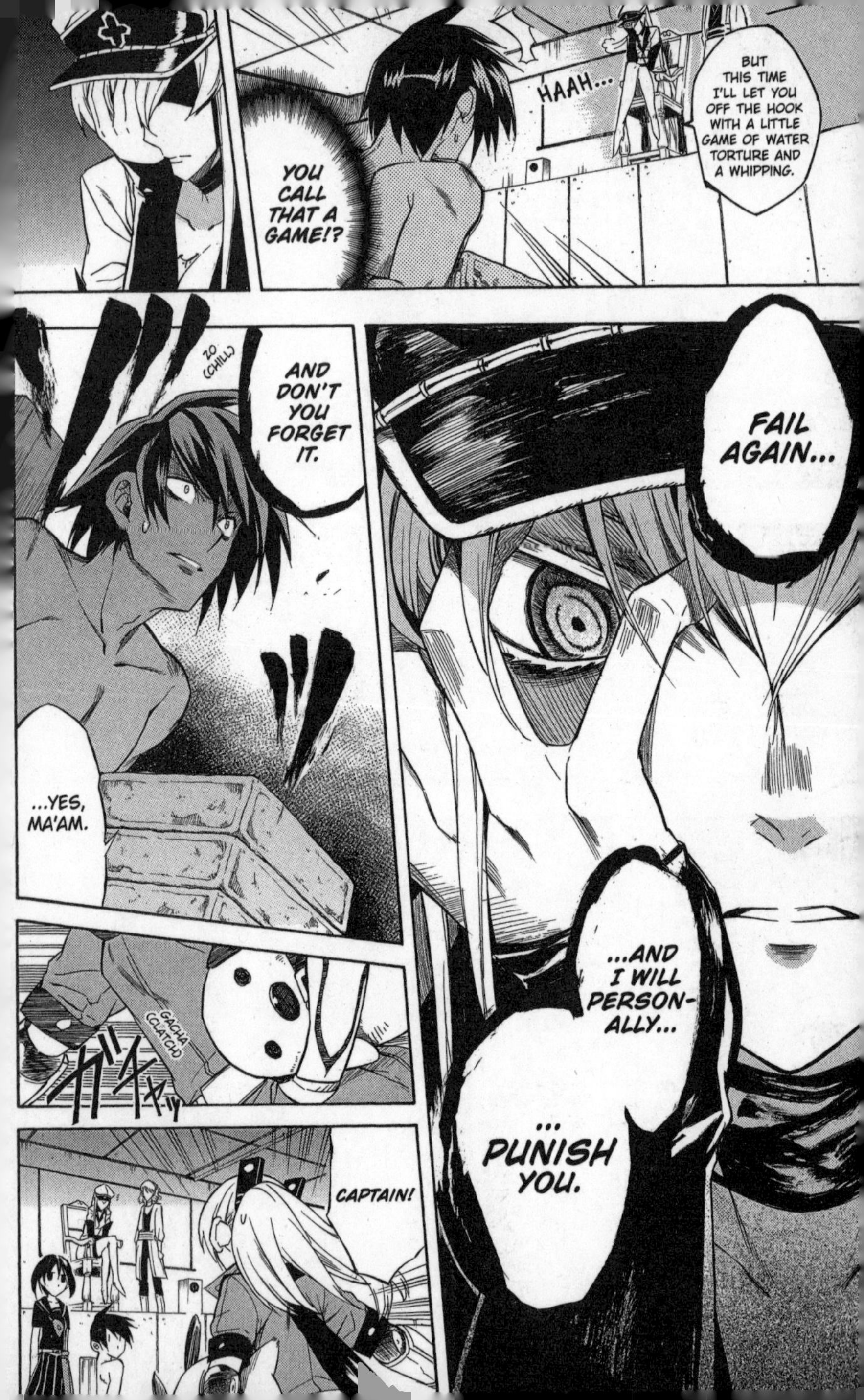
BUT THIS TIME I'LL LET YOU OFF THE HOOK WITH A LITTLE GAME OF WATER TORTURE AND A WHIPPING.
HAAH...
YOU CALL THAT A GAME!?
FAIL AGAIN...
...AND I WILL PERSON-ALLY...
... PUNISH YOU.
AND DON'T YOU FORGET IT.
ZO (CHILL)
...YES, MA'AM.
GACHA (CLATCH)
CAPTAIN!

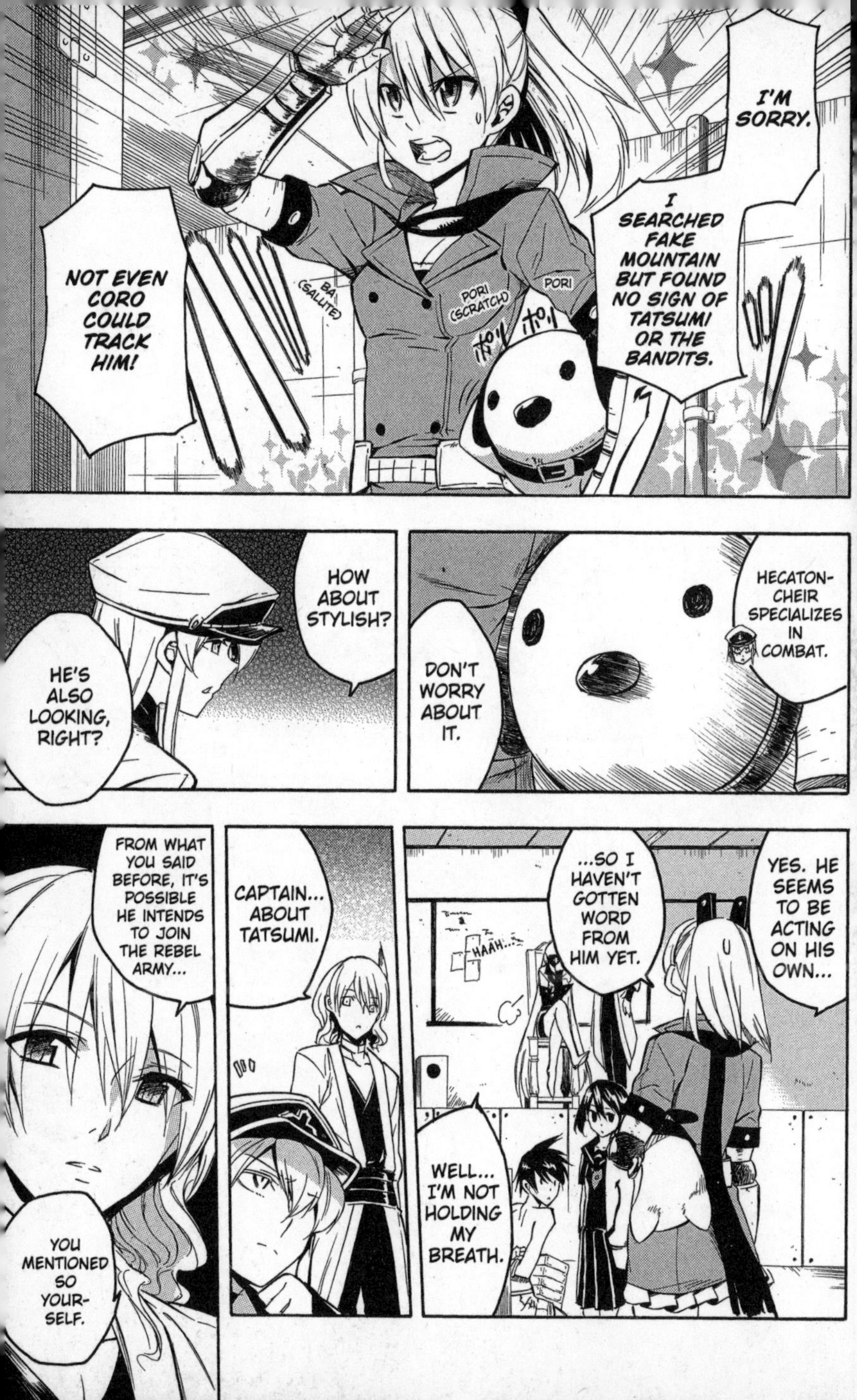
I'M SORRY.
I SEARCHED FAKE MOUNTAIN BUT FOUND NO SIGN OF TATSUMI OR THE BANDITS.
PORI
PORI (SCRATCH)
BA (SALUTE)
NOT EVEN CORO COULD TRACK HIM!
HECATON-CHEIR SPECIALIZES IN COMBAT.
DON'T WORRY ABOUT IT.
HOW ABOUT STYLISH?
HE'S ALSO LOOKING, RIGHT?
YES. HE SEEMS TO BE ACTING ON HIS OWN...
...SO I HAVEN'T GOTTEN WORD FROM HIM YET.
HAAH...
WELL... I'M NOT HOLDING MY BREATH.
CAPTAIN... ABOUT TATSUMI.
FROM WHAT YOU SAID BEFORE, IT'S POSSIBLE HE INTENDS TO JOIN THE REBEL ARMY...
YOU MENTIONED SO YOURSELF.

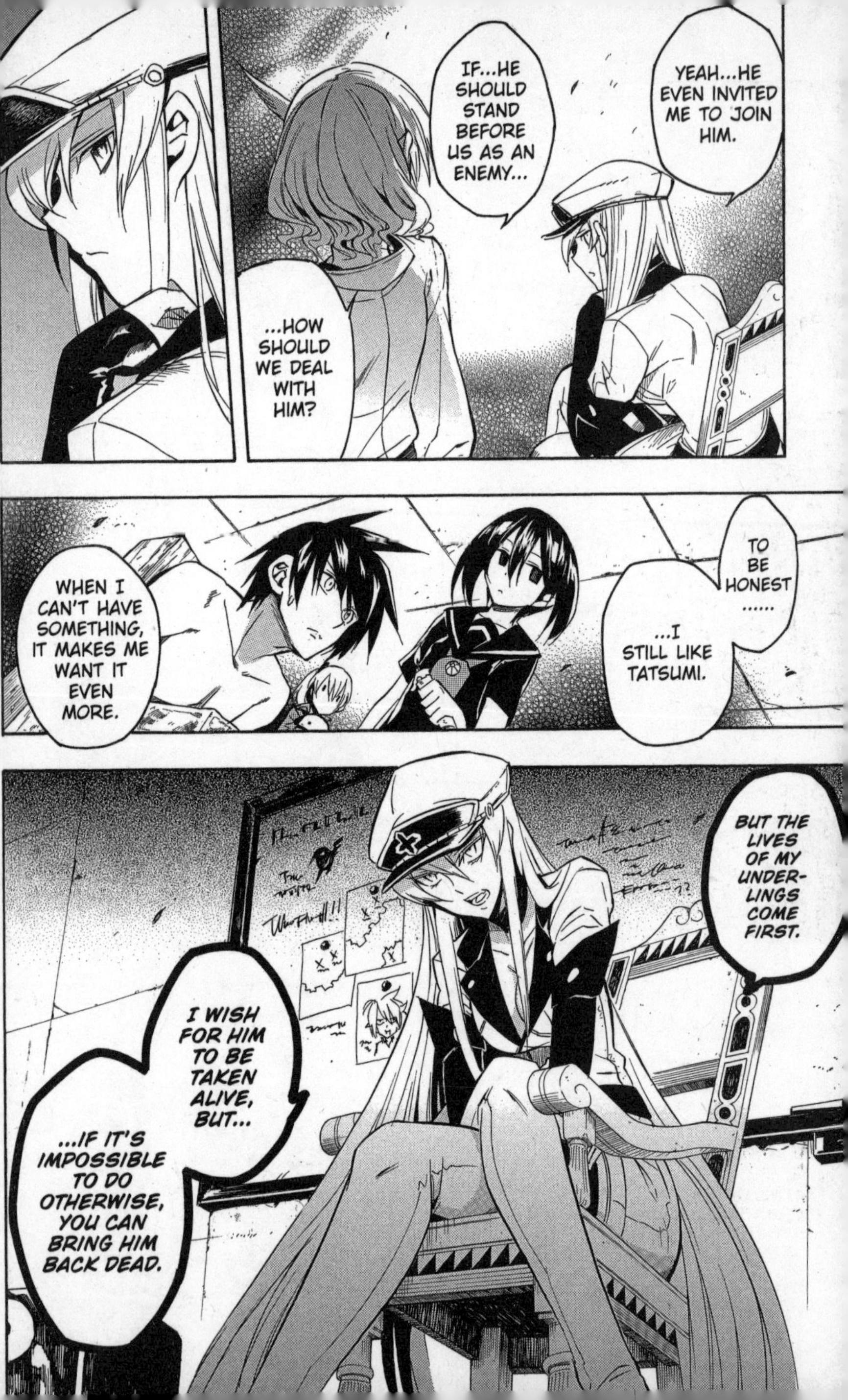
YEAH...HE EVEN INVITED ME TO JOIN HIM.
IF...HE SHOULD STAND BEFORE US AS AN ENEMY...
...HOW SHOULD WE DEAL WITH HIM?
TO BE HONEST ......
...I STILL LIKE TATSUMI.
WHEN I CAN'T HAVE SOMETHING, IT MAKES ME WANT IT EVEN MORE.
BUT THE LIVES OF MY UNDER-LINGS COME FIRST.
I WISH FOR HIM TO BE TAKEN ALIVE, BUT...
...IF IT'S IMPOSSIBLE TO DO OTHERWISE, YOU CAN BRING HIM BACK DEAD.

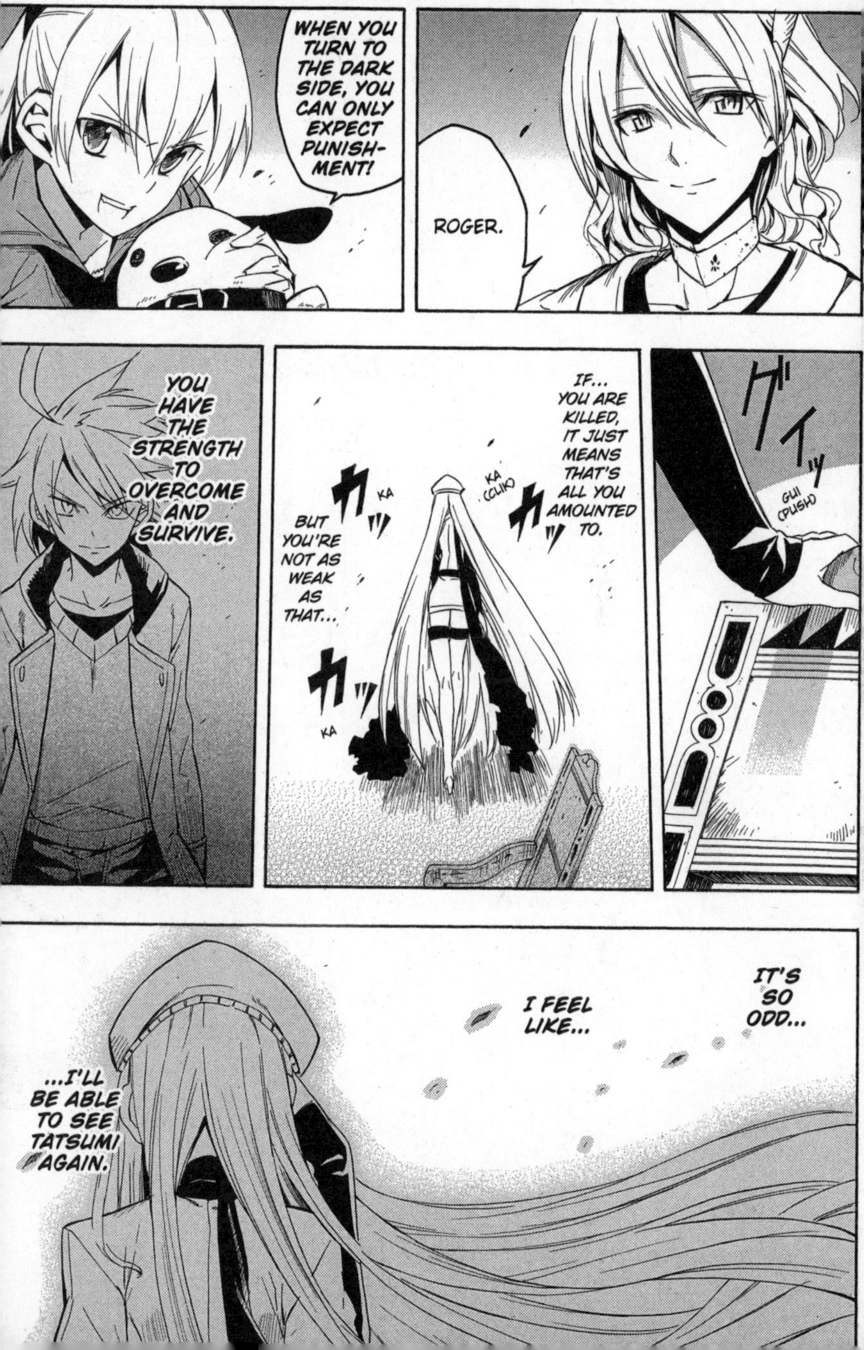
ROGER.
WHEN YOU TURN TO THE DARK SIDE, YOU CAN ONLY EXPECT PUNISHMENT!
GUI (PUSH)
IF... YOU ARE KILLED, IT JUST MEANS THAT'S ALL YOU AMOUNTED TO.
KA (CLIK)
KA
BUT YOU'RE NOT AS WEAK AS THAT...
KA
YOU HAVE THE STRENGTH TO OVERCOME AND SURVIVE.
IT'S SO ODD...
I FEEL LIKE...
...I'LL BE ABLE TO SEE TATSUMI AGAIN.

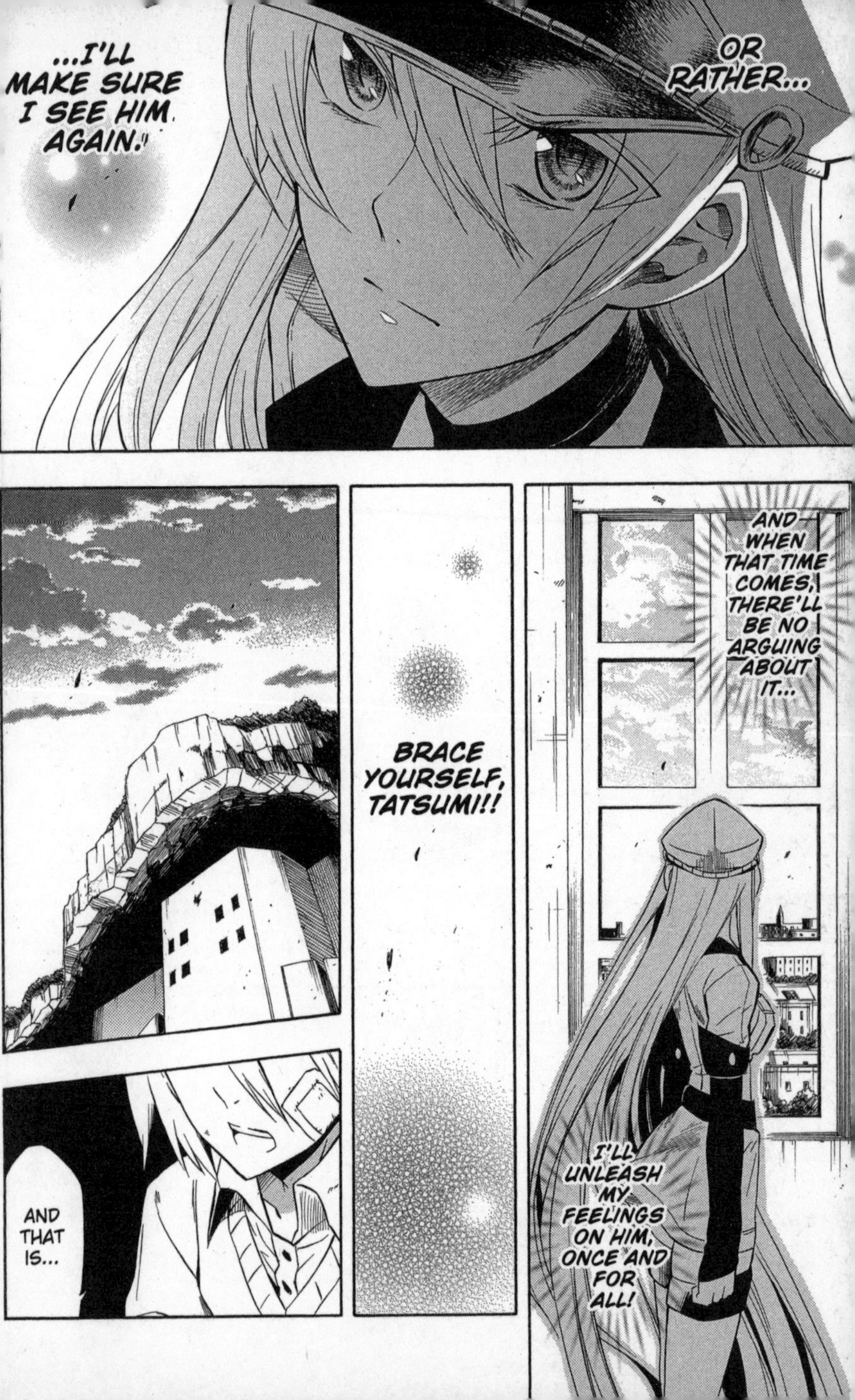
...I'LL MAKE SURE I SEE HIM AGAIN.
OR RATHER...
AND WHEN THAT TIME COMES, THERE'LL BE NO ARGUING ABOUT IT...
I'LL UNLEASH MY FEELINGS ON HIM, ONCE AND FOR ALL!
BRACE YOURSELF, TATSUMI!!
AND THAT IS...

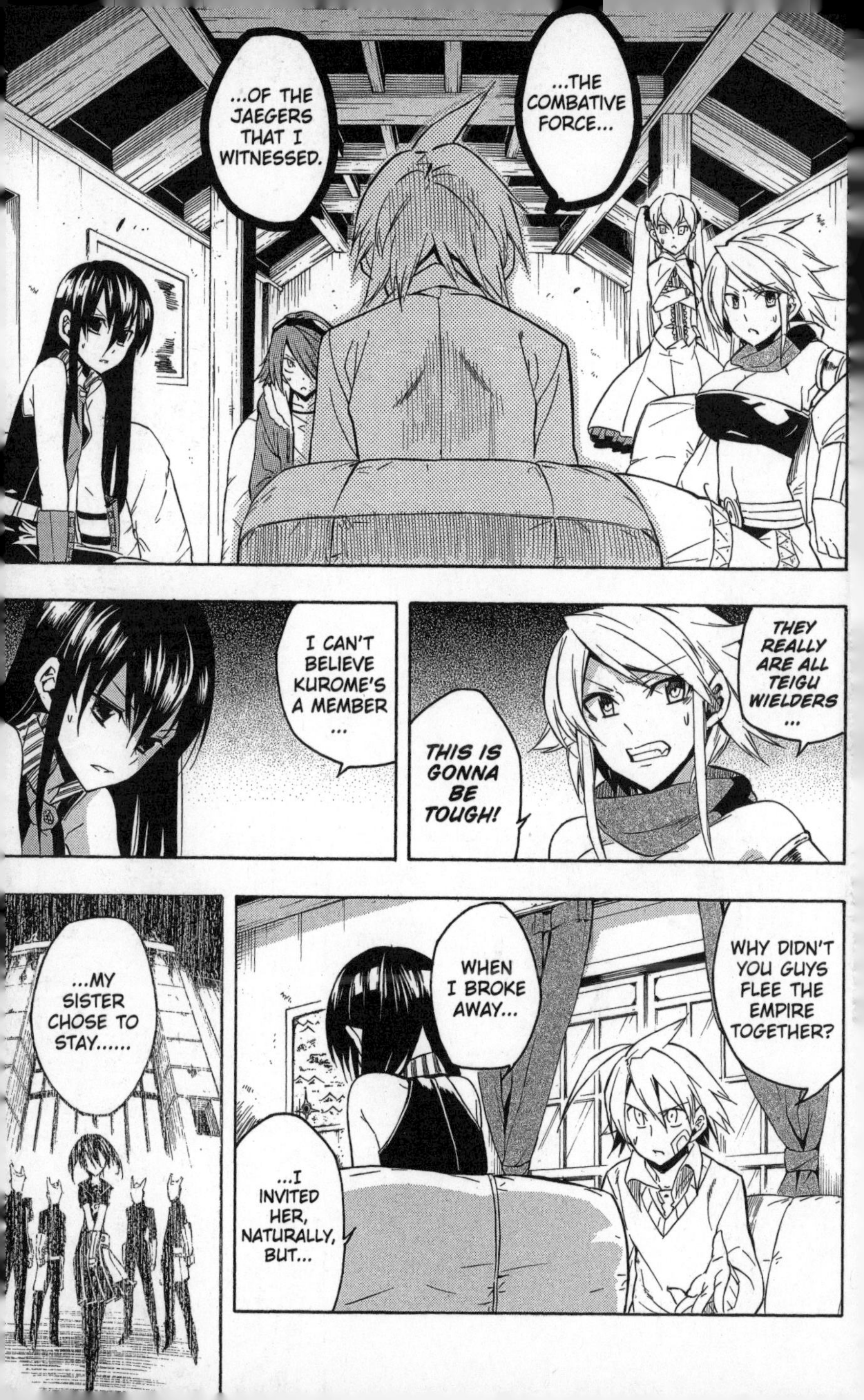
...THE COMBATIVE FORCE...
...OF THE JAEGERS THAT I WITNESSED.
THEY REALLY ARE ALL TEIGU WIELDERS...
THIS IS GONNA BE TOUGH!
I CAN'T BELIEVE KUROME'S A MEMBER...
WHY DIDN'T YOU GUYS FLEE THE EMPIRE TOGETHER?
WHEN I BROKE AWAY...
...I INVITED HER, NATURALLY, BUT...
...MY SISTER CHOSE TO STAY......

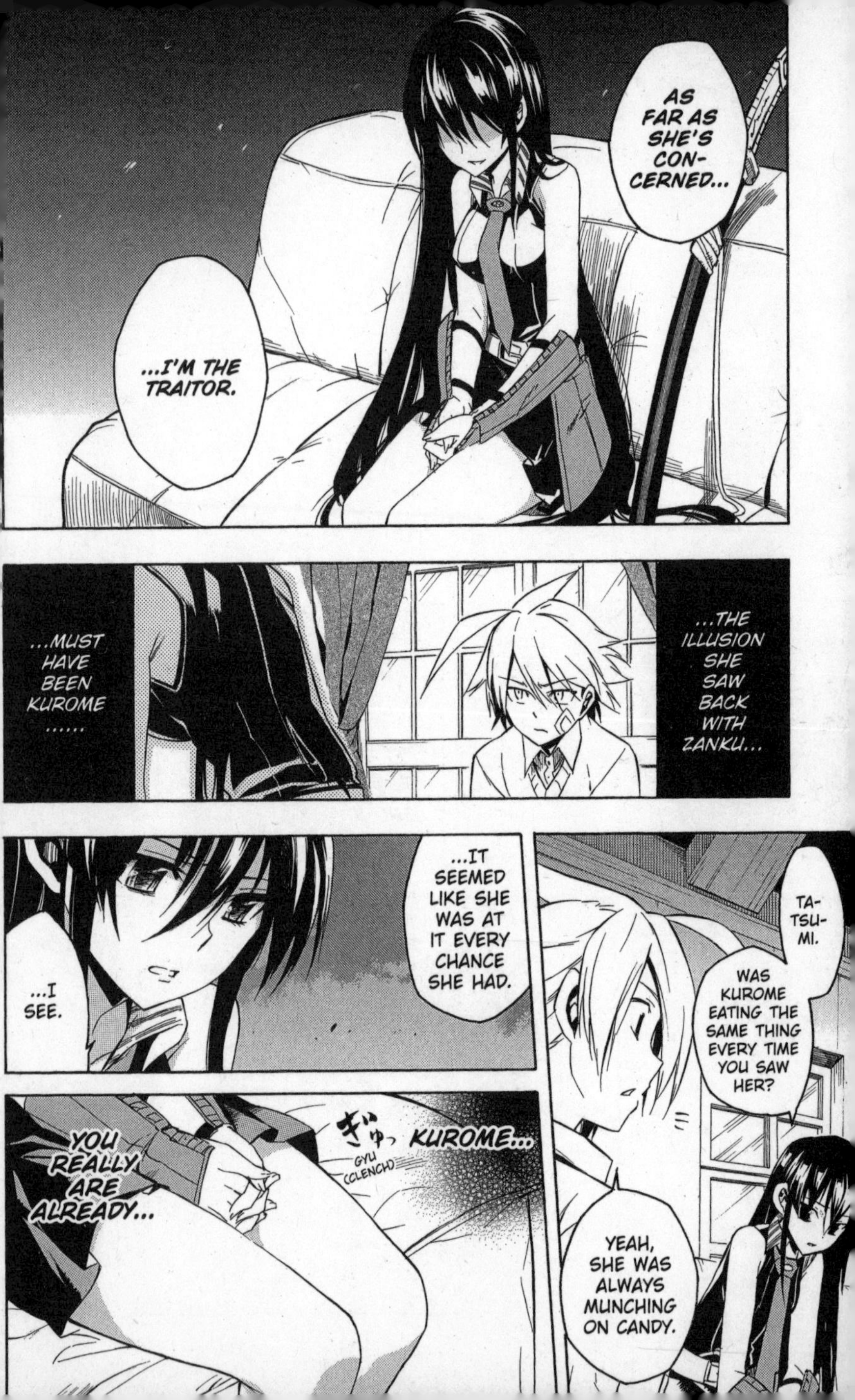
AS FAR AS SHE'S CON-CERNED...
...I'M THE TRAITOR.
...THE ILLUSION SHE SAW BACK WITH ZANKU...
...MUST HAVE BEEN KUROME ......
TATSU-MI.
WAS KUROME EATING THE SAME THING EVERY TIME YOU SAW HER?
YEAH, SHE WAS ALWAYS MUNCHING ON CANDY.
...IT SEEMED LIKE SHE WAS AT IT EVERY CHANCE SHE HAD.
...I SEE.
きゅっ
GYU (CLENCH)
KUROME...
YOU REALLY ARE ALREADY...

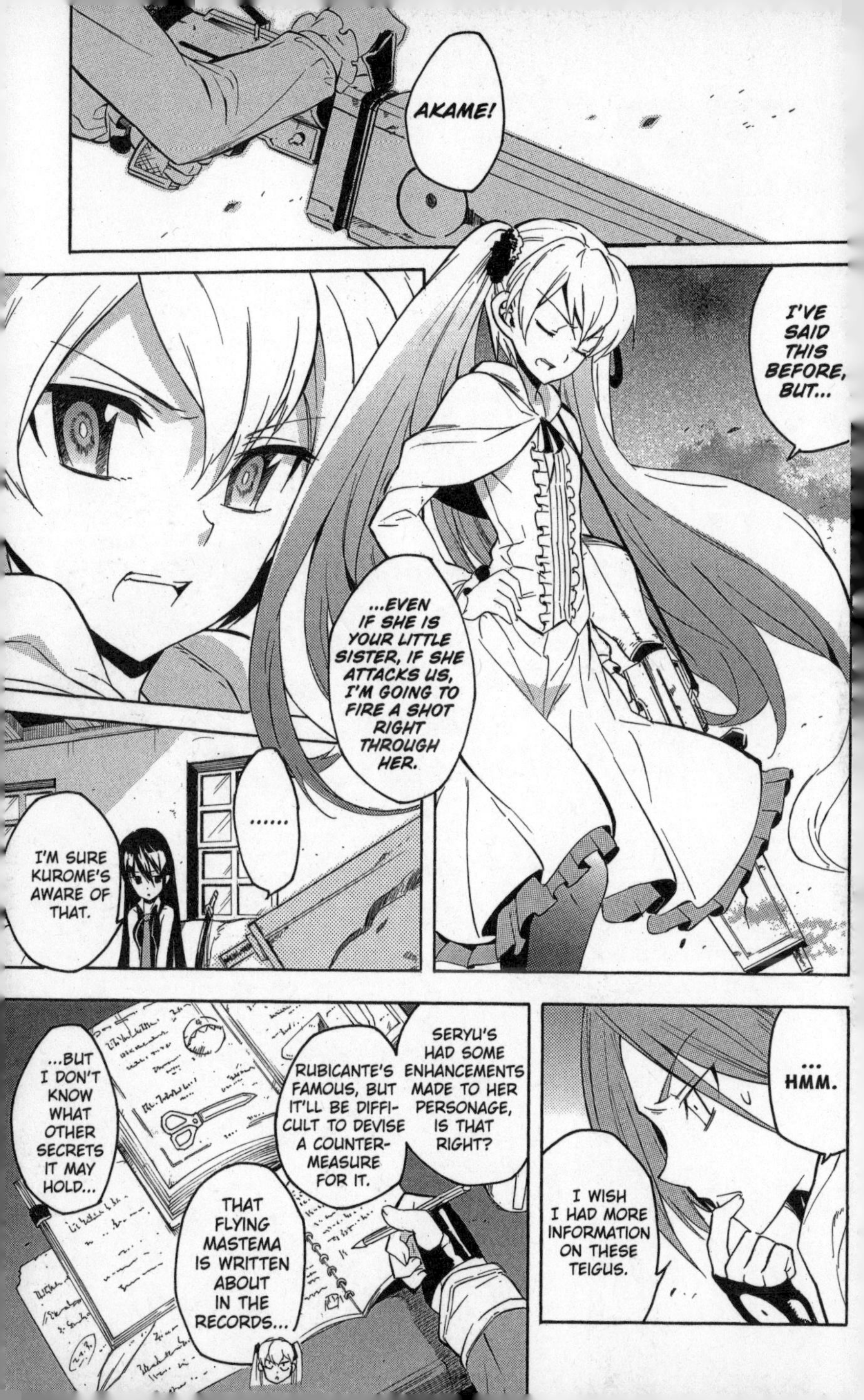
AKAME!
I'VE SAID THIS BEFORE, BUT...
...EVEN IF SHE IS YOUR LITTLE SISTER, IF SHE ATTACKS US, I'M GOING TO FIRE A SHOT RIGHT THROUGH HER.
......
I'M SURE KUROME'S AWARE OF THAT.
... HMM.
I WISH I HAD MORE INFORMATION ON THESE TEIGUS.
SERYU'S HAD SOME ENHANCEMENTS MADE TO HER PERSONAGE, IS THAT RIGHT?
RUBICANTE'S FAMOUS, BUT IT'LL BE DIFFICULT TO DEVISE A COUNTERMEASURE FOR IT.
THAT FLYING MASTEMA IS WRITTEN ABOUT IN THE RECORDS...
...BUT I DON'T KNOW WHAT OTHER SECRETS IT MAY HOLD...

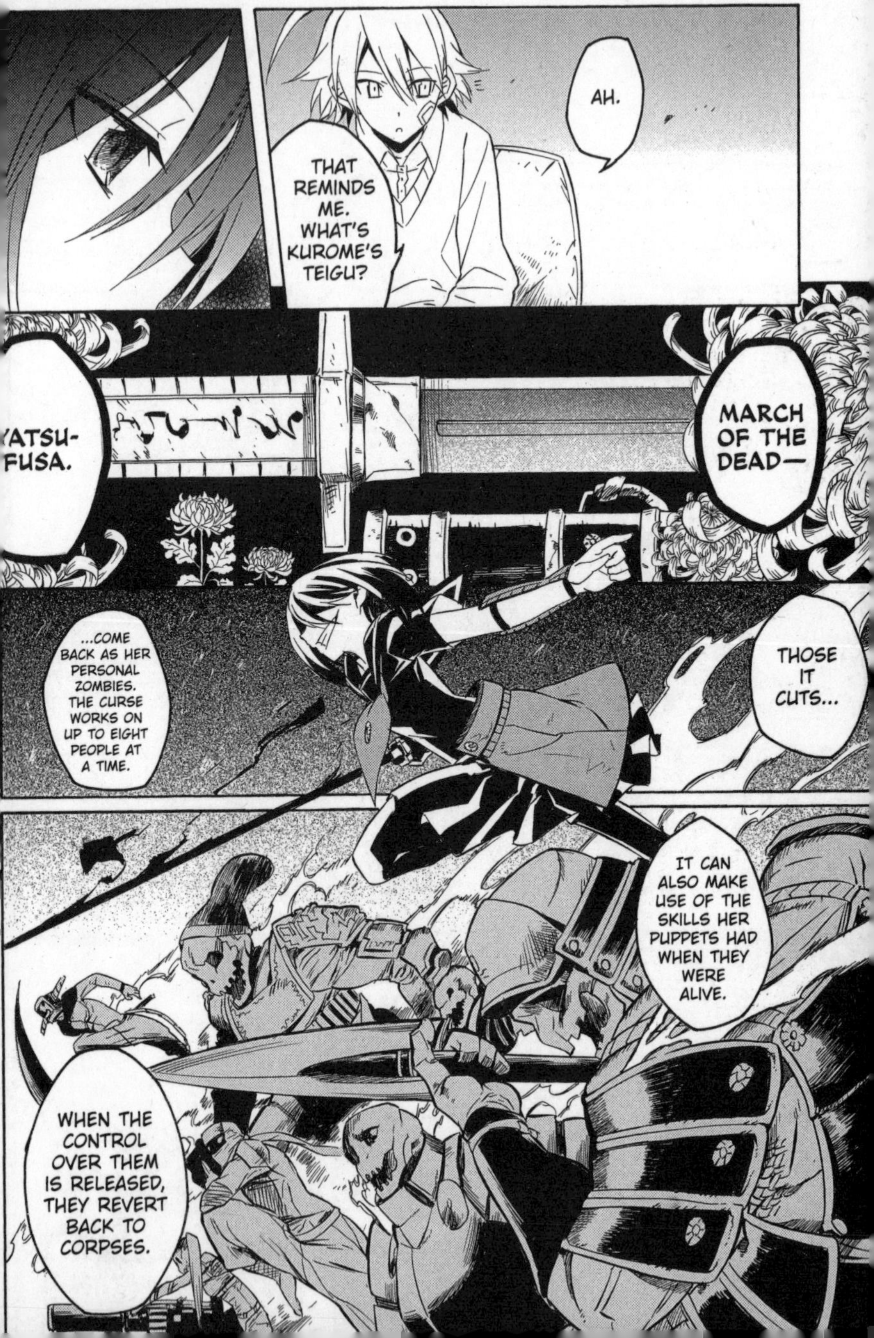
AH.
THAT REMINDS ME. WHAT'S KUROME'S TEIGU?
MARCH OF THE DEAD—
YATSU-FUSA.
THOSE IT CUTS...
...COME BACK AS HER PERSONAL ZOMBIES. THE CURSE WORKS ON UP TO EIGHT PEOPLE AT A TIME.
IT CAN ALSO MAKE USE OF THE SKILLS HER PUPPETS HAD WHEN THEY WERE ALIVE.
WHEN THE CONTROL OVER THEM IS RELEASED, THEY REVERT BACK TO CORPSES.

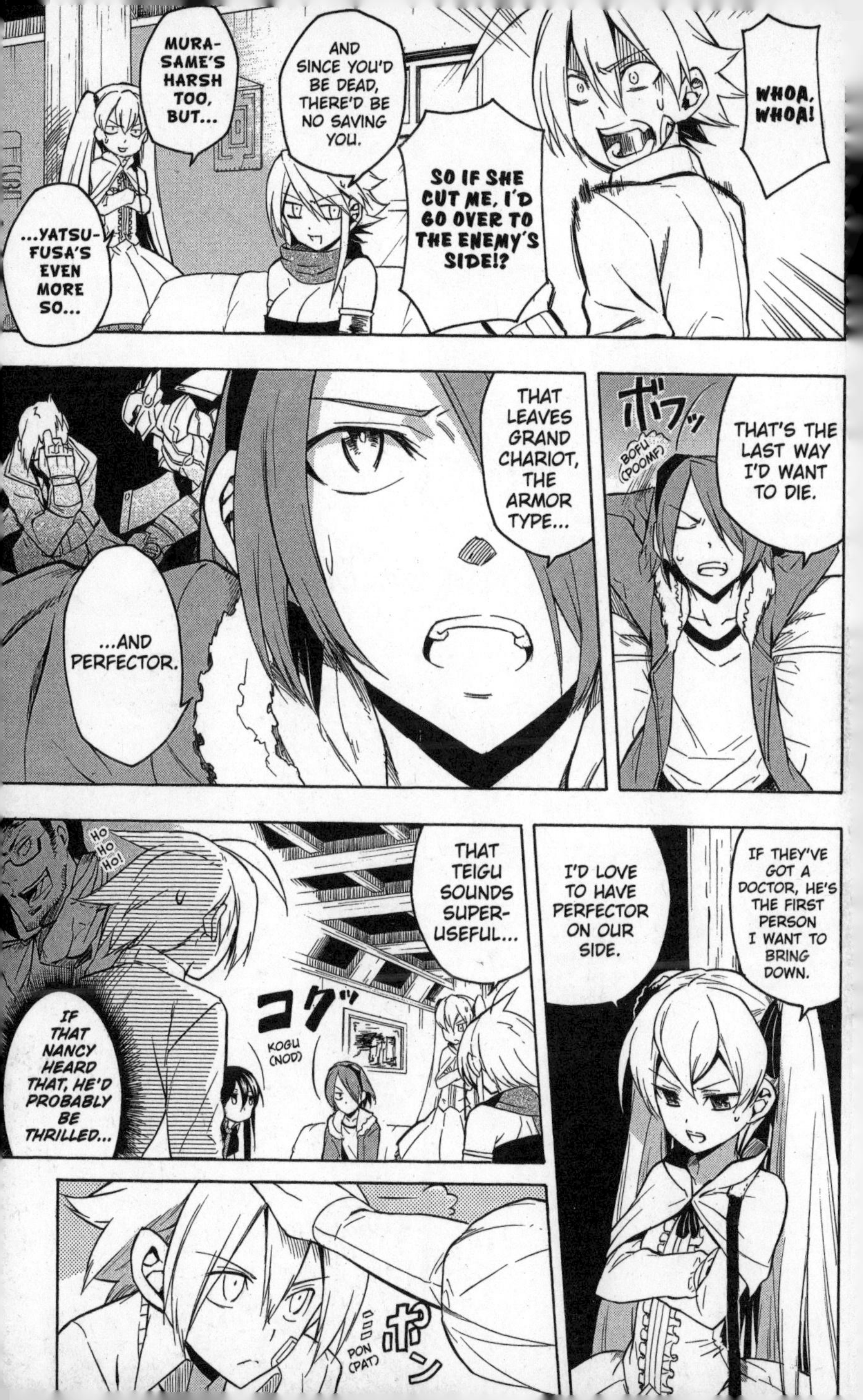
WHOA, WHOA!
SO IF SHE CUT ME, I'D GO OVER TO THE ENEMY'S SIDE!?
AND SINCE YOU'D BE DEAD, THERE'D BE NO SAVING YOU.
MURA-SAME'S HARSH TOO, BUT...
...YATSU-FUSA'S EVEN MORE SO...
ボフッ
BOFU (POOMF)
THAT'S THE LAST WAY I'D WANT TO DIE.
THAT LEAVES GRAND CHARIOT, THE ARMOR TYPE...
...AND PERFECTOR.
IF THEY'VE GOT A DOCTOR, HE'S THE FIRST PERSON I WANT TO BRING DOWN.
I'D LOVE TO HAVE PERFECTOR ON OUR SIDE.
THAT TEIGU SOUNDS SUPER-USEFUL...
コクッ
KOGU (NOD)
HO HO HO!
IF THAT NANCY HEARD THAT, HE'D PROBABLY BE THRILLED...
ポン
PON (PAT)

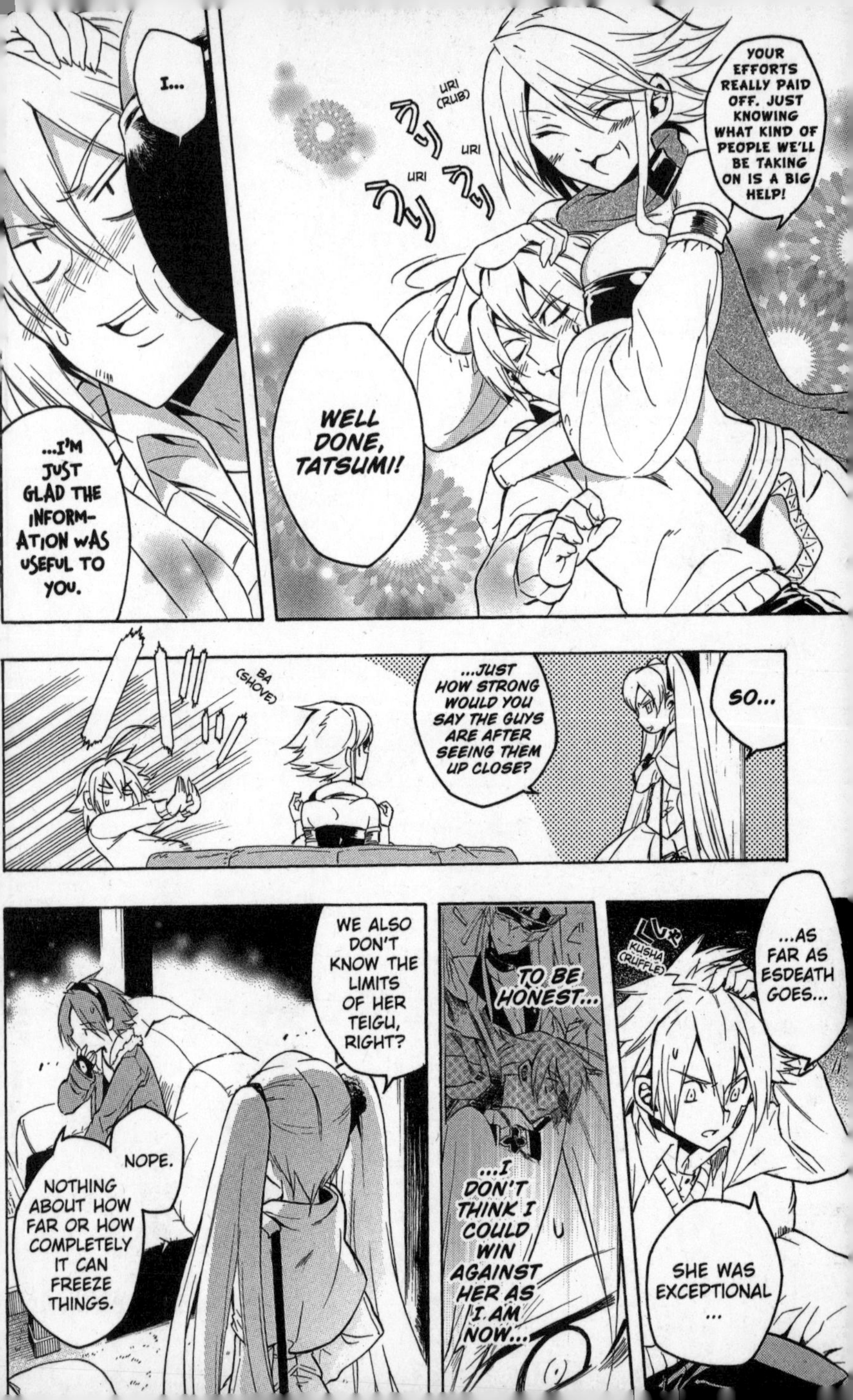
YOUR EFFORTS REALLY PAID OFF. JUST KNOWING WHAT KIND OF PEOPLE WE'LL BE TAKING ON IS A BIG HELP!
URI (RUB)
URI
URI
WELL DONE, TATSUMI!
I...
...I'M JUST GLAD THE INFORMATION WAS USEFUL TO YOU.
SO...
...JUST HOW STRONG WOULD YOU SAY THE GUYS ARE AFTER SEEING THEM UP CLOSE?
BA (SHOVE)
KUSHA (RUFFLE)
...AS FAR AS ESDEATH GOES...
SHE WAS EXCEPTIONAL ...
TO BE HONEST...
...I DON'T THINK I COULD WIN AGAINST HER AS I AM NOW...
WE ALSO DON'T KNOW THE LIMITS OF HER TEIGU, RIGHT?
NOPE.
NOTHING ABOUT HOW FAR OR HOW COMPLETELY IT CAN FREEZE THINGS.

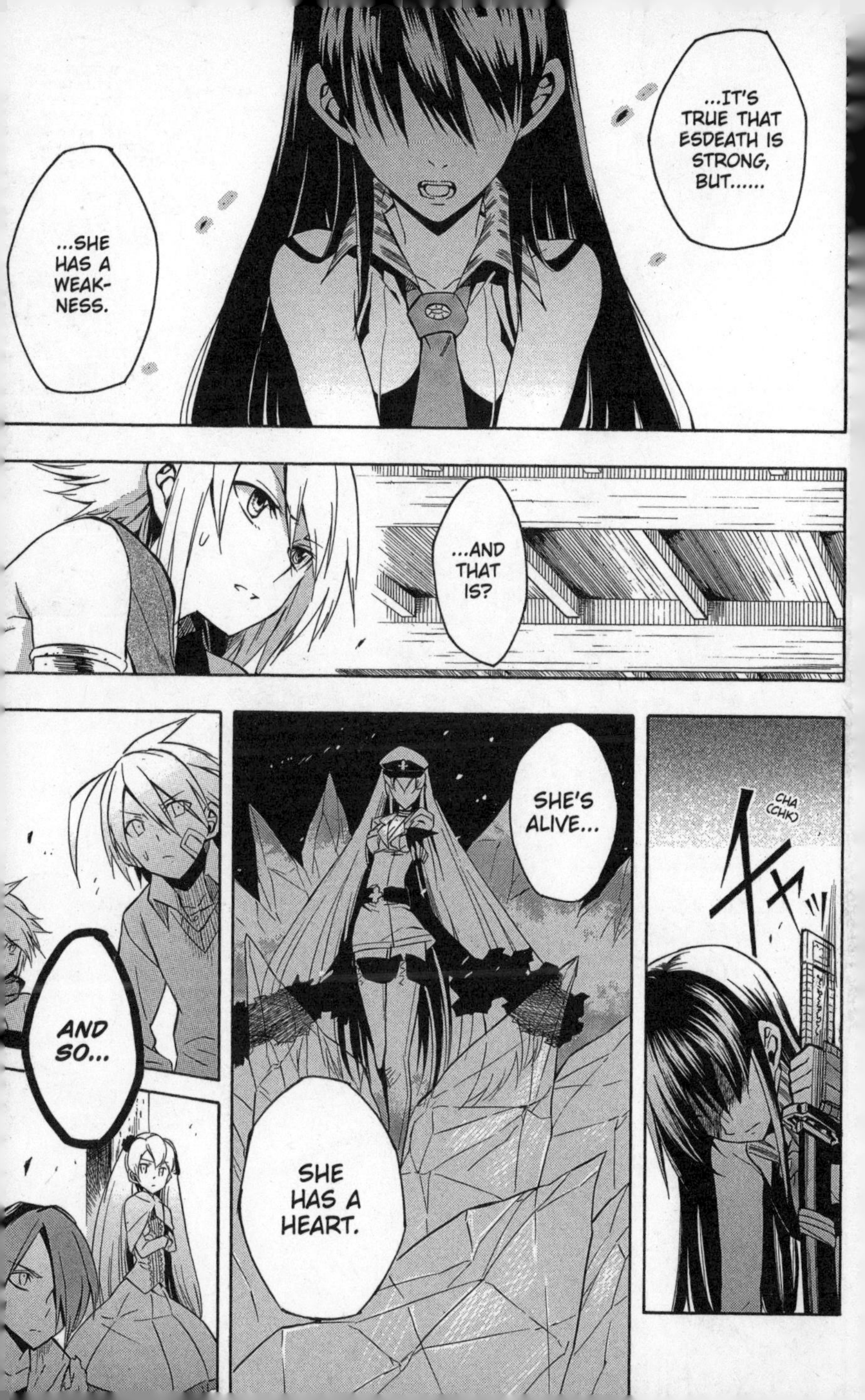
...IT'S TRUE THAT ESDEATH IS STRONG, BUT......
...SHE HAS A WEAKNESS.
...AND THAT IS?
CHA (CHK)
SHE'S ALIVE...
SHE HAS A HEART.
AND SO...

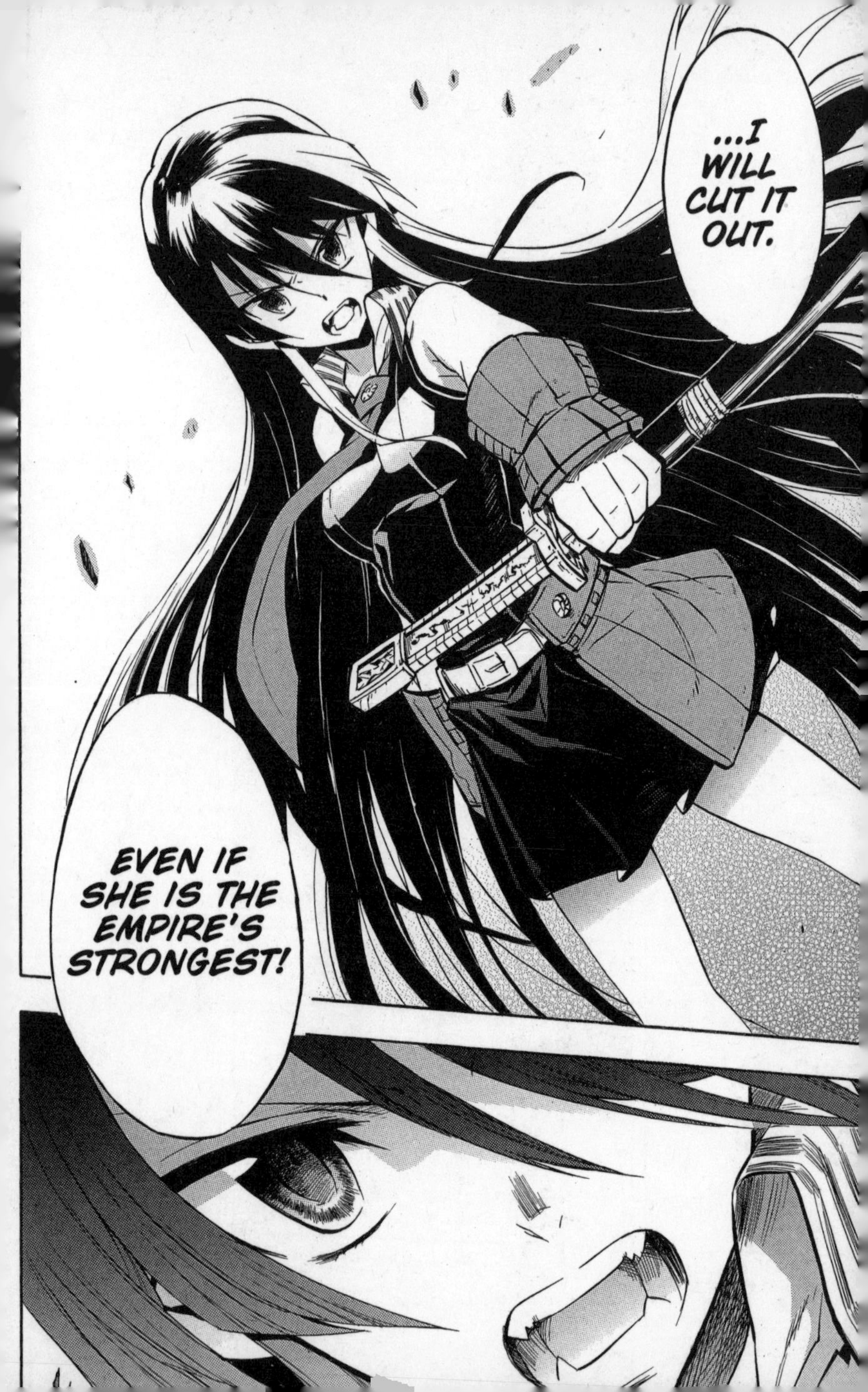
...I WILL CUT IT OUT.
EVEN IF SHE IS THE EMPIRE'S STRONGEST!

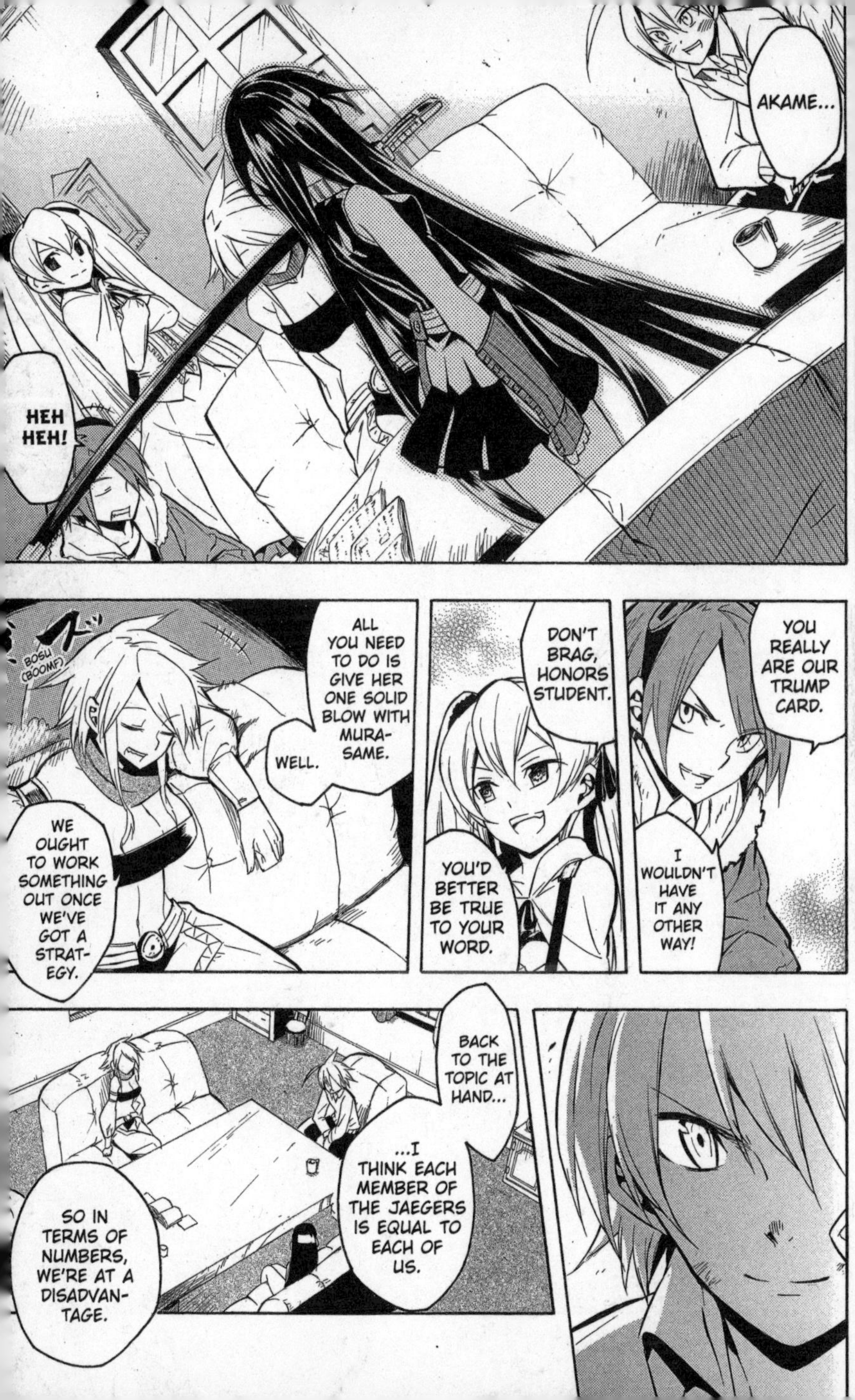
AKAME...
HEH HEH!
YOU REALLY ARE OUR TRUMP CARD.
I WOULDN'T HAVE IT ANY OTHER WAY!
DON'T BRAG, HONORS STUDENT.
YOU'D BETTER BE TRUE TO YOUR WORD.
ALL YOU NEED TO DO IS GIVE HER ONE SOLID BLOW WITH MURASAME.
WELL.
BOSU (BOOMF)
WE OUGHT TO WORK SOMETHING OUT ONCE WE'VE GOT A STRATEGY.
BACK TO THE TOPIC AT HAND...
...I THINK EACH MEMBER OF THE JAEGERS IS EQUAL TO EACH OF US.
SO IN TERMS OF NUMBERS, WE'RE AT A DISADVANTAGE.

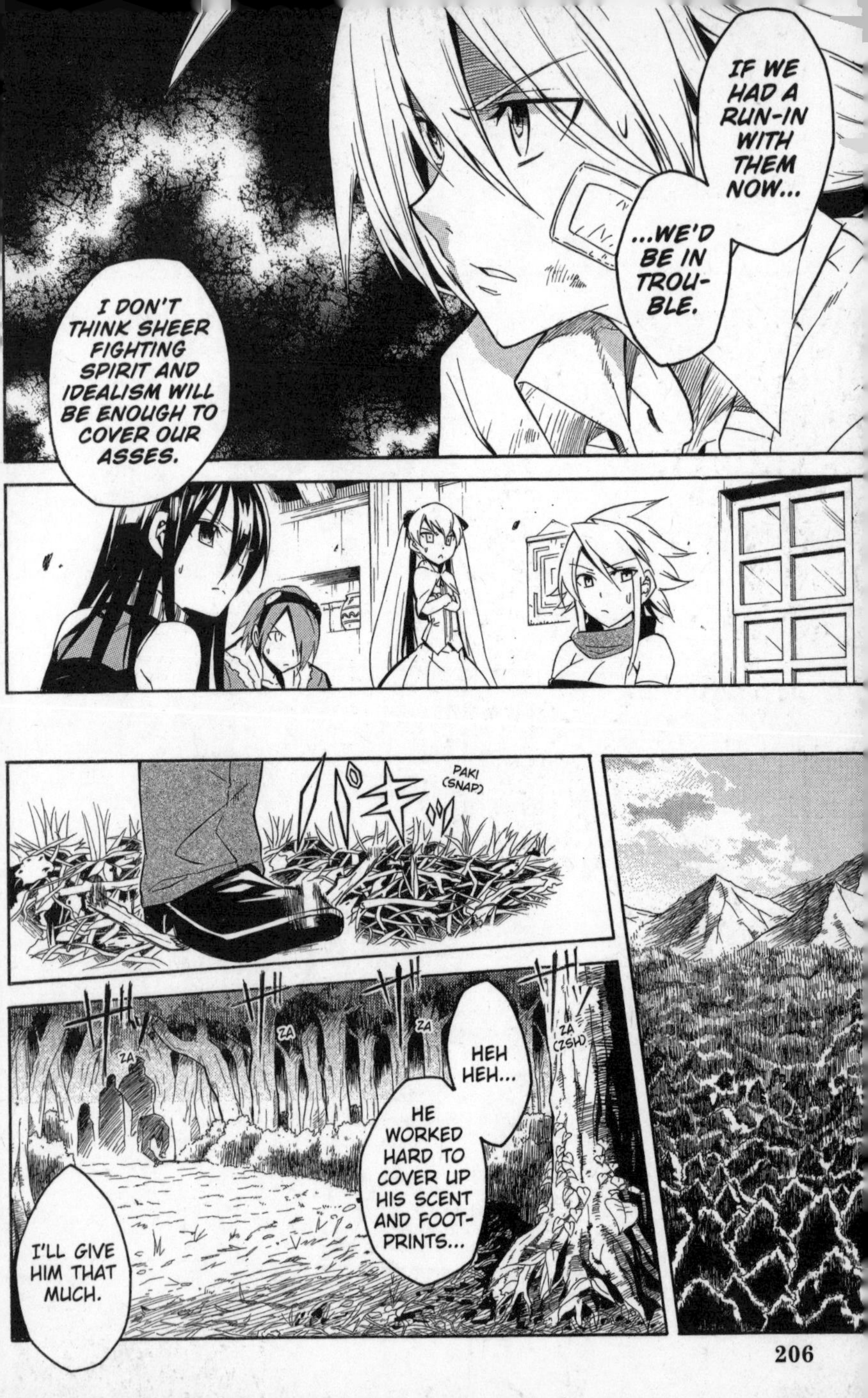
IF WE HAD A RUN-IN WITH THEM NOW...
...WE'D BE IN TROU-BLE.
I DON'T THINK SHEER FIGHTING SPIRIT AND IDEALISM WILL BE ENOUGH TO COVER OUR ASSES.
PAKI (SNAP)
ZA (ZSH)
ZA
ZA
ZA
HEH HEH...
HE WORKED HARD TO COVER UP HIS SCENT AND FOOT-PRINTS...
I'LL GIVE HIM THAT MUCH.

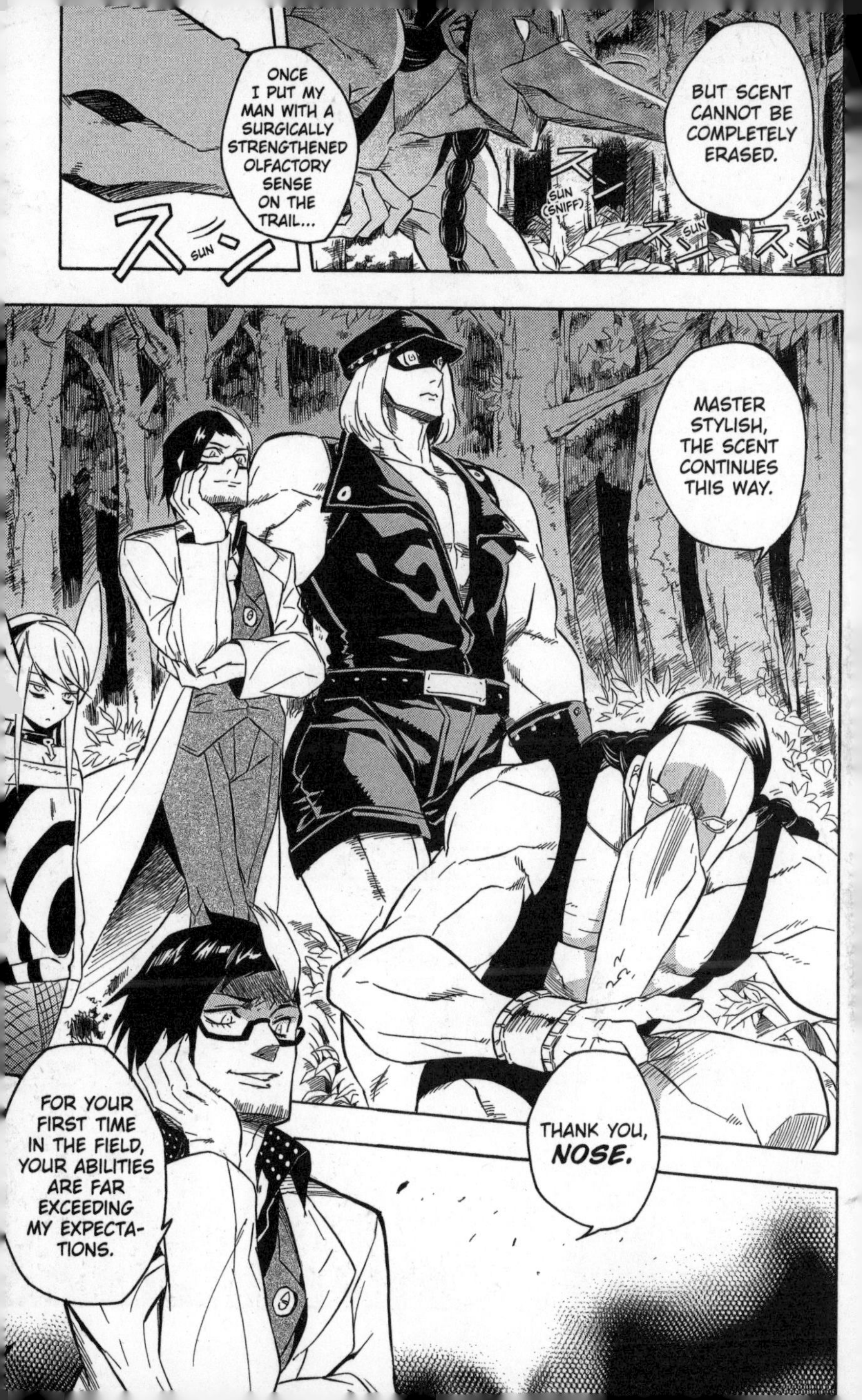
BUT SCENT CANNOT BE COMPLETELY ERASED.
SUN
SUN
SUN (SNIFF)
ONCE I PUT MY MAN WITH A SURGICALLY STRENGTHENED OLFACTORY SENSE ON THE TRAIL...
SUN
MASTER STYLISH, THE SCENT CONTINUES THIS WAY.
THANK YOU, *NOSE.*
FOR YOUR FIRST TIME IN THE FIELD, YOUR ABILITIES ARE FAR EXCEEDING MY EXPECTA-TIONS.

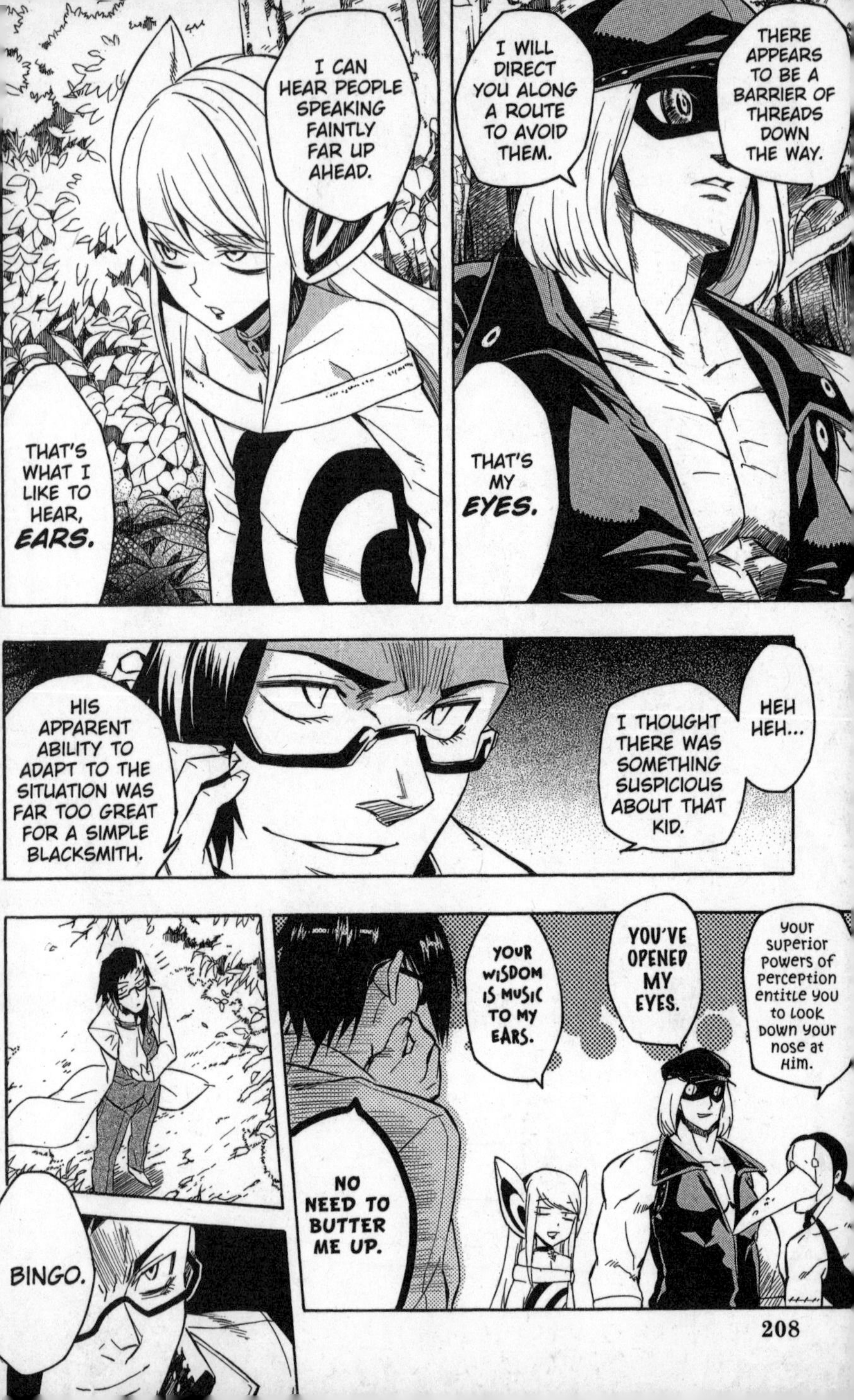

THERE APPEARS TO BE A BARRIER OF THREADS DOWN THE WAY.
I WILL DIRECT YOU ALONG A ROUTE TO AVOID THEM.
THAT'S MY EYES.
I CAN HEAR PEOPLE SPEAKING FAINTLY FAR UP AHEAD.
THAT'S WHAT I LIKE TO HEAR, EARS.
HEH HEH...
I THOUGHT THERE WAS SOMETHING SUSPICIOUS ABOUT THAT KID.
HIS APPARENT ABILITY TO ADAPT TO THE SITUATION WAS FAR TOO GREAT FOR A SIMPLE BLACKSMITH.
Your superior powers of perception entitle you to look down your nose at Him.
YOU'VE OPENED MY EYES.
YOUR WISDOM IS MUSIC TO MY EARS.
NO NEED TO BUTTER ME UP.
BINGO.

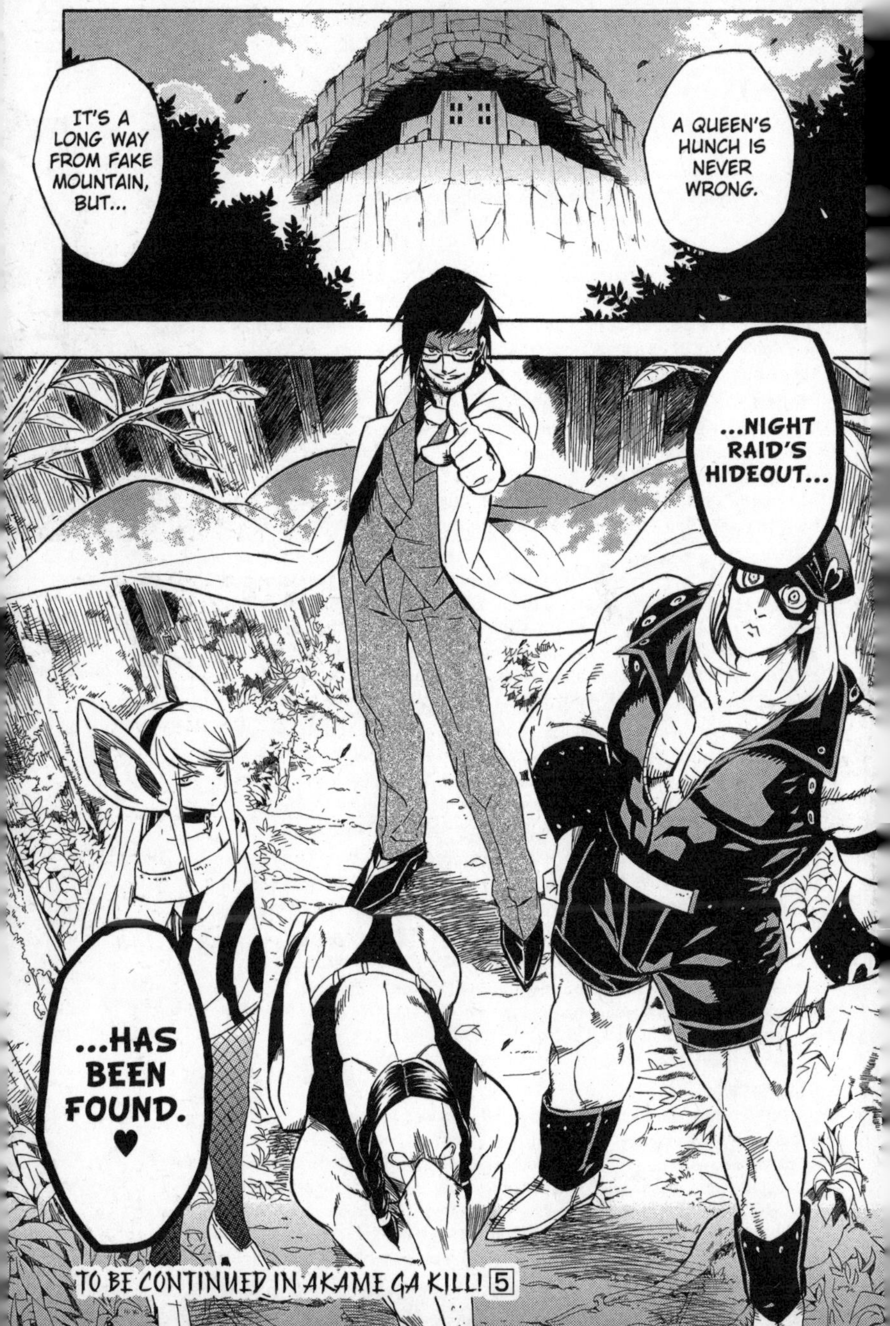
A QUEEN'S HUNCH IS NEVER WRONG.
IT'S A LONG WAY FROM FAKE MOUNTAIN, BUT...
...NIGHT RAID'S HIDEOUT...
...HAS BEEN FOUND. ♥
TO BE CONTINUED IN AKAME GA KILL! 5

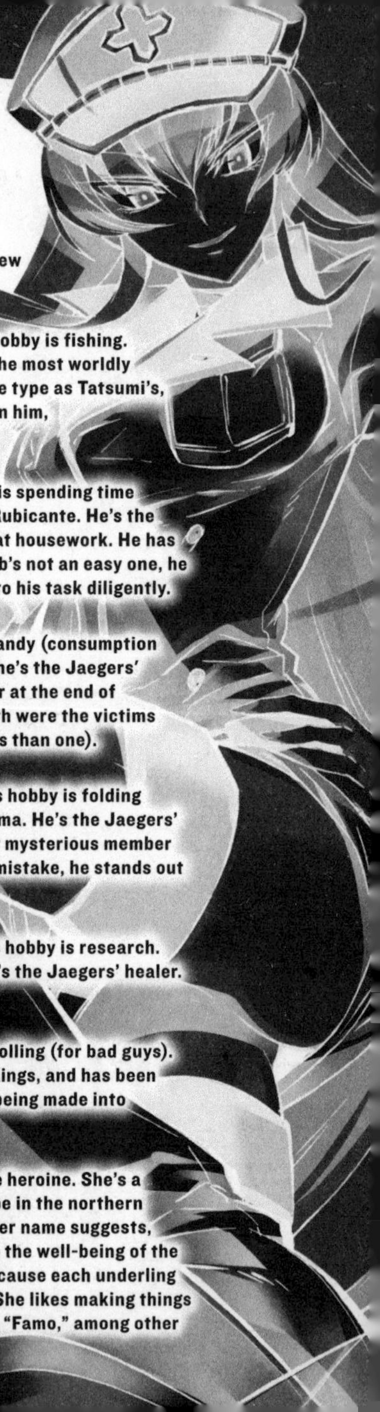

TAKAHIRO's POSTSCRIPT

Thank you very much for buying Volume 4.
This is Takahiro. This supplement is devoted to the new characters introduced in this volume: The Jaegers.

[Wave]
Blood Type: A. He's about twenty years old. And his hobby is fishing. His teigu is Carnage Incarnate: Grand Chariot. He's the most worldly member of the Jaegers. Because his teigu is the same type as Tatsumi's, he's something of a rival character. Everyone picks on him, but he sticks by Run since Run was kind to him.

[Bols]
Blood Type: AB. He's thirty-two years old. His hobby is spending time with his family. His teigu is Invitation to Purgatory: Rubicante. He's the straightforward member of the Jaegers. And a whiz at housework. He has a beautiful wife and adorable children. Though his job's not an easy one, he feels the work has to be done by someone and takes to his task diligently.

[Kurome]
Blood Type: A. She's in her mid-teens. Her hobby is candy (consumption of). Her teigu is the March of the Dead: Yatsufusa. She's the Jaegers' mascot(?) and Akame's little sister. When we saw her at the end of Volume 3, those corpses she was messing around with were the victims of Yatsufusa. She loves her older sister (in more ways than one).

[Run]
Blood Type: O. He's about twenty-three years old. His hobby is folding origami. His teigu is the Thousand Mile flight: Mastema. He's the Jaegers' butler. He is always cool and collected. He's the most mysterious member and is very soft-spoken, but since he never makes a mistake, he stands out from the rest.

[Dr. Stylish]
Blood Type: B. He's about twenty-eight years old. His hobby is research. His teigu is the Glorious Hands of God: Perfector. He's the Jaegers' healer. He's the person who modified Seryu in Volume 2.

[Seryu]
Blood Type: A. In her mid-twenties. Her hobby is patrolling (for bad guys). She's acquired a new weapon, Judgment of the Ten Kings, and has been greatly strengthened by it. Coro often finds himself being made into Kurome's plaything.

[Esdeath]
From this single volume, she could totally pass as the heroine. She's a young prodigy general who comes from a hunting tribe in the northern frontier, where she used to hunt Danger Beasts. As her name suggests, she's quite sadistic, though she's closely attentive to the well-being of the underlings she fights with. However that's mostly because each underling is linked to the effectiveness of her unit as a whole. She likes making things fun and will also do things like calling Fake Mountain "Famo," among other charming points.

AKAME KILL! 4

☆ **ALL MY STAFF** ☆

YAMASHITA-SHI   ITOU-SAN
MIYAZAKI-SAN, thank you!! 🐱
MINAMI-SAN, thank you!! 🐱
HIRAIWA-KUN   OKUDA-KUN
NOZUE-SAN   FUJINO-SAN
IMAI-SAN   TAKAGI-SAN

☆ **SPECIAL THANKS** ☆

PINE-SAN 🐧   YAMAMOTO-SAN 🐱

✿ **THE ORIGINAL AUTHOR** ✿

TAKAHIRO-SAN

✿ **THE EDITOR** ✿

KOIZUMI-SAN

THANK YOU FOR READING! ♡

| TATSUMI | COURAGE | LOOKS | SPIRIT | HEARTTHROB METER ♡ | 20% |
| | 30 | 20 | 20 | FATALITY METER 💀 | 90% |

ESDEATH ♥ ♥ ♥

Esdeath: "Tatsumi, how do you feel about me!?"

Tatsumi: ⇒"I think I love you."
⇒"I'm afraid of you."
⇒"I think it's your turn."

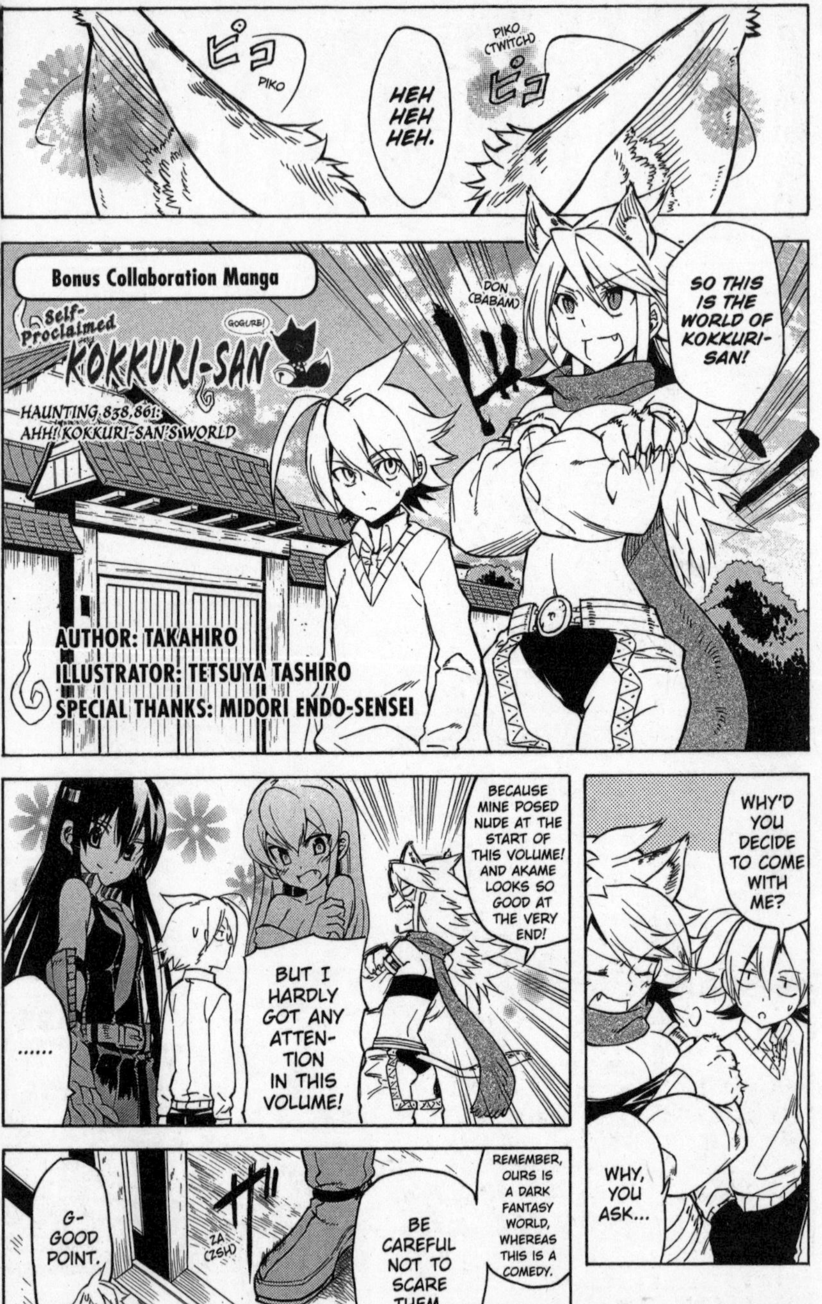
PIKO (TWITCH)
ピコ
HEH HEH HEH.
ピコ
PIKO
SO THIS IS THE WORLD OF KOKKURI-SAN!
DON (BABAM)
Bonus Collaboration Manga
Self-Proclaimed KOKKURI-SAN
GOGURE!
HAUNTING 838,861: AHH! KOKKURI-SAN'S WORLD
AUTHOR: TAKAHIRO
ILLUSTRATOR: TETSUYA TASHIRO
SPECIAL THANKS: MIDORI ENDO-SENSEI
WHY'D YOU DECIDE TO COME WITH ME?
WHY, YOU ASK...
BECAUSE MINE POSED NUDE AT THE START OF THIS VOLUME! AND AKAME LOOKS SO GOOD AT THE VERY END!
BUT I HARDLY GOT ANY ATTENTION IN THIS VOLUME!
......
REMEMBER, OURS IS A DARK FANTASY WORLD, WHEREAS THIS IS A COMEDY.
BE CAREFUL NOT TO SCARE THEM.
ZA (ZSH)
G-GOOD POINT.

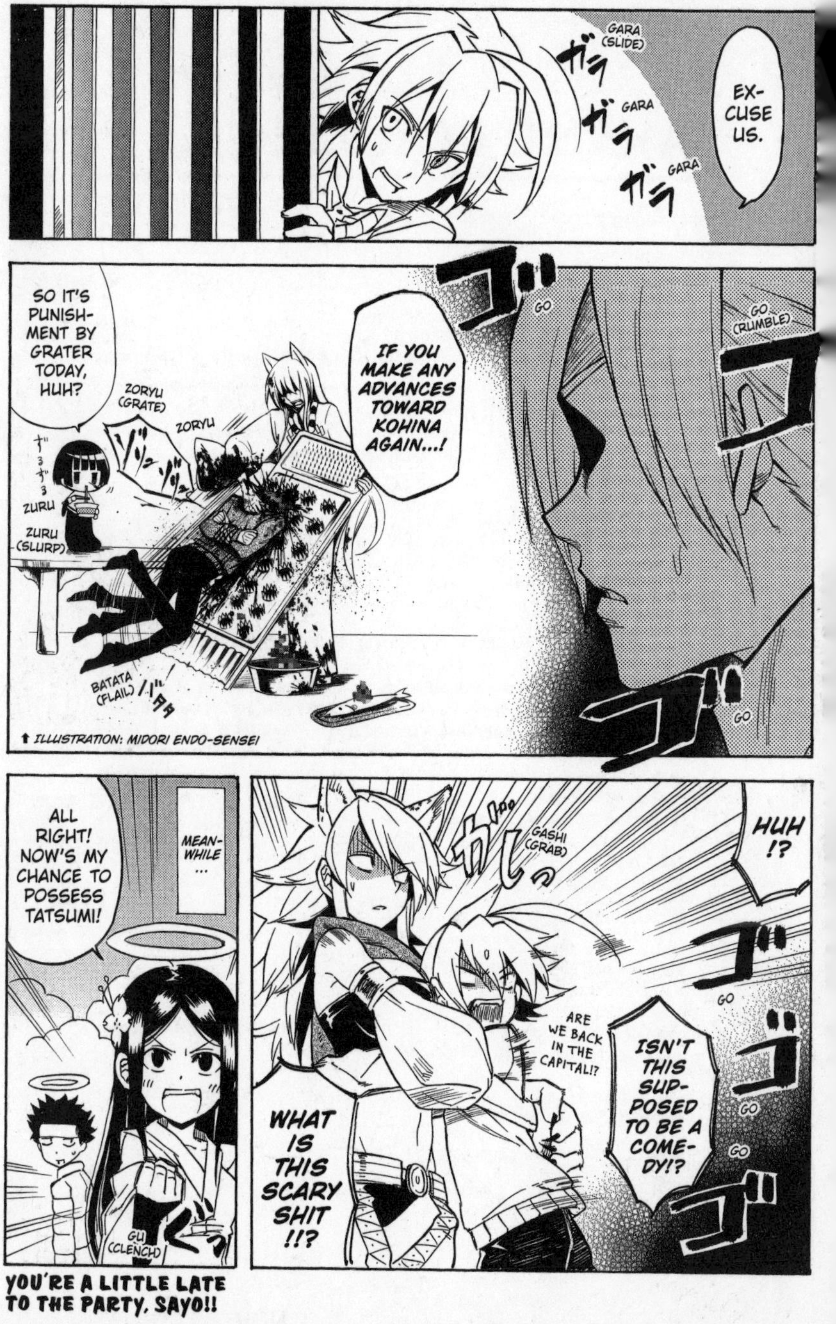
GARA (SLIDE)
GARA
GARA
EXCUSE US.
GO (RUMBLE)
GO
GO
IF YOU MAKE ANY ADVANCES TOWARD KOHINA AGAIN...!
SO IT'S PUNISHMENT BY GRATER TODAY, HUH?
ZORYU (GRATE)
ZORYU
ZURU
ZURU (SLURP)
BATATA (FLAIL)
⬆ ILLUSTRATION: MIDORI ENDO-SENSEI
HUH!?
GASHI (GRAB)
ISN'T THIS SUPPOSED TO BE A COMEDY!?
ARE WE BACK IN THE CAPITAL!?
WHAT IS THIS SCARY SHIT!!?
GO
GO
GO
MEANWHILE...
ALL RIGHT! NOW'S MY CHANCE TO POSSESS TATSUMI!
GU (CLENCH)

YOU'RE A LITTLE LATE TO THE PARTY, SAYO!!

AKAME GA KILL! ④

TAKAHIRO
TETSUYA TASHIRO

Translation: Christine Dashiell • Lettering: Erin Hickman

AKAME GA KILL! Vol. 4
© 2012 Takahiro, Tetsuya Tashiro / SQUARE ENIX CO., LTD. First published in Japan in 2012 by SQUARE ENIX CO., LTD. English translation rights arranged with SQUARE ENIX CO., LTD. and Hachette Book Group through Tuttle-Mori Agency, Inc., Tokyo.

Translation © 2015 by SQUARE ENIX CO., LTD.

Yen Press
Hachette Book Group
1290 Avenue of the Americas
New York, NY 10104

www.HachetteBookGroup.com
www.YenPress.com

Yen Press is an imprint of Hachette Book Group, Inc. The Yen Press name and logo are trademarks of Hachette Book Group, Inc.

The publisher is not responsible for websites (or their content) that are not owned by the publisher.

First Yen Press Edition: October 2015

ISBN: 978-0-316-34005-2

10 9 8 7 6 5 4 3 2 1

BVG

Printed in the United States of America